THE REVELS PLAYS COMPANION LIBRARY

The works of Richard Edwards

POLITICS, POETRY AND PERFORMANCE
IN SIXTEENTH-CENTURY ENGLAND

Ros King

Manchester University Press

Manchester and New York

distributed exclusively in the USA by Palgrave

The right of Ros King to be identified as the author of this work has been asserted
by her in accordance with the Copyright, Designs and Patents Act 1988.

Published by Manchester University Press
Oxford Road, Manchester M13 9NR, UK
and Room 400, 175 Fifth Avenue, New York, NY 10010, USA
http://www.manchesteruniversitypress.co.uk

Distributed exclusively in the USA by
Palgrave, 175 Fifth Avenue, New York,
NY 10010, USA

Distributed exclusively in Canada by
UBC Press, University of British Columbia, 2029 West Mall,
Vancouver, BC, Canada V6T 1Z2

British Library Cataloguing-in-Publication Data
A catalogue record for this book is available from the British Library

Library of Congress Cataloging-in-Publication Data applied for

ISBN 0 7190 5299 8   hardback

First published 2001

10 09 08 07 06 05 04 03 02 01   10 9 8 7 6 5 4 3 2 1

Typeset in Sabon by
Best-set Typesetter Ltd., Hong Kong

Printed in Great Britain
by Bookcraft (Bath) Ltd, Midsomer Notton

The Revels Plays COMPANION LIBRARY

E. A. J. HONIGMANN former editor
J. R. MULRYNE. R. L. SMALLWOOD and PETER CORBIN general editors

For over thirty years *The Revels Plays* have offered the most authoritative editions of Elizabethan and Jacobean plays by authors other than Shakespeare. The *Companion Library* provides a fuller background to the main series by publishing worthwhile dramatic and non-dramatic material that will be essential for the serious student of the period.

The Works of Richard Edwards

MANCHESTER
UNIVERSITY PRESS

For my friends

CONTENTS

PLATES

GENERAL EDITORS' PREFACE

Since the late 1950s the series known as the Revels Plays has provided for students of the English Renaissance drama carefully edited texts of the major Elizabethan and Jacobean plays. The series includes some of the best-known drama of the period and has continued to expand, both within its original field and, to a lesser extent, beyond it, to include some important plays from the earlier Tudor and from the Restoration periods. The Revels Plays Companion Library is intended to further this expansion and to allow for new developments.

The aim of the Companion Library is to provide students of the Elizabethan and Jacobean drama with a fuller sense of its background and context. The series includes volumes of a variety of kinds. Small collections of plays, by a single author or concerned with a single theme and edited in accordance with the principles of textual modernisation of the Revels Plays, offer a wider range of drama than the main series can include. Together with editions of masques, pageants and the non-dramatic work of Elizabethan and Jacobean playwrights, these volumes make it possible, within the overall Revels enterprise, to examine the achievements of the major dramatists from a broader perspective. Other volumes provide a fuller context for the plays of the period by offering new collections of documentary evidence on Elizabethan theatrical conditions and on the performance of plays during that period and later. A third aim of the series is to offer modern critical interpretation, in the form of collections of essays or of monographs, of the dramatic achievement of the English Renaissance.

So wide a range of material necessarily precludes the standard format and uniform general editorial control, which is possible in the original series of Revels Plays. To a considerable extent, therefore, treatment and approach is determined by the needs and intentions of individual volume editors. Within this rather ampler area, however, we hope that the companion Library maintains the standards of scholarship that have for so long characterised the Revels Plays, and that it offers a useful enlargement of the work of the series in preserving, illuminating and celebrating the drama of Elizabethan and Jacobean England.

J. R. MULRYNE
R. L. SMALLWOOD
PETER CORBIN

PREFACE

This book began when the research and education committee for Shakespeare's Globe in London, led by Andrew Gurr, delegated to me the task of devising a programme of activities for the 1996 Prologue season which would celebrate and integrate the theatre and the research wings of the project. At the same time Mark Rylance, the Artistic Director, was looking for a 'rare' play that could, with a couple of weeks' rehearsal, be given a single, fully staged performance to complement the play chosen for the season, Shakespeare's *Two Gentlemen of Verona*.

Edwards's source for *Damon and Pythias* occurs in *The Book Named the Governor* by Sir Thomas Elyot, next to the story of Titus and Gisyppus, the source for *Two Gentlemen*. Both stories illustrate the bond of friendship so that, both in terms of relevance to the Shakespeare play and as an emblem for continued artistic and academic co-operation at the Globe, it seemed to me to be a good choice. Mark Rylance agreed and asked me to edit the text and advise on the production as dramaturg. The play was performed on 10 September 1996, as the centrepiece of a programme which comprised a symposium for theatre professionals on the use of the Globe stage, an academic conference on sixteenth-century drama including workshops with members of the acting companies, and a public lecture recital on Edwards's songs.

I am therefore deeply indebted to Andrew and to Mark; to the production's director, Gaynor Macfarlane, the cast and production team; Beth Deitchman; and to everyone connected with the Globe who enabled this week of extra frenetic activity to go so smoothly even while the theatre was still being built. These include: executive director, Michael Holden; Patrick Spottiswood, Deb Callan and the staff at Globe Education; Tiffany Foster, Press Officer; Alan Butland, Chairman of the Friends of the Globe and of the archive committee; Jon Greenfield, architect; Peter McCurdy and the builders. In addition, I would like to thank: Kate Bennet; Michael Bogdanov for goading me into 'researching a comma'; Mike Edwards for his advice on Latin and Greek literature and language; soprano Catherine King for helping me to sing the songs; Nigel Alexander (repeatedly), Nigel Glendinning, Victoria Rothschild and Andrew (again) for reading and commenting on various drafts of the introduction; the staff at Queen Mary and University of London Libraries; the British Library; the Folger Library, Washington; the Public Record Office; the Surrey History Centre; the Bodleian, Christ Church and Corpus Christi libraries, Oxford; J. R. Gurney of the Historic Manuscripts Commission; Matthew Frost and Lauren McAllister at MUP; John Banks; and, not least, Ernst Honigmann for his rigorous and unfailingly helpful criticism.

ABBREVIATIONS

Add.	British Library, Additional MS.
AH	Arundel Castle, Arundel Harington MS.
Bereblock	Description of Queen Elizabeth's visit to Oxford, in Plummer, below.
Bradner	Leicester Bradner, *The Life and Poems of Richard Edwards*, Yale Studies in English 74 (New Haven: Yale University Press, 1927).
Cheque Book	*Old Cheque-Book or Book of Remembrance of the Chapel Royal from 1561–1744*, ed. Edward F. Rimbault, (London: Camden Society, 1872).
Cott. Vesp.	British Library, Cotton Vespasian MS.
CSP, Spanish	*Calendar of State Papers, Spanish Series.*
CT	British Library, Cotton MS Titus A.xxiv.
D&P	*Damon and Pythias.*
DNB	*Dictionary of National Biography.*
Edward and Mary	Albert Feuillerat, ed., *Documents Relating to the Revels at Court in the Time of King Edward VI and Queen Mary* (Louvain: A. Uystpruyst, 1914) (Kraus Reprint, 1963).
Elizabeth	Albert Feuillerat, ed., *Documents Relating to the Revels at Court in the Time of Queen Elizabeth* (Louvain: A. Uystpruyst, 1908) (Kraus Reprint, 1963).
Governor	Sir Thomas Elyot, *The Book Named the Governor*, 1531 (London: Dent, 1962).
Jack Juggler	in Marie Axton, ed., *Three Tudor Classical Interludes* (Woodbridge: D. S. Brewer, 1982).
Mulliner	The Mulliner Book, Add. 30513.
Nic. Eth.	Aristotle, *Nicomachean Ethics*, tr. David Ross (Oxford: Oxford University Press, 1953).
Nichols	John Nichols, *Progresses of Queen Elizabeth I* (London, 1823), vol. 1.
OED	*Oxford English Dictionary.*
P&A	*Palamon and Arcyte.*
Patent Rolls	*Calendar of the Patent Rolls Preserved in the Public Record Office* (London, 1891–1901).
PDD	*The Paradise of Dainty Devices*; specific editions referred to by date. Numbers refer to poems included in this edition.
Plummer	C. Plummer, ed., *Elizabethan Oxford: Reprints of Rare Tracts* (Oxford: Oxford Historical Society, 1887).
Plutarch	*Lives of the Noble Grecians and Romans, Englished by Sir Thomas North*, 1579 (London: David Nutt, 1895–6, 6 vols).
PRO	Public Record Office.
RCM	Royal College of Music.
Scholemaster	Ascham, Roger, *The Scholemaster*, in *English Works*, ed. William Aldis Wright (Cambridge: Cambridge University Press, 1904, reprinted 1970).
Stopes	C. C. Stopes, *William Hunnis and the Revels of the Chapel Royal* (Louvain: A. Uystpruyst, 1910).
Tilley	Morris Palmer Tilley, *A Dictionary of the Proverbs in England in the Sixteenth and Seventeenth Centuries* (Ann Arbor: University of Michigan Press, 1950).

Tusc.   Cicero, *Tusculan Disputations*.
Windsor   Corpus Christi College, Oxford, Corpus Christi MS 257.

Classical references are from editions in the Loeb Classical Library unless otherwise stated. Quotations from Shakespeare are taken from the edition by Peter Alexander (London and Glasgow: Collins, 1951); those from Chaucer from the edition by F. N. Robinson (Oxford: Oxford University Press, 1957); and those from the Bible from the Great Bible of 1540.

INTRODUCTION

Richard Edwards is something of an enigma. Highly esteemed during and immediately after his lifetime, his work is now almost unknown and survives only in a single play, a handful of poems and a little music. Both Edwards and Shakespeare were described by their contemporaries as rivals to the Roman dramatists Plautus and Terence. Francis Meres includes both Edwards and Shakespeare in his list of English writers best for comedy, describing Edwards as 'eloquent and wittie' (*Palladis Tamia* (1598), Oo3v). Yet Edwards is now dismissed as one of the old-fashioned academic poets from whose dreadful scansion and conventional platitudes Shakespeare mysteriously sprang. He died in 1566 when Shakespeare was two, yet thirty years later Shakespeare was satirising his work. Why should he feel the need?

We now live and work with a language and culture that owes a large part of its development to the writing of Shakespeare. It is therefore difficult for us to appreciate or even to recognise the liveliness and importance of the cultural experimentation that was going on immediately before him. The problem is compounded because so much of this work has disappeared. Yet, unusually, glimpses of Edwards's work as a performer, and his behaviour as a person, were written down and have survived. There are tantalising snippets of some lively banter he exchanged with Queen Elizabeth, and several descriptions of a performance of the lost play, *Palamon and Arcyte*, which he not only wrote but directed. Together, these provide perhaps the fullest account of a production of any play in the early modern period. They also highlight how little we know for certain about theatre and performance in the sixteenth century.

The bare facts of Richard Edwards's life are recorded in the registers and account books of Oxford University where he was a student, in state records relating to his office as a Gentleman, later Master, of the Chapel Royal, and in the descriptions of the Queen's visit to Oxford in 1566 in which he was so heavily involved. These can be amplified by what we know about the school and university education of the time, as well as the political and religious upheavals of the period through which he lived, which would have had profound and immediate effects on his working life as a church musician. All this, together with an appreciation of how the texts have come down to us both in print and in manuscript form, provides us with the context which helps us to understand how it was that they came to be written and how they should be read.

The systematic study of archive material relating to the sixteenth-century drama has been hampered because it is widely scattered in a variety of different manuscript sources that have not been fully collated in one single modern publication. Conversely, and ironically, any attempt to do this inevitably makes the material look more complete than it is. No one working on any of the public theatre dramatists of the later Elizabethan period would expect to find more than a small proportion of their evidence in the court records. What is instructive is how little these records preserve for those dramatists who spent the bulk of their working lives at court. In fact, our understanding of the drama as a whole has relied too much on written documents. We have to learn to read more inclusively, bringing details of literary criticism, performance practice, cultural studies and history to bear in a single argument.

This book is therefore in the nature of an archaeological investigation. Like the disturbed ground of an ancient site, the documents bear the imprint of human activity that they were not actually intended to record but which can nevertheless be deduced. Looking for the anomalies in the records that might accommodate the career of this once highly regarded sixteenth-century poet has given me a fresh understanding of the cultural life of the Tudor court and its household. It has enabled me to identify certain specific holes in the documentation, which, considered in context, go some way to explain its apparent sketchiness and thus provide new evidence for the working of the Revels Office and the function of drama at court.

It is the purpose of this book to try to reconstruct the story of the cultural and political life of the 1550s and 1560s in which Edwards took part as poet, performer and educator. While I do not wish to make inflated claims for him as a writer, it is important to realise the extent to which English language, literature and theatre were being shaped during the brief period in which he was working. His contribution to that development should be recognised.

Education and early career

Richard Edwards was born in the county of Somerset, probably in September 1524, and admitted in 1539 to Corpus Christi College, Oxford, where he studied under the composer and Greek scholar George Etherege.[1] Vacation times, particularly at Christmas (when most students would still be in residence) and Candlemas (the Feast of the Purification of the Virgin Mary in February), were often times for actual play performance, although there have always been (and were increasingly to be) those who regarded such activity as sinful. College life itself was essentially theatrical, both in its customs and in its teaching methods. At school, and in the universities, public performance by students of all kinds of plays and shows was, as Thomas Heywood later claimed, 'held necessary for the emboldening of their Junior schollers, to arme them with audacity, against they come to bee imployed in any publicke exercise as in the reading of the dialecticke'. It trained the student in the practical arts of presentation and rhetoric, and made him 'a bold sophister, to argue *pro et contra*, to compose his sillogismes . . . to reason and frame a sufficient argument to prove his questions'.[2]

When Elizabeth travelled to the universities of Cambridge and Oxford on her progresses, which she first did in 1564 and 1566 respectively, she spent her days sitting on a stage listening to the scholars engaged in their disputations, and receiving and returning spoken addresses in both Latin and Greek. She spent her evenings—when she wasn't too exhausted by this—listening to them performing a range of ancient and modern plays in Latin and in English. Most of this literature is lost. The rest is largely ignored because it is in Latin or perhaps because the term 'academic' is so widely used as synonymous with 'boring'.

Students were trained in the Trivium (Grammar, Rhetoric and Logic), which furnished them with the linguistic and debating skills to undertake the Quadrivium (Arithmetic, Music, Geometry and Astronomy), together with the three Philosophies: Physical, Moral and Metaphysical. Books were scarce, so it was necessary to commit huge swathes of text to memory. A student's own composition involved 'fishing' relevant texts from a variety of authors out of the memory, and then literally 'positioning' them together in a logical argument.[3] Students progressed by performing such rhetorical exercises orally and in public.

Corpus Christi itself was not particularly noted for its play productions while Edwards was a student there, but next door Merton College had a flourishing tradition. The poet Nicholas Grimald arrived there as a probationer fellow in 1541. He is now best known for the forty lyrics that he contributed to the first edition of Tottel's *Songs and Sonnettes* in 1557, the earliest of all the Tudor poetic miscellanies, but he also wrote at least seven plays, two in English. Only two Latin plays on religious themes still exist.

Edwards supplicated for his BA in May 1544 (admitted 3 November), and was elected a Probationer Fellow at Corpus Christi on 11 August. Two years later, Henry VIII, who had already given his own name to Cardinal College (originally the foundation of the disgraced Cardinal Wolsey), now completely reconstituted it as part of the new Christ Church Cathedral under Dean Richard Cox, who was also one of the advisers on the education of Prince Edward. Etherege became Regius Professor of Greek in the new foundation, while Edwards was given the lectureship in logic at a salary of 40s per year paid termly, plus 20s as bachelor of the foundation and 20s livery.[4] The following year, 1547, the year of accession of Edward VI, Cox became Vice-Chancellor of the University and Edwards advanced to a Master's Degree.

He would probably have won his lectureship at Christ Church by submitting verses, speeches or even a play written in Latin or Greek. Cox had apparently been inundated with applications of this kind. Grimald's, which gained him the lectureship in rhetoric, was a romantic and lyrical Latin play entitled *Archipropheta* on the life of John the Baptist, and still survives in both manuscript and printed form.[5] It presents the biblical story of Herod, Salome and John with considerable passion, music and spectacle and not a little humour. With both Grimald and Edwards on the staff, it is perhaps not surprising that Christ Church immediately became a centre for theatrical performance in Oxford.

Edwards also evidently took on additional tasks in the college of an organisational nature since the keeper of the college disbursement book for 1548 records that he paid Master Edwards 20d 'to helpe me at Dyvers tymes'. Unfortunately the disbursement books for later years until 1577 are missing, but, after Edwards had left the college, play performance seems to have become a source of anxiety for the Dean and chapter, no doubt caused by some run-away expense and perhaps concern about the moral advisability of such activity. An occasional entry, dated 12 December 1554 in another college ledger, finds them limiting expenditure on the Christmas plays to £6 (20s a piece for two comedies, one Latin and one Greek, and 40s each for two tragedies, again in Latin and Greek).

The last record of Edwards in the hierarchical lists of members of Christ Church is in 1550. It is not clear exactly when he arrived at court or in what capacity, but various pieces of circumstantial or otherwise doubtful evidence combine to place him there during the reign of Edward VI, who died in 1553. The Christ Church connection makes it possible that he was preferred through the patronage of Richard Cox, who was briefly imprisoned on Mary's accession for his support of Lady Jane Grey, later going into exile for the rest of her reign. In her book on William Hunnis, Edwards's successor as Master of the Chapel, C. C. Stopes cites a payment to Edwards in a book of Fees and Annuities of Edward VI of £6 13s 4d, an amount which happens to be the standard payment for a stage performance at court during the period.[6] Unfortunately this document can no longer be found. Finally, a copy of Edwards's poem 'In youthful years' (p. 201), describing how he set off to make a life for himself at court, occurs in a manuscript in the British Library (Add. 15233). The manuscript, which is in a variety of hands, is supposed to have been copied in the early 1550s. It contains a play, keyboard music and poems by John Redford, one-time Master of St Paul's School who died in 1547, and other poems by John Heywood, a favourite of Queen Mary who left England after her death. The *persona* in Edwards's poem tells that he was warned by his father not to trust the promises that people at court will make to him, 'for fair words make fools fain'. The advice about fair words and false friends is entirely proverbial and forms the basis for other poems in the period, but what distinguishes Edwards's lyric is the verisimilitude afforded by the particularity of the scene. Here is an ordinary family, a prepossessing young man, and a father who is proud of his son's talent, willing him to succeed through the patronage system at court, offering him parting advice, and blessing him 'with trembling hand'. Finally, the speaker observes that the advice is valid:

> Woe worth the time that words so slowly turn to deeds,
> . . . let words be words which never wrought me gain,
> Let my experience make you wise, and let words make fools fain.
> (PDD, 4.25–32)

It is of course inadvisable to draw a life from a lyric poem, but the lines suggest the experience of someone for whom preferment and reward was a long time coming. They also bear out what can be gleaned about the workings of the Chapel at that period. The *Cheque Book* of the Chapel Royal begins only in 1561 and initially keeps very scanty and sparse records. In the 1590s, however, it seems that people were regularly appointed to substitute or 'extraordinary' places, often by order of the Lord Chamberlain but without pay, while waiting for an 'ordinary' place to become available. Ordinary gentlemen would be on probation for the first year. A place must have been worth waiting for as there was a queue. Once conferred, it belonged to the holder until death and could be sold, although a permanent place would not be bestowed without the permission of the sub-dean and, it seems, the agreement of the existing gentlemen.[7] The name George Edwards appears amongst the members of the Chapel Royal in a list of wages paid to members of the royal household, compiled during Edward VI's reign (BL MS Stowe 71, fol. 36v). It is therefore possible that this man was a relative who then bequeathed Richard the place. Whether or not Edwards's poem was autobiographically true, it has the ring of truth and seems to have been popular. The words can be found in three surviving manuscript miscellanies as well as the printed *Paradise of Dainty Devices*, while the music occurs in two manuscripts.

Documentary evidence for the provision of drama at court

The history of sixteenth-century drama relies almost entirely on records of payment, both for the dating of the few plays that are extant and for an indication of the subject matter and indeed the very existence of those that are lost. The problem with this, as I shall try to show, is that people who wrote for court entertainment in their capacity *as courtiers* did so as part of their 'service' or 'duty', and would not necessarily be paid directly. Theirs was a social act, a gift. Payment, if it came, would come in like manner, *ex gratia*. Edwards's life as a working artist at court is, I suggest, inevitably poorly documented because it was by nature amateur. This is a description of fact, not quality. In order to fill in the gaps we need to examine the practices relating both to play production and to the circulation of poetry in educated circles.

Theatre historians have tended to talk about performances 'at court' without considering that these may have fallen into a number of different categories requiring different types of expenditure. On the one hand, entertainments provided by members of the royal household as part of their service would not necessarily result in direct payments to the performers. Depending on the nature and scale of the entertainment, however, there might or might not have been production costs. On the other hand, visiting companies would normally expect payment and also might or might not have incurred production costs.

There were a number of different sources of materials and funding for court entertainments. The fanciful costumes needed for masques were made and stored by the Office of the Revels. Equally rich but real clothes might be borrowed from the Great Wardrobe. There must also, as with any theatrical enterprise, have been a good deal of borrowing of more ordinary garments from friends and acquaintances. Tents and pavilions for outdoor shows would come from the Office of Tents (from which the Revels Office itself had separated out as recently as 1545). The task of erecting and dismantling scaffolding structures for temporary indoor theatres in existing halls would be the responsibility of the Office of the Works. The 'apparelling' of these chambers with tapestries, hangings and cloths of estate for special occasions such as plays and revels was the job of the Chamber, the division of the royal household responsible for running the sovereign's living quarters. Payments to players might be made either from the Chamber or from the Privy Purse depending on whether the entertainment was a state or private occasion. This is complicated both by successive attempts to reorganise such funding and the resulting 'chaotic state of the records', and by the fact that when the private household is also a royal household it can be difficult to distinguish between private and state occasions.[8]

Specific payments of £6 13s 4d to Richard Bower and before him to William Crane (Edwards's predecessors as Master of the Chapel) for plays by the Chapel children are regularly found in those court account books that survive up to 1549. They resume only after Edwards's death in 1566. With the exception of the entry seen by Stopes, there is no record of any payment to Edwards himself. It is inconceivable that someone with Edwards's reputation as an accomplished and prolific playwright, and with his documented connection with the Chapel, was not performing with those children during that blank period. The start of the hiatus in recorded payments to the Master of the Chapel for play performances coincides with reorganisation of the financing of entertainments. It also roughly corresponds with the date of Edwards's departure from Oxford.

During the period from Elizabeth's accession in November 1558 to Edwards's death in October 1566 there are regular payments from the Chamber to visiting companies for performances at Christmas, Candelmas and Shrovetide. Thus in 1564–5, the year of the probable performance of *Damon and Pythias*, the Office of the Works supplied 'skaffoldes, and other woorks for tryumphes at Christm[a]s' at Hampton Court. The Chamber Accounts record payments to the Earl of Warwick's players and to Sebastian Westcote, Master of the Children of St Paul's for two plays each (three at Christmas and one at Candlemas).[9] Yet, as I have already indicated, there was no payment to Edwards or the Chapel. The visiting company performances had been ordered by the Privy Council in the name of the Queen, and payment was made by the Treasurer of the Chamber on production of the Council's warrant at the standard rate of £6 13s 4d per play. The Revels Accounts for the Christmas period, however, show expenditure on props and costumes for plays by Westminster School as well as the Children of Paul's, together with a masque, a show and a play noted as 'Edwardes tragedy' by the Children of the Chapel. On 18 February the Revels also provided for a play made by 'Sir Percival Hart's sons' with a masque of hunters and various devices, while at Shrovetide (4–6 March) they helped the gentlemen of Gray's Inn with a play concerning Diana and Pallas and other shows.[10]

Within four months of Edwards's death, with William Hunnis as the new Master, the Chapel children start to appear alongside the visiting companies as regular payees, although the popularity of the children's companies gradually declines in favour of adult companies. Hunnis, in addition to his role as a Gentleman of the Chapel, was Head Gardener at Greenwich, a post that was not simply a sinecure since he was paid for bushels of roses, pinks, privet flowers and honeysuckle, strewing herbs and rose water for decorating a banqueting house to entertain the French Ambassador in 1572.[11] He was therefore perhaps more used to being on the payroll as a servant rather than being treated as a gentleman amateur. Indeed he tried hard to professionalise the post, writing to the Queen deploring the penurious state of previous Masters. This led both Stopes and Bradner to suppose that Edwards had died penniless since his burial place is unknown and he seems to have left no will.[12] On the contrary, we shall see that the grants of land and of sinecures recorded in the Patent Rolls constitute an untapped source for the study of the drama. The evidence of such patents as rewards 'for his service' suggests that he gradually amassed a reasonable living, although what precisely the services were that were being recognised in this way is always left unrecorded. Financial success, if indeed he achieved it, thus required a mix of personal and entrepreneurial skills as landholder and businessman in order to make the most of these opportunities and provide the necessary addition to the meagre income that he drew as a gentleman, and later Master, of the Chapel. Such an existence is precarious, however, and sadly he would die before being able to enjoy the reversion of at least two of the leases that he acquired in this way.

The only other record of costs specifically associated with a play by the Chapel, during the time when we know for certain that Edwards was in post there, is in a Revels inventory from 1560 charting changes in the stock since March 1555. Against an entry for seventy-one yards of white sarsenet which had been acquired at about Christmas 1559, it is noted that five yards had been used to furnish a play by the Chapel Children, the rest used on a variety of other projects, with one yard given as a fee.[13]

It was a relatively common practice for players in masques to be given costumes as fees,[14] but sometimes costumes were lost, or retained without permission. A Revels inventory, dated 1 April 1547, the first year of Edward's reign, notes that two named members of the Chapel, Stone and Gravesend, are holding on to a crimson damask costume for a 'priest or cardinal' and a long white damask gown. In both cases these are marked as 'unserviceable' and yet as being 'with' a named person, which suggests that the costume was still regarded as belonging to the Revels.[15] The gentlemen might have regarded the clothes as legitimate perquisites for their generally underpaid service but the Revels Office did not agree. It is not the performance or even the borrowing that is being recorded in these cases but the fact that the costume has not come back to the store. Had it been returned, we would not know that Chapel gentlemen had recently been performing in plays at court.

It is important to remember that the Chamber and Revels accounts are not literary records. It is the payee, usually the company or its director, the number of performances and the date that are pertinent to the Chamber accountant, not the play or playwright. Although the Revels might sometimes take on the role of a theatrical production company as we might now understand it, a more exact equivalent is perhaps a quartermaster's store, responsible for procurement and the care of equipment. Yearly Revels 'paybooks' or accounts thus show the itemised daily wages of named workers—embroiderers, seamstresses, painters, carpenters etc.—as well as lists of the sums paid out for different types of cloth or other supplies, together with reimbursements to Revels officers for their payments for transport from the store to wherever the court was in residence. They rarely name either the writer or the entertainments. Where these are recorded, they usually occur as marginal notes, as *aides mémoires* to the identification of the costumes. In addition to drawing up summary end-of-year accounts for submission to the Treasury, the Revels Office undertook yearly audits of stock. These give brief descriptions of costumes, noting whether they are 'serviceable' or 'unserviceable', and sometimes, as we have seen, indicating their whereabouts if, for some reason, they have not been returned to the store. Their purpose is to track the cloth as it is successively bought, cut, re-used or 'translated', worn out, lost and given away.

Other details about the workings of the early years of the Office are mostly culled from papers belonging to Sir Thomas Cawarden, Master of the Revels from the inception of this Office (c.1544) until his death in 1559. These were hoarded at Loseley House in Surrey for three hundred and fifty years and then, mostly, sold to the Folger Library in Washington, but in reality they are little more than the contents of Sir Thomas's waste-paper basket. The pioneering work of A. Feuillerat in printing these various documents in ordered and accessible book form made them accessible to scholars, but the material was lent a coherence and aura of completeness which it actually does not possess. Sifting through the actual scraps, scribbles and jottings of the Cawarden papers for the first time can therefore be something of a shock.

With a few notable exceptions, several of which are cited below, most of these papers are lists of goods—candles, properties, shoes, spangles, lengths of cloth—bought from external suppliers who may or (more often) may not be named, with the cost of each item and usually a total. Many of them are in fact debentures, itemised lists of goods received, given to the supplier on delivery, such as those that Grim the collier has in his purse (D&P, 13.189). The supplier would later need to submit them to the Revels Office in exchange for payment. Sometimes he or she would sign them to say that this had been received, sometimes they would be crossed through. Occasionally, since the Office was chronically in deficit, payment was made in part and the debenture submitted more than once. The debentures describe the goods themselves in some detail—cloth is denoted by quality, yardage and colour. Very occasionally they mention the masque, play or the character for which the particular item was intended but, as before, this is incidental to the real purpose which is to document trade in commodities.

Cawarden's papers were generated by change: mostly change in stock, represented as a financial charge, but occasionally change in working practice, or special measures to cope with an unusual event. We can therefore only really expect to find recorded in these documents payments for new materials, loss or damage to old materials, and any extra-ordinary costs or requirements for mounting a production. As historians, our most difficult task is therefore to determine the normal practice of the Office, particularly in its dealings with the gentlemen amateur playwrights attached to the court. The following abnormal warrant from Mary to Cawarden and his deputies in respect of Nicholas Udall, dated 13 December 1554, in fact enables us to deduce a whole history for which there is no record:

wher as our welbelovid Nicholas Udall haith at sondry seasons convenient hertofore shewid and myndeth herafter to shewe his diligence in settinge forthe of dialogwes and Entreludes before us for our Regall disport and recreacion to thentent that he may be in the better redynes at all tymes when it shalbe our pleasure to call. wee will and comaunde you and every of you that at all & every soche tyme and tymes so ofte and when so ever he shall neade & requier it for shewing of any thinge before us ye delyver or cause to be delyvered to the said Udall or to the bringer herof in his name out of our office of Revelles soche apperell for his Auctors as he shall thinke necessarye and requisite for the furnishing & condigne setting forth of his Devises before us and soche as may be semely to be shewid in our Regall presens / And the same apperell after the exhibitinge of any soche thing before us to be restored and redelyvered by the said Udall into your handes and custody againe.[16]

Udall (1504–56) was the translator of Erasmus's *Apophthegms* or 'sayings' (1542), and author of several school texts, including the *Floures of Latine Spekyng* (a selection of phrases, in parallel Latin and English translation, culled from three plays by Terence, 1533), and a commentary on Cicero's *Tusculan Disputations*. Having been sacked from the headmastership at Eton, probably for his abuse of the boys, he redeemed himself by publishing various religious and political works. These include a translation of Erasmus's *Paraphrases* of the Gospel, which he began with the then Princess Mary, and perhaps an *Answer* to the grievances of the West Country rebels who rose against the new Protestant prayer book in 1549.[17] His known dramatic output consists of the verses in English for the pageants for Anne Boleyn's coronation procession in 1533, some plays in Latin on religious subjects and, according to an attributed quotation in Thomas Wilson's *The Rule of Reason*, the English comedy *Ralph Roister Doister* (c.1553, published 1566). On the grounds of stylistic similarity with this play, he can also be credited with both *Thersites* (published c.1562), based on a Latin play by the French writer Ravisius Textor, and the moral interlude *Respublica*. It is probably this interlude that occasioned this warrant. The warrant, however, states that he had already written 'sundry' court entertainments, and its purpose is to circumvent whatever bureaucratic procedure he had needed to go through in the past in order to produce these. It would not be possible to attribute any of the three English plays to Udall without the quotation in Wilson's book, and apart from this warrant and the bills connected with the masques and plays he 'set owte' that Christmas,[18] no financial, procedural or descriptive records remain of his play-producing activities. The warrant thus demonstrates that a courtier like Udall, and indeed like Edwards, might be writing and producing plays for the various royal households for years without this being visible in the accounts.

This warrant also raises another question about the custody of costumes, all of which were of considerable value, borrowed from the Office for household purposes. An early Elizabethan civil servant trying to rationalise and reform the Office cites the need for an 'employ book' to record the use to which cloth is put, demanding much greater supervision by the officers to avoid wastage, and recommending that costumes should no longer be lent.[19] Given the evidence of the Loseley papers, Cawarden and his officers probably did no more than retain a receipt for any costume borrowed, which would have been handed back to the borrower when the item was returned. Our evidence that such borrowing took place therefore comes from letters written to Cawarden requesting costumes, not from any day-to-day stock control book.[20] It is only in such a book that we could expect to find consistent records for shows that incurred no new costs.

On 8 March 1554 the Patent Rolls record 'a grant for life in consideration of his service to Richard Edwards one of the yeomen of the chamber, of the office of keeper of the Castle of Kirkby in Kendal Co.

Westmorland and of the park there, which office was lately held by Ralph Grymshay deceased'.[21] Kirkby, otherwise known as Kendal Castle, was the birthplace of Catherine Parr, one of Henry VIII's wives, but was abandoned since William Parr had been attaindered for his support of Jane Grey and his estate sequestered by the Crown. The post carried wages and fees of 4d per day plus rights to 'lopings and brusyngs and windfalls' from the park. No duties were laid down, which suggests that it was a sinecure, a post literally 'without responsibility', and could thus have been held *in absentia*. Court officers at this period were often remunerated in this way with rents from property held by the Crown.[22]

Official posts were usually held under a patent, which granted certain freedom of action and even entrepreneurial rights to the office holder. No one without private means could survive on an officer's salary alone. The same Revels Office reformer to whom I have already referred wrote: 'The fee and wages whiche anye one of the officers hath will not in my symple opynyon suffice to maynteyne any man beinge of meane and symple estate accompted the Princes officer (havinge nothinge els to take to) albeit he were a sole man without charge of wife or children' (*Elizabeth*, 7). Cawarden himself, for example, had a yearly basic salary as Master of the Revels of only £10, plus fees of 4s per day when directly engaged on the work of the Revels. More important was his mastership of the Office of the Tents for which he was paid £30, and the rents he received from the manorial courts of Nonsuch, Banstead and Walton as steward of these manors, those from his properties in the Blackfriars which he had been granted on the dissolution of the monasteries, and benefits accruing from his keepership of Donnington Castle and of two areas of the park at Hampton Court.[23]

The easy bantering tone of a poem addressed to eight ladies of Queen Mary's court (CT 1) shows that, by the end of 1555 at the latest, Edwards had become familiar with the Queen's closest circle. This group of ladies was a mix of aristocrats and gentlewomen, some of whom had served her for many years and become her long-term friends (see pp. 231–2). It is therefore not impossible that it is our Richard Edwards who is referred to in the previous year as a yeoman of the chamber. This post would normally carry a daily salary and responsibilities, but it would also be possible for the sovereign to confer it in an honorary fashion, in which case there would be no record of it in the account books. The same name also recurs in the same capacity in the first year of Elizabeth's reign.[24] It is not sufficiently unusual as a name for us to be sure that it does not represent two different people. On the other hand, there is a strange poem in one of the Tanner manuscripts in the Bodleian Library, Oxford, in which the poet petitions to be a woman's 'chamber fool'. This precedes one about Queen Elizabeth attributed to Edwards (see pp. 227–30) and is in the same hand. Maybe an honorary position as gentleman of the bedchamber under Mary was initially continued under Elizabeth, perhaps confirmed by a grant of board wages in the year after her coronation (see

p. 26). Maybe he lost the title when one of his satirical plays took one liberty too many since the prologue to *Damon and Pythias* (pp. 7–12) suggests that one of his previous comedies had got him into some kind of trouble. And maybe his success with *Palamon and Arcyte*, performed during Elizabeth's visit to Oxford in 1566, encouraged him to sue for reinstatement. It is a tempting scenario, though quite unprovable.

RELIGIOUS POLITICS IN DRAMA AND POETRY

Mary's coronation play

If the 1554 patent is indeed in favour of our Richard Edwards, it might well have been a reward for working alongside Udall in the provision of the entertainments that accompanied Mary's coronation, and which continued through the following Christmas and New Year. On 16 August 1553, within days of her accession, the Privy Council prepared a proclamation for the 'reformation of busy medlers in matters of religion, and for redresse of prechers, printers, players'. It sought to regulate 'the playing of Interludes, and printing of false fond bookes, ballettes, rhymes and other lewde treatises in the English tongue concerning matters now in Question and controversy'.[26] Theatrical shows were not simply entertainment. They had political, religious implications.

Two warrants followed in September, one to the Master and Officers of the Revels and one to the Master of the Wardrobe, both requesting costumes. Both state that the Chapel Royal was to produce a play for the coronation 'as in tymes paste haithe bene accustomed to be done by the gentillmen of the Chappell of owr progenitours'.[27] Both Offices were issued with a list of costumes for this play which, although the text is lost, shows that the proclamation was being carefully heeded. The main character was a figure of mankind, *Genus Humanum*, who in the course of the play would meet five virgins in cassocks of white 'Bruges' satin. There will evidently be a struggle for his soul between a good angel and an evil angel. In the process he will encounter on the one hand Reason, Verity and Plenty (all in purple satin), and, on the other, Self-love, Care, Scarcity and Deceit (in red, green, russet and red satin respectively), and be beset by Sickness, Feebleness and Deformity (in tawny, ash-coloured and black satin). It is not known who wrote this play. Stopes suggests Udall, but he was never a gentleman of the Chapel and the royal warrant addressed to Cawarden instructs him to deal with 'toe [two] of the seide gentillmen'. A marginal note in Cawarden's copy of the instructions indicates that the play was postponed until Christmas.

Edward VI's Christmas entertainments

This morality play is in marked contrast to the Christmas entertainments of the previous reign. In 1551–2 and 1552–3 the Revels Office had been requested by King Edward VI's councillors to spend enormous sums of money on costumes for a revival of the traditional Christmas carnival of the Lord of Misrule. The part of the Lord of Misrule himself was undertaken by George Ferrers, Master of the King's Pastimes under Henry VIII. He would later be connected with *The Mirror for Magistrates*, a collection of 'tragedies' illustrating the dangers of bad government, probably suppressed by Mary in 1555. Ferrers's retinue of mock councillors, 'dizzards' or fools was played by courtiers dressed in extravagant motley costumes. They were equipped with a pillory, stocks, gibbet, 'heading axe and block' and numerous whips, clubs, staves and other weapons. We do not know what texts they spoke, but their costumes and reported actions incorporate satire on false religion and bad government. This, together with the extraordinary expense and the haste in which Ferrers was first appointed to the job, suggests a political as well as a recreational purpose, connected with the fall of Protector Somerset and the jockeying for power amongst Edward's advisers that attended this. The fun included various masques, a procession through the City of London, a mock tournament on hobbyhorses, and a parade of the holy sacrament, described by the Spanish Ambassador in a letter to the King his master, as 'perfumed in most strange fashion, with great ridicule of the ecclesiastical [i.e. Roman Catholic] estate'. He added that this scandalised some English people as well as the French and Venetian ambassadors.[28]

In all his dealings with the Revels Office, Ferrers acted in role, robustly reminding Cawarden that he had the authority of the Privy Council behind him and writing on one occasion to complain about the quality of the costumes provided:

> Mr Carden we have receaved from you the Apparell for *our* owne *person which* we mislyke not muche . . . but it seemeth unto vs that as towching the Apparell of *our* Counseillo*ures* yo*u* have mistaken ye *persons* that sholde were them as S*ir* Robe*rt* Stafforde and Thom*as* Wyndeham w*ith* other gentlemen that stande also apon their reputac*ion* and wolde not be seen in london so torchebererlyke [i.e. torch-bearer-like] disgysed for asmoche as they ar worthe or hope to be worthe. (*Edward and Mary*, 59)

Cawarden was charged by the King's councillors to give Ferrers every support and he took care to copy their warrants into his accounts to explain the extraordinary expense. The Spanish Ambassador reports that Ferrers and some others were rewarded with good pensions from the King in addition to the ready money they received at the time.

The authorship of Jack Juggler

The anonymous, learned but actually very funny comedy *Jack Juggler* belongs in the same religious context as Ferrers's Lord of Misrule shows and may have been written the year before (1550–1). It was evidently written to be performed at Christmas since Jack's opening speech calls on Christ, St Stephen and St John (celebrated on 25, 26 and 27 December respectively), but it is no mere seasonal comedy. There are dark references to hidden meanings, to four deaths seven years previously, and to being 'washed in warme blod' (364–8).

The play is a rewriting of Plautus's *Amphitruo*, which concerns Jupiter's adultery with Alcmena, achieved by turning himself into a copy of her husband Amphitruo, while Mercury, disguised as the family slave, Sosia, guards the door. Most of the humour in Plautus's play derives from Sosia's puzzlement and frustration at coming face to face with his double. *Jack Juggler* has occasionally been ascribed to Udall but it does not contain his characteristic trademarks: alliteration, regular metres and lines split between different speakers. On the contrary, I consider that its metrical irregularity, humour, facility for wordplay, ability to adapt classical literature to an English domestic situation and numerous instances of its phraseology and choice of rhyme are characteristic of Richard Edwards's known work.[29]

Like *Damon and Pythias*, this play for child actors begins with a disclaimer. The author stresses that the only reason for the present comedy is to provide a bit of fun and that the content is 'not worthe an oyster shel'. He repeats that the play will treat of 'mattiers of non importaunce' (l. 54) and that no one should 'looke to heare of mattiers substancyall / Nor mattiers of any gravitee' since such things are not appropriate for 'litle boyes handelings' (ll. 73–6). These protestations of inconsequentiality are in fact necessary because this play's play on language will allow audiences to hear it as a metaphor for the most 'substantial' matter of the sixteenth century: the question as to whether the bread and wine of the communion service came to 'represent', to 'carry the memory of' or to 'be' the body and blood of Christ. In the change of the story from ancient Rome to London, Jupiter and his adultery is discarded, Amphitruo's character is renamed Master Boungrace, Mercury becomes Jack Juggler and a supper invitation significantly developed. In October 1551 Archbishop Cranmer himself cited Alcmena's deception by Jupiter in *Amphitruo* as an example of 'an illusion of our senses, if our senses take for bread and wine that whiche is not so indeed'.[30]

The character Jack Juggler first appears in the reforming satire of the fifteenth-century poem *Piers Plowman*, and the term 'juggling' was regularly used to attack Roman Catholic practices (particularly the belief in transubstantiation in the Eucharist). The play is vigorously Protestant, which must mean that it dates from the reign of Edward VI. At Christmas 1550 the haunting reference to seven years before would refer back to the blackest period in the struggle for the reformation of the English church. This was the so-called 'Prebendaries Plot' fomented amongst the reactionary staff of Canterbury Cathedral and its Oxford institution, Canterbury College, by Dr John London and Bishop Gardiner. The immediate result was the burning of evangelicals connected with the Chapel at

Windsor in 1543, and accusations of heresy against Archbishop Cranmer. Two years later the tables had turned and Canterbury College buildings were ceded to next-door Christ Church, a fact that cannot have been lost on Edwards, who was in post there, alongside Roger Marbeck, the son of one of the Windsor victims (see n. 51).

Later Marian morality drama

Such was the success of the 1551–2 Lord of Misrule shows that Ferrers was commissioned again the following year. The Revels Office ran up bills of over £900 for these two Christmases, much of it apparently remaining unpaid. These accumulated debts contributed to a total debt for the royal household of £220,000.[31] After the necessary expenditure on Mary's coronation in 1553 and her marriage the following year to Philip of Spain, the yearly audited Revels Office accounts suggest that Cawarden was practising a policy of make-do and mend. There are the usual post-Christmas charges for cleaning, airing, 'translating' and mending the costumes, and for removing them to and from the court for shows, but few new purchases. For several years running, rewards are given to workers for 'woorkinge and framinge of to dyvers patrons [patterns] of Maskes devysed by the *Master*'.[32] Masques were generally far more expensive than plays, and no doubt Cawarden wanted to be sure that he could re-use costumes already in store. The economies, however, enabled him gradually to pay himself and others the arrears of rent on their property in the Blackfriars used as Revels Office stores, which had been owing since the Lord of Misrule extravagances.

There is an interesting letter in Cawarden's papers, dated Christmas Eve 1556, from William Baldwin, the main author of the *Mirror for Magistrates*. He is sounding out Cawarden on the possibility of the Revels Office providing costumes for a play. The play, which concerns 'the way to lyfe', is already in rehearsal and he intends to present it to the Queen in ten days' time. He says that the Inns of Court are interested in presenting it but that he is giving first refusal to Cawarden, since Cawarden has previously expressed interest in his devices. He also warns that the 'settyng furth wil be chargeable because the matter is stately'. Given the economies already noted in the accounts, this is an important point because it again indicates that there was drama being performed at court that was *not* chargeable. The play is three hours long and contains sixty-two characters, all with names beginning with the letter L:

> The matter is this, I bring in a yong man whome I name Lamuel who hath a servant called Lob, these two will attempt the worlde to seke theyr fortune, they mete with Lust lucke and love, Lust promiseth them lecherie, Lucke lordship, Love Lyf, they folow lust and through lechery be lost, th[e]n through Lucke they recover, Luck bringeth them to lordship from whiche through Larges and larracine [larceny] they cum to Lacke / Th[e]n

through Love, the[y] go to Light & therby attayne Lyfe. (*Edward and Mary*, 215–17)

The play is in Mary's approved morality style, but we do not know whether Cawarden agreed to spend money on it or indeed whether it was performed at all, although an endorsement on the paper suggests that it may have been presented the following year. I think, however, that it may provide us with the identity of one of the more enigmatic contributors to *The Paradise of Dainty Devices*, the anthology of poems collected by Edwards and published after his death. The first poem in the collection is based on some Latin verses by St Bernard on the state of the world. This, with four other poems on unrequited friendship, appears under the alias 'My Lucke is Losse'. The identity of this poet has been an unanswered puzzle but the pseudonym and the preposterous play seem to go together, particularly since Baldwin had, in more congenial times, signed the Address to the Reader for his *Canticles or Balads of Salomon . . . in Englysh Metres* (1549) with the phrase 'love and lyve'. If this allegorical morality play was his bid to restore himself to favour after the suppression of the historical, tragic narratives of the *Mirror for Magistrates*, it seems that he might have failed.[33]

Loyalty inscribed: an Oxford manuscript of the 1550s

Our best hope for understanding both the politics and the literature of this period is to try to trace the networks of friendship and patronage embedded in them. Manuscript collections are frequently the result of such networks and demonstrate both continuity and community—different hands, different owners contributing poems, notes, observations (sometimes recipes or household bills) over a period of time. Such a manuscript, containing five poems by Edwards, survives in the British Library, now part of a collected volume known as Cotton MS Titus A.xxiv. It must originally have been a notebook composed of sheets of folded paper, and now consists of twenty-four leaves, some still connected and some now separately mounted.[34] Its contents, and the group of authors represented in it, locate the manuscript in Oxford somewhere in the middle of Mary's reign, and reveal the very precarious nature of life in Tudor England.

Two of the poems by Edwards, 'O lord that rulest' and 'To Mr Wilson', concern foreign travel, even exile. Both are written in his distinctively vigorous and personal tone, although the first is a virtual reality since it involves the death by drowning of the poet, and the observations made over his dead body by the man who finds him washed up on a beach. The agony described, however, is not just that of the process of drowning. There is a strong sense that part of the torment is connected with dying unknown in a foreign place, although the poet is ambivalent as to whether this follows from his having to *fly* the country, or from a simple desire for foreign travel, 'our fancies for to please':

But woe worth me yet once again
that thus shall lie unknown,
And shall not place my wretched corpse
under some English stone.

(CT 4, 57–60)

The poem's address to the Lord, its apocalyptic promise of salvation and its verse structure are reminiscent of the Psalms of David. Translation of the psalms into English metre so that they could be sung and said, at home and in church by ordinary people, was one of the most important projects of the Reformation. The poem's first line is a quotation from Psalm 89.9, a psalm which praises God for raising the lineage of David 'hyer than the kinges of the earth'. Other quotations come from those psalms specifically recommended as prayers against those enemies that would destroy one's soul (Psalms 71 and 102). The effect of Fortune on human life was commonly likened to a ship in a storm at sea. This, together with the resonance of the underlying psalms, means that the poem can be understood not simply as a description of an actual journey but as an expression of the physical and spiritual dangers confronting someone living through the religious and political turmoil of the mid sixteenth century. It is thus an illustration of Fortitude, one of the four cardinal virtues, which 'makes souls pre-eminent and indifferent to worldly fortune' (Cicero, *De officiis*, 1.20.67; cf. *PDD*, 11n).

The poem to Mr Wilson is more ambiguous, and even more potentially disturbing. On one level it is a conventional love complaint, the lover burning with unconsummated love as if in the volcanic fires of Mount Etna, but it is evidently more complex than that and gives the impression that much more is intended than is readily apparent. Ultimately, interpretation must depend on the context afforded by the identity of the man in its title. The only notable Mr Wilson of the period is Thomas (1525–81), author of *The Rule of Reason Containing the Art of Logique* (1551) and *The Art of Rhetorique* (1553), the earliest extended treatise on literary theory written in English. He was almost the same age as Edwards and began his career in a similar way. A Greek scholar at Cambridge, he was associated with John Cheke, another of those like Dr Cox called to court to advise both on the reformation of the church and on the education of Prince (later King) Edward. Cheke had become Secretary of State to Lady Jane Grey for the brief fortnight of her ill-fated reign after Edward VI's death in 1553. On Mary's accession, both Cheke and Wilson therefore fled to Padua. Imprisoned in 1556 on the orders of Mary's husband, Philip II of Spain, Cheke was returned to England where he recanted, converted to Catholicism and died—it is said from the grief that this recantation caused him—in September 1557. Wilson remained at liberty until 1558 when Mary ordered him to return to face a charge of heresy. He was arrested and tortured by the Inquisition, but escaped, returning home only after Elizabeth's accession when he became successively a Member of Parliament, a diplomat and ultimately a Privy Councillor and Secretary of State.

If the Mr Wilson of the title is indeed Thomas Wilson, the poem is no conventional complaint on the miseries of being in love. Instead, it is an agonising appraisal of the 'burning' conflict between loyalty to Mary (expressed in terms of courtly love) and loyalty to one's conscience, coupled with the real risk of being burnt for heresy. The 'sacred dame', referred to in l. 31 below, then becomes either death or even Mary herself, for whom the loyal subject may need to lay down his life.

> O death ere she that death shall cause
>   come change my case at last. . . .   20
> Alas Leander, why do I   25
>   impute to thee a blame
> For yielding life to earnest love
>   where I do mean the same?
> Nothing can quench my aching flames,
>   in vain for help I call,   30
> In fine therefore, O sacred dame,
>   thou shalt have life and all.

Leander was the mythical lover who nightly performed the feat of swimming the Hellespont to visit his beloved Hero until he was drowned in a storm. The reference to his heroic story here implies some other, recent, real-life martyr, whose 'earnest love' (for his country? his religion?) has led to his death while travelling over the seas. The ambiguity of the poem resides in the poet's recognition that he must stay in love with the beloved even though he wishes he were not in such thraldom; his readiness to die before she can cause his death; his fear of unnatural death yet his unwillingness to live; his wish to change his 'case' (inward circumstance? outward body/appearance?); the blame he attaches to 'Leander' for giving in, yet his recognition that he must do the same; and simultaneously his admiration for Mr Wilson's steadfastness in exile. There seem to be only two choices: either to die for the beloved or to die because of her.

The first section of the manuscript has ruled margins and contains a variety of poems, probably all in the same hand, some anonymous, others ascribed to Thomas Norton or to the Earl of Surrey, and concluding with four poems all signed M. (i.e. Master) Edwards (CT 1–CT 4 in the present edition). It opens with a poem addressed to God, praising him for granting the 'seate imperial' to the noble Queen (i.e. Mary), and celebrates her safe delivery from 'dubul dark dissayte' (i.e. deceit)—presumably the plot to give the throne to Lady Jane Grey and Sir Thomas Wyatt's subsequent rebellion. But the poem also urges God to give Mary grace so that she may rule wisely and in peace:

> And give O lorde until her grace
>   from thy supernall throne
> longe lyfe to rayne and rule in rest
>   her subjectes all and one

The group of four poems by Edwards begins with the one in praise of
Mary's ladies to which I have already referred. Judging from the dates of
their various marriages, this must have been composed by the end
of 1555, and probably by March that year (see p. 231). Then follows a
transcription, in the same hand, of Archbishop Thomas Cranmer's last
confession before his execution on 21 March 1556—officially for heresy,
but also for his part in the divorce of Mary's mother and his upholding
of King Edward's will which stipulated that Jane Grey, not Mary, should
inherit the throne. At the end of the confession the scribe of the manuscript has appended the comment, 'You have written falsly', which led
Leicester Bradner to suggest that the manuscript belonged to an actively
Catholic supporter of the Queen. Cranmer, however, was one of those
responsible for writing the *Sermons or Homilies* (1547) published as a
major plank in the reformation under Edward. One of these, 'Of Obedi-
ence', states:

> Christe taught us plainly, that even the wicked rulers have their power and
> aucthoritie from God. And therefore it is not lawfull for their subjectes,
> by force to resist them, although they abuse their power, much less then
> it is lawfull for subjectes to resiste their godly and Christian princes, which
> do not abuse their aucthoritie.

By this premise, princes' lawful and absolute authority extends to the
right to determine the religious faith of their subjects. The first genera-
tion of English Protestants was therefore caught by the logic of their own
religious instruction, as well no doubt as a state of fear, if they refused to
conform to the re-establishment of the old faith. It is perhaps the trauma
caused by this logic, as much as the immediate bodily fear, that caused
Cranmer to recant, which he did in writing on six separate occasions.
This last confession was prepared in order to be spoken at the service
staged in St Mary's University Church in Oxford, which preceded his execution at the stake (although he also wrote it down in order that it could
be distributed). The authorities had been expecting him to confirm his
previous recantations but this new statement entirely repudiated them and
caused uproar in the church. A dramatic woodcut in Foxe's *Book of
Martyrs* shows him being hauled from his platform in the nave. The confession expresses his remorse for the recantations, which he describes as
'written withe my hande contrari to the truthe whiche I thoughte in my
herte, and written for feare of deathe and to saue my life if it mighte be'.
He concludes by saying that he will extend that hand into the flames of
the fire at his execution so that it will be burnt first—which indeed he
did. The scribe's comment is ambiguous but, with the stress that Cranmer
is giving to the word 'writing' in reference to his previous recantations,
it is probably best interpreted as agreeing with Cranmer, affirming the
truth of this the spoken confession and displaying his own Protestant
sympathies.

After the transcription of the confession in the Cotton MS, there follows a page (fol. 91a) ruled down the centre. At the top, scribbled in a different hand, are a few Latin phrases with English translations. The reverse side is ruled in the same way, with Edwards's poem to Wilson squeezed into the column widths. This is very neatly written but is probably in the same hand as that of the Latin phrases. It is signed *per mē R E*, a phrase which can sometimes suggest an autograph, as with Edwards's signature in the Christ Church disbursement book (plate 1), but these two examples of writing are not obviously by the same hand.

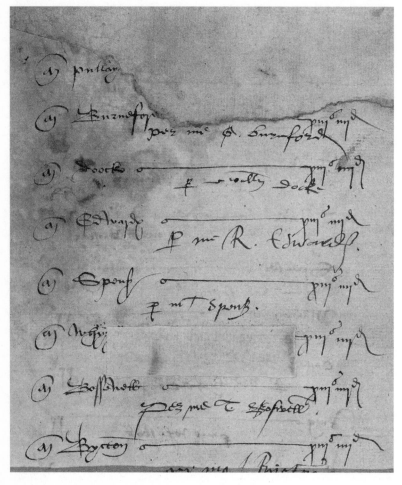

1   Edwards's signature in the Christ Church disbursement book for 1547–8, confirming receipt of his termly salary.

Up to this point, although the MS is in several pieces, its various sections are all linked—either by folds in the paper or by a single poem spread over two or more leaves. The leaves that follow, all written in Latin, contain first a series of poems celebrating the marriage of Queen Mary and King Philip II of Spain in 1554, then what seems to be the draft of a disquisition on the nature of humanity, and lastly some notes under chapter headings, apparently from a book on natural philosophy. The poems are signed R.M., Ri. Alen, Thomas Carrus and Cox, with a couplet signed 'Hadd'. R.M.'s initials appear below two lines that are heavily crossed out. The words *Ex Ecclesia Christi* ('from Christ Church') can be made out, but the second line is almost entirely illegible. Most of the names can be found in the Christ Church records for this period. A Richard Allen went up in 1552, probably as a commoner, taking his BA in 1555 and his MA in 1558. Thomas Carr, born in Bristol, was a student there between 1552 and 1557, taking his BA in 1556, and was perhaps the Thomas Carr who was presented to the living of Postwick in Norfolk in 1562. Cox is presumably Richard Cox, former Dean of Christ Church and Vice-Chancellor of Oxford who remained in the country until May 1554, two months after the royal betrothal. There are eight contenders in the college records for the identity of R.M., the most appealing being Roger Marbeck who was later public orator for the University and gave both the welcoming and valedictory speeches to Queen Elizabeth at her visit in 1566.[35] The brief appearance of 'Hadd' may, however, be the most significant of them all. Walter Haddon had spent most of his career at Cambridge, but he was a friend of Cox and, with Cheke, a reformer of ecclesiastical law. In 1552 Edward VI made him Master of Magdalen, Oxford, supplanting the incumbent who was considered insufficiently reformist. On Mary's accession he, perhaps wisely, resigned, although he became prominent again during Elizabeth's reign (*DNB*). Given his history, his presence here as the only non-Christ-Church man seems particularly interesting.

The threat to English sovereignty caused by Mary's marriage to a foreign king was a source of considerable anxiety to many, even those who were happily re-embracing the old religion. All the betrothal poems therefore stress that the marriage they are anticipating is between two equal princes and that Mary will continue to hold imperial power in her own kingdom. They aver that this equality will bring peace and joy to both countries. There are several references to Mary's virginity and deliberate comparison with the Virgin Mary.

The manuscript thus contains material dating from before January 1547, when the Earl of Surrey was executed for treason, through to at least March 1556 (the death of Cranmer), although it is not in chronological order of composition nor, probably, of copying. This need not surprise us since we all keep notebooks in which we make entries in different places according to subject. The change of hands likewise does not indicate a change of owners since the owner of a commonplace book will often invite others to make entries in it. The overall structure of the manuscript, however, begins to look like a political statement, or at least a political quest—an attempt to square patriotic loyalty to England, political loyalty to Mary and personal religious integrity. This context in turn gives a curious frisson to the poems by Norton and by Surrey (several of which are still much anthologised). Norton was Cranmer's son-in-law. He is also the third person in this narrative (along with Ferrers and Baldwin) associated with stories in the *Mirror for Magistrates*.[36] Surrey had been executed for quartering his arms with those of the royal house, thus giving his detractors opportunity to suggest that he was preparing to claim the throne for himself. He was noted for his personal extravagance and fast living. In other contexts these poems on the return of spring and expressing the need to live the good and simple life might therefore seem merely conventional. Here, in the context of the manuscript, they seem to take on a more profound meaning: a desire for truth, a recognition of the fragility of wealth, health, indeed life itself, and a metaphor for the deep political uncertainties of the time:

> Therefore let no man put his truste
>   in that that will decay
> for sliper wealthe will not abyde
>   pleasure will weare away.

(fol. 82)

In the same way, two other poems by Edwards in this collection, which take a humorous look at women's power, can be seen as having more than private significance. Femininity had been at the heart of royal politics in England since Henry VIII had begun the tortuous business of begetting a male heir, but the mid-century saw the beginning of absolute female power. It is hardly surprising if male courtiers, and indeed the women themselves, were unsure how to handle it. Jane Grey had been young, a pawn in the hands of her powerful and ambitious relatives. Mary was both fully adult when she came to the throne and righteous in her right to it, but she was nevertheless a mass of contradictions: both her father's daughter, and determined to right her mother's wrongs; both absolute monarch and needing to be dutiful wife. Edwards's poems, both in this manuscript and in the *Paradise*, show a willingness to view women as independent, thinking, educated beings, although, coming from the all-male environment of Oxford as he did, it is hardly surprising if he was both intrigued and slightly surprised by this.[37]

Through his choice of a range of different types of writing, the compiler of the Cotton manuscript can be seen to be consciously negotiating a way through the enormous political upheavals, dangers and agonies of the mid-1550s. He has placed Edwards at the centre of that cultural exploration. This is where we should expect to find him if the later public effusions about his talent have any credence.

EDWARDS OF THE CHAPEL

The next chronological reference to Edwards in the state papers was noted by the antiquarian John Nichols, although the original is again lost (Nichols, p. xxxv). It is the record of a New Year's gift to Philip and Mary: 'Sheparde, of the Chapel, three rolls of Songs; Richard Edwardes, of the Chapel, certain verses'. It was a common practice to make gifts of writing at New Year, and a way of cementing friendships and allegiances. Nichols gives the date as 1556–7. If the gifts in fact marked the year change 1557/58 they bore fruit a few months later, since an entry in the Patent Rolls dated 13 July 1558 grants a lease:

> in consideration of their service to John Shepard and Richard Edwardes, gentlemen of the Chapel, of the said manor of Deane and the lands of Hengrove with the reservations specified from Michaelmas [i.e. 29 September] 1563 or the expiry of the above recited indenture at the yearly rent of £42 1s 5½d and two hens to be paid half yearly at the Receipt of the Exchequer.

This is the earliest surviving document that unequivocally refers to Edwards in a role at court, although the poem to Mary's ladies demonstrates that he must have been a familiar there for a number of years. The land is in Kent on the Isle of Thanet. The lessees were to keep the premises in repair, ensure the grain was stored and the dung 'spread on the said land and not elsewhere' and to bear the charges of the officers of the Crown in surveying the manor and holding the manorial court. Shepard, who was a prolific composer, particularly of church music, never enjoyed the benefits or indeed the responsibilities of this lease, for he died in December 1558.

The coronation of Elizabeth I

In November that year Edwards and other members of the Chapel, together with the hundreds of other people associated with the court, were individually listed for their allocation of black livery material for Mary's funeral, each in a quality and yardage determined by rank. For Chapel gentlemen, as for other clerks and yeomen in departments as diverse as the pantry and the woodyard, it was seven yards of black cloth at 1s 2d a yard.[38] Two months after that, in the very reverse mood, it was four yards of scarlet material for the coronation of Queen Elizabeth.[39] Here the gentlemen of the Chapel received the same yardage as the yeomen in the domestic offices but in scarlet, not plain red. Meanwhile the Dean of the Chapel was entitled to ten yards of scarlet. This is the rigidly codified language of dress against which we must understand the joke of the little boys playing Will and Jack in *Damon and Pythias*, whose grotesquely out sized breeches contain an extravagant seven ells (eight and three-quarter yards, approximately eight metres), but of ultra-coarse cloth. A proclamation in 1562, indeed, limited material in breeches to a yard and three-quarters.[40]

Again, the coronation theatricals reflect the political changes occasioned by the change of monarch. One of the most interesting of Cawarden's papers is a memorandum of expenditure by one Tho. Northam (Thomas Norton?), incurred between Christmas 1558 immediately after Elizabeth's accession and the following Shrove Tuesday. It gives a personal glimpse into the workings of the Office and the frenzied to-ing and fro-ing in the run-up to a performance. Items include: payment for properties for the first masque at Christmas; 'cardinalls bulles' and 'bishopes articles'; payment for carriage of items 'home to the Blackfriars'; another for his costs in travelling 'on shrove teusday at night to the court'; one 'for yo*r* message to Miles hys wife'; and finally a few pennies 'for my supper that night'.[41] This small scrap is extremely suggestive and shows a return to the anti-Catholic propaganda of Edward's reign. The Venetian Ambassador confirms that a Christmas show presented cardinals as crows, bishops as asses and abbots as wolves.[42] In turn it also suggests that the masque on the following Shrove Tuesday, which we know from another paper was a masque of fishermen and fishwives, was likewise a religious satire.[43] Such a subject would be suitable for the carnival evening before Lent. Edward VI's coronation had been similarly celebrated with a play involving priests, cardinals and friars.[44] There is also a plot for an interlude that must date from his reign in which pride, wrath, envy, covetousness and gluttony are paired with a pope, a bishop, a friar, a parson and a 'sole prest'. These are respectively contrasted with a king, a knight, a judge, a preacher (accompanied by a woman carrying a bible) and a scholar, representing honour with wisdom, loyalty, justice with mercy, religion with God's word and science with reason.[45]

As we have seen, the Master of the Revels was expected to help plan the visual aspects and devices or subject matter for such shows, but he was not himself a writer. I suggest that all court entertainments and state shows not attributed to visiting companies are likely to have been the work of courtiers such as Udall and Edwards, working to satisfy the specific political needs of successive monarchs. One of the most important, because the most public, of these official, unascribed shows was the triumphal entry into the City of London on the day before Elizabeth's coronation in January 1559. Udall, who had been jointly responsible with Leland for writing the script for the coronation entry for Elizabeth's mother, was of course dead by this time. An 'eyewitness' account was published anonymously by Richard Tottel just over a week later, for which Richard Mulcaster MP was paid by the Corporation of London.[46] Mulcaster later became the first Master of the Merchant Taylors' School (founded 1560) and presented his charges in plays at court several times in the 1570s and 1580s. His book comprises descriptions of the various allegorical pageants erected upon scaffolds along the route, the texts of welcoming verses spoken on the behalf of the City by various children, the behaviour of the crowd, the Queen's requests to be briefed on the nature and content of each pageant just before she reached it, and her reactions, both to the entertainment itself and to the greetings of the ordinary people along the route. The Corporation had delegated the organisation to a committee of four leading merchants from appropriate guilds whose skills, trades or wares would all be needed for the preparations: the mercer Lionell Duckett; the Merchant Taylor Richard Hilles MP; Francis Robinson, a grocer; and Richard Grafton, printer. But although the show was ostensibly given to Elizabeth by the City, a great proportion of the costumes for those in the tableaux were in fact provided by the Revels Office, as was customary. The most spectacular part of the entire afternoon, of course, was the Queen herself and the thousand people and their horses in red livery accompanying her. This, together with the immense political importance of the entire event to the crown, and the problematic nature of the political and religious changes that it might signify, means that we should perhaps be considering the spectacle more as a joint exercise, if not one actually controlled by the government. As Mulcaster says: 'if a man should say well, he could not better tearme the citie of London that time, than a stage wherin was shewed the wonderfull spectacle, of a noble hearted princesse toward her most loving people, & the peoples exceding comfort in beholding so worthy a soveraign. (*The Queenes Maiesties Passage through the Citie of London to Westminster the Day before her Coronation*, ed. James M. Osborne (New Haven: Yale University Press, 1960), A2v).

The various Latin and English poems, both spoken and displayed in writing on the triumphal scaffolds erected along the route, probably represent several different authors. Mulcaster's introduction to the Latin oration and verses delivered by the child from St Paul's School indicates that that part of the entertainment was the responsibility of the Master there. This was Sebastian Westcott, who regularly performed with the St Paul's children at court. There is, however, a conspicuous thematic progression from one triumphal arch to the next which was lacking in Mary's procession five years earlier and which might suggest an overall dramaturg.[47]

The writer of the description seems to have a sympathetic and intimate understanding of the proceedings and indeed to have been within earshot of the Queen for the duration of the entire event, even while she was still in the Tower before she entered her carriage (E4). Strangely, for a document supposedly emanating from the City, the one speech that is not recounted in full is the one spoken in welcome by the City's own Recorder. Mulcaster may have been paid for this book, but a person or persons much closer to the Queen and to the organisation and writing of the pageant must have furnished him with the necessary materials. What is clear is that the event demanded immense co-operation between court and City, and the schools in London, and was carefully co-ordinated and directed by someone with an eye for theatrical effect and for what would now be termed photo opportunities. This effect would be ruined by ascribing it to an author. The political point is that the City 'without anye sovereyne persone, of it selfe beautifyed it selfe' (E2v).

After the procession had wound its way almost to the western edge of the City, it came to what is described as an unscheduled stop: the Queen herself calls a halt in order to receive an oration from one of the children lined up outside the school attached to St Dunstan's in the West. This school was a charitable foundation for the poor. The Queen graciously moves nearer to hear better, receives a copy of the Bible in English, clasps this to her breast and raises her eyes to heaven. It is a politically significant and also a genuinely affecting moment. One is tempted to suppose not only that the stop itself was not unscheduled but that the Queen's own gestures had been considered carefully in advance. A similar impromptu but inevitably stage-managed occasion occurred for very good political reasons on Good Friday 1998, when Mo Mowlam, Secretary of State for Northern Ireland, appeared outside Stormont Castle, where the peace talks were in progress, to join groups of waiting schoolchildren in a song expressing optimism for the outcome. There too the use of children was semiotically significant: a fresh start after a period of political turmoil and sectarian violence; a sense of the future. Child actors were a standard feature of sixteenth-century coronation processions, but in Elizabeth's they are used exclusively.

Edwards was of course present in the procession but there is no way now of gauging whether he was involved in helping to write and plan this show. There is no record of any immediate extraordinary payments to him but in the next year and a half he had become sufficiently valuable to the young Queen that he was granted an extra allowance for board, in addition to his daily chapel wages:

> Grant for life, for his service, to Richard Edwardes, a gentleman of the Chapel, of wages of $7\frac{1}{2}$d a day, which he has for the said office, and board wages of 12d a day, 'without any checke defalcacion deduccion or abatemente of the same ... by the name of the fee', payable by the cofferer of the household.[48]

This may suggest a role in the royal household over and above that of singing man in the choir and prepares the way for his promotion to Master.

Master of the Chapel

Edwards was made Master of the Chapel after Richard Bower's death in 1561 in preference to William Hunnis, who had the seniority and was a noted anti-Catholic (whereas, of course, Edwards had been an insider in Mary's court). Hunnis did in fact succeed to the job on Edwards's own death in 1566, although his appointment was not for life, as was customary, but only for so long as he was of good behaviour. Those who rebelled, even for the Protestant cause as he had done, were perhaps considered more untrustworthy than those who had faithfully served Elizabeth's Catholic sister.

The Masters habitually operated under two patents. The first, in Latin, would grant the appointment for life with the standard payment of £40 yearly, payable from the exchequer. This was not just a salary but the entire budget for the school and also had to cover food and clothing for the twelve children. It had remained unchanged for many years and can scarcely have been adequate. The patent goes on to grant to the Master the (unspecified) wages, fees and profits, jurisdictions, authorities, privileges, commodities, rewards and advantages due to the office or henceforth to be due, in like manner and form as the previous incumbent had enjoyed, 'or ought to have had'. This comprehensive list is frustratingly vague, but it suggests both that the Master's income would be made up of a portfolio of different items and that people were not always paid what was due to them.

The second patent was written in English so that it could be produced as a warrant to local officials up and down the country and was addressed 'to all mayours sherifs bayliefes constables and all other our officers'. It granted the right to conscript into the Chapel Royal 'well-singinge' children from any chapel or cathedral choir in the country plus the authority to hire transport at a reasonable cost so that the choir could accompany the monarch on progresses. Edwards's two patents are respectively dated 27 October 1561, backdated to Michaelmas, and 10 January 1562.[49]

The Chapel Royal: rites and privileges

Under Elizabeth, most church trappings, vestments, altar cloths and plate were officially relinquished, although some churches hid their treasures away in the expectation that they would be needed again in the future. The Chapel Royal, however, was part of the monarch's magnificence and its members would sometimes be required to dress accordingly. The Great Wardrobe therefore furnished them with copes for special occasions such as the Feast of the Garter on or near St George's Day, which at that period was not, as it is now, exclusively celebrated at Windsor. The Chapel members for the ceremony in 1561, which must have included Edwards, were all dressed in cloth of gold—a literally glittering occasion, suggesting the iconographic importance of this yearly religious event for the English monarchy.

> all her Majesty's Chapel came through her Hall in copes, to the number of thirty, singing, 'O God, the father of Heaven,' etc. the outward court to the gate, and roundabout being strewed with green rushes. After came Mr Garter and Mr Norroy, and Master Dean of the Chapel, in robes of crimson sattin, with a red cross of St. George; and after, eleven Knights of

the Garter in their robes; then came the Queen, the Sovereign of the Order, in her robes; and all the guard following in their rich coats; and so to the Chapel; and after service done, back through the Hall to her Grace's great Chamber; and that done, her Grace and the Lords went to dinner, where she was most nobly served; and the Lords, sitting on one side, were served in gold and silver. (Nichols, 88–9)

The problem is that it is usually only extraordinary activities that are described. The special yearly ritual of the Garter ceremony was regularly written down so that protocol could be guaranteed, but ordinary procedures are rarely remarked upon unless someone is trying to change them. Daily practices are likely to be as fully arcane as extraordinary ceremonial ones—it is just that people know what they normally do and do not bother to record it. Memory of normal practice soon fades and later ages therefore have to deduce or reconstruct it. Occasional entries in the *Cheque Book* of the Chapel Royal, written when the Chapel was being reconstituted after the interregnum, indicate that day-to-day garments were provided out of the yearly budget paid to the Sergeant of the Vestry (for the Gentlemen) and the Yeomen of the Vestry (for the Children):

> It is ordered that the old bookes and surplices shall be to the use of the Gentlemen . . . paying to the Serjant of the Vestry twelve pence for the old booke and ten shillings apeece for their old surplices. Upon the testimony of Mr John Harding, Gentleman for 30 years standing. As also Mr Thomas Purcell, Mr Alfonso Marsh and Mr William Tucker, who averre they have often heard Mr Nightingalle to testife the same as an antient privelidge belonging to the said Gentlemen. (*Cheque Book*, 85)

In other words, these current members believed that once new books and surplices had been issued, the gentlemen had the ancient right to purchase and take away the old stock. This 'old custom' is restated in 1720 'for the removing of all doubts and disputes that possibly may arise for want of such determination or registering' (*Cheque Book*, 88).

There were also other payments in kind to the Chapel. It was customary, for instance, for the children to be provided both with breakfast and with gloves when they performed special services or plays at court[50]— a practice also extended to performances for other bodies such as the Inns of Court. Gentlemen, Priests and Organists were also entitled to bring a guest to the yearly Chapel Feast. By ancient tradition, the monarch contributed to this by providing venison and wine—although, as so often, this gift also involved the recipients in considerable expense since it did not cover the full cost. This had to be defrayed by the members and the entire event supervised by two of their company elected as stewards who might have to bear the brunt of any shortfall, an 'honour' which could be refused only on payment of a fine (*Cheque Book*, 122–6, 236).

Singing the word

Changes to the form and content of church music occasioned by the changes in monarch, and therefore religion, during this period are extremely far-reaching. Under Edward VI, Archbishop Cranmer had directed that only the very simplest of music should be sung in church with no more than one note per syllable. The objective was for the priest to enunciate every word, indeed every syllable, equally clearly and for the congregation to be able to join in. This does not mean, however, that the Latin language was dropped from church services, particularly in places of learning or for grand occasions at court. Latin, after all, was still the language of both scholarship and diplomacy. As we shall see, sermons were given in Latin as well as English during Elizabeth's visit to Oxford in 1566 and a *Te Deum* sung with an accompaniment of cornets. Nevertheless, a switch to a simpler style might be a cause for regret for anyone whose love was music *as music*, or who enjoyed the particular intellectual challenge of the older, highly complex polyphonic writing. The injunction about the setting of words was in fact made repeatedly by church authorities, indicating that it was not being observed. Changes in the repertoire must still have caused the masters of chapel choirboys quite a headache.

John Merbecke's *The Book of Common Praier Noted* (1550), published in the reign of Edward VI, was the first to print the daily services in English with music.[51] His is an extremely plain form of plainsong. There is little variation in pitch or in the length of notes, and therefore little sense of melody. There is no time signature and therefore no predetermined pattern of stress, so the singer is able to intone words with the accent of normal speech. It is the basis for modern Anglican chant. In Catholic practice, by contrast, the plainsong could be extensively ornamented with a single syllable set to long runs of notes (melisma), and with different voices weaving in and out (polyphony) above and below the tenor line, so called because it 'holds' the tune. The metre in such music is also often 'proportional'. Simply put, this means that, depending on whether what we would now call the time signature of the music is 'perfect' or 'imperfect', there can be either three semibreves to the breve, and three minims to the semibreve, or two. This proportional technique can be used to create complex variation and development of the simple plainsong theme. Sometimes different voices can be carrying perfect and imperfect rhythms simultaneously. The only known piece of Edwards's own music for the Catholic service, a proportional Latin motet for five voices, *Terrenum sitiens*, of which only four parts survive, must date from Mary's reign.[52]

Mass had been re-established at court and was being celebrated in London churches within a month of Mary's accession—with some concomitant civil unrest. Elizabeth was a little more cautious, for a while continuing the celebration of mass but with increasing restrictions.

Machyn's diary records the gradual but determined changes effected after her accession, starting with the removal of rood screens from churches so that congregations could be allowed to see the ritual. But it was not an easy process. Edwards would have been present in her Chapel on Christmas Day 1558 when she walked out because the celebrant had rejected her injunction not to elevate the host.[53] By law the English service was due to begin on St John's Day (23 June) 1559, but was celebrated in the Royal Chapel on 12 May only four days after it was enacted by Parliament (Nichols, 67).

In 1562 Merbecke's pioneering work gave place to one of the most enduring publications of all time: *The Whole Booke of Psalmes* translated into English metre by Sternhold and Hopkins. 'Day's Psalter', as the book is often known, after the printer who owned the patent for its publication, includes some tunes—mostly adapted from continental Protestant hymns. It is also prefaced with an exemplary introduction to elementary musical theory. This explains the gamut (the scale in sol fa), the clefs and the time values of notes, so that everyone might learn to sing at sight. The following year another edition appeared with a complete set of tunes, harmonised by English composers for four voices, 'set forth for the encrease of vertue and abolishyng of other vayne and trifling ballades' and handsomely printed in four separate partbooks. This edition includes three arrangements of the famous chorale tune '*Vater unser*' for the Lord's Prayer, including one by Edwards (pp. 237–8). The edition contains a pictorial frontispiece that succinctly illustrates its project (plate 2). It shows a family group. On the right a middle-class woman sits on a stool, her hands resting on her stomach as if she is pregnant. At least four children cluster around her, hiding in her skirts, one son holding an open book and another, younger one, clutching a hobbyhorse. On the left her husband sits on a high-backed chair with a cushion, teaching his family to sing by pointing out the intervals on his hand in the recognised Guidonian system.[54] It is a touching, earnest, if somewhat paternalist scene of family self-improvement.

The great anxiety about the translation of the Bible into the vernacular was the scope that it gave to ordinary people to interpret it in ways that would have political as well as religious implications. Translation into metre gave the authorities a sense of control: 'Therefore is Gods will delivered to us in Psalms, that we might have it the more cheerfully, and that we might have it the more certainly, because where all the words are numbred, and measured, and weighed, the whole work is the lesse subject to falsification, either by substraction or addition.'[55]

John Day was fortunate to have the patent for printing this officially sanctioned Psalter and could therefore afford to produce it in various formats. The patent monopoly on music printing, however, combined with the technical difficulty of printing both the lines for the stave and the notes, meant that most music and song circulated in manuscript. None of Edwards's other music was printed.

2   A man teaching his family to sing the psalms, using the Guidonian hand signs for sol fa. He is making the sign for bottom G. *The Whole Book of Psalms* (1563), K.1.c.2, fol. A1v.

'Some . . . may match but none shall pass (no doubt)'

This judgement of Edwards's skill as a writer occurs in the eulogy 'Of Edwardes of the Chappell' published by Barnabe Googe in his book *Eclogs* (1563). Googe's poem describes him as someone whose skill would make even Plautus and Terence burn their own works in dismay if they were alive to see it. We are in no position to judge the merit of this reputation since (with the possible exception of *Jack Juggler*) not one of the stage comedies on which it is based is known to have survived. The *fact* of his considerable reputation, however, is undeniable. That same year he was granted the reversion of two further leases of land: the rectories of Swaton and Thornton, once the property of monasteries at Barlings and Thornton, both near Lincoln. These leases were both for twenty-one years, but dependent on the future expiry of the leases held by the current incumbents. The reversion on the former property would not fall due for another ten or eleven years, and that for the Thornton rectory was even more vague. He also had to pay a 'fine' or fee of £40. This is a considerable sum and points to income far above that for which records remain. Once in possession, he would also have to pay yearly rents in spite of the fact that the leases were 'for his service'.[56] Within two years, however, he was embroiled in a lawsuit in the court of Chancery over the Thornton property. Edwards's lawyer submitted that the original lessee had held the land directly from the Abbot and that the current tenants' lease, derived from the subsidiary College of Thornton, was therefore 'false, fained and forged'. It is a small but not unusual footnote to the dissolution of the monasteries.[57]

On 25 November 1564 Edwards was admitted to Lincoln's Inn as an honorary fellow.[58] This connection was of mutual benefit. It meant that the Inn could be furnished with a performance of a play at their annual celebration on the Feast of the Purification at only a moderate cost to them, although the extra performance presumably represents profit to Edwards and the Chapel. Like students in the universities, the gentlemen of the Inns of Court regularly acted in plays, sometimes performing before the Queen or members of the government. Edwards's fellowship thus gave the gentlemen at Lincoln's access to an accomplished playwright whose skills might be expected to enhance their theatrical shows. Since he was not a former student of the Inn, he would have been required to pay a 40s admission fee, although there is no record of this unless it is reflected in a reduction in his payment for a play the following February. The Black Book of Lincoln's Inn, in which the governing body of the Inn recorded their activities, initially minutes a council decision that he should be paid 53s 4d for this play (a sum which was also paid to a group of musicians that year), and that his usher should have 10s, with a further 10s paid to the children.[59] This seems to have been partially rescinded by the time it was paid in August, when the treasurer's accounts record expenditure on the play of 38s 2d. This also had to cover a supper for the boys and the cost of torches, although the 20s reward to the boys was undiminished. The following year the account records a mere '40s to the boys of the queenes Chapel and their master for their play at the purification'.[60]

On 28 November 1565 the Patent rolls record that a Richard Edwards, who we might assume was the poet, was granted leases for twenty-one years on former monastic lands in the Wirral and Derbyshire. Again he was to pay rent to the Crown and also undertook to make extensive repairs to the 'waterworks' at the Wirral property at his own cost. Tenants were in place who would pay their own rents yearly to him. Keeping track of such scattered landed interests as our Richard Edwards certainly enjoyed cannot have been easy.

DAMON AND PYTHIAS

Props and costumes for the earliest performances

The 1565 play at Lincoln's Inn may have been *Damon and Pythias*, fresh from its performance at court the previous Christmas. It is only the need to purchase rug, the coarse material needed in such ludicrous quantities for the pages' breeches, coupled with the marginal note, 'Edwardes tragedy', that allows us to connect this particular play with a Christmas 1564–5 performance by the Chapel children that contributed to expenditure of £87 7s 8d noted in the end of year Revels Office accounts:

> Christmas Anno Septimo Elizabeth. wages or dieats of the officers and Tayllours payntars workinge divers Cities and Townes carvars Silkewemen for frenge & tassels mercers ffor Sarsnett & other stuf and Lynen drapars for canvas to cover divers townes and howsses and other devisses and Clowds ffor a maske and a showe and a play by the childerne of the chaple ffor Rugge bumbayst an cottone ffor hosse and other provicions and necessaries. (*Elizabeth*, 116)

This is far from unambiguous. It rolls at least three of the 1564–5 Christmas and New Year entertainments together, and maybe more, since the subsequent entry is for the cost of airing the stock costumes used that Christmas in plays given by the children of Westminster and St Paul's schools. Special provision for these shows might therefore also be included under 'other provicions and necessaries'. It indicates, however, that, when the *Damon and Pythias* Prologue pointed out Dionysius's palace and the town of Syracuse, he would have been standing in front of scenic representations of those places: wooden frames, perhaps with cut-out outlines made by the 'carvars', covered with painted canvas.

The next entry, relating to expenditure of £57 10s for entertainments in February, may also be relevant to *Damon*. This lists:

> divuers Cities and Townes and the Emperours pallace . . . for A play maid by Sir percivall hartts Sones with a maske of huntars and diuers devisses and a Rocke, or hill ffor the ix musses to Singe uppone with a vayne [?vayle] of Sarsnett Dravven upp and downe before them &c. (*Elizabeth*, 117)

This entry likewise refers to several different entertainments—a play, a masque and various shows—but the rock for the Muses (probably the most expensive individual item) looks a bit like an afterthought. This together with the frames for town and emperor's palace makes a closer match for the scenic requirements for Edwards's play than the list in the earlier entry. There are several possible mutually exclusive explanations, all of which could arise from practices in the Revels Office that we have already noted. Firstly, the yeoman and clerks whose job it was to prepare the end-of-year financial summary from the mass of scraps of paper floating round the office, most of it undated, will simply have been anxious to ensure that they accounted for all the expenditure under reasonably convincing headings. They were not trying to compile a performance diary or a theatre history, and it is the expenditure that is pertinent, not so much the date on which the goods were used. Secondly, since debentures from external suppliers might often be submitted for payment some time after the goods themselves were delivered, such amounts would rightly be included in the period when the bill was paid, rather than that in which the goods were received or used. Thirdly,

Edwards would want to be able to use the same props and costumes if *Damon* was indeed the play that he took to Lincoln's Inn in February, and it is perhaps the re-use that associates the items with the February date in the clerk's memory. Fourthly, the two plays might have used the same property.

A rock, or a rock and a fountain, representing the mountains of Helicon, or of Parnassus with its Castalian spring, both traditional homes of the Muses, would be almost prerequisite for any representation of them at this period. A rock and fountain were supplied for a masque at Shrovetide, 1560. Twelve years later the French ambassador was entertained with a spectacular show which included a chariot, fourteen feet long and eight feet broad, bearing a rock with a fountain and furnished for Apollo and the Muses, which alone cost £66 13s 4d.[61]

The stage directions in the printed edition of *Damon and Pythias* are normally very adequate but there is none to mark the actual entrance of the Muses, simply the direction '*Then the Muses sing*' (15.20.1). A scenic device whereby they could get into position seated, screened from the audience by a veil of fine silk sarsenet, and then be revealed just as they began to sing, would help create the necessary sense of apotheosis for the end of the play. It would also explain the lack of an entrance in the stage directions.

Eubulus's song to the Muses in the play refers to their 'yellow, rented hairs'. The boys were evidently wearing wigs, probably made of silk threads and perhaps frizzed to denote their distraught feelings at Pythias's imminent death. The French Ambassador's show perhaps re-used these properties. On that occasion nine 'heades' for the nine Muses 'owte of th'office' were retrimmed with silk thread of sundry colours and 'Heads of Heare drest and trymmed' at 23s 4d each were purchased. Discord's wig for that masque was made of 60 oz of black silk thread which was then curled at a cost of 7s 8d.[62]

With the exception of Will and Jack's comic breeches, the other special costumes required by the production of *Damon* could well have been in stock. Carisophus, identified on the list of characters as a parasite, would have been marked out as such by a parti-coloured costume such as had been worn by those in Ferrers's Lord of Misrule retinue.[63] Similarly, the mariners' costumes required for Damon and Pythias's first entrance must indicate a stylised garment (analogous to the nineteenth-century fashion in sailor suits for children) rather than realistic seamen's clothing. Mariners had several times been the subject for court masques during the 1550s, always with fantastically rich costumes in watery colours. On one occasion these consisted of jerkins and sleeves of purple cloth-of-gold 'barred over' (banded) with 'gardes' (strips) of green cloth-of-silver, with hoods of blue cloth-of-gold edged with red silk lace, and parti-coloured breeches with one leg in blue cloth-of-gold, and the other of green cloth-of-silver. The Revels Office inventory of 1560 describes these particular garments as having been 'translated' into other costumes, with the green cloth-of-silver later turned back into mariners' costumes. Alternatively, Damon and Pythias could have been wearing the remnants from the six 'straighte gownes of clothe of golde blew velvet with roses of gold raysed', originally for 'Alboma's warriors', that had been 'translated' into costumes for a mask of Irishmen, then a mask of fishermen 'and againe into Marryners and after into players garmentes'.[64] Both sets of garments had been so often 'shewen and forworne' that they had been taken as fees and could therefore even have been in Edwards's possession. Whereas a spectacular new masque would be marred by bringing the same old costumes out once too often, Damon and Pythias's entrance in recognisable cast-offs would have comic potential.

Anti-theatricality

Up to this point I have stressed the esteem in which Edwards was held by his contemporaries. But not everyone was so happy about plays and players. Anti-theatricality in late sixteenth-century England is a well-known phenomenon which, it is often assumed, began with Northbrooke's *Treatise Against Dicing, Dancing, Plays and Interludes* (1577), Gosson's *School of Abuse* (1579) and Philip Stubbes's *The Anatomy of Abuses* (1583). These publication dates, following as they do the opening in 1576 of the Theatre, the home of what was to become Shakespeare's company and the prototype of the Globe, led Jonas Barish to suggest that 'the stage provokes the most active and sustained hostility when it becomes a vital force in the life of a community'.[65] Repeated internal references in *Damon and Pythias*, however, indicate that anti-theatricality was already posing a serious threat, even to the continued enjoyment of normal *courtly* diversions, by the time of the play's original performance during the Christmas festivities of 1564.

Anti-theatrical (to which can now be added anti-film and anti-Internet) polemic forms a distinct genre which has changed little over the course of two and a half millennia. In the Christian tradition it can be traced back through a letter from Bishop Grindal to Cecil (23 February 1564), Bishop Alley's St Paul's Cross sermon of 1561, and Calvin's sermons on Deuteronomy (1556, published in English, 1583), to St Augustine's *City of God*. But the same arguments appear in ancient Greece. The surface accidentals may alter slightly according to the current obsessions within society but the object remains the same: control, not simply of the medium under attack but of society at large.

The tracts generally agree, with tortuous tautology, that plays are the work of the devil and were invented by the heathen in praise of the pagan gods. Being the work of the devil, they must therefore be wicked even when apparently praising or depicting virtue, because 'it is the juglinge of the devill, to turne himselfe sometimes to an angel of light to deceive us the sooner'.[66] The most extensively repeated objection, however, is that plays involve dressing up. Our contemporary anxiety about sex-and-gender identity has tended to focus on the cross-dressing aspect of this 'abuse', but the original concern is with wider issues of social control. Dressing as someone of a higher rank constitutes, quite literally, dressing 'up' the social scale, which contravenes the sumptuary laws dictating the proper order of clothing for each section of society.

It is not generally remarked by those primarily interested in theatre history that almost all of the first half of *The Anatomy of Abuses* (1583) is devoted to the sin of Pride, whose most flagrant manifestation, according to Stubbes, is 'excesse in apparell' (B5v). The rest of the book, dealing with abuses as various as usury, football-playing and dancing (as well as the more usually extracted short section 'Of stage-playes and enterludes, with their wickednes'), likewise tends to dwell wherever possible on the implications of dress for that particular abuse. Thus the recent explosion of interest in the subject of transvestism on the stage in early modern England owes more to our own society's anxieties concerning sexual identity and gendered behaviour than it does to our understanding of sixteenth-century culture. There has been a failure to situate the phenomenon of dressing up either against the broader content of the tracts themselves or against the many different types of disguise (not just transvestism) in the plays.[67]

The earlier supposition that the anti-theatrical writers were Puritans was successfully refuted by Margot Heinemann: Stubbes dedicated the first edition of the *Anatomy of Abuses* to Philip, Earl of Arundel, who, in the year after publication, was under house arrest for his Catholicism; Stephen Gosson actually bitterly attacked the 'new Presbytery' in his virulent sermon *The Trumpet of War* (1598); and the avowedly puritan Martin Marprelate tracts made extensive joking reference to stage plays, obviously assuming 'an audience which, like the writer, enjoys a play'.[68] Much anti-theatrical literature was in fact written by people who themselves came from some kind of theatrical background. Gosson had written a couple of pastoral plays before turning his pen against the theatre, while, as a young man, John Rainoldes, author of *Th'Overthrow of Stage-Plays* (1599), which was part of a sustained attack against performances of plays at Oxford University, had taken a leading role in Edwards's play *Palamon and Arcyte*. In London the City fathers, while on the one hand paying Gosson to write his attack, on the other paid out substantial sums of money both for private theatrical entertainments and for public relations spectacles like the yearly Lord Mayor's shows. These indeed increased in cost and splendour over the time-span covered by the publication of the pamphlets in question.[69]

Because of the inflexible nature of any moral pronouncement, everyone in the controversy on both sides is trapped in a double bind. The City fathers may deplore the existence of theatres as permanent places of public resort, but they need the resources of theatre to present their view of social and moral order to as many people as possible during City celebrations like the installation of the Lord Mayor. Similarly, the wearing of rich clothing, which it would be easy to describe as sinful, has to be defended in the interests of social order, as the mark of proper distinction between different ranks. It is thus represented in Gosson's *Plays Confuted* as a representation of God's gifts to mankind, since flowers, rich cloths and precious stones, all of which are 'delightful' rather than 'necessary', have been provided for us: 'that we may use them well, and by these transitorie benefits be led as it were by ye hand, to a consideration of those benefits that are layde up for us in the life to come' (G1v). It is worth remembering that the need to republish the proclamations on the sumptuary laws at regular intervals is indicative that they were not being heeded, and also that it was found necessary to make a special dispensation to allow court servants to be suitably richly dressed.

The problem as far as the stage is concerned is that it is not possible to refute these rabidly polemical arguments on their own terms without appearing to be either depraved or a fool—or both. Thomas Heywood fell into such a trap in his *Apology for Actors* when, in trying to defend theatre from the charge of effeminacy, he observed stoutly that it was in a theatre that the Sabine women were raped. Game, set and match to Stephen Gosson, one might say, except that of course it is not a joke. Theatres and amphitheatres are indeed convenient places to hold and slaughter political opponents, and have been used as such in our own times.

Sixteenth- and seventeenth-century anti-theatricalists identify theatre as contravening the religious injunctions to stay within one's own calling or station in life (St Paul, 1 Cor. 7.20), as well as the 'abomination' of wearing the apparel of the other sex (Deut. 22.5). But their understanding of dramatic form is one that also underpins much modern literary criticism of drama: the 'suspension of disbelief'. This theory is based on the premise that the most convincing theatre is that in which the staged representation most closely resembles the thing represented so that the audience can comfortably forget the difference between them. The corollary to this results in a commonly held misconception that what the audience *knows* (that female parts are played by boys) is what the audience *sees* (boys and young men dressed up as the female love interest in the play, thereby embodying both heterosexual and homoerotic licence).

Disinterested eyewitness accounts of performances are sadly much rarer than the partial, conventional, self-righteously angry and therefore distorting outpourings of those who wish that those performances were not happening. The only descriptions of boy players in action both come from Oxford. The first is the description of the grace and singing ability of Peter Carew who played Emilia in *Palamon and Arcyte* (p. 80).

The second is Henry Jackson's account in Latin of a performance of *Othello* by the King's Men in 1610. According to him, the skill of the actors was such that 'not only by their speech but also by their deeds they drew tears.—But indeed Desdemona, killed by her husband, although she always acted the matter very well, in her death moved us still more greatly; when lying in bed she implored the pity of those watching with her countenance alone.'[70] The language here indicates that the writer is both aware of the artifice involved in what he was watching (he knows that it is acting) and moved by the reality of his imaginative involvement in it. It is surely this simultaneous consciousness that theatre demands that is so unsettling to those in authority, particularly once plays have ceased being vehicles for religious instruction and have begun to explore purely human stories and therefore, inevitably, issues of moral relativism. The collective empathy in which this Oxford audience apparently participated in its reaction to Desdemona's tragedy, whatever else it may be, does not seem to be an expression of 'dominant ideology' with regard to the subjugation of women. Nor does it suggest a homosexual fantasy concerning the boy beneath the clothes. It is perhaps too much to claim that theatre can change society, but it can promote the collective imagining of a society different from the one in which the participants (actors and audience) live. Theatre is not simply mimesis, it is dialectic. The knowledge that they are 'only' watching a play actually encourages audiences to make more direct political comparison with their own lives and experience. The only effective attack on this freedom of thought is the calumny that the action is sexually immoral, since this reduces the act from the socio-political sphere to the personal. It is also almost impossible to refute since 'mud sticks' and 'there is no smoke without fire'.

Those who try to defend theatre in the terms set by the attackers therefore tend to get mired in the same areas of the controversy, combating like with like. Thomas Nashe in *Pierce Penniless his Supplication to the Devil* (1592), uses a conventional diatribe against the old medieval line-up of the seven deadly sins while suggesting that the lawyers and the merchants of the City of London are quite successful enough as devils themselves to be able to do without any extra supernatural help. After an extensive attack on Gluttony and its related sin of Drunkenness, he asks which is the more evil man, one who sits gluttonising at home, or one who goes revelling, exercising his body at dancing, fencing and tennis schools, and going to the play, sharpening his wits in the company of poets. Activity is better than sloth and men who have no employment (like courtiers, Inns of Court men and soldiers) are bound to spend it in pleasure, gaming, whoring, drinking or seeing a play. Is it not better that they should frequent the least of these evils, which is the playhouse? This is, of course, satirical but it is probably an ineffective way to defend the theatre against a charge of licentiousness. Plays themselves can offer a better critique.

Damon and Pythias: *a defence of the theatre*

The extraordinary Grim-the-Collier scene in *Damon and Pythias* is by far and away the longest in the play. It is also apparently almost completely unconnected to the play's main story—the pair of friends trapped in a tyrannical court. It is, however, a rather more effective defence of the drama than any attempt to take on the polemicists on their own terms, and seems to have inspired a series of plays by other people. The scene starts as a dialogue between Jack and Will, lackeys to Carisophus and Aristippus respectively. They square up to each other, each abusing the other's master, until stopped by Snap the constable for brawling in front of the court gates. They then see Grim the Collier. Much play is made in the ensuing dialogue about the relative sizes of Grim and the two lackeys—their sexual immaturity marked by the pun on *lack-ey*. The children's enormous breeches are ultra-fashionable in style (though not, as we have seen, in cloth), but Grim says they look like leather water buckets (since they are causing the children to sweat profusely as well) or perhaps prostheses for people with no buttocks. He is now well into his stride, joking that schoolboys invariably have ruddocked (reddened) buttocks from being breeched or beaten (13.82ff). What a pair of robin redbreasts (little innocents)—ho, ho!

These breeches do not cross the gender distinctions to be found in the Deuteronomy dress code but, ludicrously, the difference between species. But, as Grim well knows, talking about such things risks giving offence. It seems that such monsters were invented for 'ghostly' (spiritual) purposes so that they can be turned into a subject for sermons. There is daily proof that the male member is ever ready to go poking about in other people's breeches—someone was saying as much just the other day in a sermon from the back of a hay cart. But the foregoing bawdy conversation between Grim and the children has already provided an opposite meaning. These children may be the 'male' (strong box) for other people's filthy thoughts but they are as yet, in the sixteenth-century understanding of physiology, sexless children.

The phraseology is elliptical but the effect, signalled by Jack and Will's annoyance at this uncool treatment by an overweening, ignorant yokel, is quite clear: extreme fashion may be ridiculous, but immorality is in the mind of the beholder.[71] Grim's objections, borrowed from some schismatic preacher, are not to be taken seriously by such as are present at court watching this performance by the Children of the Chapel. Thus, rather than being the *cause* of religious objection, the writing of this scene of the play is a direct satirical *response* to earlier pronouncements on abuses.

The play's dramatic structure is finely balanced, with now one, now another character in the ascendant, and although each will state in no uncertain terms how he thinks the world works, that view is soon contradicted vehemently by someone else. It is not the function of a play to tell you a moral—leave that to those who speak from pulpits. It is the function of a play to present you with an absorbing situation to which you as an audience member may bring your own explanation. This, I believe, is the true philosophical defence of drama, and it is voiced when Damon credits Pythagoras with inventing the famous proverb that the world is like a stage (*D&P*, 7.71)—although Cicero states that Pythagoras's inspiration came from observing the behaviour of real people at the amphitheatre where games were played:

> Pythagoras . . . replied that the life of man seemed to him to resemble the festival . . . ; some men whose bodies had been trained sought to win the glorious distinction of a crown, others were attracted by the prospect of making gain by buying or selling, whilst there was on the other hand a certain class, and that quite the best type of free-born men, who looked neither for applause nor gain, but came for the sake of the spectacle and closely watched what was done and how it was done . . . ; and just as at the games the men of truest breeding looked on without any self-seeking, so in life the contemplation and discovery of nature far surpassed all other pursuits. (*Tusc.*, 5.3.9)

By the end of Edwards's play even Dionysius has learnt this lesson. Damon, Pythias and Eubulus have all, in their different ways, directly *told* Dionysius what to do, thus demonstrating Sir Thomas Elyot's injunction, 'Thinke not them to be loial or faithfull, that doe preise all thyng that thou doest, but them that do blame the thing, wherin thou errest' (*The Doctrinal of Princes* (1534), B3). Dionysius himself, however, remarks that it is not this sermonising but the poignant tragedy that Damon and Pythias have *played out* before him that has taught him the true meaning of friendship and of virtue:

> My heart, this rare friendship has pierced to the root,
> And quenched all my fury. This sight has brought this about,
> Which thy grave counsel, Eubulus, and learned persuasion could never do.
> O noble gentlemen, the immortal gods above
> Has made you play this tragedy, I think, for my behove.
>
> (*D&P* 15.213–17)

THE PARADISE OF DAINTY DEVICES

A defence of music and poetry

It is, of course, not just theatre that is implicated in the attack on abuses but all modes of fiction except Bible stories, which are held to be literally true, and all music except the simplest forms of psalm singing. Edwards's poem 'In commendation of music' (*PDD*, 14), which urges the healing and restorative powers of music, is therefore not just, as it might seem to us now, a celebration of music's sweetness but a vigorous defence of an entire artform in the face of moral attack. Henry Disle, the printer of *The*

Paradise of Dainty Devices, the book of poems that Edwards was credited with compiling, was also acutely aware of the problem. In his preface
addressed to the book's patron, Lord Compton, he anticipates the objections of those who see poetry as a wasteful, even immoral, activity. He
takes care to find safety in numbers, and states that he first 'perused over'
the poems and then:

> not without the advise of sundry my freendes, I determined by theyr
> good motion, to set them in print, who therunto greatly perswaded me,
> with these and like woordes: The wryters of them, were both of honor
> and worship: besides that, our owne countrey men, and such as for
> theyr learnyng and gravitie, might be accounted of among the wisest.
> (A2r–v)

This book of poems is no frivolity but a serious enterprise, well considered by the printer and his friends. Pushed into a corner by those
who might censor it, its aim is no less than the promotion of English
culture and letters. Philip Sidney's *Defence of Poetry* (published 1595)
is in the same tradition. Written in about 1580 as a rebuff to Stephen
Gosson's temerity in making him the dedicatee for the *School of
Abuse*, it is credited with being the first such treatise in English, a
counterpart to various French, Italian and of course classical examples.
Many of the ideas it contains, however, were already being expressed in
English and being used to inform creative writing while Sidney was still
a schoolboy.

Manuscript culture in print

The Paradise of Dainty Devices was perhaps the most successful of all
the Elizabethan printed anthologies of poetry. First printed in 1576, it ran
to at least nine further editions: 1577 (now all lost), 1578, 1580, 1585,
1590, 1596 (twice), 1600 and 1606. The 1576 title page advertises the
book as:

> aptly furnished with sundry pithie and learned inventions, devised and
> written for the most part, by M[aster] Edwards, sometimes of her Majesties
> Chappel: the rest, by sundry learned gentlemen, both of honor and
> worship, viz. S[t]. Bernard, E[arl of] O[xford], L[ord] Vaux, D.S., Jasper
> Heywood, F[rancis] K[indlemarsh], M. Bew, R. Hill, M. Yloop with
> others.

In fact, only ten poems out of a total of ninety-nine in the 1576 edition
are assigned to Edwards, three fewer than those given to Vaux (1509–56).
Edwards's tally rises to fifteen with a single couplet in 1578, with further
poems in 1580 (no. 21 here), and 1585 (no. 2 here), both, I think, doubtful. William Hunnis (d. 1597), Edwards's successor as Master of the
Chapel Royal, has a mere seven poems in 1576 rising to eighteen in 1578,
six of these new to the anthology and five reascribed from other authors.
In addition a Hunnis poem from the first edition is dropped and one

previously anonymous poem assigned to him. In all there are at least eighteen authors in 1576 (depending on the interpretation of various combinations of initials). Subsequent editions each added, deleted or reascribed poems, introduced a further eight authors and gave an overall total of 127 poems.

This printed book was in fact in a state of flux for more than forty years and is actually evidence for manuscript culture in action. Its various manifestations mark a continuing process of exchange: a community of poets, and later of poets and printer, sharing ideas, collecting each other's work, using each other's poems as sources for their own writing, praising by imitation and sometimes criticising each other directly. Many of the poems share the same titles, although these may sometimes have been added as part of the process of transforming the collection from private manuscript into public print, with the titles standing in for a context that was formerly supplied by real-life social networks. This theme of friendship which runs throughout, both in the subject matter of individual poems and in their relation to each other, and which was the impetus for the initial manuscript collection, also continued to shape the printed book, with the printer, as we have seen, taking the careful advice of his friends before committing the volume to print. Edwards may have begun the collection, but others carried it on.

Post-Romantic habits of reading poetry, with an insistence on the individual genius of the poet, have dulled our receptiveness to this sense of community. It is essential to read this book not as a series of individual poems but more three-dimensionally, alive to the links both between poems by different authors and between different poems by the same author. These relationships are, in fact, sometimes signalled by the physical juxtaposition and appearance of the verses on the printed page. A poem by Hunnis (*PDD*, 18), which is present in the first edition, appears in the second with an additional couplet commenting on it, signed M[aster]. Edwards. Since the second edition also includes a number of additional poems by Hunnis, new to that edition, perhaps it was he who supplied the printer with the comment by his former Chapel Royal colleague, along with the additional verses. The change of typography for the final four lines of 'Of a friend and a flatterer' (*PDD*, 20, in this edition), which was entirely new to the 1578 edition, probably likewise signals that they too are a comment by Edwards on the preceding lines written by another. The main body of the poem is an entirely conventional and straightforward rendition of some of the many proverbs on friendship. The italicised comment is likewise proverbial, but here the choice is bizarrely eclectic and colloquial, the effect being, ironically, to satirise the use of proverbs.

I have included the poem by M.S. (*PDD*, 2, in the present selection) because it is a direct critical response to one of Edwards's most famous and popular poems, 'When May is in his prime'. It is the only poem in *PDD* attributed to M.S., but this may be the D.S. or D. Sand included in the lists of authors in all editions, who contributed some four or five poems, or the E.S. who contributed five poems. The letters 'M' and 'D' could stand for 'Master' and 'Doctor' respectively, so all three sets of initials could signify the same person. Sand is listed as a poet in William Webbe's *Discourse of English Poetrie* (1586):

> I might next speake of the dyvers workes of the olde Earle of Surrey: of the L[ord] Vaus, of Norton, of Bristow, Edwardes, Tusser, Churchyard. Wyl: Hunnis: Haiwood: Sand: Hyll: S.Y. M.D. and many others, but to speake of their severall gyfts, and aboundant skyll shewed forth by them in many pretty and learned workes, would make my discourse much more tedious.[72]

Webbe wrote his apologetically opinioned *Discourse* while a personal tutor in a country house in Essex, some thirty miles from London and, as he says himself, without benefit of a library. All but Surrey, Norton of Bristol (who has been made to look like two people in Webbe's list) and Tusser are *PDD* poets (Wyl: Hunnis being a punctuational quirk for William Hunnis). The list is therefore more likely to be drawn from a copy of the *PDD*—or from what he could remember of it—than to be contributing any independent information.

Two poems (*PDD*, 17 and 19, here) share the same dialogue form (reminiscent of some of the satires of Horace) which became fashionable in later Elizabethan pastoral and also popular ballads. Several instances can be found in the poetic eclogues that punctuate each book of Sir Philip Sidney's political prose romance *Arcadia*, and one is performed in the sheep-shearing scene of Shakespeare's *The Winter's Tale*. Other musical examples survive from the seventeenth and the end of the sixteenth centuries in both England and Italy. Setting to music would intensify the humour of both these pieces as the repetition of the same musical line from one stanza to the next would bring the memory of the words in previous stanzas into simultaneous juxtaposition with their opposites in the final stanza. In *PDD*, 17, 'Complaining to his friend, he replies wittily', which is signed M. Edwards in all editions, the conflicting points of view are unmistakable, thus encouraging the reader to form his or her own judgement, while the final witty reply is a tour de force of rhetorical conceit.

The second poem (no. 19) is attributed to M.B. in the first edition, but ascribed to Edwards from 1578 onwards. Here, in contrast to *PDD*, 17, the lady gives in, albeit after a fairly spirited stand-off. There is, however, no real reason for her to do so. The poem has no witty rhetorical trap, and no confrontation of the gender divide that we see in CT 2 and CT 3, so it may be that the first edition's ascription to M.B. is correct. M.B. and M. Bew are signatures given to five poems in the 1576 edition. Two are not reprinted in later editions and the remaining three are reassigned to William Hunnis, Richard Edwards and the Earl of Oxford.

Poems in sets

While there are thematic links between many of the *Paradise* lyrics, Edwards's own contributions to the collection also comprise two consecutive groups of poems that seem to have been conceived as sets. The first group, nos 6, 7 and 8 in this edition, are all composed of four line stanzas in fourteeners, and chart a moral progression from worldly good fortune to spiritual wisdom. The first poem in the group, 'Of Fortune's power', engages humorously with the philosophical arguments concerning the tensions between virtue, happiness and good fortune in any definition of the 'good life': 'Polycrates of Samos was called "the fortunate". Not a single untoward circumstance had ever befallen him, except that he had thrown his favourite ring overboard at sea . . . But Polycrates, if he was foolish (which he certainly was, since he was a tyrant) was never happy' (Cicero, *De finibus*, 5.30.92). The theme is continued in the next poem, for Croesus (l. 12), the richest of men, also considered himself to be the most fortunate, and was angry when he was told that he could not be counted happy until the manner of his death was known (Herodotus, 1). Edwards Christianises this idea, perhaps in Catholic terms. His poem is concerned not with the physical manner of death but with the nature of the life after death, as determined by a person's behaviour in this life. The title of this poem also contains a clue as to the structure of the sequence: '*Though triumph after bloody wars, the greatest brags do bear, / Yet triumph of a conquered mind, the crown of Fame shall wear.*' The Roman practice of parading the spoils of military victory in a triumphal procession had been adopted by Renaissance princes across Europe as a way of displaying power. Petrarch transformed the idea in his *Trionfi*, a series of six narrative poems written between 1338 and 1374, outlining the progress of the soul in terms of a series of triumphs. These are, in turn: Love, Chastity, Death, Fame, Time and Eternity, each one triumphing over the one before. The *Trionfi* are essentially medieval poems, but the concept of the procession as an allegorical expression of transcendent virtue had enormous cultural influence throughout Europe for several hundred years, both as political propaganda and as a structural device or decorative motif in the arts. Petrarch's *Trionfi* were translated into English by Henry Parker, Lord Morley (published some time between 1553 and 1556) but their iconography was well known in England much earlier.[73] Roger Ascham deplored the fact that there were so many who held 'in more reverence, the triumphes of Petrarche, than the Genesis of Moses' (*Scholemaster*, 232), but Edwards's sequence of three poems uses the form for Christian purposes.

The first is a celebration of worldly good fortune that lights on individuals irrespective of their deserts. It ends by quoting the proverb that it is better to be fortunate than wise. The second poem argues that Fortune can never satisfy 'will' or desire. A virtuous, equitable life of the mind, that exercises justice and triumphs over witless self-will and the pursuit of bodily gratification, will alone allow the rich and powerful man's fame to live on in splendour after death. The third poem goes on to say that only those who succeed in *acting* virtuously can achieve true *wisdom*. Mere worldly sophistication, the ability to talk well, is set against true spiritual wisdom, which consists in deeds and flows from total submission to God. Viewed as three individual poems in a collection of individual poems, *PDD*, 6–8, could perhaps be dismissed as a mere rehearsal of proverbial sententiousness. But viewed together as a developing trio, they acquire more complexity and present a philosophical and political dialectic on the nature of the good life.

The second group of poems that can be regarded as a sequence consists of numbers 10–13 here. It is devoted to the four Cardinal Virtues: Prudence; Fortitude; Justice and Temperance. Each moralises on a famous story from classical history. The first three poems in the series were printed without an author's name in 1576, first being assigned to Edwards in the 1578 edition. They are all written in fourteener rhyming couplets. The fourth poem, 'Temperance', alternates sixteener couplets (rhyming both at the end and in the middle) with octosyllabic couplets. The octosyllabics comment on the story contained in the sixteeners, so that the two sets of couplets can almost be read as parallel poems—a not uncommon trick in poetry of this period. 'Temperance' was signed 'M.E.' from 1578 onwards, but 'F.M.' in 1576. All editions of *PDD* give only one other poem to F.M.: 'Finding worldly joys but vanities, he wisheth death' (1576, C3). This employs exactly the same metrication as the 'Temperance' poem, and a similar straightforward and humourless treatment of its subject. In his edition of the *Paradise* H. E. Rollins simply states without further discussion that 'Temperance' is by Edwards. I consider, however, on the basis of both content and metrical style, that the fourth poem is best left with F.M., whoever he may be, and that whoever prepared the second edition was simply trying to make up a coherent group of poems.

The first three poems in the group all set individual behaviour against wider issues of law and justice in a direct encounter with a dictator. This is ticklish ground, and the author uses an urbane humour to raise more questions than he is able to answer. In the first poem a young man, Damocles, thinks what fun it would be to live with the trappings of royalty like Dionysius. Dionysius grants his wish and the young man is enjoying a splendid banquet when he glances up and sees a sword suspended by a single horsehair over his head. The sword represents both the fear of assassination that afflicts Dionysius and also Dionysius's doom, in the sense of his absolute power, which is arbitrary, not equitable. Although the final line of the poem warns subjects not to rise above themselves, the penultimate line 'kings be put in mind their dangers to be great' does not offer a solution to Dionysius's real problem, which is that he is hated for his cruelty and his neglect of natural justice.

The second poem shows a cruel ruler whose attempts at mercy are both motivated and effected through corruption and partiality. The Emperor Valerian, struck by the beauty of a young Christian man, tries to save him from the mandatory death penalty exacted on all Christians by arranging for him to be seduced, thus making him fall from Christian grace. The humour in this poem comes from a dig at untempted moralists in the first eight lines, and the fact that the young man is on the point of giving in to the beautiful temptress when his 'stout and manly mind' overcomes his (evidently equally stout and manly) yielding flesh, in a gruesome connection between two boneless parts of the male body.

The third poem turns from self-mutilation to prevent an inducement to fornication by a ruler, to legal punishment by mutilation for fornication. Zaleuchus is credited with being the first person to make a written code of law, without which equal justice for all is impossible. His code, however, stipulated a fixed (and harsh) penalty for each crime. This may appear to be equality before the law, but such a system in fact prevents the operation of equity, the form of justice superior to common law (and sometimes equated with natural justice, or a sense of humanity) which considers the particular circumstances of the crime and the offender (cf. Aristotle, *Ethics*, 5.c.10). Legal systems are under constant pressure, even in our own times, to operate under fixed penalties in the mistaken belief that this is the best way to ensure the just treatment of offenders. English law, however, had developed during the Middle Ages into a dual system, with courts of common law governed by statute and by precedent, operating in parallel with courts of equity. The result was muddle and confusion, although the system lasted for hundreds of years.

The source for this poem is probably *The Arte of Rhetorique* (1553), by Thomas Wilson (the same Mr Wilson as the likely subject of CT 5, see p. 17). He is in no doubt that Zaleuchus's action in giving one of his own eyes as part of his son's strict punishment represents a personal mitigation of the law by the humane love of the father, which nevertheless allows the law to stand in its entirety—an idiosyncratic definition of equity. He states:

> Thus through equitie of the lawe, he used the dew meane of chastisement, showyng hymself by a wonderful temperature both a merciful father, & a just lawe maker. Nowe happy are thei th*a*t thus observe a law, thinking losse of body, lesse hurt to the man, th[a]n sparyng of punisheme*n*t, mete for the soule. (D4)

Diodorus Siculus (12.20), however, describes Zaleuchus differently and lists a much wider range of rather more subtle legal measures than the story in Wilson. A knowledge of this, which is also hinted at in Cicero (*De legibus*, 2.5.14), might have encouraged the *PDD* author to question both the sense of Zaleuchus's law and his operation of it. The poem rephrases Wilson's statement as a question:

> Say now who can, and on my faith Apollo he shall be,
> Was he more gentle father now, or juster judge, trow ye?
> (*PDD*, 12, 27–8)

This introduces a touch of irony and allows us to wonder whether Zaleuchus's behaviour as a *father* was indeed gentle. Since one of the most powerful images of statecraft at this period presents the relationship of ruler to ruled as that of father to children and family, it also prompts the question as to whether his law can be considered capable of promoting natural justice.

While 'Temperance', the fourth poem in the series, continues the theme of mutilation as a result of sexual appetite, it does so in a different metre and does not raise any of the more difficult ethical and legal questions of the first three in the set. Temperance should be understood not only as the mean between the two extremes of excess and defect but as the means whereby the rational man can control both his own emotions and the forces of external nature. This poem, rather sloppily, sets up Temperance as a mean between an attribute (comeliness) and a virtue (chastity). Spurinna's act is similar to that of the young Christian in the earlier poem, but lacks the political dimension and therefore seems anti-climactic. The great political, Protestant, epic poem *The Faerie Queene* builds book by book through the virtues of Holiness, Temperance, Chastity, Friendship, Justice and Courtesy. This sequence is of course tiny in comparison but, if Edwards was responsible for the first three poems and not for the fourth, we can only speculate as to how he might have realised the potential of the political sequence that he had set up.

EDWARDS'S POETIC TECHNIQUE

Edwards's familiarity with classical subjects and facility in his treatment of them are a direct result of the nature of his education. His early life as a schoolboy would have involved studying classical authors through the process of double translation, first turning Latin (or Greek) into English and then retranslating back into an imitation of the original.[74] This was designed to teach not just the content but the style of expression, although it inevitably results in paraphrase. It had a lasting effect, which can be seen in the handling of the many Latin quotations in *Damon and Pythias*, where the practice allowed him both to make certain loose translations for ironic purposes, and to remove individual words and phrases that might be offensive. Damon's particular translation of the classical quotation he uses at 7.80, for example, draws attention to an unwarranted pride in his own wisdom. Conversely, at *D&P*, 1.102, Edwards truncates and adapts Cicero's *Nihil autem est amabilius nec copulatius quam morum similitudo bonorum* ('nothing, moreover, is more conducive to love and intimacy than compatibility of character in good men', *De officiis*, 1.17.56) rendering it simply as *Morum similitudo conciliat amicitias*. There are several possible reasons for this paraphrase. Firstly, the sentiment is repeated frequently throughout Cicero's works in a variety of formulations as an essential tenet of his philosophy on friendship (*amicitia*). Secondly, Edwards, like Cicero himself, was aware of the sexual implications in male friendship. The Latin verb *copulatio* and its English derivative 'copulate' originally meant 'join together', but the sexual sense—always present as a trope or metaphor—was already in the sixteenth century beginning to take over the English word as its primary meaning. Edwards's version may be an attempt to remove any suggestion of homosexual love. As Damon says, they love each other 'only for virtue' (*D&P*, 10.280).[75]

The absence of any more direct source for what appears to be another Latin quotation may instead indicate the most complex example of this creative use of classical texts. In the middle of the play Aristippus enters revelling in the success he's having at court and breaks into Latin. He's living the good life: good food, luxurious couches and a king's money belt stuffed with glittering gold (*Dapsiles cenas, geniales lectos, et auro / Fulgentem tyranni zonam*, 9.3–4). It sounds like one and a half lines of poetry by the Roman poet Horace, with a further half line added later (*Auri talentum magnum*), but it may not be a quotation. This is, indeed, one of the very few occasions in which the play does not supply an immediate translation or at least a paraphrase. Instead, Edwards seems to be making his Aristippus give direct expression to desires that are elliptically satirised in the first Epistle of Horace (1.1). Horace's *persona* in this epistle is concerned with establishing a philosophy of life for himself. But he is torn between two opposites. He argues for the rigours of the Stoic life but admits that he keeps 'reluctantly' sliding into the self-indulgence of Aristippus (ll. 16–19). He says that virtue is to gold as gold is to silver (52), and deplores society's pursuit of money (59–69). He repudiates his own desire for the status symbol of the *lectus genialis* (87, the elaborate couch, often of gold and tortoiseshell that would stand in the hall of a married couple)—celibacy would be better. But he ends by saying that everyone is as bad as everyone else—who is he to preach? Edwards's Latin phrase thus uses a succession of images that can be found in the Epistle, but seems to be a new composition, giving whole-hearted expression to Aristippus's position. If that is the case, it is a fine example of the Renaissance scholarly imagination and trained memory in action. But Edwards also seems to be engaging directly with Horace's satire (cf. 9.20–2n). In the play Aristippus is repeatedly described as framing or shaping himself to the situation (1.4, 4.8, 13.148, 14.59). This is the reverse of the historical Aristippus's actual philosophy (also expressed in Horace), which was to claim that everything suited him and that his inner self could not be dishonoured, even by wearing the purple, female robe, because he subjected all things to himself, not himself to things (*D&P*, 12.20, *Epistles* 1.17.23, 1.1.18–10). The opposite to this Aristippus that Horace pretends to posit as a goal for his own life would in fact be the same type of self-serving flatterer as the Aristippus of Edwards's play.

The same joke, and a similar detailed and inventive understanding of classical texts, accounts also for the epithet that Will and Jack give to Grim—if the emendation to *Colax epi* in this edition is correct (13.43). Edwards would have known that *Colax* was the title of a lost play in Greek by Menander, which was imitated in Latin plays by Naevius and Plautus (also lost), and by Terence (*The Eunuch*).[76] The preface to Terence's play (l. 30) states that Menander's original contained both the toadying Colax character and a braggart captain. Grim's self-importance and social climbing (describing his charcoal as 'for the King's mouth') and his claim to be a soldier (13.121) combine both characteristics.

Music, metre and rhythm

Critics, inevitably influenced by Sidney's polished detraction of his immediate predecessors in the *Defence of Poetry*, and by the undoubted poetical achievements of the 1580s and 1590s, have long regarded *The Paradise of Dainty Devices* as old-fashioned. Indeed, it contains no sonnets or blank verse, although these were hardly new, having been introduced into English by Thomas Wyatt in the late 1520s. Instead its poems are in traditional English rhyming forms: couplets in either four-teeners (fourteen-syllable lines) or poulter's measure (alternate twelve- and fourteen-syllable lines). Henry Disle, its printer, however, is selling the book on its up-to-the-minute entertainment value: 'Furthermore, the ditties both pithy and pleasant, aswell for the invention as meter, and wyll yeelde a farre greater delight, being as they are so aptly made to be set to any song in 5 partes, or song to instrument' (A2v).

Music settings for at least ten of the *Paradise* poems can be found in a variety of manuscripts and show that composers took Disle at his word. Even those that survive only in keyboard or lute transcriptions are mostly polyphonic, with answering and imitating phrases in different parts, which is the hallmark of having been originally composed for separate voices or instruments. The five-part 'broken' consort (so called because it may be performed by a variety of voices and/or instruments) was an important musical development because it was so adaptable; it suited those middle-class families who might muster a motley array of instruments, instrumentalists and singers. In many ways, musically, morally and sociologically, the *Paradise* is the secular equivalent of Day's Psalter.

Many years ago Winifred Maynard warned critics not to consider the *Paradise* poems separately from musical considerations, although she did not demonstrate her reasons. Critics have continued to be unable to reach back beyond the poetic achievements of the turn of the sixteenth and seventeenth centuries to appreciate the different kinds of experimentation going on in the 1550s and 1560s. Besides, even Shakespeare does not use blank verse or sonnet form for song. Rather than deplore the way in which the *Paradise* poems are written, we should perhaps reconsider the way we read them.

A Tudor writer's understanding of poetics and metrics was rooted in an understanding of Latin and, to a lesser extent, Greek poetry. The Latin *Grammar* that goes under the name of William Lily, but which was continually revised by others, became the authorised school textbook in 1540 and was still in use through the nineteenth century in English schools. It taught that the Latin language was endowed with a natural 'quantity' or length of time for each syllable, depending on the position of the syllable in the word or the number of consonants following a vowel. In poetry, however, when a vowel was followed by more than one consonant, not just in the same word but in consecutive words, it was deemed long even if its natural prose quantity was short. The length of the poetic syllable need therefore have nothing to do with the normal prose pronunciation of the word. Students were to read Latin poetry with the normal prose accent of the words but should also learn to engage in a separate intellectual study of the scansion, appreciating the way in which the raw elements of the language had been disposed with artifice to create the often very complicated pattern of the metre. This effectively created a visual pattern that acted in counterpoint to the aural pattern.

The quantitative experiment in English verse is normally associated with the 1580s and 1590s, particularly the Eclogues in Philip Sidney's *Arcadia* and the songs of Thomas Campion. Like so much else in this story, however, this is an accident that relates to what has been preserved in writing, not an accurate history of cultural practice. Ascham tells how, fifty years earlier, he, Cheke and Watson had often talked together at St John's, Cambridge, where Watson was master. He says they deplored the rude rhymes of traditional English poetry and wished that Virgil and Horace had done a better job in imitating the metres of Greek poetry in the Latin language, bringing 'Poetrie to perfitnesse also in the Latin tong, that we Englishmen likewise would acknowledge and understand rightfully our rude beggerly ryming'. He goes on to protest, 'surelie, to follow rather the Gothes in Ryming, than the Greekes in trew versifying were even to eate ackornes with swyne, when we may freely eate wheate bread emonges men' (*Scholemaster*, 289). Such insistence on theory in the face of both fact and practice is sadly what makes the word 'academic' such a term of abuse. The experiment is doomed to failure because English is not an inflected language and therefore depends on accent (i.e. stress) for meaning. In English the lengthening of a syllable inevitably creates a stress.

William Webbe likewise decried traditional English accentual rhyming verse, advocating Latinate quantitative metres by quoting from Watson's translation of the opening lines of the *Odyssey* by the Greek poet Homer (cf. *D&P*, 8.73n):

– ′ ′ / – – / – ′ ′/–   – / – ′ ′/– –
All travellers doo gladlie report great praise to Ulisses
– ′ ′ / – ′ ′ / – –/– – / – ′ ′/– –
For that he knew manie mens maners and saw many citties

Webbe (p. 72) finds that Watson has attained the 'very perfection' of all the rules of versifying but, in fact, in trying so desperately to follow classical models, he has made the syllable 'ers' long in both 'travellers' and 'maners' and thus sadly distorted the accent of the English words.

As a university fellow and a schoolteacher, Edwards spent his life grappling with the difficulties of Latin scansion, but as a musician and an actor I believe that he was experimenting with other solutions for English poetics. Edwards's spoken poetry for the stage is extraordinarily uneven. Lines vary from two to twenty-one syllables in length and have no regular metrical pattern. The unifying element is the rhyme, which he often goes to some lengths to maintain.[77] His lyric poetry on the other hand is completely regular with almost invariably the correct number of syllables in the line and with regular placing of the mid-line caesura.[78] The result often overrides the natural prose rhythm of the words and makes the poems *read* monotonously, but, if one turns one's attention to the musical settings that survive, his practice becomes clearer. The music invariably underscores the sense and rhythm of the words, not the metre. I therefore suggest that Edwards is attempting to achieve an English idiom of counterpointed rhythm and metre which matches but does not seek to imitate the quantitative form of classical poetry. He is trying to go with the language and not against it, and this would account for his immense contemporary appeal. It is as if his training in classical poetry, in which the quantitative metre is understood intellectually in counterpoint to the natural prose rhythm of the words, has been reinforced by his training as a musician in the demands of proportional church music (see above, p. 29).

Edwards's writing combines the intellectual understandings of both music and classical metre with the quick ear of someone who is a popular performer in the vernacular. Speakers (and readers) of his verse need to be aware of its formal, metrical features such as the line length, the strength of the caesural point and any rhymes, whether at the ends of lines or internally. But they need to pronounce the prose rhythms of the words. For instance, readers are likely to slip into reading the poem 'When May is in his prime' (*PDD*, 1) as a monotonous run of equal syllables. The musical setting shows how it should be read instead (p. 250–4). The music has a delightfully varied, lively rhythm which perfectly underscores both the sense and the natural rhythms of the words, breaking up the tyranny of the poulter's measure. This is a period in music when neither tonality nor rhythm was fixed in the forms that are now familiar to us. The setting accordingly slides from something that feels to us like two in a bar to something that feels like three and back again. Sometimes triple and duple rhythms occur in different voices simultaneously. Having set up an expectation of the pulse, the music dances around it—a bit like jazz syncopation.[79] The same principle of prose pronunciation, which in English means giving emphasis or accent to syllables according to the meaning of the sentence, achieves a surprising result when applied to the

apparently wayward, rambling lines of *Damon and Pythias*: it paradox-
ically reveals the underlying four-stress metre. Here, however, the varying
number of unstressed syllables between stresses (which is a reflection of
colloquial English prose) means that the true rhythm of the line is not
enslaved to this underlying metrical organisation but again works in counterpoint to it. To us now the rhyming couplet conjures up the expectation of the regularity of eighteenth-century poetry. Edwards is not aiming
at that effect. The extraordinary variation in the length of his lines
achieves the kind of sprung rhythm that in his regular verse for song
is accomplished through the music. Edwards's dramatic poetry is a kind
of orchestration for the spoken voice, utilising a variety of techniques
designed to simulate different linguistic registers, but which all play with
the tension between poetic metre and natural word rhythms.

The dramaturgy of rhyme and metre in Damon and Pythias

Amongst its rhyming couplets *Damon and Pythias* contains a significant
number of single unrhymed lines. Textual editors who approach the dramatic poetry of this period from a written, literary perspective inevitably
see irregularities in poetic form as faults to be corrected. I think that
in many instances such anomalies may contain dramaturgical, indeed
directorial, clues for actors that need to be approached by editors from a
theatrical rather than a bibliographical standpoint.

One of these unrhymed lines (10.153) is perhaps explained as part of
a dialogue that has been going on before the character's entrance. Elsewhere, non-rhymes occur whenever speech is broken off or changes direction (10.148 and 152), or is in some way disconnected. As he struggles
to counter Eubulus's plea that Damon should not 'die' (10.217ff.),
Dionysius's paranoid fears about assassination become fixated on the
loose rhyme 'ie/y' in the words *mercy*; *only*; *quietly*; *violently*; *lie*, which
connects back to Eubulus's 'die'. But his fantasy about yielding his throat
to 'Damon's sword' is unrhymed and thus seems to stab him into a decision to carry out the sentence of execution. He has scarcely settled into
the security of regularly rhyming couplets, however, before he is inter-
rupted by a veritable clamour of separately motivated utterances: Damon
and Pythias greeting each other with much emotion; Snap anxiously
trying to control the crowd; Groano dispassionately reporting to Dionysius. All are kept disconnected by virtue of being unrhymed.

A similar technique is used later in the middle of the section in which
Damon and Pythias are vying with each other for the right to die. Here
both Groano and Eubulus make half-line comments that are outside the
rhyme scheme. These can be understood dramaturgically not as utterances
of equal importance with Damon and Pythias's lines but as interjections
to be thrown into the building momentum of the scene (15.203, 208).
They are not asides, because they are not secret utterances. They are
tangential to the content of the main flow of the verse but nevertheless
contribute to its intensity. This use of rhyme and non-rhyme is a subtle,

intrinsic, rhythmic way of marking commentary that is slightly independent of the main thrust of the scene.

Other instances occur where a character addresses himself or the audience without other characters hearing him, in what is now conventionally termed an aside. This is a particularly interesting example:

> You do wisely to search the state of each country
> To bear intelligence thereof whither you list. [*Aside*] He is a spy.—
> Sir, I pray you, have patience awhile, for I have to do hereby.
> View this weak part of this city as you stand, and I very quickly
> Will return to you again, and then will I show
> The state of all this country, and of the court also.
>
> (8.81–6)

Carisophus's private remark, 'He is a spy', rhymes with the overt explanation for his temporary absence, 'I have to do hereby.' This in turn is embedded in the overt advice to Damon that rhymes 'country' (l. 81) with 'quickly' (l. 84). Because of the rhyme, we who have heard the word 'spy' are, however, enabled to understand Carisophus's doings 'hereby' in a much more sinister (and more humorous) way than Damon. Carisophus's duality, and humour, effected by both rhythm and rhyme, is repeated in the second half of his exit line where we, but not Damon, are invited to understand 'court' as 'court of law'.

Poetic form can also be used to indicate character. Left on his own, Stephano's good but uneducated nature causes him to speak in regular ballad metre: generally eleven syllables (divided five plus six) with four stresses to a line (e.g. 5.1–48). He has the common person's natural, wary intelligence, and this is the poetry of the people. Elsewhere, however, he takes objection to Damon's received notions of philosophical aestheticism, and the ensuing argument is marked by lines of variable rhythm. In this passage Stephano's disagreement is twice marked by a refusal to rhyme with his master:

> *Stephano.* 'A short horse soon curried'—my belly waxes thinner,
>   I am as hungry now as when I went to dinner.
>   Your philosophical diet is so fine and small
>   That you may eat your dinner and supper at once, and not surfeit at all.
> *Damon.* Stephano, much meat breeds heaviness, thin diet makes thee light.
> *Stephano.* I may be lighter thereby, but I shall never run the faster.
> *Damon.* I have had sufficiently discourse of amity
>   Which I had at dinner with Pythias, and his pleasant company
>   Has fully satisfied me. It does me good to feed mine eyes on him.
> *Stephano.* Course or discourse, your course is very coarse, for all your talk,
>   You had but one bare course, and that was pike, rise and walk,
>
> (8.13–23)

There is also a marked contrast between Stephano's forthright colloquialisms and Damon's more self-consciously mannered expressions. Damon here sounds a bit of a prig. Stephano is palpably disgruntled.

Aristippus, a philosopher, but one who enjoys the good life rather too much, is inevitably at odds with himself. His long speech that forms the entirety of Scene 12 starts as an account of court life and his own cleverness in negotiating its difficulties. His self-satisfaction causes him to quote the song the ladies sing about him, presumably breaking into song himself. It is a wonderfully ludicrous moment in performance and he has to pull himself back to reality: 'But in all this jollity one thing mazes me.' This line does not find its rhyme until after the next couplet (12.21–4). The rhyme scheme for the rest of the speech is unusual. Two lines are entirely unrhymed. One of these mentions Dionysius's lack of equilibrium (l. 34); the other (l. 40) is an admission of personal anguish—quite a change of direction for someone whose philosophy is the pursuit of happiness. Twelve of the forty-one lines again make the loose rhyme between 'die' and words ending in y. This section also contains two of the longest lines in the play (ll. 25–6), twenty-one and nineteen syllables, so that the restlessness of the verse, unable to settle down to any regular metre, contrasted with the death-knell fixation on the rhyme, seems to reflect the fearful restlessness of the character.

By contrast, Eubulus (whose very name means 'good counsellor') is a model of balance, control and poetic mastery. His finest moment occurs at the opening of the penultimate scene. This speech, like Pythias's song, is a lament in *anticipation* of death—a variation on elegiac form that Edwards seems to have invented. It is printed in Q as a single block of verse, but metrically it divides into groups of four alternately rhyming iambic pentameters (*abab*), with a distich (rhyming couplet) which divides the text into six-line stanzas. The poetic formality of Eubulus's lament thus invokes the very Muses themselves who begin to sing during his fourth stanza. Damon too uses formal, metrical structures to convey his advice to Dionysius about the importance of friendship (15.176ff.), breaking out of his normal conversational register as if quoting from the kind of verse found in the *Paradise*. It is not set to music but it has much the same effect as a pause for song. It is potentially both triumphal and self-reflexively parodic and thereby achieves the lightness of approach required for the moral lesson to be acceptable to Edwards's audience, as well as to Damon's. Once converted to friendship, Dionysius too resorts to a short stretch of serenely regular, sententious fourteeners (15.219–24)

A tragi-comedy also needs humour of a more straightforward nature. This too can be accomplished through rhyme or rather lack of it. Groano is a man who enjoys his job and is proud of his professionalism: he could execute many more people if only those in charge would get their act together (15.124–5). Thus while Eubulus is sorrowing after the departure of the Muses, Groano comes in with a job to do:

> Sir, all things are ready. Here is the place, here is the hand, here is
>   the sword,
> Here lacks none but Pythias whose head at a word,
> If he were present, I could finely strike off—
> You may report that all things are ready.
>
>   (15.58–61)

Again, the break in the rhyme indicates an abrupt change in direction—from being carried away with his job to the simple statement of readiness—but this time it regulates the timing and is potentially very funny.

THEATRE AND THE ART OF GOOD COUNCIL

The philosophy of friendship in Damon and Pythias

The mutual reciprocity which, as we have seen, was such an important part of Edwards's own life and livelihood is reflected in the theme of friendship which recurs throughout his work, forming the main subject of *Damon and Pythias* and of the lost play *Palamon and Arcyte*. The range of human interaction covered by the one term 'friendship' is vast. It can be made to encompass everything from a lasting affectionate relationship characterised by a unanimity or complementarity of outlook—with or without sex, and within or across the gender divide—to the casual sexual encounter, or to a purely pragmatic network of power and influence. Usage depends on the broad cultural practice of particular societies as well as the individual point of view. The importance and the complexity of the concept are demonstrated by the extraordinary number of proverbial expressions devoted to discerning the nature of the 'true' friend. Tilley's *Dictionary* of proverbs lists eighty-one on friends and friendship in use during the sixteenth and seventeenth centuries, many of them dating from classical times. As Aristotle says, 'Not a few things about friendship are matters of debate. Some define it as a kind of likeness and say like people are friends, whence come the sayings "like to like", "birds of a feather flock together" and so on, others on the contrary say "two of a trade never agree"' (*Nic. Eth.*, 8.1.1155a). Any attempt to define friendship is thus beset with difficulty. David Konstan's *Friendship in the Classical World* stresses the difference between Latin and Greek cultural understanding and practice, in that Greek uses the one word *philia* for both 'friendship' and 'love' while Latin differentiates between *amicitia* and *amor* (p. 122). Contemporary British society tends to restrict the expression 'love' to the romantic and sexual, which for most has meant 'heterosexual'. This has occasioned a corresponding euphemistic reduction and then appropriation of the term 'friendship' for homosexual relationships. Non-sexual loving friendship between peers, siblings, teachers and students, even parents and children can, perhaps as a result, sometimes be difficut to express in words, let alone show physically. Scholarship in the field has meanwhile become a political act: Jacques Derrida's book *Politics of Friendship* is an attempt to interrogate the male-centredness of the French revolutionary concept of *fraternité* and define friendship as a new, democratic, political force. Others, working in the opposite direction, but for equally modern, personal and political reasons, have argued that the constant reference to male friendship in Renaissance culture is evidence of widespread homosexual practice.[80]

The poem 'In going to my naked bed' (*PDD*, 9) is one of Edwards's most touching songs. It also engages with some central problems in the philosophy of friendship: child rearing and education. The woman in the poem, in trying to comfort her fretful infant by breast-feeding and singing to it, has to overcome her own feelings of frustration and weariness. The poet, necessarily making his way to bed alone, is deeply struck by the aptness of the woman's song and the parallels she draws with the usually male preserves of political power and military might. Her child will imbibe wisdom along with mother's milk.

Aristotle (*Eudemean Ethics*, 8.8.1159a 28–33), had sought to draw a distinction in the concept of love (*philia*) between the reciprocal love of friends and the elemental love that a mother feels for her child whether it is reciprocated or not. He, however, was trying to describe maternal love in a society in which children were not raised at home with their mothers:

> Some [mothers] give out their children to be raised, and they love . . . and know them, but they do not seek to be loved in return . . . but it seems to them to suffice if they see them [i.e., their children] doing well, and they love them even if they, as a result of their ignorance, provide in return none of the things that are due a mother. (Cited Konstan, p. 69)

Aristotle's problem on this score is compounded because Greek culture does not allow the equality of women or therefore the possibility of friendship between the grown male and his mother. By contrast, Plutarch's *The Education of Children*, written four hundred years later and published in English translation by Sir Thomas Elyot in 1533, urges mothers to bring up and nurse their own children, rather than employ a wet nurse. He could see that 'familiar company in livynge and fedynge is an encrease of love and amitye' (B2v), although he does not envisage a role for a woman in her son's education after the child's seventh birthday. In mid-sixteenth-century England, however, the reluctant admonition in Plato's *Republic* (5) that women should be educated to the fullest possible extent had entered humanist practice. Not everyone, even among the rich and powerful, necessarily valued education, but those who did regarded it as important for girls as well as boys—if only because it contributed to the well-being of men. Edwards could have read Hyrde's preface to Juan Luis Vives's book *Instruction of a Christian Woman*: 'For what is more fruitful than the good education and order of women, the one half of all mankind, and that half also whose good behaviour or evil tatches [taints] giveth or bereaveth the other half, almost all the whole pleasure and commodity of this present life' (Foster Watson, ed., *Vives and the Renascence Education of Women* (London: Arnold, 1912), p. 30). Vives, adviser on the education of the Princess Mary, had dedicated his book to her mother, Catherine of Aragon, on the grounds that it was but a portrait of her virtues. He concluded that, although they must be educated, women should yet be silent and not presume to teach lest they be in error. But two of the most famous English educationalists of the period, Ascham and Mulcaster, were both enthusiastic champions of women's education. As a teacher in court circles, serving two powerful queens in succession who had both had the benefit of an extensive education, who could converse in Latin, and read and write in both Latin and Greek, Edwards must have become used to the idea. The women who make their appearance in his poetry are certainly not silent. He has some uneasy humour on the subject of women's 'schools' (CT 3, p. 191), but a recognition that men and women have similar passions, desires and intellectual capacities (cf. *PDD*, 17) is generally what lifts Edwards's work from the usual run of sixteenth-century poetic complaint.

Edwards's grammar-school education would have introduced him to Cicero's *De amicitia* (*On Friendship*), as well as his *De officiis* (*On Duty*) and his *Tusculan Disputations*, both of which contain references to the story of Damon and his friend (originally called Phintias), disciples of the ancient Greek philosopher Pythagoras.[81] All three of these works had been translated into English by 1561—the *De officiis* by Grimald, Edwards's erstwhile colleague at Christ Church. Cicero himself was not an original philosopher but a Roman rhetorician whose writings rehearse and weigh up the arguments of the Greek philosophers. It is therefore through Cicero's Latin that an Elizabethan boy (and occasionally girl) would have initially become acquainted with a range of philosophical ideas.

The *Tusculan Disputations* is a dramatic dialogue on the nature of the 'Good'. It is set in a country house over a period of days. In the course of the dialogue Epicurus's philosophy of the good life (which Cicero reduces to the idea that pleasure is the greatest good and pain the only evil), is largely refuted through the arguments of Stoicism. According to these, the virtuous man alone can be happy, because, no matter in what terrible or painful situation he may find himself, his sense of virtue will lend him strength. This same conflict between pleasure and virtue runs throughout Edwards's play and is developed with quite sophisticated dramaturgy. Edwards himself was evidently aware of the complexity of the philosophical arguments and their historical development, but he also possessed a humorous deftness of touch that did not allow him to be swamped by academicism.

Pythias's joy in the face of death can be seen as an exemplum of the Stoic ideal: his virtue in offering his life for his friend both gives him joy in itself and will grant him future renown. For Aristippus on the other hand, the best condition of life is the one that grants him the greatest ease and luxury. Such a way of life has always been loosely referred to as 'epicurean', although it is actually a falsification of Epicurus's profoundly humanitarian ideal that the good life is virtuously simple but free from pain. The historical Aristippus was reputedly the founder of the Cyrenaic school of philosophy, a more materialist forerunner of Epicureanism.

By drawing on his schoolboy training and imitating Cicero's character-istic stylistic combination of chain logic and rhetorical question (cf. *Tusc.*, 5.6.15–16), Edwards makes Aristippus 'prove' that looking after number one is in fact the greatest good (*D&P*, 1.1–12). Elsewhere Aristippus's conversation with Carisophus (*D&P*, 14.29–46), while quoting directly from Cicero's *Amicitia*, has also digested the form and content of the argu-ment in the *Tusculan Disputations* and proceeds stychomythically (in alternate lines linked by a verbal chain from line to line), in order to prove that honesty is in fact the chief link in friendship. Carisophus is appalled and amazed—as well he might be, since this is a version of the Stoic ideal that what is right is the only good (*Tusc.*, 5.8.21) and is counter to Aristippus's avowed hedonism. Carisophus has asked him to stretch a point—that is, be dishonest. Aristippus responds, 'I love no stretching', but his wordplay, which in itself is a form of dishonesty, makes the word slip from meaning that he refuses to put himself out for Carisophus to a pun on being stretched on the rack: 'so may I breed my own pain'. This exposes him in his own colours as the libertarian dilettante that Cicero so despises. Aristippus and Carisophus are, on one level, as *unlike* 'as Jack Fletcher and his bolt' (1.104), yet, on another, they are *equal* rivals at Dionysius's tyran-nical court. They call their temporary alliance 'friendship' but it is entirely self-serving and indeed deceitful in both cases.

Having asked the question, 'Do men love, then, *the* good or what is good *for them*?' Aristotle answers that, 'each man loves not what is good for him but what seems good' (*Nic. Eth.*, 8.2), later concluding, 'Friend-ship for utility's sake seems to be that which most easily exists between contraries, e.g. between poor and rich, between ignorant and learned' (8.8). Difference in status between king and commoner might thus logi-cally imply that true friendship between them is impossible. In Edwards's play, however, friendship repeatedly crosses class boundaries: Dionysius is, comically, accepted into friendship by Damon and Pythias; they in turn repeatedly show friendship to their slave, Stephano, eating with him and listening to his complaints—although of course still expecting him to carry the bags. In this they are following a mode of behaviour advocated by the stoic philosopher and playwright Seneca:

> I'm glad to hear ... that you live on friendly terms with your slaves. It is just what one expects of an enlightened, cultivated person like yourself. 'They're slaves,' people say. No. They're human beings. 'They're slaves.' ... No, they're friends, humble friends. 'They're slaves.' Strictly speaking they're our fellow-slaves, if you once reflect that fortune has as much power over us as over them. (Letter 47.1)

Seneca's reasons are not entirely altruistic: one needs as many friends as one can get, and a slave can be an enemy behind your back if you are not careful. Damon and Pythias's behaviour accordingly pays off: Stephano would do anything for them.

Damon is the older of the two friends and thus, in the Pythagorean tradition, he should make up for the dissimilarity in age by being Pythias's mentor as well as his friend. Unfortunately he flatters himself on the extent of his own wisdom, and falls prey to the traveller's delusion that he can be *in* the country but not *of* it. He takes a detached, tourist's interest in the town, not anticipating the ease with which he can be swept up in Syracusan politics. Stephano, on the other hand, has not got much time for philosophy (cf. 8.13–30), but does keep his eyes and ears open, and uses his common sense. Damon refuses to listen to Stephano's sensible warnings, condescendingly berates him as a 'bond-man' (not just in fact but in his lack of sensibility and intelligence), and shows off his own education with a quotation from Horace:

Not in vain the poet says, '*Naturam furca expelles, tamen usque recurret*',
For train up a bondman never to so good a behaviour,
Yet in some point of servility he will savour.
As this Stephano, trusty to me his master, loving and kind,
Yet touching his belly, a very bondman I him find.

(8.38–42)

He has a lot to learn, and it is a mark of the play that he learns from his slave and his younger companion.

Carisophus and Dionysius have the most to gain from the friendships in which they engage in the play, while it is Pythias and ironically Stephano, the least powerful of the three visiting Greeks, who find it most natural to give. Aristotle stated that it is more worthwhile to give love than to receive it (*Nic. Eth.*, 8.8), and most people would probably initially assume that giving love is entirely altruistic. Further reflection shows that this imposes a moral debt on the object of affection so that, as Jacques Derrida observes (while dancing suggestively around Aristotle's famous conundrum, 'My friend, there is no friend'), it is the *giver* of love who has the most to *gain*. This is destabilising and 'renders dissymmetrical the equilibrium of all difference' (*Politics of friendship* (London and New York: Verso, 1997) p. 7).

Destabilisation is exactly what we get at the end of *Damon and Pythias* as the two friends in the depths of a tragic situation and in the height of love for each other argue as to which should die so that the other may live. The effect in performance at the Globe Theatre in 1996 was extraordinary. During the afternoon dress rehearsal, the few cast friends and acquaintances sitting in scattered isolation in the vast auditorium had been avowedly moved by the pathos inherent in the situation. In the evening, a crowd of nine hundred typically active Globe audience members (who could all see each other as clearly as they could see the characters on the stage) refused to be drawn in by the emotion of the scene. Instead they revelled in the ludicrousness of a situation in which each character strives to gain the moral advantage in self-sacrifice. The few people who knew the play in advance before seeing it at the Globe may have been surprised that such a serious and such a moral tale could have generated such gales of laughter. They could be forgiven for wondering whether we had got it right. But the reaction was revealing, for it defined the term tragi-comedy not as something that is potentially tragic but turns out well but, more interestingly, something which finds comedy *within* the tragic situation. The Globe archive fortunately possesses a video record of the performance and of some rehearsals.[82] Those who doubt my judgement as someone too closely involved to be objective will at least be able to go back to that source.

The play begins with the disclaimer that it is not about Elizabeth's court (Prologue 39–40). It ends with a paean of praise to Elizabeth, wishing her good friends as the chiefest defence against those who would endanger her. In so doing it rehearses the moral injunctions to be found in books on good government such as those by Sir Thomas Elyot: 'Get thee frendes, not all them that dooe seke frendship of the: but suche as be most agreable unto thy nature, neither those, with whom thou shalte live plesantly, but with whom thou maiest governe thy countrey most surely' (*The Doctrinal of Princes* (1534), B2v).

Dionysius, who is an undoubted tyrant, becomes transformed by the vision of goodness in the two friends.[83] Our moral selves might expect to have to find this moving, exemplary, the epitome of everything that a humanist or Christian education would teach. It is indeed all of these things, but at the same time it is ludicrous, risible, impossibly other-worldly, indeed simply 'other'. This is not just a twentieth-century view. It is signalled to us by the comic figure of the executioner, Groano, his appallingly literal name and his caustic commentary on events. Throughout the play individual characters make moral pronouncements, some resort to extensive passages of poetic formality, yet the total effect is, in its comic performativity, ambivalent and contradictory. It therefore becomes a piece of philosophy in its own right—a dialectic in which moral truisms and courtly shortcomings are placed side by side for re-evaluation. We have watched something that we know to be part history, part legend, part impossibility, but within the logic of this particular comic structure it has obeyed Aristotle's precepts and achieved probability.[84] We also want it to be true. We want Damon to come charging in like the arrival of the cavalry just in time to save Pythias. We want the tyrant to change his mind, although logically, outside the theatre, we know that he probably could and would not. It is this kind of optimism that keeps us going and raises the image of what Derrida in *Politics of Friendship* calls the 'perhaps': the 'if only it were possible'. It is not in our interests as human beings to believe that such an event is actually impossible since that would prevent us from striving for better things. Friendship is a political necessity, a way of climbing the ladder of success, but it can also be a political act of faith, a bond against tyranny. This vital political tool, then, accounts for what can seem to us now as the plethora of 'merely conventional' poems on friendship in the poetry collections of the period.

The change in religion in England was of course motivated at least in part by the desire to separate secular power from that of the church. The monarch, as head of the Church of England by God's will, logically needs no church from which to gain authority. Cranmer's address at the coronation of Edward VI thus amounted to a denial of the need even for the consecration service: 'the solemn rites of coronation have their ends and utility, yet neither direct force or necessity; they be good admonitions to put Kings in mind of their duty to God, but no increasement of their dignity'.[85] The only sanction on royal behaviour, short of insurrection, which for the stability of the country must be classed as a sin, is thus the monarch's own sense of responsibility for the wellbeing of the commonwealth combined with his or her human desire for a good reputation. Friendship, in both its materialist and altruistic senses, is the only mechanism that can save an autocratic system from dissolving into outright tyranny. Yet there is acute tension between the concept of friendship as pure altruistic love and friendship as personal political need. This is the heart of the philosophical discourse concerning friendship from Aristotle to Derrida. Edwards is fully aware of the problems. By exploiting the contradictions in the easy moral messages of traditional proverbial sayings, he is able to go beyond them.

Modern readers, however, may well be exposed to the evolutionary genetic theory that self-interest is not a moral failing but the actual cause of behaviour previously termed altruistic. Self-interest is likewise the median term in all of the dichotomies of friendship identified in philosophical discourse. The play's playfulness, its determination to create a happy ending in the face of normal expectation, requires the characters to move from the pursuance of their own immediate short-term plans to an appreciation that their *real* self-interest can be achieved by other means. Damon and Pythias want to live, not to die for each other. Dionysius wants the security that has hitherto eluded him. Groano wants his executioner's right to the condemned prisoner's clothes and is delighted that he can get them without killing anyone. The play thus ends in a celebration of pleasure, with everyone winning. The only person who cannot be accommodated is Carisophus, whose trade is based on flattery, that inversion of true friendship. This is arguably the vice most damaging to society as a whole because it distorts the flattered person's perception of genuine self-interest.

As we shall see, arguing the pros and cons of monarchical versus republican government may have furnished the legitimate exercises in logic, law and moral philosophy for members of the universities, but Elizabeth was most definitely running a monarchy. While it might be possible to quote from Cicero so that his republicanism appears to be unexceptionally sound morality, the persuasion of a single autocratic prince demands more subtly insinuating rhetorical skills than those needed for public oratory, hence the fine line between courtliness and parasitical sycophancy. Making the monarch herself see the funny side is surely the safest guard that subjects have against absolutism. Despite the initial disclaimer, 'We talk of Dionysius's court, we mean no court but that' (Prologue, 40), *Damon and Pythias* is very much applicable to Elizabeth's court. Or at least it would be if she were so foolish as to be a tyrant, which she is not—of course. A tragic version of the story, in which one or both of the friends was killed, might run the risk of being perceived as an attack. Edwards's playfulness, by contrast, achieves what Castiglione in the *Book of the Courtier*[86] calls '*sprezzatura*'—the practised, nonchalant ease that enables one to present genuine ethical and political dilemmas in a non-threatening way.

The Bedford wedding tournament and the Queen's marriage

Edwards's theatrical activity was not confined to working with the Chapel children. He performed himself and must also have written and devised the iconography for a range of court masques, disguisings and tournaments. The tournament was no longer simply a trial of strength but a show which would often play out an allegorical story in words and music as well as in the physical competition of the joust itself. These events often established a narrative told at intervals of time. Such a sequence occurred in 1565, and linked a significant diplomatic visit connected with proposals for the Queen's own marriage with the marriage of one of her maids of honour.

Cecilia, Margravine of Baden, had just arrived in the country with her husband after a hazardous sea-voyage when she gave birth to a son. More significantly, the Margravine was sister to the King of Sweden, a long-term suitor to Elizabeth. Elizabeth naturally became the baby's godmother and was present at a feast to celebrate Cecilia's churching after childbirth at Bedford House (home of the Earl of Bedford) where she and her husband were staying. After the banquet the York herald announced the arrival of a messenger from a foreign country. Elizabeth agreed to his admittance and, after the herald had sounded a trumpet three times, in walked Richard Edwards, dressed as the post in boots and spurs. He knelt and told the Queen, no doubt in verse, and no doubt in a foreign accent, that four foreign knights would hold a joust, tourney and barriers to celebrate the forthcoming marriage of Bedford's daughter, Lady Anne, with the Lord Ambrose, Earl of Warwick. He invited her and the Margravine to attend. Elizabeth accepted and more than twenty gentlemen stepped forward to take up the challenge, including the Earl of Leicester, another of her long-term suitors.[87] A challenge in verse was also fixed upon the court gate at Westminster.

On 11 November the bride was escorted to the Queen's great closet, where the marriage ceremony was to be performed, by a company of young lords and the other maids of honour, all dressed in yellow satin trimmed with green velvet and silver lace. The groom, and then the Queen herself, arrived in separate processions. Afterwards a marriage feast was held in the council chamber hung with arras. In the afternoon in the tilt-yard, Edwards, 'with a trumpet' rose, and asked the Queen, who was in a gallery at the upper end of the jousting area, if the tournament might begin. The four challengers then rode in, each preceded by a supporter and followed by an Amazon 'with long hair hanging down to her sandals', a gown with crimson satin sleeves, a sword at her side, a vizor on her face, a shield bearing her master's arms and her horse caparisoned with white tinsel sarsenet, appliquéd and embroidered. Each challenger's party was completed with a spare horse caparisoned with black tinsel, likewise embroidered.

The iconography is sufficiently complex to be both suggestive and diplomatic. The 'foreign' knights (played by English gentry) with 'Amazons' in their entourage, challenge other English gentlemen in the name of love and country. The real Amazon, playing hard to get as usual, was in the royal box. The tournament consisted of six courses at the tourney, twelve strokes with the sword, three pushes at the punchion staff and twelve blows with the sword at barriers—or twenty 'if any be so dis-posed'. But even after three days they had run out of time and not all the bouts were completed. The valuable accoutrements of the losers, and any garments or equipment that fell to the ground, were forfeit to the officers of arms as their fees, and were redeemed 'according to the usages of olden time', presumably for cash. At 10 p.m. on the first night a 'valiant ser-viceable man', a master gunner, fired a three-gun salute to honour the marriage and, particularly, the groom who was General of the Ordinance. Unfortunately the second explosion killed one of the onlookers. This whole charade must have been in the same tradition as the masque-cum-show of arms on 9 June 1564 to honour the French Ambassador which had involved a castle for the court ladies, 'a harboure' (place of shelter or retreat) for the lords, three heralds and four trumpeters to 'bringe in the devise with the men of Armes'.[88] If George Peele, Ben Jonson and Francis Bacon could write verses for tilts and tourneys later in the reign, and Shakespeare provide an *impresa* (an iconographical device and motto) for the Duke of Rutland,[89] there can be no doubt that Edwards's courtly service kept him fully employed in doing the same. We can there-fore assume reasonably safely that the unattributed poetic challenge for the Bedford tournament printed in Stow's *Summarie of English Chronicles* came from his pen. It is certainly in his style and is included in this edition (p. 225).

OXFORD 1566

The politics of a progress

The most extensive piece of total theatre in which Edwards was involved was probably the Queen's visit to Oxford, the culmination of a two months' progress in the summer of 1566. Normally the Master of the

Chapel and the children would be part of the enormous retinue involved, but this year, when Elizabeth set out from Greenwich in July on her winding progress through Middlesex, via Northamptonshire and Warwickshire,[90] he went straight to his old university to start preparations.

Two fundamental issues hung over the Queen's visit to Oxford in 1566: the question of the succession and therefore of her marriage; and the question of what constituted good, secure government. While all her courtiers desperately wanted her to marry, she had probably already come to the conclusion that the two issues were incompatible and that if she was to achieve the latter she would need to remain single. Her visit to the University is partly in the nature of an inspection: she needed to ensure that her academics were doing their duty in underpinning the intellectual life of the kingdom and the re-established church. It was also an attempt to confirm and encourage those people personally in her service. As with the performance of *Damon and Pythias* and the Bedford marriage celebration, it also served to allow those taking part to remind her of her duties to the kingdom and to her subjects. One of the happy results of the visit was a letter from the Chancellor asking the Queen to reaffirm the powers and privileges of the University.[91] One of the less happy results was a series of letters to All Souls from Archbishop Parker and the Queen's Commissioners ordering them to deface their plate and surrender their 'superstitious books', including a specified number of psalters, pricksong books, massbooks, antiphonals and processionals.[92] Almost all of the week's events—the processions, orations, disputations, plays and sermons—were variations on a theme of government, whether of the country, the natural world or the individual self.

The royal party itself, however, was inevitably far from united or well disciplined. Cecil's diary for June that year records a violent argument between the Earls of Sussex and Leicester occasioned by the question of the Queen's marriage. It was apparent to all that Leicester still longed to marry her himself. Sussex was urging the match with the Archduke Charles of Austria. The Spanish Ambassador, who was likewise with the Queen, was also hoping for that match and sent regular reports on its progress to King Philip II of Spain, her sister's widower, who had briefly considered marrying her himself. One of the perhaps half-serious reasons that he had given to his ambassador for not wanting to make a match with another English queen was that he would again be expected to pay his share of the prodigiously expensive English style in court entertainment.[93] But Elizabeth evidently took delight, and derived control, from playing these men off against each other. Several times in the course of the week she went out of her way to tease Cecil, who was Chancellor of the rival University of Cambridge, that things were much better done at Oxford.

Edwards's play that week, *Palamon and Arcyte*, confronted this situation head-on. It likewise dealt with two men battling for the love of a single woman, with its story taken from Chaucer's 'The Knightes Tale'. Edwards's skill as a courtier in this environment is displayed in the poem

'The Muses nine' (p. 228). This poem may have been a separate gift, but conceivably it could have formed the play's final paean, connecting the fictional world with that of the court, just as the final song in *Damon and Pythias* extends that play's theme of the importance of friendship to rulers without implicating Elizabeth as Dionysius. It manages an appealing mix of eulogy and humanity blended with humour, plus a tribute to Henry VIII, whose popularity amongst his subjects, and skill as a ruler, she was trying hard to emulate. Its final line, wishing 'him to have her that *loves* her best' is a subtle change from Emily's prayer to Diana in 'The Knightes Tale': 'sende me hym that moost *desireth* me' (*Canterbury Tales*, 2325, my italics). Thus the poem places the ball firmly, indeed permanently, in the suitors' court, requiring them to compete to prove their worth without demanding that she should make a decision. In so doing, it counterbalances the outcome of the play (and Chaucer's story) in which both men get the girl in turn without her having any choice in the matter. If this is indeed the way in which Edwards's play could be read by the court, it would be no wonder that one of the descriptions we have of Elizabeth that week shows her enjoying the company of her poet (p. 86).

Throughout her visit the Queen was on show to the University as much as the University was on show to the Queen. Extensive arrangements had to be made for her comfort, security and privacy. She was to be housed in the Deanery at Christ Church, that symbol of the reformed English Church, reconstituted by her father Henry VIII as both a cathedral and one of the largest of the University's colleges. College accounts reveal months of building works:[94] load after load of gravel was bought and transported to make clean hard standings for the many horses and the wagons full of equipment and furnishings that she would bring with her. Large quantities of timber were cut down, sawn and squared up. Walls and partitions were torn down, new doors and new locks were provided, the kitchens whitewashed, repairs made and women paid to clean the church. Rob Bote was paid £3 7s 10d 'for diverse women makinge garlandes and gatheringe ivye'. This is an extraordinary sum, equivalent to an unskilled male labourer's wages for more than seventy days, assuming that the ivy was free for the gathering.[95] He was paid a further 14s 10d for 'dayly paynting king henryes name in golde'. Work continued for more than a week after the Queen's departure, putting everything back together again after the damage inflicted by so many visitors. This included repairing a bridge, the range and the sink in the kitchens, Mr Calfhill's stable (which had been altered and disordered by the yeomen of the larder), and, as we shall see, rebuilding the wall to the hall stairs.

Elizabeth took her place on a variety of stages that might reveal her, conceal her or represent her as appropriate. For example, two partitioned enclosures were made for her within the cathedral at Christ Church so that she could, in private, say her prayers and listen to the sermon, that hallmark of the new religion. But the latter was raised well above the ground near the pulpit so that the word of God was mediated both visibly and audibly by his minister and silently by the invisible but nevertheless evident presence of his anointed. Similarly, the stages prepared for her to sit and watch the disputations and the plays were so adorned with cloths of state that they marked her presence even on the occasions on which she pleaded indisposition and was absent.

Everyone in Oxford that week seems to have been an actor in a play and, as with the coronation entry procession, it is sometimes difficult to determine who is performing for whom. The principal participants were all dressed for their parts with appropriate costumes and props: the members of the University in the gowns and hoods according to their degrees; University officers with staves; aristocratic visitors in their finery. A splendid litter was provided for the Queen to sit in relative comfort, listening to the various speeches of welcome made at intervals along her route as she moved from the outskirts of the city to Christ Church. Even the buildings were dressed up, not only repaired and renewed in honour of the event but fluttering with cloths painted with commendatory verses, encased in panels of gold, and festooned with garlands of leaves, cloths of state, canopies and ornamental tapestries. Significantly, this excess in apparel was the means whereby the University showed itself, not as an actor but as a repository for the word, at a time when the word needed to be the received religious and political truth.

The eyewitness descriptions

There are three detailed descriptions of the visit, two in Latin, and one in English from which several others also derive. All give day-by-day accounts but with variations depending on the respective interests of their writers. Together they form a good record of the public parts of the visit, giving the order of events, and some indication of the disputations and of the content of the orations made to welcome the royal party. Their descriptions of the three theatrical spectacles (Toby Matthew's Latin play *Marcus Geminus*; Edwards's *Palamon and Arcyte*; and *Procne*, a Latin play by Mr Calfhill) provide us with some of the most detailed information about plays in performance for the entire early modern period. But even so, all three play texts are lost and it is notoriously difficult to describe both visual effects and architectural details in words. Interpretation is therefore problematic, and my understanding of the content of Edwards's play and of the staging arrangements sometimes differs from that of other historians.

The English account is by Miles Windsor, a student actor in Edwards's play and a great-nephew of the third Lord Windsor who was travelling with the Queen and would be entertaining her at his country estate the following week. Windsor provides a very personal record, including some typical actor's reminiscences of near disasters on the night, together with some details of official events and the reactions of the royal party that probably came from his great-uncle. It exists in a rough draft and a fair copy, both holograph and bound together in the same volume.[96] Some of the most interesting features of the first draft were added later, squeezed into the margins (plate 3). Windsor then had third thoughts and omitted much of this from his fair copy.[97]

Windsor left his papers to Brian Twyne (the son of Thomas who had also been a student actor in *Palamon*). He copied the description of the visit, slightly shortening it but adding other documents in 1636 for the benefit of the University authorities, who were then preparing for the visit of Charles I.[98] This version was again copied by the antiquarian Anthony à Wood, but with some errors of transcription. There is a further related version, copied by Richard Stephens, but this is greatly truncated, concentrating mostly on the disputations.[99]

The Latin records are by John Bereblock and Nicholas Robinson.[100] Bereblock was a fellow and perhaps already Dean of Exeter College, and was one of two Masters of Arts who delivered an oration to Elizabeth as she entered Christ Church at the start of her visit. He was also responsible for the drawings of the colleges interspersed throughout a book of Latin verses praising the University, written by Thomas Neale and presented by him to the Queen during her visit.[101] This book takes the form of a dramatic dialogue between the Queen and Leicester, the Chancellor of the University. Bereblock's drawing of Christ Church is reproduced here (plate 4), although it has considerable inaccuracies even after accounting for its variable scale and impossible perspective. His descriptions of the plays are also untrustworthy as his notions of authority mean that he is more concerned to retell the original source stories rather than accurately describe the particular plots and productions he saw. Thus he makes no mention of the character Trevatio that Edwards adds to his Chaucerian source, and ekes out his description of Calfhill's *Procne* with direct recourse to Ovid's *Metamorphoses*.

Nicholas Robinson, Bishop of Bangor, had been educated at Cambridge and had written a Latin comedy for performance there.[102] Later he became Dean of Queens' College, and wrote an account in Latin of the Queen's visit to that University in 1564. But he displays little interest in, and less knowledge of, the plays at Oxford, being more concerned to compare the disputations in St Mary's Church with those two years earlier in Cambridge. Nevertheless, it is he who tells us that Edwards had been in Oxford for two months previously, helping to make the sumptuous preparations in the hall at Christ Church, and preparing for the 'English play'.[103]

These descriptions appear in different permutations in the various editions of John Nichols's *Progresses of Elizabeth I*, suggesting that the multiplicity of related texts confused even him. Bereblock, Robinson, Stephens and Neale's verses are included in Plummer's *Elizabethan Oxford*. I have taken Windsor's account from both his manuscript rough draft and his fair copy as necessary, modernising the spelling, and translated Bereblock's and sometimes Robinson's Latin from Plummer. The

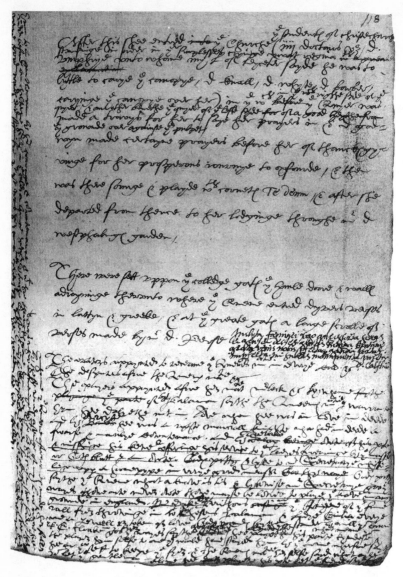

3   A page from the rough draft of Miles Windsor's description of the Queen's visit to Oxford in 1566. The top of the page describes the appearance of the college buildings hung with verses. A verse by Dr Calfhill is quoted in the middle. The Queen's comments on the actors and the burning of the cloak are squeezed into the bottom of the page. The vertical section tells what she said to Lord Windsor about Miles after they had left Oxford. Corpus Christi MS 257, fol. 118 (Original size: 210 × 155 mm).

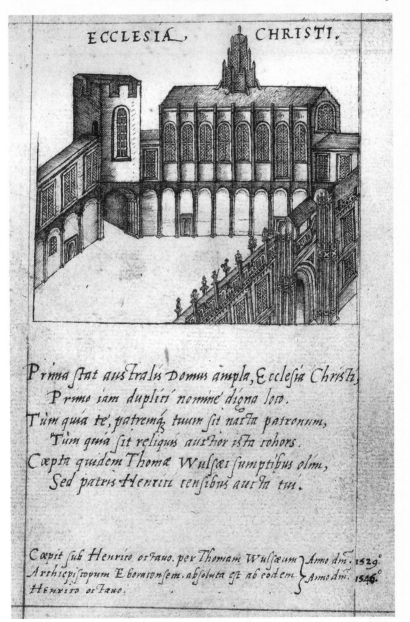

4 Bereblock's drawing of Christ Church showing the arrangement of the hall, stair turret, and Deanery with Neale's accompanying verse. MS Bodl. 13, fol. 5v.

description that follows here is an attempt to situate Edwards's work as both dramatist and director within the total theatricality of the royal visit.

Staging the visit

On 29 August 1566 Secretary of State William Cecil, with Robert Dudley, Earl of Leicester, Chancellor of the University, arrived with a small entourage at Christ Church to check on the arrangements. They were supposed to have been greeted by the whole company of students all ranked in order and dressed in their gowns, but it was pouring with rain. Mr Potts of Christ Church made an oration of welcome to Leicester, and Mr Ponson one to Cecil, 'who after he had talked with Mr Potts of the causes why Aristotle in his Politics wrote *De monarchia* (being at that time no monarchy in the world) entered into further talk of the privileges of Oxford' (Windsor, fol. 105). The following day the Bishop of Salisbury, Dr Jewell, arrived in the college but went straight to his room without stopping to hear the orations that had been prepared.

On 31 August the Queen, accompanied by the Spanish Ambassador and a large company of noblemen and ladies, approached Oxford from the north. At the furthest extent of the University liberties (or area of jurisdiction), near the village of Wolvercote, the Queen's party was met by the Earl of Leicester in his role as Chancellor, accompanied by four doctors in their scarlet gowns, eight Masters of Arts and three Esquire Beadles. In a delicate enacting of the balance of authority and jurisdiction between Crown and gown, Leicester received the staves of office from the Beadles and offered them to the Queen who immediately delivered them back to the Beadles. Then an oration was made by Roger Marbeck of Christ Church, 'enduring one quarter of an hour, which was very well liked of her majesty, saying that she had heard of him before, but "Now, we know you"'. The Spanish Ambassador added, '*Hic non pauca multis, sed multa paucis complexus est*' ('This is not a few words of a great deal but a great deal encompassed in a few words'). The Queen gave each of the doctors her hands to kiss, pointedly singling out Dr Humphrey, a noted puritan, with a joke linking habit of thought with form of dress, before giving him her hands, 'Methinks this gown and habit becometh you very well, and I marvel that you are so straight-laced in this point; but I come not now to chide' (Windsor, fol. 106).

A little further on, they were met by the Mayor and aldermen. He presented the Queen with a gold cup, such as she customarily received from civic dignitaries on these occasions, and made an oration in English. They then progressed via the north gate into the city, where the streets were lined with members of the University, until they came to the main gate to Christ Church. Here the entire college stood 'standing in order according to their degrees'. Two representatives from the undergraduates 'exhibited an oration in writing and certain verses'. They were followed by two of the bachelors (that is, graduates) who did the same, then two Masters of

Arts (Mr Ponson and Mr Bereblock), who spoke their orations and were thanked by the Queen in Latin, and finally two doctors. All were dressed in gowns and hoods. Then, 'the scholars in order kneeling cried "*Vivat Regina*" [Long Live the Queen], which she taking very thankfully with a joyful countenance, said often times sitting in an honourable riche litter "*Gratias ago*" [thank you]' (Windsor, fol. 117v). The arrangements in Oxford were in marked contrast to those that had pertained during Elizabeth's visit to Cambridge almost exactly two years earlier. At this point in the proceedings on that occasion the undergraduates had been told to disperse to their lodgings and to stay there on pain of punishment, scarcely allowed to walk in the streets, let alone be present at the plays and disputations.[104]

The royal party then progressed to Carfax, the crossroads at the centre of the town, where an oration was made in Greek. Elizabeth gave thanks, also in Greek, and continued, 'We would answer you personally but with this great company we are somewhat abashed; we will talk more with you in our chamber.' Once inside Christ Church, she was met with another oration about which she was critical, though conciliatory, saying, 'You would have done well if you had good matter.' She entered the cathedral accompanied by four doctors carrying a canopy over her, 'the students of Christ Church standing orderly in their surplices and crying "Vivat Regina"'. The service included a sung *Te Deum* accompanied by cornets, after which she departed to her lodgings in the Deanery.

At this point both Bereblock and Windsor describe the physical appearance of the college buildings hung with verses in Latin, Greek and Hebrew, a celebration of language meant to express both the University's loyal love and its intellectual strength. Copiousness was therefore the order of the day but the visual and verbal riches that Oxford provided were never, or so Bereblock claims, guilty of excess or pomposity. On the contrary, they were simply appropriate to the solemnity of the occasion. His Ciceronian phrases are an attempt to match this message, although his prose structure is more akin to Elizabethan English than to classical Latin and does not appeal to modern classical scholars. He does not divulge the financial assistance to which the University would be entitled from the exchequer to offset the charges incurred, nor the extent to which the Queen's own lodgings would have been equipped and furnished with what she brought with her.[105]

> The College of Christ was indeed a sufficiently magnificent [lit. 'brilliant'] and spacious House,[106] and truly so prepared by its own people that it appeared from that, as clear as day, how much it hated luxury privately, and how much it adored magnificence publicly. For nothing there was haughty, nothing puffed up or swollen with arrogance, but everything was prepared aptly and fitly to her sovereign power, with the immortal gods approving her arrival by the abundance, copiousness and usefulness of those things which pertain either to need or the means to live. And while she now relaxed, setting aside her great, anxiety-inducing responsibilities,

the royal party thinking it shameful to waste the chance of rest in a long solitude, dispersed in all directions through the streets into the town. They observed with great circumspection, looking at its situation and arrangement; they admire, they are amazed, they become astonished at the neighbourhoods there, very spacious in a certain continuous broadness of the streets, very splendid in the ornateness of its buildings, very magnificent in the beauty of its colleges. The entrance courts then, and front gateways of the colleges, were adorned with poems; there were indeed a thousand copies of the finest verses fixed to their individual doors. Therefore they are immediately much occupied in inspection of the verses; they are seized in amazement, reading them, and it is absolutely incredible how they are immediately entranced by our shared enthusiasm for the Queen (for which, from these verses, like a shining monument, they had testimony).

(Bereblock, 122–3)

The verses decorating the University Church, St Mary's, which at that period was also used for the day-to-day running of the University and would be the venue for the week's disputations, included celebrations of the Kings of England since William the Conqueror, and histories of the Oxford martyrs—Bishops Cranmer, Ridley and Latimer—who had all met their deaths by burning in the town in Mary's reign.[107]

The following day, Sunday 1 September, the Queen kept to her lodgings in the Deanery all day, missing both the morning and afternoon sermons preached in Christ Church. Windsor, however, records that young master Peter Carew, 'a fine boy', son of the former Dean of Christ Church,[108] who was also in the cast of *Palamon*, made her a private oration in Latin and Greek. Peter gained his BA from Exeter College in 1572, and was probably about fourteen at this time. The Queen, sensing the opportunity to make an anti-Cambridge joke at Cecil's expense 'sent for Mr Secretary and willed the boy to pronounce it again the second time, and said before he began, "I pray God, my boy, thou mayest say it so well as thou didst to me." And when he had ended she said "That boy doth as well as many masters of Cambridge"' (Windsor, fol. 118v).

Bereblock has the fullest description of the architectural preparations for play performance in Christ Church hall although his Latin is far from unambiguous.

With night approaching, the most magnificent spectacles were given, which, to some who had been idly looking forward to them all day long, were, in their splendour, ample reward. And nothing now could be devised more extravagant or more magnificent than their preparation and construction. First there, with an entrance thrown open through a massive, solid wall, there was a remarkable porch,[109] and a wooden bridge, suspended from it, set upon piles, extends by means of a small, polished track over the transverse steps to the great hall of the College. It is adorned with a canopy, with a carved and painted festive garland of leaves, so that by this means, without disturbance or jostling of the pressing crowd, the Queen could, with almost even step, reach the prepared spectacles.

(Bereblock, 123–4)

The hall at Christ Church is on the first floor and is approached up a flight of stairs housed in an adjoining stair turret, and then through a small ante chamber. The stairs have since been rebuilt and perhaps re-oriented. A disruption in the stonework at first floor level in the side wall of the Deanery where the Queen was lodging still marks the opening that was made from her rooms directly into the stair turret. The accounts show that three joiners were paid for eight days with their board to build a 'porche for the quenes entrance into the greate chamber' and that it required 'two great planks'. The bridge and polished track would have extended in a straight line immediately to the right, parallel with the south wall of the turret, delivering the Queen through a still extant sixteenth-century doorway into the antechamber. This doorway is now balustraded as a window on to the stairwell, the stairs currently ascending towards a door in a corresponding position to the north where the stonework is more recent. There is now only a single, central door from the ante-chamber into the hall itself, but modern stonework blocks up what may originally have been two or three openings, as would be normal.[110] The Queen's access could thus have been kept entirely separate from that of the rest of the audience.[111]

The hall itself had been fitted with 'a gilded, panelled ceiling [*laquearo aurato*], and with the roof painted and curved inside;[112] in its grandeur and loftiness you would say it imitated the scale of an ancient Roman palace, and in its magnificence the very image of antiquity' (Bereblock, 124). The roof of the hall is still supported by very fine, early sixteenth-century, low-pitched hammer beams with curved braces. It has no ceiling. The curved, gilded and painted ceiling that Bereblock describes seems to be closing off the void of the roof above the hammer beams, perhaps resting on top of them. It was presumably coffered—that is, with recessed panels of painted plaster, supported by a grid of timber joinery, covered in gesso and gilded.

> In the upper part [*superiori*] of the hall which looks back [*respicit*] to the West, a stand [*theatrum*] is built [*excitatur*], large and upright, and high with many steps[113] [*gradibusque multis*]. Against all the walls, balconies [*podia*] and platforms were built out. There were tiers of many benches higher than these, whence important men and ladies could be seen from below [*suspicerentur*], and the ordinary people could look at the plays from all sides [*circum circa*]. (Bereblock, 124)

The Hall is on an east–west axis with the entrance from the staircase and antechamber to the east and the dais at the western end. It is the dais end that is described as the 'upper' part, both because it is raised and because it takes the high table for senior members of the college. Bereblock's use of the word *excitatur* in connection with the *theatrum* may simply be rhetorical variation, that is, the need to find more than one verb for 'to build'. More interestingly it could, in its primary sense of 'brought out' or 'aroused', indicate that the *theatrum* is something which the college already possesses for its regular theatrical shows and that it has been brought out from storage. Bereblock describes the *theatrum* and the other stands in separate sentences which is consistent with the idea that he thought of them as separate structures. Christ Church had a thriving tradition of play production and it is reasonable to assume that it already had some demountable scaffolding structures for both performers and audience. The loss of so many of the disbursement books means that there is no evidence for this. If the other stands were specially built for the occasion, they would account for some of the quantity of timber that we know was felled in the college's own meadows and squared up in preparation for the visit.

All these wooden stands must have been built like any Elizabethan timber-frame construction in sections or bays. The term *podia* could thus have various interpretations, which are not mutually exclusive. Firstly, the top storey might project forward in a jetty, as in many Elizabethan timber-frame houses, so as to create a row of 'balconies'. Secondly, the division between each section on the top tier might be filled in and plastered so as to form individual rooms. Thirdly, although the hall is the largest in Oxford, it is much longer than it is wide (35.5 m by 12 m). Perhaps the structures with the *podia* are said to be against (*juxta*) the wall, because they were comparatively narrow and needed to be fixed for stability, whereas the *theatrum* was deep enough to be free-standing.

We know that Queens' College in Cambridge had a set of scaffolds that was brought out once or twice a year for play performances.[114] These lined the entire hall and incorporated a stage, which Alan Nelson places at the dais end of the hall. In a later article, he extrapolates from this to argue that the *theatrum* on the dais at Christ Church was likewise the stage.[115] Bereblock, however, also uses the term *theatrum* to denote the scaffolding erected for audience seating at the disputations in the nave of St Mary's Church. Here he additionally uses the terms *amphitheatrum* and *circus*, suggesting that, there, it was a circular or, more likely, a rectangular structure, surrounding the spot from which each disputant in turn delivered his argument. Robinson says that it was very like the scaffolding normally used for such events at St Mary's in Cambridge. Windsor and Robinson confirm that 'a fair large scaffold' occupied most of the nave, and that a room was constructed either in or over the chancel so that the Queen and the ladies could retire if they desired. The Queen's place was flanked with her councillors on one side, and the Spanish Ambassador and the ladies on the other. Bereblock puts it rather more expansively, although again it is not unambiguous:

> And now between the columns of the temple a huge amphitheatre was built, broad and magnificent with steps on high. Divisions and benches were built higher. Its breadth extended from the south to the north, its length, truly, from the east to the west. From the upper place, men and women of honour and renown could look down at the public exercises in rhetoric with very great enjoyment; in the eastern part of it was an ample

wooden platform, and a chamber was built, protected and dignified by a curtain and a tapestry in which ancient and antique stories were seen, woven in silk and gold. In the centre platform [*medio suggesto*] in a higher place was a very high seat, clothed and covered with gold, and ornamented with a precious tapestry. The enclosure [*septa*] of the bottom of the *theatrum* was crammed full of stools for the masters, a platform provided amongst the respondents' stools [*mediis scabellis respondentis*]. In the north, a company of the elected officers (which we call proctors) occupied the remaining higher places . . . The seats of the doctors on either side of the *circus* were higher and larger. Next to these, on the south side of the east-facing part of the theatre, another seat was seen to overhang, covered in red silk in triumphal manner. The Earl of Leicester, our Chancellor, was conducted to his seat there by the Beadles of the University. In stalls outside the amphitheatre, bachelors of arts, younger scholars and strangers [that is, non-University-members] truly sat with remarkable eagerness and extensive comprehension. (Bereblock, 130)

The Queen's chair was therefore placed high up with its back to the chancel, looking westwards down the nave. While Robinson simply says that the Chancellor sat amongst the Doctors, Bereblock's formulation, 'south of the east-facing part', indicates that the scaffolding across the back of the church was in two parts either side of a central opening. The fact that his seat is said to overhang again suggests that the upper tiers were jettied forward. The plural term '*septa*' (enclosure) must here mean the floor of the church in the middle, surrounded by the scaffolding. The respondents sat all together, ready to take their turn on the platform provided for them.

In both hall and church the seating arrangements presented a visual representation of social hierarchy. The most important people, the nobility, sat on the top tier of the scaffold. At the disputations, the Doctors of the University also sat high up, while the stools for Masters were crowded into the floor space at the bottom. Bachelors of Arts and the youngest scholars were not even admitted into the scaffolding, crowding eagerly, so we are told, into the spaces of the church behind. In both hall and church the highest seat, suitably ornamented with a cloth of estate, was reserved for Her Majesty, while in the church a draped stage facing her was provided for the University Chancellor, the Earl of Leicester.

In the hall, for the people on the floor, the show consisted of looking *straight* at the stage and *up* at the beautiful people in their benches at the top. Indeed the text suggests that the only seating was in these *podia*. The phrase '*circum circa*' indicates that people were standing all round the acting place. The fact that Bereblock found this noteworthy might also suggest that the normal Christ Church *theatrum* was a single scaffold, front-on to the acting area.

The platforms and scaffolds to which Bereblock refers are all for the use of the audience. Windsor the actor, however, confirms that the plays were performed 'upon a fair large scaffold', while attempts later in the week to hold disputations in the hall were frustrated because of the presence of the stage (Windsor, fol. 108). Both *Palamon* and *Procne* seem to have required a trapdoor and infernal sound effects coming from below, while *Palamon* also called for subterranean fire shooting out of the ground. The stage must have extended at least to the centre of the hall since that play involved a funeral pyre on which certain objects were really burnt, the smoke from which would need to be able to escape through the roof louvre (see Bereblock's drawing). The accounts record a payment for taking down the 'haarth in the hall and makinge it up agayne'.

Bereblock describes the scenery for the first night's play:

> On each side of the stage [*ex utroque scenae*], magnificent palaces and the most splendid buildings were put up for the use of the comedians and actors. On high was fixed a seat [*sella*] adorned with cushions [*pulvinaribus*] and tapestries and covered with a golden canopy. This place was for the Queen. (Bereblock, 124)

A stage erected immediately in front of the entrance doors to the hall would inevitably obstruct access. Bereblock, however, says that the audience stands were on *all* the walls. This suggests to me that the audience entered the hall underneath scaffolding that might, as in the church, provide the Queen with a retiring room at the upper level. It would also support the back wall of the stage on to which would be built both stage scenery and the Queen's box. The audience would thus make their way behind the scenes at the back and down the sides of the stage to their viewing positions.

The scene, with buildings on either side, recalls the opposition of town houses and palace in *Damon and Pythias*. That play, like most classical comedy, and most of the surviving university drama from Cambridge, has fixed locale staging and takes place in the street with entrances permanently assigned to specific places. In Cambridge, Nelson has argued that the required houses were formed from the scaffolding on the two opposite sides of the stage, and so faced each other. Such an arrangement would work perfectly well for the two Latin plays performed in Oxford that week. But, as we shall see, *Palamon and Arcyte* had fluid setting and required extensive scene changes during the performance. It is also important to register that this description refers to the performance of the first play and does not necessarily describe the precise scenic arrangements for them all. One Berell was in fact paid for four days' labour 'about the plays and alterations of the stage', which coincides with the number of days of actual play performance that week and suggests that the scenes were changed from night to night. The question remains whether, in Oxford, Bereblock's phrase signifies 'on the two opposite sides of the stage' or, as I am inclined to believe, 'on either side of the back of the stage'.

The Queen's throne is a '*sella*', a term used for both a schoolmaster's chair and that of a magistrate. It thus suitably represents her role as judge at all the week's linguistic entertainments in this seat of learning. Her chair also has the trappings of a *pulvinar*, a cushioned seat for the gods or for one who has received divine honours. Robinson says that her seat was '*in scena praesente*',[116] i.e. on view either 'in the scene' or 'on the stage'. It is clear from Bereblock, however, that her place was set on high, in a position above the stage, and that whether occupied or empty it was intended to represent the noblest and most splendid show of all. Whether this effect was enhanced by restricting scenery to the back of the stage, visually separating the audience standing 'round about' the stage from a spectacle that incorporated the Queen herself, cannot be stated for certain, but it is a possibility in Bereblock's description of the arrangements.

One of the enormous extravagances of the occasion was the lighting. Windsor observes that as many candles were used in one night as would normally serve for five, although this may be poetic licence since the same proportionate numbers are used in *Damon and Pythias* (1.52). Bereblock gives the impression that torch and candleholders had to be imported from numerous different sources:

> Lamps, torches [*lichni*] and wax candles burning made an extremely bright light there. With so many sources of light distributed in branched and circular chandeliers, and so many tapers everywhere with flickering brilliance [*inaequali splendore*] supplying changeable light, the place was gleaming so that the lights seemed both to shine like the day and to enhance the clarity of the spectacles by their dazzling brightness. (Bereblock, 124)

The accounts confirm that it took two men and a boy two days to repair the holes made by the light fittings, although perhaps these holes included those made to support the panelled ceiling.

But that Sunday night, despite all this effort and expense, the Queen's seat was empty. What she missed was a tragi-comedy in Latin, 'made and set out by one Mr Mathew and other the students of Christ Church' (Windsor, fol. 118v). Toby Matthew, then a twenty-year-old student of Christ Church and an actor in the play, was later to become President of St John's, Dean of Christ Church and finally Archbishop of York.[117] He is also listed as one of the two opponents in the Tuesday afternoon disputations in moral philosophy where the questions were, 'A prince should be declared by succession not election' (*Princeps declarandus est successione, non electione*), and 'It is better to be governed by the best law than the best king' (*Praestat gubernari ab optima Lege, quam ab optimo Rege*). Robinson says that Matthew was the final speaker in the first of these, arguing against succession with taste and distinction, winning great praise (Plummer, 182). This might initially seem to be quite a feat, appearing as he was before a monarch who claimed right of succession from her father. If Elizabeth were not to marry and produce an heir, however, as she had already indicated that she might not, her successor would have to be chosen by some form of election. Both she and her courtiers needed to hear the politics, legality and ethics of the various options rehearsed, but naming a successor was to be something that she steadfastly refused to do.

According to Bereblock, Mathew's play concerned the wrongful accusation 'through envy and rivalry' of one Geminus Campanus, and his eventual acquittal owing to the honest action of some honourable freedmen 'whom neither punishment nor reward could induce to wrongful accusation'. The antics of the accusers, brawling amongst themselves and subsequently 'deploring their misfortunes with tears and lamentation like women', seem to have been entertainingly ridiculous. This story takes place at the court of Alexander Severus, a Roman emperor who was probably rather better known in the sixteenth century than he is now. He was a reputededly virtuous and honest ruler and, significantly, a supporter of the power of the Senate. The story of Marcus Geminus occupies two lively chapters in *The Image of Governance Compiled of the Actes of Alexander Severus*, a translation of a Greek text by Isocrates, by Sir Thomas Elyot (four editions between 1541 and 1556). The sayings of Severus are also extensively quoted by William Baldwin in his most popular and influential work, *A Treatise of Morall Phylosophie, Contaynyng the Sayinges of the Wyse* (eighteen editions between 1547 and 1640). The topic of the play was thus central to the cultural and political concerns of the Queen's visit, and indeed of the period, and was carried off with energy and humour. The Spanish Ambassador and all the nobility who were present at the performance, including Lady Cecil (sister to one of the ladies addressed in Edwards's poem CT 1.15, cf. Appendix p. 232), 'commended the same so highly to the Queen insomuch that her Grace said that she heard so good report of their doing that she would lose no more sport' (Windsor, fol. 118v).

The following day, Monday 2 September, began with the ordinary term-time lectures of the University, starting with Greek and Hebrew translations and then variously lectures in grammar, rhetoric, dialectic, arithmetic, geometry, music, astrology, natural philosophy, moral philosophy and metaphysics (Bereblock, 125). Later, John Rainoldes, who would play the part of Hippolyta in *Palamon* that night, delivered one of two orations at New College. He was to become a celebrated puritan divine, President of Corpus Christi, Oxford, one of the translators for King James's Bible and, ironically, one of the most outspoken opponents of the stage.[118]

The most frequently reported drama of the whole week, however, occurred inadvertently that night before the play began, on the stairs outside the hall. The fact that the Queen had been absent from the proceedings for two days, in addition to the reputation for spectacle that this production had already acquired, meant that the stairs were thronged with people. In the crush the side wall collapsed, killing a young scholar from St Mary Hall, a brewer named Penny and a cook from Corpus Christi, and injuring five more.[119] Bereblock characteristically stresses the strength and solidity of the college building and blames the plebs for causing a foul scuffle. Windsor's first draft likewise includes some unsympathetic dialogue that is dropped from later versions: 'my Lord Chamberlain when he found that they were dead said, "Bury them"', although the Queen sent her own surgeons. The show went on regardless, and 'the Queen laughed full heartily afterward at some of the players' (fol. 119v).

Palamon and Arcyte, *part 1*

The salutary point about the two descriptions of *Palamon and Arcyte* in performance is that Windsor's acting anecdotes and Bereblock's concentration on the states of mind of the two protagonists scarcely match at any point. They can, however, be reconciled by recourse to Chaucer's original narrative and to the one song that we can be certain still survives from the play.

Chaucer begins by stating that Theseus has married Hippolyta, Queen of the Amazons, and has brought her back with her sister Emily to Athens. His first scene is a street in Athens where the royal party is met by a company of ladies weeping for the loss of their husbands at the siege of Thebes. The Theban ruler, Creon, is refusing to allow the bodies to be buried. Theseus sets off immediately for Thebes. He sacks the city, restores the bones of their husbands to the ladies, and finds the cousins Palamon and Arcyte on the battlefield. They are both wounded. He sends them back to perpetual imprisonment in Athens. Several years pass until one May morning Palamon looks out of his prison window and sees Emily in the garden, singing a song and gathering flowers.

> And in the gardyn, at the sonne upriste,
> She walketh up and doun, and as hire liste
> She gadereth floures, party white and rede,
> To make a subtil gerland for hire hede;
> And as an aungel hevenysshly she soong.
> *(Canterbury Tales*, 1051–5)

He cries out in admiration, inadvertently waking Arcyte who also looks out and falls instantly in love. The pair then start to quarrel about who loved her first: 'Greet was the strif and long betwix hem tweye' (*Canterbury Tales*, 1187).

Perotheus, an old childhood friend of Theseus, arrives. He also knew Arcyte at Thebes. At his request Theseus frees Arcyte without ransom but on pain of death if he remains in Theseus's kingdom. Arcyte, however, is suicidal because he will never see Emily again. He weeps whenever he hears music:

> He wepeth, wayleth, crieth pitously;
> To sleen hymself he waiteth prively.
> He seyde, 'Allas that day that I was born!
> Now is my prisoun worse than biforn.
> *(Canterbury Tales*, 1221–4)

Palamon, left alone, likewise bewails his lot with 'youlyng and clamour' (*Canterbury Tales*, 1278).

Bereblock simply introduces Palamon and Arcyte as people who had become like brothers from having shared the same country of birth and the same perils. Now, sharing the same prison, they fall in love with the same woman, Emily, sister of the Duke of Athens, with the result that their minds are set in 'backwards and contrary motion'. He does not mention Hippolyta at all. Sadly, in his description of the first part of the play, he is more concerned to express himself and the young princes' psychological turmoil in polished antithetical Latin than to give a precise account of the structure of the plot or the staging. It is therefore not possible to say whether Edwards followed Chaucer's arrangement of scenes from Athenian street to Theban battlefield back to Athenian prison, or whether, as in *Two Noble Kinsmen* (the later play on the same theme attributed to Fletcher and Shakespeare), there was a scene before the battle in Thebes in which Palamon and Arcyte demonstrated their friendship and noble natures by deploring Creon's tyranny. By contrast, we get a strong sense that the two young men's behaviour was both ridiculous and meant to be so: 'What more? They are prohibited by order; they do not heed the order; they are incarcerated; they break out; they exult; love does not allow them to go further; two days is too much; three days is insupportable' (Bereblock, 128). From Windsor, however, we know both that Hippolyta played a significant role and that, as in Chaucer, there was a scene in a garden, because the Queen singled out the two actors playing the female roles for special recompense.

> When all the play was done, she called Mr Edwards, the maker thereof, and gave him great thanks with promise of reward. And afterwards her majesty gave unto one John Rainoldes, a scholar of Corpus Christi College who was a player in the same play, eight [g]old angels in reward. The lady Emilia for gathering her flowers prettily in the garden and singing sweetly in the Prime of May, eight angels for a gracious reward. (Windsor, fol. 121)

Although it seems likely, we cannot say for certain that the play showed Palamon and Arcyte witnessing Emilia in the garden or, if so, whether they did so from an upper playing level as in *The Two Noble Kinsmen*. We can speculate, however, that Edwards's poem 'When May is in his prime', with its reference to the flowers having been kept in prison (*PDD*, 1), may have been the song that Emilia sang at this point. If so, the line 'take May in time', which caused M.S., the poem's imitator, such anxiety, becomes a specific piece of advice to the Queen to marry, something which her courtiers might have some difficulty in saying to her directly.

The anonymous poem 'O death, rock me asleep' (p. 226), which has occasionally been ascribed to Edwards, with its desire for death and its expression of being alone in a prison, may also derive from the play. It would admirably suit the lamentations made by either of the princes after

Arcyte's release—Arcyte for a figurative imprisonment, removed from the sight of Emily, and Palamon because he remains incarcerated alone. This song is both strikingly beautiful and completely over-the-top. In one of the two extant settings the music conjures up the sound of a tolling bell: in the Christ Church MS version, occasional tremolo markings give a musical impression of fear and cold while another version of the same setting (Add. 15117) repeats the words 'I die' consecutively six times. The language was satirised by Shakespeare both in Pyramus's death scene in *A Midsummer Night's Dream* and in *2 Henry IV* in the mouth of bombastic Pistol: 'Then death rock me asleep, abridge my doleful days! / Why, then, let grievous, ghastly, gaping wounds / Untwine the Sisters Three! Come, Atropos, I say!' (2.4.188). Bereblock's laconic explanation, 'The prince does not care for death', is perhaps consistent with Arcyte being converted to life through lying down to die in extravagant song, rather than from a dream, as is the case in Chaucer.

Bereblock continues, concurring with Chaucer that Arcyte returns, disguised in a 'rough habit' having changed his name to Philostrate, and gets a job as Emily's chamberlain, instructing himself in all kinds of duties. There is no duty so vile or irksome to his nature which Emily's presence does not make agreeable. Without that 'most delightful girl', all is laborious and hateful. Meanwhile, Palamon gives his jailer a narcotic drink and escapes under cover of darkness—Chaucer says that he has a friend to help him do this—taking refuge in a wood where Arcyte eventually finds him. Such is the tumult that Emily has aroused that soon they are fighting.[120]

No doubt some of the quantity of ivy that the college paid to have gathered (p. 65 above) was used to create this scene. Theseus with Hippolyta, Emily and ladies now enter, hunting a hart. Windsor lets us know that the hunt was represented in the play by off-stage sound effects achieved with a real pack of hunting dogs, and no doubt horns, outside in the quad. This created pandemonium inside the hall. His first draft says, 'the ladies in the windows cried out "Now!" and hallowed', though 'ladies' is changed to 'boys' in the second draft. Both concur that the Queen exclaimed, 'O excellent, those boys are ready to leap out at the window to follow the hounds' (Windsor, fol. 118v). The first draft, with intermittent legibility, then goes on to compare Edwards's achievement in the verisimilitude of the setting for this scene with that of three of the most famous ancient Greek artists: the sculptors Praxiteles and Polycletus and the painter Apelles. This is the highest compliment that could be paid in the context of classical and Renaissance theory on art as mimesis. Windsor is insisting that the hunting effect was not real life—as the audience response seemed to assume—but true art, imitating the very essence of life.

Theseus stops the fight and asks the young men who they are. Palamon identifies them both and says they both love Emily. In Chaucer he asks that they both be slain; in the play, Bereblock writes, he 'does not pray for death although he has committed a grave error' (phrasing which suggests that he has been checking the source). Hippolyta, Emily and the ladies weep and kneel, begging pardon for the two young men. This is granted but Theseus demands that in fifty weeks (Chaucer) or forty days (Bereblock) they must return to joust for Emily's hand. Everyone rejoices. That was the end of the first part of the play. A shout went up in prayer for the Queen and then everyone went to bed.

Palamon and Arcyte, *part 2*

The second part of the play was due to be given on the following night, but the disputations went on so long that Elizabeth 'sent word if they would play, the nobility should be there present, but she could not come: unto whom Mr Edwards made supplication that it might be deferred unto the next night which the Queen granted out of hand' (Windsor, fol. 120v).

On Wednesday, after four hours of disputation in civil law, the second part was duly given. Bereblock now seems to provide more detail, although we cannot be sure how much is derived directly from Chaucer. The audience settled down and a 'great silence' followed. Palamon and Arcyte appear dressed for battle, with their supporters (supposedly, as in Chaucer, one hundred knights each), including Emetrius, King of India, on Arcyte's side and Lycurgus, King of Thrace, on Palamon's. Theseus decrees that they should fight in single combat which 'did not displease the kings'. 'A marble enclosure [*septa marmorea*] is therefore made in the woods. There, three sacred altars are built' (Bereblock, 138). Bereblock has already used the plural noun *septa* to denote the single enclosure made by the *theatrum* on the floor of St Mary's church. It therefore seems that a single wooden fence, painted to look like marble, was erected around three separate altars, which turn out to be dedicated to Diana, Mars and Venus. Emily approaches Diana's altar. She prays for chastity but, Bereblock says, is unfortunate, 'The Goddess predicted matrimony.' Arcyte prays to Mars, who thunders out, 'Victory' (*intonuit victoriam*); Palamon prays to Venus and is immediately promised the girl. These mutually incompatible promises cause strife amongst the Gods, which Saturn breaks up (*disrumpit*).

Neither of the witnesses gives any clue as to where the actors representing the gods were positioned—although logically we might assume that they were on an upper level. Nor do we know the precise nature of the sound effects, and perhaps visual effects, emanating from the altars. The lovers have to hear (or witness) the latter but not the former, which indicates that the gods themselves were on a different plane.

The princes' supporters are meanwhile preparing the arms for battle; there is a strident call of trumpets. There follows a ferocious fight with much crashing and glittering of swords. At first neither wins the upper hand and both rest, exhausted. Then, in what is evidently time-honoured stage-fight tradition, they get locked together, their bodies motionless, their weapons shaking with tension, their wounds and blood (Bereblock says) providing a spectacle for everybody. Palamon collapses at the foot of the victorious Arcyte who is greeted with acclaim. Breathless, hopeless, and out of control, he rages passionately at the altar and curses Venus. Venus cannot bear it, nor can she suffer Mars standing in front of her, and laments 'like a woman'. Moved by her tears, Saturn strikes Arcyte 'with subterranean fire', even while he is triumphing round the stage in a laurel crown. He dies at once.

Another scene change brings on a structure representing a tomb and another pyrotechnic effect. There is a procession in which the kings follow Arcyte's body as it is carried to a funeral pyre. It is probably at this point that Emily sings her song appealing to the weeping nymphs (pp. 225–6). These must be the women who lament their husbands at the start of Chaucer's poem and have presumably, therefore, also been part of the play since the beginning, although we are not told this. Arcyte's body 'is cremated with due pomp' (Bereblock, 139), Theseus, Palamon and Emilia each casting some jewel or token of love into the flames (Windsor, fol. 118). Chaucer adds that Arcyte's shield, spear and vestments were burnt (2947–8). In the production one of the players threw into the flames a cloak once belonging to Edward VI. This must have come from the royal wardrobe and was presumably worn by Arcyte in the second part of the play.[121] Fire on stage is always an exciting, not to say dangerous, effect. A play at court in 1579 staged fire issuing from a large 'rock'. Decorated with ivy and holly, the rock was equipped with concealed crevices in which *aqua vitae* was burnt, with rosewater 'to Alay the smell'.[122] In Oxford, it caused consternation in the hall, with one audience member physically intervening. The fullest rendition of this is only found squeezed into the bottom of a page in Windsor's draft (plate 3) and, with its contractions and erasures, becomes increasingly unreadable:

'God's wounds,' said a stander by, 'will ye burn ye K[ing] E[dwards] cloak?'—'Go thy ways,' said Edwards, 'go fool, he knows ⟨plays⟩ his part kindest, what mean you?' The player himself to one that would have stayed him by the arm, 'Wherefore,' said he, 'are you [?]set to keep the fire?' And the Queen's Majesty herself said, 'What are you? W[oul]d let the gentleman alone? He ⟨does⟩ plays his part, let the firers [i.e. incendiarists] as [?]well do theirs. (Windsor, fol. 118r–v)

After that, in a final scene and by common consent, Emilia is given to Palamon in marriage. Bereblock gives no details, but Chaucer assigns to Palamon a speech on the nature of life, which argues that 'thynges and progressiouns / Shullen enduren by successiouns' (*Canterbury Tales*, 3013–14). God has bound everything together with a chain of love and has allotted certain days and duration to everything on Earth:

Thanne may men by this ordre wel discerne,
That thilke Moevere stable is and eterne.
(*Canterbury Tales*, 3003–4)

Whatever the reasoning behind the conclusion in Edwards's play, and however it related to that week's themes of order and stability, it delighted the spectators in the now extremely crowded theatre. There was tremendous applause.

Palamon and Arcyte in context

Echoes of some of the effects used in this play can be found in some later Revels accounts. Leashes and doghooks were provided for hunters in a play of Narcissus in 1571 'that made the crye after the fox (let loose in the Coorte) with their howndes, hornes, and hallowing' This play by Hunnis and the Chapel children also called for thunder and lightning effects. Hunnis again staged a hunting scene with dogs in 1574.[123] The fact that the clerk described the loosed fox in the first of these in such detail is, I hope, an indication that it was a one-off novelty.

There is no indication that Edwards's play was revived. Philip Henslowe's account book records very respectable takings at four performances of a play called 'palaman & arset' by the Admiral's Men and the Chamberlain's men between September and November 1594, but this is more likely to be an independent version. As we have noted, Chaucer's story is also the source for *Two Noble Kinsmen*. This introduces a subsidiary plot in the form of the jailer's daughter who, rejecting her suitor, goes mad for love of Palamon. The suitor perseveres, exploiting her crazed belief that he is in fact the young knight.

Edwards's play too must also have incorporated a subsidiary plot, for Windsor's rough draft describes the antics of a character who does not appear in Chaucer and is likewise absent from Bereblock. This is Trevatio, played by John Dalaper. His moment probably came in the first part, though we cannot be sure. He could perhaps have been a third and emphatically unsuitable suitor to Emily. 'Lord Trevatio, Dalaper, being out of his part and missing his cue, and offering his service to the ladies swearing, "By the Mass!" and, "God's Blood I am out!" "God's pity!" and the like to Mr Secretary and whistling up a hornpipe in very good measure' (Windsor, fol. 118). This caused some vocal response from the courtly audience, the Queen shouting out from her high seat, ' "Go thy way, God's pity, what a knave it is!" and likewise Mr Secretary, "Go thy ways, thou art out, clear out. Thou may'st be 'lowed to play the knave in any ground in England" '—both of which, we can be sure, would have caused much merriment. The question is whether this was caused by the actor actually 'drying' or whether it was a deliberate metatheatrical, humorous effect (similar to the acting of the mechanicals in Shakespeare's *A Midsummer Night's Dream*) designed to undercut the ridiculous sadness of the love story.[124] The whistling up of a hornpipe and the direct accosting of the ladies and the Secretary of State either show remarkable *sang froid* in an acutely embarrassing situation or indicate carefully rehearsed clowning. There is some similarity with Henry Medwall's *Fulgens and Lucres*, written at the end of the fifteenth century, which also concerns a woman faced with two suitors. Medwall frames the action with two people, apparently members of the audience, who tell us that there is about to be a play, but who then proceed to intervene in the action. For actors to switch in and out of character in this way might seem to us now a daringly modern device but it is a natural thing to do when actors and audience share the same light conditions. It is highly unlikely that Edwards would have known Medwall's play.

The theme of the two suitors is of course a stock folk-tale motif, and Chaucer likewise treats it humorously. But the fact that it is also a real-life story for the court at this time means that the interface between the real world and the play world needed to be thoroughly blurred. Elizabeth was never slow to register when a play was intended to represent her and her activities. At the Gray's Inn play of Juno and Diana performed on Shrove Tuesday 1565, in which extensive argument on the pros and cons of marriage ended with Jupiter's ruling in favour of matrimony, she turned to the Spanish Ambassador and exclaimed, 'This is all against me.'[125] This time, however, she was evidently unfazed by the significance, commenting first on Palamon, 'I warrant him he dallieth not in love when he was in love in deed', and then on Arcyte, 'He was a right martial knight who had indeed a swart and manly countenance' (Windsor, fol. 118).

As we have noticed, she made a point of singling out for special reward both of the actors who had played the two main female parts. This even-handed generosity of course may have had as much to do with the political allegory with which she had been presented as with the relative acting skills of the two young men. Emilia evidently reflects Elizabeth's own situation faced with two suitors but, as with the Bedford wedding tournament, Hippolyta, the Amazon, is just as relevant. John Nichols preserves a story concerning Roger Ascham who had written a letter to Sturmius, 'the learned man of Strasburg', concerning Elizabeth's marriage which he had himself shown to her, no doubt in hope of some reward:

> which the Queen read over thrice, smiling, but very bashfully and mod-estly, and said nothing. Then he added, that for her disposition towards wedding, he nor none else could know any thing certain, nor tell what to say. And that it was not without reason he had told him, that all her life she was more like to Hyppolite than Phaedra; which, he said, he meant in regard of the chastity of her mind; and that of her own nature, not by the Council of any, she was so strange and averse from marriage. (Nichols, 107)

As Nichols explains, Hyppolita was a warrior, whereas Phaedra, Theseus's other wife, was 'very amorous'. Whatever she did for Ascham, Elizabeth certainly thanked Edwards for his pains and seems to have promised him a reward after each part of the two-part performance.

Aftermath

The following day Elizabeth delivered her own address to the University in Latin, full of compliment for their teaching and their learning and modestly deprecating her own linguistic skill (which, she said, was marred with barbarisms). This was, of course, received with tumultuous applause. Afterwards, as Windsor recounts, Edwards's old tutor Etheridge, who had lost his Chair at Oxford because of his Catholic sympathies when Elizabeth came to the throne, approached her as she was leaving St Mary's and presented a book of poems in Greek in praise of Henry VIII. Edwards, 'standing by said, "Madam, this was my master"'. Elizabeth's speedy riposte was that Etheridge had not given him 'whipping enough'. Her comment suggests that Edwards had sailed very close to the wind. He pulled it off, I think, because of a strong sense of the ridiculous, honed by years of experience of fantastical court shows—something which was perhaps so foreign to Bereblock that it took him the two evenings of the production to begin to get used to it.

That night, by contrast, there was a performance of *Procne*, a tragedy of rape and murder, based on the story from Ovid's *Metamorphoses*, and written in Latin by Dr Calfhill. This is the least informative of Bereblock's descriptions, relying as it does so heavily on direct quotations from Ovid. The visual effects he describes (such as references to the 'boiling sea', *spumas agere in ore*) are too conventional to be valid descriptions of the performance.

The next day, 6 September, the University presented the Queen, her noblemen and several officers of her household with fine pairs of gloves, and made her courtiers honorary Masters of Arts. After dinner she was accompanied to the extent of their respective liberties by the Mayor and Aldermen (as far as Magdalen Bridge), and by various representatives of the University (to the village of Shotover), where, after an oration by Mr Marbeck and a final kissing of hands, she continued on her way.

Palamon and Arcyte closed Edwards's career in the place where it had begun. It amazed and delighted those who saw it, but the strain must have been enormous. Windsor tells that, to their credit, the masters of Christ Church recognised the capability and the hard work of the former fellow when they audited the show prior to performance:

> which was so well liked afore the Queen's Majesty's coming, being played by the players in their gowns in Mr Marbeck's lodging, that some said it far surpassed *Damon and Pythias* than the which nothing could be better and who likewise said if he did any more afore his death he would run mad when indeed it was the last and the best that Edwards did. (Windsor, fol. 118v)

One of these players was Thomas Twyne, who was studying medicine at Corpus Christi.[126] After Edwards's death he wrote a lengthy and affectionate elegy, mentioning 'Damon and his friend' as well as Palamon and Arcyte, and referring vaguely to 'more full fit for princes' ears'. He calls

Edwards 'the flower of all our realm and Phoenix of our age' and states that not only London and Oxford but 'all good, gentle hearts' will mourn for him.[127]

The *Cheque Book* of the Chapel Royal, in the impersonal manner of account books, briefly notes that Edwards died in October.

EDWARDS'S LEGACY AND INFLUENCE

Damon and Pythias *and later drama*

Damon and Pythias may be the one surviving example of a strand of English drama which can be thought of as a missing link between Shakespeare and the English medieval tradition. It syncretises elements from four different types of drama: the classical new comedy of Plautus and Terence; the English vernacular morality plays; the tradition of courtly disguising; and the dialectical dialogues of classical philosophy in which different characters argue partial or conflicting aspects of a philosophical problem. It displays a surprising facility with wordplay but, in the absence of other evidence, its most important innovation is perhaps the introduction of the truly multiple plot into English drama.

The plays of Terence, of course, tell stories with parallel strands, as do some earlier English plays, even as early as the Towneley Second Shepherd's Play. But in these examples characters from the main action simply carry out supplementary details of the same story. The way in which, as we have seen, masques, plays, disguisings and tournaments at court went together thematically over extended periods of time may have given Edwards the idea of using a multiple form within a single piece. Marie Axton described Henry VIII's own participation in successive court masques as an example of what she calls the 'divided self':

> Henry's roles were not idealisations of the Prince; rather, each figures forth an aspect of the man ... Henry was fond of donning several disguises in one evening. To a knowledgeable courtier the temporal sequence of Henry's contrasting roles ... might imply *simultaneous* conflict ... Henry's courtier could relate the separate disguises of a mask fiction to each other as well as to the play which preceded it and to the tournament which followed the next day.[128]

By analogy, I think that Edwards put himself into *Damon and Pythias* in the guise of both Aristippus and Grim, thus spreading the satire and providing himself with some level of immunity. Aristippus's habit of making verses to the ladies draws an obvious parallel with Edwards's poem to the ladies of Mary's court (cf. *D&P*, 6.3–5; CT 1). Edwards himself may well have played Grim—the contrast between Grim and the young pages, and the requirement for a bass singing voice, both seem to demand an adult actor.

These two characters offer strange mirror images of each other and of attributes that we know Edwards possessed. Together, they send up: learning and education (in the sophistical philosopher and in the jokes surrounding Grim's 'mother wit', *D&P*, 13.67–71); the role of supplier of goods and services to the court (9.1–16; 13.189–98); and perhaps a love of the good life. Neither Grim nor Aristippus, of course, adequately fulfils the role of teacher or guardian of morals. While a coterie audience might have enjoyed making a connection between the writer/performer and the characters, however, the characterisations are not dependent on such meta theatricality.

It is the repetition of corresponding features in strongly contrasting characters that is important. Grim is entirely tangential to the main story, but he is far from extraneous. He supplies both an essential aspect of the play's subject and, in his bizarre and comic difference, a dialectical perspective on the play as a whole. The play is in fact filled with characters that have varying degrees of association with the main story, thus providing it with a sense of complex reality. Will and Jack, and Groano too, have lives and private concerns that have nothing to do with the thrust of the big idea of Pythagorean friendship. Will and Jack are in actuality friends, but unlike their masters, or indeed Damon and Pythias themselves, they do not make a thing of it. The three very different pairs of friends work in apposition to each other, and thus provide material for audience contemplation of what, as we have seen, is a complex philosophical problem. They achieve very different outcomes depending on their particular circumstances and on the motivations supplied by the individual characterisations. Plays with multiple plot lines generally have the effect of raising questions about meaning rather than imposing interpretation. This modality of representation—in which one idea is presented in different contexts and with different degrees of seriousness—is matched by a corresponding playfulness in language (different tongues and registers, a variety of metre, multiple simultaneous meanings) and also by a range of theatrical styles, from high camp tragedy to low farcical comedy.

Grim the collier

The old morality plays teach a theology of salvation by good works. Sin is a choice. If you choose to sin you will be damned. The devil is extrinsic, as are the other good or bad representative types that *Genus Humanum* or Everyman meets on his pilgrimage through life. Once religion has changed to justification by faith alone, however, the devil no longer has a theological function. Human salvation is pre-ordained and the only sanction on our behaviour in the world is our sense of our own *humanity* and the laws we make to reflect this.

The blackened face of the collier or charcoal maker, his smoky trade carried out within the forest, away from settled habitation, naturally gives him an outlandish and scary aura. A connection with the devil is almost inevitable. Grim thus constitutes a very human figure with which to ridicule the accusation that plays are the work of the devil. He is also a representative of the lower classes whose hard work, financial acumen and scorn of high fashion can be used to poke fun at the excesses and ineptitudes of courtiers (13.155–79). He has the same comic, country bumpkin accent as People in the interlude *Respublica* (attributed to Udall)—and also Edgar in disguise in *King Lear*. But whereas People is simply an emblem for the oppressive effects of bad government, Grim is an autonomous agent who inflicts his barstool philosophy on anyone he meets. Our sympathies are therefore simultaneously with the quick-witted children. Grim is perhaps a product of the English reformation, but he is a non-sectarian one.

Judging by the number of later imitations and references, it was indeed Grim who captured imaginations rather than Damon and Pythias themselves. Nearly eighty years after the play was written, Ralph Kettle, the idiosyncratic President of Trinity College, Oxford, seizing a bread-knife and singing the refrain from the play's shaving song, cut off the hair of one of his wealthy, upper-class students as he sat at table.[129] In the intervening period numerous plays took their inspiration from the character or the scene in which he appears. Ulpian Fulwell responded with a satire written in the form of a traditional morality play entitled *Like Will to Like*—quoting the proverb 'like will to like quoth the devil to the collier'. This text is entirely episodic, the only unifying structural devices being the proverb and the vice figure—significantly called Nicholas Newfangle, who thus ironically confirms the straightforward and old-fashioned nature of the play. It was printed in 1568, the year *Damon and Pythias* was revived at Oxford, and ridicules the propensity of Edwards's play to quote proverbs at every turn by tediously repeating just the one. The famous breeches are there in extended passages of quite revolting scatology (although this is also familiar from the famous bawdy song in the play *Mankind* and, to a lesser extent, *Jack Juggler*).

A slightly more creative use of the character is made by one J.T. in *Grim the Collier of Croydon*—another play in which the collier is only loosely if at all connected to the main story line, although here he is made the eponymous hero. In this play the enormous breeches become inverted, as it were, in the name for the corrupt hedge-priest, Parson Shorthose, who makes a serious attempt to steal Grim's sweetheart, the lovely Jug, from under his very nose. The devil/collier correspondence is strengthened with real devils in the main story, which is likewise also a tale of men attempting to snatch a beautiful, but here speechless, young woman from each other's possession. The devil in disguise wins her as a prize in return for restoring her speech, but is then duped by a bed trick into marrying her maid. Both mistress and maid vent their female spleens on all the men in sight, mortal and devilish, the lady, ironically, in torrents of verbal abuse, and the maid with quite staggering promiscuity. Eventually the devil retires thankfully back to hell, horrified at the iniquities of womankind,

although the experiences have, in theory at least, had a salutary effect—
the lady learning to love and cherish her elderly husband. John Webster's
The Devil's Lawcase and Dekker's *If This Be Not a Good Play the Devil
Is in it* both have similar stories. The latter isn't a particularly good play
and the devils are in it—in enormous numbers—although the stage directions are wonderful: *Enter Scumbroth, ringing a bell, Alphege a friar and
Shacklesoul in a friar's weed, with cloth to lay.* The Prologue places the
play firmly in the pattern I have been mapping out. It makes claims to
high art and poetic skill which are triumphantly and, one must assume,
satirically *not* achieved in the play that follows, in order to prove yet again
both that the devil has no function in the production of serious drama
and that humans do not need devils to be depraved.

Ben Jonson's *The Devil Is an Ass* (1616) rather more successfully uses
the same device of real devils outwitted and literally beaten by City of
London merchants and speculators. This play cunningly turns itself inside
out. The main character, who so much wants to conjure up a devil, is too
self-absorbed in his social climbing to recognise one when it appears
dressed up as a servant. The dressing-up theme indeed runs throughout
the play. This character is prepared to parade his wife in front of a
prospective lover in order to win a fancy cloak from him so that he can
show off when he goes to the theatre that afternoon to see—yes!—*The
Devil Is an Ass.* The lover in turn dresses up as a Spanish lady and gives
advice to an all-female soirée on make-up and fashion.[130] Again the
message is that real people do not need to be influenced by devils or the
theatre; they can be quite sufficiently corrupt on their own.

Jonson's *Bartholomew Fair* (1614) ends with a puppet show in which
Damon and Pythias, together with the famous lovers Hero and Leander,
with Dionysius and one Cole (both a pander and a collier), are not child
actors but puppets, with equally high voices, brought to life by Lantern
Leatherhead, the hobbyhorse seller in the fair. This is no presentation
of virtuous friendship or true love. Hero is a whore and both Damon
and Pythias are quite prepared to fight Leander and each other for her,
although their behaviour is nothing compared with the corruption of the
human inhabitants of the fair. When the local Puritan, Zeal of the Land
Busy, seeks to expose the 'abuses' of the fair, Leatherhead claims to have
a licence from the hand of the Master of the Revels himself. Busy's
response is, 'The Master of the Revels' hand, thou hast? Satan's!' (5.5.17),
but then puppet Dionysius takes him on, saying that the Revels workers
in the Blackfriars, the feather makers and comfit makers, may pretend to
be 'brethren' (Puritans) but through their trade are just as bad as any
actors. Busy (quoting Deuteronomy) replies that the puppets are abomi-
nations, the male putting on the apparel of the female, but Dionysius
responds by lifting his coat in triumph to display his sexlessness: 'It is
your old stale argument against the players, but it will not hold against
the puppets, for we have neither male nor female amongst us. And that
thou may'st see, if thou wilt, like a malicious purblind zeal as thou art'

(5.5.95–8). Busy has no answer to this and declares himself converted. Jonson's play significantly begins with an induction setting out a contract between performers and audience concerning proper interpretation and the extent of the audience's right to criticise. The play itself is thus literary, dramatic and social criticism in action.

It is left to Shakespeare to pick up the exact promise of Edwards's creation, while transforming it. Shakespeare's *Twelfth Night* (c.1599) has no devils and, we are specifically told, no puritans either, but there is a killjoy, Malvolio, who is duped into wearing cross-gartered hose—the later fashion equivalent of Will and Jack's breeches. Recent criticism has narrowly picked over the cross-gendering of Viola and the possible homosexual tendencies of Orsino and Antonio, but it has failed to situate this against the fact that virtually every character is engaged in some kind of dressing-up, disguise or play-acting. Malvolio, perhaps oppressed by the structure of his society, is obsessed with degree and position. In this he also incorporates something of the Colax character underlying Grim (p. 49), while his fancied elevation into favour with Olivia encourages him in an excess of apparel and demonstrably foolish pride. Sir Toby then casts him in the role of devil-possessed madman and 'foul collier', and imprisons him in a dark cell. There, in a parody of the prayerbook service for the visitation of the sick, he is catechised by a fool dressed as priest who asks him about the transmigration of souls according to Pythagoras and tells him that he is in a state of ignorance, since his dark cell is a 'clerestory' of light. The clerestory, a series of windows in the upper section of a wall, is a feature of larger churches and thus crowns this very mixed message satire on religious difference. Malvolio has little to do with the main love story except as a gatekeeper. His own story parodies both Orsino's love for Olivia and Viola's hopeless love for Orsino—since she is actually separated from him by no more than clothing. He also has a darker function: to situate the fanciful love interest within a problematic examination of social hierarchies, radically expanding the subject matter of the play.

Another theatrical venture on the Damon and Pythias theme is now lost. Between mid-February and the beginning of May 1600, Henry Chettle received four payments totalling £6 from Philip Henslowe for a 'damon and Pytheas' which he was writing for the company at the Rose Theatre.[131] This sum was the normal payment for a new play at the Rose, and on 16 May Henslowe paid 7s to 'the Master of the Revels' man for licensynge' this play, which confirms it as new and not a revision.

The Irish novelist, dramatist and poet John Banim had a success with his own *Damon and Pythias*, a tragi-comic melodrama, at London's Covent Garden in 1821. Macready played Damon and Charles Kemble, Pythias. The play was published in Dicks's Standard Plays. Here the two Pythagorean friends are both natives of Syracuse. Damon is married with a child and Pythias has returned from the wars to marry his betrothed, Calanthe. Dionysius proclaims himself King. Damon, his old enemy, protests about this in the Senate and is arrested and condemned to death. In order that Damon may go to tell his wife himself of his impending doom, Pythias offers himself as hostage. Dionysius in disguise first tells Calanthe that Dionysius (*sic*) will prevent Damon's return, and then tries to tempt Pythias to escape. Back in his villa, Damon takes a heart-rending farewell of his wife and child. His former slave kills his horse in order to prevent his return. In the final scene, with Dionysius still in disguise, Pythias is led out to execution. At the last minute Damon returns, having hijacked a traveller's horse. Dionysius, amazed at the rigorous honesty of the two friends, reveals himself and pardons Damon.

Analogues of the same story but with a fully tragic treatment and outcome were used by Handel in the eighteenth century. The opera *Orestes* takes the ancient Greek story of the friends Orestes and Pylades, who are likewise prepared to die for each other. His oratorio *Theodora* deals with a similar theme, although here the friends are Theodora, a Christian woman asserting her right not to worship Jupiter on his festival day and her lover Didymus, a Roman soldier. He rescues her from prison by substituting himself, but she then returns to plead for his life. In the end both are killed. Oratorio was Handel's way of treating subjects that were too dangerous for the theatre of his day. It is intensely dramatic, but was never staged until Peter Sellars's deeply moving production at Glyndebourne in 1996.

Edwards's Damon and Pythias *in later performance*

Damon and Pythias may well have been performed at Lincoln's Inn six weeks after the first performance at court, was certainly known to the fellows at Edwards's old college by 1566 (see p. 86) and was revived at Merton College, Oxford, in 1568.[132] There is no way of knowing how many other schools, colleges or households took up the invitation of the printed title page to perform it for 'private audience'.

The 1996 performance of Edwards's play at the Globe was probably the first for well over three hundred and fifty years. As dramaturg to a production of such an unknown text, and in a theatre where the question of what constitutes 'authenticity' is never far away, I was keen for us to address both contemporary and historical issues of performance. I wanted to explore the dislocation between actor and character that the original audience watching a performance by children might have experienced. But I believe that the authenticity of any performance must also reside in the circumstances and society of the performers and audience. For us, now, it is important to extend the range of parts available to women actors in classical theatre. I therefore suggested that we should have an entirely female cast. Gaynor Macfarlane, directing, added a nicely complicating twist which combined this with the play's other themes of cultural tourism and appropriateness of dress: our female actors were to present Damon and Pythias as a couple of Scotsmen—in kilts. The play

5 Damon (Maureen Beattie, left) and Pythias (Patricia Kerrigan), Globe Theatre, 1996.

was performed on the evening of 10 September 1996 to a two-thirds capacity crowd of nine hundred people. It was jubilantly received by the audience and attracted enthusiastic reviews in *The Guardian*, and, appropriately, the national Scottish paper, *The Herald*. In the event, an academic reviewer found that 'within a very short while the gender of the players was virtually forgotten'.[133]

Once the decision had been taken to use an all-female cast and to update to the 1950s, the problem was to find a suitable metaphor to express the connotations of youthful swagger, sexual licence and excessive fashion encapsulated in Jack and Will's pride in their outsize breeches. The designer, Jo Van Schippen, came up with the zoot suit. True, the extended lines in this fashion belong to the jacket rather than the trousers, but the image turned Jack into a teddy boy with slicked-back hair and encouraged an aspirationally-Elvis pelvic roll for the song at the shaving of the collier. Meanwhile Carisophus developed all the charm of a dodgy used-car salesman, and Aristippus that of a nattily dressed media don: the one in a sharp, double-breasted blue pin-stripe doing duty for the parti-coloured parasite's costume that would probably have originally marked the character; the other in velvet jacket and elegant scarf (cf. p. 172n.51).

Our cast of women was *dressed as* men, but there was no attempt to pretend that they *were* men—rehearsals were devoted to presenting the issues of the play, not to impersonating the characters in terms of supposedly male characteristics. Macfarlane and I were also both equally keen to find a way of playing the new Globe stage. We were warned that the sightlines were bad and that women's voices would not carry in the space. Of course the play would originally have been performed indoors in a hall at court, a much smaller space, but if my interpretation of Bereblock's Latin description of the staging of *Palamon and Arcyte* is correct, the original playing space for *Damon* may have been similarly surrounded by the audience. Pythias certainly needs to be able to hide amongst members of the audience (10.150–1), who are again transformed into the throng of people in Dionysius's court later in the scene (10.231).

We spent some time in the theatre early in rehearsals, both on-stage and in the auditorium, acclimatising ourselves to all aspects of the space, its acoustics and the position of the stage pillars. I believe that Shakespeare's plays, written for such a theatre, utilise his much remarked-upon

6   Carisophus (Ruth Lass), Globe Theatre, 1996.

imagery as a memory system, both to help the actor to remember his lines and to encourage him to direct different sections of his speech to different sections of the audience. Accordingly, we ensured that long speeches were played in sections towards different areas of the auditorium, and scenes were blocked on the diagonal so that all parts of the house were treated to equal shares of actors' faces. From one scene to the next, the conceptual 'front' of the stage was rotated with the sides (there was to be no audience in the gallery over the stage that season). Audience members were addressed directly wherever the text warranted it. Although these may seem like obvious measures, the overriding instinct of actors on that stage is to gravitate to the space between the two pillars at the front. This is probably because the distance between the pillars across the stage is unfortunately wider than the distance between the pillars and the tiring house wall. This is true of the stage configuration both in its 1996 prologue season manifestation and in the subsequent finished design in which the pillars are positioned slightly closer together and slightly more upstage. The pillars therefore feel to those standing on the stage like a proscenium arch. They draw actors to what seems to be the spot in which the maximum number of audience members can be commanded. In actuality the pillars block the strip of stage between them to a depth of about three metres from the view of about 15 per cent of the audience. Macfarlane dubbed this strip the 'valley of death' and no one was allowed to linger there for very long. Most of the other productions in the 1996–8 seasons had whole scenes blocked within the space between the pillars. Even in 1999 audiences in the side bays—in Shakespeare's day the most expensive areas of the house—were rarely treated to more than a fleeting glimpse of an actor's face.

DAMON AND PYTHIAS IN PRINT

Damon and Pythias was entered in the Stationers' Register as the property of Richard Jones, on or around 22 July 1567. It was printed in quarto format in 1571 (Q1) to be sold in Jones's shop at the south door of St Paul's. A second edition (Q2) appeared in 1582, also printed for Jones. Only one copy of the second edition is known to survive. This belonged to David Garrick and is in the British Library. There are three surviving copies of the first edition, one in the British Library (which likewise once belonged to Garrick), one in the Huntington Library in California and one in the Folger Shakespeare Library in Washington. The Folger copy lacks the first six and the last two printed pages (i.e. the two leaves that constitute gathering A containing the title page, the Prologue and the list of Speakers' names; the first leaf (two pages) of gathering B; and leaf H3). The lower half of E4 in that copy is also torn and lost.

The first quarto is printed in black-letter type with all the Latin quotations printed in roman. This, and the layout of the title page, follows a typographical style common to a number of Jones's publications, both those he claims to have printed himself and those printed for him, most notably by William How. Blank space on the title page and on the final page of printing is filled with small square woodcut vignettes which have nothing to do with the text but are similar to the decoration on the broadside ballads that both How and Jones also printed. Since the list of speakers' names is preceded and followed in Q by thick bands of ornamental type, and since it omits both Prologue and Muses, it was probably likewise supplied by the printer to fill up the blank half-page at the bottom of A2v. The play itself starts on gathering B. The title page states that the Prologue had been 'somewhat altered' for the benefit of its new audiences, but it is impossible to tell how, or indeed whether, this was actually done.

The text presents no particular bibliographical problems. One line is repeated, spread over two half-lines (3.4n). This might be a copying error but it perhaps rather indicates that the copy text was an authorial MS with a first thought imperfectly marked for deletion. There is possibly evidence of moral censorship at 13.12 and 13.66 (see collation and commentary) and a couple of other instances where Q makes no sense and needs emendation, but otherwise it appears to be remarkably full and substantively accurate. The text is, however, scattered with turned letters (e.g. n/u, and even the occasional 't' or comma printed upside down). There is some confusion between letters (h/b, f/long s, even t/c and d/o which are difficult to distinguish in black letter). Occasionally the ligatures 'ee' or 'oo' are substituted for their respective single letters, resulting in spellings like 'Beees' for 'bees' (4.23), while on one occasion 'nnn' is used to represent 'mm'. The typesetting has numerous instances of inaccurate spacing, which sometimes vary between the extant copies and led the Malone editors to suppose that it was loose, although this seems unlikely. These have all been silently amended in this edition.

The stage directions in Q are full and accurate. Evident omissions (cf. 9.0) and occasional additional directions (cf. 15.20.1) are supplied in square brackets. Q routinely omits the speech heading for the first speech in each scene. These speech headings have been supplied in this edition but are not in square brackets. None is problematic.

The second quarto is set from the first. It has no independent authority. It corrects some obvious errors of printing and, as is to be expected, introduces others. Some of its variants might conceivably be the result of having been set from a copy of Q1 that contained additional proof-corrected pages to those found in the three extant copies. A possible example of this is page C4v (9.70 to 10.10).

The play has been only rarely edited. It was included in Dodsley's *Old Plays* (1744), which used Q2 as the copy text. This was revised first by Isaac Reed in 1780, with notes by George Steevens, then by O. Gilchrist with notes by John Payne Collier, and finally by William C. Hazlitt in 1874. J. S. Farmer included it in his series for the Early English Drama Society, 1906, and in *Tudor Facsimile Texts*, 1908. A reprint of the 1571 edition was published by the Malone Society (1957), edited by Arthur Brown and F. P. Wilson, and an old-spelling edition by D. Jerry White in 1980.[134]

The present edition uses the British Library copy of Q1 as the copy text, collated with the Folger copy. Occasionally Q2 variants have been adopted but (with the possible exception of 9.70) these are invariably the kind of common-sense correction that any careful reader would be likely to make. Variants are generally only recorded in the collation where the copy text has been amended. Pythias's song, 'Awake you woeful wights' (10.28ff.), is preserved in two manuscripts in the British Library: Add. 15117, fol. 3 (words and music); and Cotton MS Vespasian A.xxv, fol. 135 (words only). The variants are inferior and non-authoritative and have not been collated, except in one instance which might have a bearing on the musical setting (10.44).

EDITORIAL APPROACH TO MODERNISATION

Spelling

Original spellings have been retained only where the word itself is obsolete. Archaic forms of extant words have all been modernised except where this would seriously reduce the possible range of meanings. Where the result is a distortion of the rhyme, this is noted in the commentary. Thus 'whiles', 'sith', 'ne', and 'doth' have been modernised to 'whilst' or 'while' (depending on the sounds in neighbouring words), 'since', 'nor' and 'does'. Occasionally 'doth' is used with a plural subject (*PDD*, 15.1, 15.7 and 17.30; *D&P*, 15.108), and in these instances has been modernised to 'do'. Archaic forms of past tenses such as 'brake' and 'spake' are modernised to 'broke' and 'spoke'.

Edwards uses 'you' for plural or formal modes of address, and 'thee' for the singular informal mode. Occasionally he uses the vocative 'ye'. This has been retained only where necessary to achieve a rhyme. The archaic verbal ending 'eth' is modernised to 'es' or 's', as appropriate, where this does not disrupt a set metre or destroy a rhyme. The old form has therefore been retained, for example, in *D&P*, 10.168–9; 13.279; 14.17, and rather more frequently in the poems. In many cases, in both play and poems, these modernisations actually reveal greater metrical regularity, or similarity of rhyme, indicating that the poet expected readers to elide the vowel (cf. CT 2.1–3 where the rhyme words are originally spelt tryeth/price). The second person singular ending 'est' cannot of course be modernised since it is obsolete. Here too, more often than not, the reader should probably elide (cf. 10.275, 279, 289). With two exceptions (7.0 and 13.108.1, where the command 'Enter' is used) the standard formulation in *Q* for entrances is 'Here entreth'. Since modernisation to 'Here enters' simply draws attention to the archaism, I have standardised to 'Enter' throughout except for 15.129.1 because of the presence of another verb in the stage direction.

I have modernised Sicilia (sometimes Cicilia) to Sicily, and Syracusae, the Latin name for this town (spelt Siracusae throughout), to Syracuse. There are four instances of Siracusae in the play including one (2.16) where it was intended to rhyme with 'by'. Readers should be aware that, while it would normally be pronounced with four syllables with the third syllable long, at 5.35 the 'ae' would have needed to be elided with the vowel starting the next word, 'Siracus' in'. At Prologue, l. 35, however, it was probably pronounced in full, but with the preceding 'here is' elided to 'here's' and, as printed in Q, 'the ancient' elided to 'th'ancient', i.e.: 'Lo, here's Syracusae, th'ancient town which once the Romans won'.[135] The fourth instance is at 2.3, where the Latin form would provide a slightly more tripping rhythm than modern 'Syracuse'. Modernisation with annotation seems the preferable solution because of the variation that a sixteenth-century reader would naturally have brought to the pronunciation. Indeed, the extent to which sixteenth-century speakers would have elided non-essential syllables has probably been under-estimated.[136]

By contrast, there are some instances in which the full complement of syllables would require the inclusion of voiced 'èd' endings. These tend to occur in words in which the main syllable is naturally long and which occur before a monosyllable. They are particularly common in 'In going to my naked bed' (e.g. sighed sore, cried still, proved plain, failed them). The original music for this song provides an extra note in each case, which could be used to pronounce the 'ed' syllable or, sometimes perhaps more effectively, could slur with the preceding note to lengthen the main syllable. This would enhance the rocking rhythm of the song and, given the high incidence of such cases in this poem about a mother singing to her child, may have been what Edwards intended.

Grim speaks with a country accent rendered in Q by regularly spelling I'm as 'cham', I've as 'cha', and I'll as 'chyll' or 'chyl', with 'I' and 'ich' used interchangeably. He also uses 'vortie' for forty (13.69, 144) and 'tway' for two (13.47). These are all here regularised for the sake of clarity and to allow the use of an accent of choice in modern performance. Spellings indicating Grim's later drunkenness have been retained. There are a few other isolated instances of this usage by Carisophus ('Cha', 9.60), Groano ('iche … chould ich', 10.320) and Stephano ('schil', 11.34).

Scene divisions

Q does not number or otherwise mark scene divisions. In a dramaturgy such as Shakespeare's, designed to cope with the unlocalised setting of the later Elizabethan public theatres, the scene changes whenever one group of characters leaves the stage to be replaced by a different group. This change is conceived as a different place. *Damon and Pythias*, by contrast, is set throughout in a street in front of two scenic frames, one painted to represent the court and the other the town. Here, therefore, the place remains the same and the dramaturgy is designed to promote the convincing passage of characters through this space in time. The scene does not, strictly, change at all, but these units of time are marked by numbered scene divisions in the present edition. On three occasions characters get out of the way of others who are about to enter, either by hiding (to overhear what is about to be said, 10.86 and 151) or by making a sharp exit (10.15, 13.307–9). In these cases, although the stage may be momentarily cleared, the entrance of the new character(s) is conceived as a continuation in both place and time. Brown and Wilson mark scene changes at these points, although, strangely, they omit the more evident scene change at Scene 16.

Punctuation

If we have perhaps not appreciated Edwards's use of metrical form, we have certainly misunderstood the use of punctuation employed so liberally by the printer of *Damon and Pythias*, Robert Jones. This however, is not so surprising. Originally intended as an elocutionary aid to speakers, punctuation marks inevitably came to be used to delineate grammatical structure and, in poetic language, metrical structure. While these three functions may overlap, they are not fully compatible and from the earliest times theorists on the subject have confused them all.[137] Francis Clement in *The Petie Schole* (1587) describes punctuation as the 'distinction and pointing of sentences, by the observation whereof the breath is relieved, the meaning conceived, the eye directed, the eare delited and al the senses satisfied'. He goes on to outline the function of each of the standard marks:

> The underpause [*comma* in margin] is a point of the shortest rest in reading, so bearing the voyce at the stay of silence, that the sentence may appear to remain unfinished . . . The middle pause [*media distinctio* in margin, i.e. colon] is a longer rest, holding forth the voice likewise at the pause of silence in expectation of as much more to be spoken, as is already rehearsed . . . and usually put before these words: for, but, yet, then, so, even so . . . The perfect pause, or full point is set down . . . when the sentence is fully and perfectly finished. (B5)

Of these, only the last is unequivocally clear. Early modern writers, scribes and compositors were also in the habit of using those same signs to mark the purely metrical features of the verse—mid-line caesurae, and the ends of couplets—irrespective of both sense and grammar. Thus it is that the punctuation of the Quarto of *Damon and Pythias* seems heavy and often arbitrary by modern standards. Here commas are used conventionally at the end of lines and at the caesura, with heavier stops routinely marking the ends of couplets, even in those cases in which the sense evidently runs on. Conversely, commas are sometimes used where the sense demands a new sentence. Full stops are generally (although not exclusively) reserved for the ends of speeches, leaving sentence-breaks mid-speech to be marked by colons. All this makes the text extremely difficult to read, sometimes obscuring the sense entirely, and has, I believe, contributed to the play's reputation of being pedestrian and 'academic'.

Poetry has the added resource of line length, rhyme and rhetorical struc-ture to point up the sense and does not always need punctuation *per se*. Thus the punctuation of the first four of Edwards's poems in the Cotton Titus MS is extremely light, sometimes even without stops at the end of stanzas. By contrast, the fifth (which is in a different hand) is marked con-ventionally with a medial stop positioned some little way from the end of almost every line and raised slightly above it. This mark is purely met-rical and is made irrespective of the sense. Punctuation in *The Paradise of Dainty Devices* is mostly metrical, with colons or stops at the end of couplets (again even where the sense runs on). Sometimes, however, the colons might be considered as obeying Clement's oratorical definition of a 'pause of silence in expectation of as much more to be spoken, as is already rehearsed'. Modernisation thus entails finding a consistent reso-lution for these conflicting practices.

Poetry is a highly effective medium for drama because its structure of line, rhythm and rhyme can make connections that create the illusion of instantaneous thought processes, and reproduce the informal structures of speech. This helps to give a sense of the 'reality' of a character, despite the fact that we know that real people do not conduct their everyday busi-ness in verse. It is inappropriate to attempt to marshal this multidirec-tional language by formal grammatical punctuation. In this edition, therefore, punctuation has been reduced to a minimum. The objective has been to mark out the connections in the text, rather than to divide it into grammatical units, particularly where these might be interpreted by a speaker as demanding a pause. Thus, wherever possible, I have avoided using the conventional comma before the name in forms of address (e.g. Why sir? not Why, sir?), and have used dashes to mark parts of a sentence which are tangential or explanatory to its main thrust, but would otherwise have necessitated a heavier stop. This makes the structure of long sentences more immediately apparent, and has enabled me to avoid almost entirely the use of semicolons. These are unhelpful to readers and actors as they break the flow of the language and thereby obscure the way in which different parts of a complex poetic sentence are connected.[138] This edition uses colons only where a speaker introduces an exemplum (e.g. *D&P*, Prologue, 14), and its single semicolon (10.191) is there as the only possible way to mark separate phrases subsequent to a colon.

NOTES

1 Bradner, 7–11.

2 Thomas Heywood, *An Apology for Actors* (London, 1612), C3v.

3 See Mary Carruthers, *The Book of Memory: A Study of Memory in Medieval Culture* (Cambridge: Cambridge University Press, 1990).

4 Bradner, 10. Records of Edwards's admission, progression and employment are preserved in: Corpus Christi, *Liber Admissorum*, 11 May 1540; Register of the University of Oxford; Christ Church, Computus Roll (1546–7) and Disbursement Book (1547–8); see plate 1.

5 Published Cologne: Martin Gymnicus (1548); BL, Royal MS 12 A xlvi; F. S. Boas, *University Drama in the Tudor Age* (Oxford: Clarendon Press, 1914), 33ff.

6 Cited as 'Treasurer of Rec. Unclassifed Miscell. No. 69. P.R.O.'. This class of MSS was recatalogued shortly after Stopes completed her work.

7 *Cheque Book*, 36ff.

8 W. R. Streitberger, *Court Revels 1485–1559* (Toronto: Toronto University Press, 1994), 190–2.

9 PRO, E 351/3202; E 351/541.

10 *Elizabeth*, 116–17.

11 *Elizabeth*, 163–5.

12 Letters of administration, dated 10 March 1567, were granted in the Commissary Court of London to a Helen Edwards in respect of her deceased husband, Richard, resident in the parish of St Faith the Virgin, by St Paul's, London (Guildhall Library, Register 12, fol. 157v). Unfortunately all records of St Faith's for this period are missing so this cannot be corroborated with a burial entry (which would in turn give an indication of the date of death). Letters of Administration were granted when a person died intestate. The wording is entirely conventional and gives no indication of the profession of this particular Richard or the extent of his estate, although it does indicate that there was property to be administered, and the date is consistent with the poet's death the previous October. Helen seems to have got married again—to a Nicholas Banks on 2 October 1569 in the neighbouring parish of St Gregory. The touching story that Bradner tells of four orphaned children of Richard Edwards of Oxford, left to the care of their uncle, must refer to another person. This administration (in the Prerogative Court of Canterbury) is actually dated 20 March 1566.

13 *Elizabeth*, 34.

14 An inventory of costumes made in 1560 makes repeated note that specific costumes had been given to players 'for ffees' or 'by composicion' (an agreement in lieu of payment, or perhaps part-payment): *Elizabeth*, 21 and 27; see also *Edward and Mary*, 20.

15 *Edward and Mary*, 12–13.

16 *Edward and Mary*, 159–60; see also 290–2 for a draft of a warrant to the Lord Treasurer asking him to pay for the expenditure incurred. U/v, i/j and the capitalisation of names have been modernised in all quotations.

17 This has also been ascribed to the evangelical Philip Nichols: cf. J. Youings, 'South Western Rebellion', *Southern History* 1 (1979), 99–122, cited Diarmaid MacCulloch, *Thomas Cranmer: A Life* (New Haven and London: Yale University Press, 1996), 439.

18 *Edward and Mary*, 166–9.

19 *Elizabeth*, 15, 16.

20 There are letters from scholars at Oxford, and also aristocratic individuals asking to borrow costumes for private masques and plays. Costumes were lent to the City of London for those participating in the pageants for the coronation entry processions for both Edward and Elizabeth; *Edward and Mary*, 249–52.

21 *Patent Rolls, Philip and Mary*, vol. 1, 241.

22 R. C. Braddock, 'The rewards of office holding in Tudor England', *Journal of British Studies* 14 (1975), 29–47.

23 *Edward and Mary*, 210, 230; BL, Stowe MS 71, fols 25v, 49.

24 BL, Lansdowne MS III, fol. 193.

25 Others have connected this passage with an entry in Machyn's diary (*Diary 1550–1563* (London: Camden Society, 1848), 31 December 1559), which records a play performance at court broken off because it had offended the Queen. Machyn does not say whether it was too licentious or just plain bad. There is no other reason to connect the incident with Edwards. The *D&P* prologue may be recalling a specific occasion or may simply be couching a general response to anti-theatricality in imitation of the Roman playwright Terence, arguing, with Horace's support, that the author must be allowed to present life as it is, not have to sanitise it for the sake of some misplaced sense of morality.

26 Cited Stopes, 39.

27 *Edward and Mary*, 149; Streitberger, 294.

28 *CSP, Spanish*, I, 444, 18 January 1552.

29 Cf. *D&P*, 8.23n; 8.37n; 13.13n.

30 *An Answer of the Most Reverend . . . Thomas Archebyshop of Canterburye . . . unto a Crafty and Sophisticall Cavillation Devised by Stephen Gardiner . . . Late Byshop of Winchester* (London, 1551), cited *Jack Juggler*, 20.

31 David Loades, *The Reign of Mary Tudor: Politics, Government and Religion in England 1553–58* (London: Longman, 2nd ed. 1991), 129.

32 *Edward and Mary*, 222.

33 Hyder Edward Rollins notes that the phrase 'luck is loss' is used proverbially by some later poets (*The Paradise of Dainty Devices (1576–1606)* (Cambridge, Mass.: Harvard University Press, 1927), lvii).

34 The watermark, an extended hand with raised thumb and a five-pointed flower, is one of a large family of similar marks found in paper from northern France, which is common in English books and manuscripts of the mid sixteenth century. It is similar to nos 11278 and 11381 in C. M. Briquet, *Les Filigranes* (Paris, 1907). It also closely resembles the mark in the paper of the Christ Church disbursement book of 1547–8, which has the letters 'hB' on the cuff whereas CT has 'B' and perhaps 'h'.

35 I am grateful to Judith Curthoys, archivist at Christ Church, for her help with these identifications.

36 The stories of Ferrex and Porrex printed in the 1573 edition of the *Magistrate* lie behind *Gorboduc* (1560), reputedly the first stage tragedy in English, which Norton wrote in collaboration with Sackville.

37 Ascham, tutor to both Edward and Elizabeth, can similarly hardly hide his surprise (and delight) when he tells us that, visiting Jane Grey at home, he found her reading Plato in Greek, which 'not many women, but verie fewe men have atteined thereunto' (*Scholemaster*, 201).

38 PRO, L.C. 2/4 (2).

39 PRO, L.C. 2/4 (3).

40 E. K. Chambers, *The Elizabethan Stage* (Oxford: Clovendon Press, 1923), vol. 3, 310.

41 Surrey History Centre, Woking, Loseley MSS, 59/170.

42 Cited Streitberger, 298.

43 Loseley MSS, 59/169. The prohibition on eating meat in Lent in fact continued throughout Elizabeth's reign. This was necessary for the support of the fishing and salt fish industries, rather than for religious reasons, and could be treated humorously at court. The Spanish Ambassador tells how a masque which continued beyond midnight on Shrove Tuesday was celebrated with delicacies involving herring. Elizabeth teased him but did not try to trick him into breaking his fast.

44 *Edward and Mary*, 5–6, 13, 190–1. Friars were usually unrealistically dressed in silk, satin, velvet or tinsel.

45 Loseley MSS 128/12, printed *Edward and Mary*, 245.

46 Corporation of London Records Office, *Repertories*, xiv, fols, 97r–99r, cited Mark Breitenburg, ' "The hole matter opened": Iconic representation and interpretation in "The Quenes Majesties Passage" ', *Criticism* 28 (1986).

47 Mary's entry procession was designed in the morality play tradition and featured the four personal, cardinal virtues (Prudence, Justice, Fortitude and Temperance), whereas the theme of Elizabeth's was good government, pure religion, love of subjects and wisdom (Breitenburg).

48 Summary in *Patent Rolls 1558–1660*, 352; full transcription in Bradner, 136.

49 *Patent Rolls 1560–3*, 100 and 335–6.

50 BL, Stowe MS 571, fol. 36b, quoted Stopes, 21.

51 John Merbecke (father of Roger Marbeck of Oxford University) was organist of the royal chapel, Windsor, and author of the first Concordance to the Bible (1550), as well as various other religious works. One of the Windsor evangelicals, he had been condemned to be burnt as a result of the Prebendaries Plot (see pp. 14–15) but was reprieved; Foxe erroneously described his actual death in the *Book of Martyrs*.

52 Cambridge University Library, Peterhouse MS 471–4.

53 J. E. Neale, *Queen Elizabeth I* (Harmondsworth: Penguin, reprinted 1961), 64.

54 Guido D'Arezzo was an eleventh-century Benedictine monk. He taught the musical sol fa by apportioning each note from G on the bottom line of the bass clef to D on the third line in the treble clef to a different joint of the hand or finger tip, using a different way of pointing to represent top E. The man in plate 2 points to bottom G.

55 *The Sermons of John Donne*, ed. George R. Potter and Evelyn M. Simpson (Berkeley and Los Angeles: University of California Press, 1953–62), 10 vols, vol. 2, 50, cited Derek Attridge, *Well Weighed Syllables* (Cambridge: Cambridge University Press, 1974).

56 *Patent Rolls 1560–3*, 501.

57 PRO, C.3.61/35.

58 *Records of the Honourable Society of Lincoln's Inn*, vol. 1, *Admissions* (London, 1896).

59 This is a total of £3 13s 4d or 11 marks, and can be compared with the 20 marks (£6 13s 4d) paid to companies for a play at court and the maximum limit of £2 for the production expenses alone at Christ Church in 1554; see p. 14.

60 *Records of the Honourable Society of Lincoln's Inn: The Black Books* (London, 1897), vol. 1, 318, 341, 344, 348, 352.

61 *Elizabeth*, 110, 157.

62 *Elizabeth*, 156, 159.

63 See, T. W. Craik, *The Tudor Interlude: Stage Costume and Acting* (Leicester: Leicester University Press, 1967), 66–70 'multi-coloured costume almost always carries condemnation with it . . . There seems also to have been a recognised use of parti-colour for parasites.'

64 *Elizabeth*, 19, 21.

65 Jonas Barish, *The Antitheatrical Prejudice* (Berkeley and Los Angeles: University of California Press, 1981), 66.

66 Stephen Gosson, *Plays Confuted* (1582), C5v.

67 E.g. Marjorie Garber, *Vested Interests: Cross-dressing and Cultural Anxiety* (London: Routledge, 1991); Susan Zimmerman, ed., *Erotic Politics: Desire on the Renaissance Stage* (London: Routledge, 1992); Laura Levine, *Men in Women's Clothing: Anti-theatricality and Effeminization from 1579 to 1642* (Cambridge: Cambridge University Press, 1994). Such arguments are appropriately questioned by Stephen Orgel, *Impersonations* (Cambridge: Cambridge University Press, 1996).

68 Heinemann, 28–31.

69 Calendar II, Lord Mayor's Shows, in *Collections*, vol. III (London: Malone Society, 1954).

70 *TLS*, 20 July 1933, 494, trans. Andrew Gurr, *The Shakespearean Stage*

(Cambridge: Cambridge University Press, 1970), 152. In the original Latin, of course, the verbs are not gender-specific, but the adjectives all take the feminine form: *non solum dicendo, sed etiam faciendo quaedam lachrymas movebant. At vero Desdemona illa apud nos a marito occisa quanquam optime semper causam egit, interfecta tamen magis movebat; cum in lecto decumbens spectantium misericordiam ipso vulto imploraret.*

71 Cf. the story from Diogenes Laertius, 2.78, quoted Horace, *Epistles*, 1.17.23–9, and *D&P*, 12.20, in which Plato declines to put on a woman's robe as being too demeaning but Aristippus does so on the grounds that true modesty cannot be put to shame by external circumstances.

72 William Webbe, *A Discourse of English Poetrie*, ed. Edward Arber (London, 1870), 33.

73 D. D. Carnicelli, ed., *Lord Morley's Tryumphes of Fraunces Petrarcke* (Cambridge, Mass.: Harvard University Press, 1971), 47.

74 *Scholemaster*, 240–6.

75 The reading '*conciliat*' is an emendation necessitated by an evident error in the original printing. It is of course the root of the English verb 'conciliate' ('gain good will by acts which induce friendly feeling', *OED vb*. 2) and is both unambiguous and understandable even by non-Latin-speakers.

76 A fragment of Menander's play has since been discovered.

77 In order to preserve the rhyme Edwards often utilises forms of words that were then nearing the end of their general circulation, and which are now archaic. Thus, wanting to rhyme 'move' with 'live' and 'geve', his standard spelling for 'give', he uses 'meeve' (15.200–1; 10.262–3) even though elsewhere he prefers the spellings 'move' and 'moved'. Later a rhyme for 'fees' is made by resorting to the old verb 'leese' rather than 'lose' (*D&P*, 15.257)—not just an old spelling but a word with a different root.

78 It is generally considered that uneven line lengths are preferable in song writing as they make for more interest in the underlay of the words and therefore a better song. The music itself will do all the evening-up that is necessary; cf. Edward Doughtie, *Lyrics from English Airs* (Cambridge, Mass.: Harvard University Press 1970), 30ff.

79 See Ros King, 'Seeing the rhythm: An interpretation of sixteenth-century punctuation and metrical practice', in J. Bray, M. Handley and A. Henry, eds, *Marking the Text: The Presentation of Meaning on the Literary Page* (Aldershot: Scolar Press, 2000).

80 Alan Stewart, *Close Readers: Humanism and Sodomy in Early Modern England* (Princeton: Princeton University Press, 1997); Jonathan Goldberg, ed., *Queering the Renaissance* (Durham: Duke University Press, 1994).

81 Pythagoras, who lived in the sixth century BC, was reputedly the first person to call himself not a 'wise man' but a 'philosopher'—literally a lover of wisdom. He taught that the universe was constructed according to universal mathematical laws of harmony and proportion and demanded that his followers should live simple, well-ordered lives of mutual dependence, but since he wrote nothing down his life and work have attained a sometimes mythical status. Pythagorean ideas about harmony and number were profoundly influential during the Renaissance and would have been known to Edwards both in general terms and through the writing of Cicero.

82 The video record of the performance consists of three tapes: two from fixed cameras in different positions, and one from a hand-operated camera which was able to pan and zoom.

83 This transformation also occurs in some of the classical sources and is the result of confusion as to whether the story of Damon and Pythias is supposed to have occurred at the court of Dionysius I, who died an unreformed tyrant, or his son Dionysius II, who was deposed and lived out his life as a schoolteacher.

84 See Aristotle, *Poetics* (in this instance most succinctly translated by S. H. Butcher

(London: Macmillan, 1895)): 'the poet should prefer probable impossibilities to improbable possibilities' (24.10).

85 Cited MacCulloch, *Cranmer*, 364.

86 Castiglione, *The Book of the Courtier* (1528), translated into English by Sir Thomas Hoby, 1561, was also the inspiration for Elyot, *Governor* (1531).

87 J. H. Wiffen, *The Russell Memoirs* (London, 1833), vol. 1, 426–30; J. Stow, *Summarie of English Chronicles* (London, 1566), 196.

88 *Elizabeth*, 116.

89 Glynne Wickham, *Early English Stages* (London: Routledge and Kegan Paul, 1972), vol. 2, pt 2, 230–1.

90 Chambers, *Elizabethan Stage*, vol. 4, 83.

91 12 October 1566, *Calendar of MSS of the Marquis of Salisbury*, vol. 1, 339.

92 Nichols, 247–50.

93 Letter to Feria, *CSP, Spanish*, 10 January 1559.

94 Bodleian Library, MSS Rawlinson C 878i and Top. Oxon. e.9.

95 This can be contrasted with the cost of transporting six loads of ivy for the decoration of a banqueting house at Whitehall to entertain the French Ambassador in 1572, which with flowers, trestles and labour for two days and a night came to only 10s 2d (*Elizabeth*, 165).

96 Corpus Christi MS 257, fols 104–14, first draft fols 115–23.

97 John R. Elliott Jr, 'Queen Elizabeth at Oxford: new light on the royal plays of 1566', *English Literary Renaissance* 18: 2 (1988), 218–29.

98 Bodleian MS Twyne 17, also Twyne 21, fols 792–800.

99 BL, Harl. 7033. fol. 150ff.

100 Bereblock, Bodleian MS Add. A 63, also Rawlinson D 1071; Robinson, BL, MS Harl. 7033, fol. 142ff.

101 Thomas Neale (c.1519–c.1590) had travelled abroad during Edward VI's reign, returning to become a chaplain to Bishop Bonner under Mary. By means of occasional conformism, he managed to continue as a Catholic in Elizabeth's time and even became Professor of Hebrew at Christ Church c.1559, although there seems to have been some dispute about his membership of the College and he resigned in 1569 to live in seclusion. His book, which can be seen as an attempt to demonstrate his loyalty to the Crown, is Bodleian MS 13.

102 Boas, 21.

103 Robinson, in Plummer, 179.

104 Nichols, 158.

105 Twyne's compilation of MSS includes a letter from Leicester as both University Chancellor and member of the Privy Council promising financial support; Robinson (Plummer, 179) says that the special alterations to the hall were at the expense of the Crown (*sumptibus regiis*); costumes were provided by the Royal Wardrobe (see pp. 83, 106n.121). At Cambridge in 1564, King's College Chapel had been equipped with tapestries, carpet and furniture belonging to the Queen (Nichols, 158).

106 'House' is still Oxford terminology for Christ Church.

107 Robinson, in Plummer, 185.

108 George Carew held numerous responsible clerical posts throughout the religious turmoil of the 1540s–60s. He was briefly Dean of Christ Church, before becoming Dean of Windsor in 1561.

109 Bereblock's description survives in two MSS which here read *Procecenium* and *Procestrium* respectively, rendered in Plummer as *proscenium* (stage). However the word *procestria* can mean 'an entrance in a wall' (C. T. Lewis and C. Short, *A Latin Dictionary* (Oxford, Clarendon Press, 1879). I have adopted the English word used in the college accounts.

110 The roof was damaged by a fire in the louvre above the central fireplace in 1720. Any repairs are indistinguishable from the original (*Victoria County History, Oxford*, eds H. E. Salter and M. D. Lobel (London: Oxford University Press, 1954), 34).

111 Glynne Wickham takes the Queen's bridge straight forward from the porch, across the west wall of the stair turret and down the north side, through an unspecified opening into the antechamber, and then through the single central door into the hall (*Early English Stages*, vol. 1, 357). This is neither economic nor private.

112 Wickham translates as 'The Hall was panelled in gold and painted within the arch of the roof' (*Early English Stages*, vol. 1, 358). Panelling the walls would have been pointless since they were covered up by the spectators' stands.

113 The *theatrum* must have had at least two upper storeys and would have required a staircase to allow access.

114 Records of Early English Drama (REED), *Cambridge*, 2 vols, ed. Alan H. Nelson (Toronto: Toronto University Press, 1989); Alan H. Nelson and Iain Wright, 'A Cambridge playhouse of 1638?: Reconsiderations', *Renaissance Drama*, New Series, 22 (1991); Alan H. Nelson, *Early Cambridge Theatres: College, University and Town Stages 1464–1720* (Cambridge: Cambridge University Press, 1994).

115 Alan H. Nelson, 'Early staging in Cambridge', in *A New History of Early English Drama*, eds J. D. Cox and J. S. Kastan (New York: Columbia University Press, 1997), 65.

116 Robinson, in Plummer, 185.

117 Elliott, 'Queen Elizabeth', 227.

118 Reynolds's memory, presumably partly developed by his acting activity, was described by Anthony à Wood as 'a living library and a third university', *Oxoniensis*, II, 14.

119 An entry in the accounts for three hundredweight of lead laid 'over the Quenes stayres and takinge downe the olde' has led some commentators to suggest that it was the extra weight of lead laid supposedly for decoration on the stairs or on the stair wall that caused the catastrophe. The same accounts later record entries of payments for new stone and for masons to repair the stair wall. It seems more likely that the lead was required for the roof of the stair turret and had nothing to do with the collapse of the wall (Bodeian MS Rawlinson C.878).

120 Chaucer adds that Arcyte has ridden out to do observance to May, accordingly singing another May song. He has sat down to bemoan his fate when Palamon hears him and, with face 'deed and pale', accuses him of being a traitor, saying that although he has no weapon he will kill him. Arcyte angrily pulls out his sword, but then says he will return with food and bedding that night and will come back again tomorrow with two sets of armour. Palamon may choose the best and then they will fight for Emily.

121 The book in which the keeper of the Great Wardrobe recorded lost and damaged garments records that certain garments belonging to Queen Mary lent for the plays at Oxford, including 'the forequarter of a gowne . . . sleeves of purple vellat with a satten grounde', were never returned (Janet Arnold, 'Lost from Her Majesty's back', *Costume Society Extra Series* 7 (1980)).

122 This play, by Warwick's men, was entitled *The Knight of the Burning Rock*. The rock incorporated machinery for raising and lowering a chair on which the knight could presumably make his entrance, and hid the stage hands who would be needed to operate the effects; *Elizabeth*, 308; John Astington, *English Court Theatre, 1558–1642* (Cambridge: Cambridge University Press, 1999), 102–3.

123 *Elizabeth*, 141–2, 145, 244.

124 Only the name of the character and the Queen's observation 'God's pity what a knave it is' make it into Windsor's fair copy, and thence into Twyne. Boas (103) therefore considered that the character was part of a comic sub-plot. Elliot, who first published details of Windsor's draft, albeit not always very accurately, argued that Dalaper simply forgot his lines and that this painful detail was therefore dropped from Windsor's fair copy.

125 *CSP, Spanish*, 12 March 1565.

126 Windsor lists the actors in the plays as: Marbeck, Banes, Badger, Rookes, Ball, Buste, Glasyer, Bristow, Thornton, Penson, Potes senior, Potes Junior, Mathewe,

Dalaper, Danet, Mauncell, Jones, Argall, Summers, Townsende, Wyndsor, Twyne, Raynoldes, Dorcet, Grey, Egerton, Carew, Poll, Younge, Ffourd, Jutsan, Dalapers boy, Smythe nutrix (fol. 107).

127 Twyne's poem is in George Turbervile, *Epitaphs, Epigrams, Songs and Sonets* (London, 1567) (fol. 77v in 1576 ed.). Turbervile's own epitaph to Edwards (fol. 142v) echoes both Pythias's lament and Googe's 1563 poem.

128 Marie Axton, 'The Tudor mask and Elizabethan court drama', Marie Axton and Raymond Williams, eds, *English Drama: Forms and Development* (Cambridge: Cambridge University Press, 1977), 25.

129 *Aubrey's Brief Lives*, ed. Oliver Lawson Dick (London: Secker and Warburg, 1949), 183–4. John Aubrey identifies the song as coming from *Gammer Gurton's Needle* and says that Kettle sang the refrain as 'Tonedi, tonedi', asking the student, 'How doe you decline tondeo? Tondeo, tondes, Tonedi?' (*tondeo* = Lat. I prune, shear, shave).

130 The part was taken by Richard Robinson who had been the most famous of the King's Men's child actors, and is self-reflexively and humorously referred to by name in Jonson's play. He might also be the boy described by Henry Jackson (p. 38 above).

131 R. A. Foakes and R. T. Rickert, *Henslowe's Diary* (Cambridge: Cambridge University Press, 1961), 63, 131, 133, 134.

132 Boas, 157–8.

133 Peter Happé, ' "Damon and Pithias" by Richard Edwards at Shakespeare's Globe', *Medieval English Theatre* 18 (1996), 161.

134 D. Jerry White, ed., *Richard Edwards' Damon and Pithias: A Critical Old-spelling Edition* (New York: Garland Publishing, 1980).

135 *Q1* reads 'here in Siracusae', but on the evidence of the likely staging with opposing houses, one representing the town and one the palace, emendation seems desirable.

136 E. A. J. Honigmann, *The Texts of Othello* (London and New York: Routledge, 1996), 124–5, 146–7.

137 M. B. Parkes, *Pause and Effect: An Introduction to the History of Punctuation in the West* (Aldershot: Scolar Press, 1992).

138 There are no semicolons anywhere in the quarto. This mark was introduced into England by the last quarter of the sixteenthcentury but it was a long time before it was generally adopted because of its absence from printers' sorts (cf. Parkes, *Pause and Effect*).

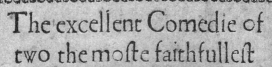

The excellent Comedie of two the moste faithfullest
Freendes, Damon and Pithias.

Newly Impzinted, as the same was shewed be=
foze the Queenes Maiestie, by the Childzen of her Graces
Chappell, except the Pzologue that is somewhat al=
tered foz the pzoper vse of them that hereafter
shall haue occasion to plaie it, either in
Pziuate, oz open Audience. Made
by Maister Edvards, then beynge
Maister of the Childzen.
1571.

Imprinted at London in
Fleetelane by Richarde Iohnes, and are to be
solde at his shop, ioyning to the Southwest
dooze of Paules Churche.

---

7   Title page of the 1571 edition of *Damon and Pythias*, C.34.c.30
(Original size: 18 × 13 cm).

DAMON AND PYTHIAS

THE SPEAKERS' NAMES

[The Prologue.]
Aristippus, a pleasant gentleman.
Carisophus, a parasite.
Damon⎫
Pythias⎭ two gentlemen of Greece.   5
Stephano, servant to Damon and Pythias.
Will, Aristippus's lackey.
Jack, Carisophus's lackey.
Snap, the tipstaff.

---

1. The Prologue] Q omits.   9. tipstaff] Porter Q.

0.1. *speakers' names*] This is placed after the Prologue in Q.
2. *Aristippus*] (c.435–c.350 BC) A contemporary of Plato, friend of Socrates and a courtier of Dionysius I, he is sometimes considered to have founded the hedonistic, Cyrenaic school of philosophy (a forerunner of Epicureanism). This teaches that the attainment of pleasure is the only reason for doing anything, and that the present moment is the only reality. Classical accounts of his life document his extravagance but demonstrate that he practised the detached mastery of pleasure rather than its simple indulgence; see Diogenes Laertius, II, 8.
   pleasant] good-humoured.
3. *Carisophus*] lit. 'the wisdom of Caria' (Gk *sophia*, wisdom). The Carians were conventionally described by some Greek writers as talking like barbarians (cf. Strabo, *Geography*, 14.2.28), or as pirates (Thucydides, 1.8), which fits Carisophus's behaviour, albeit on land, at 1.94–6, and 8.1–6).
   parasite] sycophant, flatterer; a stock figure of classical comedy.
4–5. *Damon, Pythias*] This archetypal pair of friends followed the philosopher Pythagoras. Their story can be found in: Cicero, *Tusc.* (5.22), and *De officiis* (3.10.45); Valerius Maximus (4.7.Ext.1); and Iamblichus, *Life of Pythagoras* (33). When he is named at all in the sources, the Pythias figure is called Phintias and it is usually he who takes the role given to Damon in this play. Edwards would have known the story from Cicero and from *Governor*, 2.11, which uses the name 'Pitheas' but is vague as to which friend takes which role.
6. *Stephano*] At 5.7 the metre demands virtually disyllabic pronunciation with the stress on the first syllable.
7. *lackey*] attendant.
9. *tipstaff*] constable.

Dionysius, the King.   10
Eubulus, the King's counsellor.
Groano, the hangman.
Grim, the collier.
[The Muses.]

THE PROLOGUE

On every side whereas I glance my roving eye,
Silence in all ears bent I plainly do espy.
But if your eager looks do long such toys to see
As heretofore in comical wise were wont abroad to be,
Your lust is lost, and all the pleasures that you sought   5
Is frustrate quite of toying plays. A sudden change is wrought,

---

12. Groano] *This ed.;* Gronno Q.   14. The Muses] Q *omits.*

10. *Dionysius*] Dionysius I (c.430–367 BC), King of Syracuse in Sicily. His court, which is described in Plutarch's *Life of Dion* and repeatedly cited in Cicero, was also a byword for tyranny in Renaissance writing. He was succeeded by his son, the equally tyrannous Dionysius II who was eventually deposed and lived as a teacher. Similarities between the two reigns often lead to confusion: Cicero relates the story of Damon to the elder Dionysius; Iamblichus to the younger. The philosopher Plato visited both father and son in three separate attempts to reform them, and *Epistle* 7, doubtfully ascribed to Plato, is a slightly embarrassed defence of Plato's participation in Syracusan politics. Cf. *PDD*, 10, p. 209.

11. *Eubulus*] (from Gk *eu*, good; *boulos*, counsel), Dionysius's chief minister. This is also the name given to the King's secretary in the tragedy of *Gorboduc* by Sackville and Norton (1560), who voices that play's precepts on the nature of good and lawful government.

12. *Groano*] Q spells variously Gronno, Gronoo, Grono, all compatible with sixteenth-century spellings for 'groan'.

13. *collier*] charcoal dealer. Colliers were commonly associated with the devil, thus while Q 'grimme' could signify the word 'grime', modernisation to 'Grim' is more appropriate.

14. *Muses*] the nine daughters of Zeus and Mnemosyne (Memory), inspirational patrons of the arts, and intermediaries between humans and the gods.

0.1. *Prologue*] The Q title page states that the Prologue as printed 'is somewhat altered for the proper use of them that hereafter shall have occasion to play it, either in private or open audience'. It is impossible to say what this alteration was, whether it was made by Edwards, or, after his death, by whoever arranged for the play's printing.

1. *whereas*] where (*OED*, 1, obsolete).

2. *bent*] inclined, intent; i.e. the audience is straining for silence so that the play can begin. This is, of course, a humorous way of getting such attention.

3. *toys*] trifles.

5. *lust*] desire.

6. *frustrate*] deprived.

toying] (*a*) playful, idle, (*b*) careless, (*c*) amorous.

wrought] brought about.

For lo, our author's muse, that masked in delight,
Has forced his pen against his kind, no more such sports to write.
Muse he that list, right worshipful, for chance has made this change,
For that to some he seemed too much in young desires to range.   10
In which, right glad to please, seeing that he did offend,
Of all he humbly pardon craves—his pen that shall amend.
And yet, worshipful audience, thus much I dare avouch,
In comedies the greatest skill is this: rightly to touch
All things to the quick and eke to frame each person so   15
That by his common talk you may his nature rightly know.
A roister ought not preach—that were too strange to hear—
But as from virtue he does swerve, so ought his words appear.
The old man is sober, the young man rash, the lover triumphing in
      joys,
The matron grave, the harlot wild and full of wanton toys—   20
Which all in one course they no wise do agree,
So correspondent to their kind their speeches ought to be.
Which speeches well pronounced, with action lively framed,
If this offend the lookers-on, let Horace then be blamed
Which has our author taught at school, from whom he does not
      swerve   25
In all such kind of exercise, decorum to observe.
Thus much for his defence he says, as poets erst have done,

9. list] lust *Q.*   13. worshipful] *Q2;* worwipfull *Q.*   avouch,] aduouche. *Q.*
21. Which] Whiche *Q2;* Whithe *Q.*

---

7. *muse*] poetic inspiration, genius.
masked] (*a*) took part in courtly masques and entertainments, (*b*) hid itself.
8. *kind*] nature, normal behaviour; see p. 102n.25.
9. *Muse*] think, wonder, punning on 'muse' l. 7.
list] cares, wishes. *Q* 'lust' is an old spelling.
worshipful] form of address for distinguished people.
10. *range*] (*a*) occupy himself, (*b*) change from one object of desire to another, be inconstant.
14–22.] Cf. Horace, *The Art of Poetry*, 105–16, 'Sad words are appropriate to the face of sorrow, and violent words to the face of anger; playful speech goes with merry looks, and serious speech with grave looks . . . It will make a great difference whether a god or a hero is speaking, a mature old man or a hot-headed youngster in the flower of youth, a matron of authority or an officious nurse' (my translation).
14. *touch*] (*a*) describe, (*b*) satirise, censure.
15. *to the quick*] (*a*) sharply, (*b*) to the very life or essence.
eke] also.
frame] express, depict.
17. *roister*] swaggering, riotous person.
18. *swerve*] deviate, stray, totter.
20. *toys*] flirtations.
24. *Horace*] Latin poet, 65–8 BC.
26. *decorum to observe*] to suit the writing to a particular characterisation or poetic form (not simply to be decorously moral).
27. *defence*] Attacks upon the supposed immorality of poetry in general, and drama in particular, date back to classical times and have generated a succession of 'Defences' or 'Apologies' for poetry; see pp. 39–41.
erst] previously.

Which heretofore in comedies the self-same race did run.
But now for to be brief, the matter to express
Which here we shall present is this: *Damon and Pythias*,   30
A rare example of friendship true, it is no legend-lie,
But a thing once done in deed as histories do descry,
Which done of yore in long time past, yet present shall be here
Even as it were in doing now, so lively it shall appear.
Lo, here is Syracuse, th'ancient town which once the Romans won,   35
Here Dionysius' palace, within whose court this thing most strange
        was done,
Which matter mixed with mirth and care, a just name to apply,
As seems most fit we have it termed a 'tragical comedy',
Wherein talking of courtly toys, we do protest this flat,
We talk of Dionysius' court, we mean no court but that,   40
And that we do so mean, who wisely calls to mind
The time, the place, the authors, here most plainly shall it find.
Lo this I speak for our defence, lest of others we should be shent,
But worthy audience, we you pray, take things as they be meant,
Whose upright judgement we do crave, with heedful ear and eye,
To hear the cause and see th'effect of this new tragical comedy.   *Exit.*   45

[Scene 1]

Enter ARISTIPPUS.

Aristippus. Too strange perhaps it seems to some,
    That I, Aristippus, a courtier am become.
    A philosopher of late, not of the meanest name,
    But now to the courtly behaviour my life I frame.
    Muse he that list, to you of good skill,   5

---

34. as] *Dods.;* aa *Q.*   35. is] *This ed.;* in *Q.*

28. *self-same . . . run*] i.e. ran into the same difficulties. The prologues to Terence's comedies recount similar problems between the playwright and his critics.

31. *legend-lie*] i.e. lying legend.

32. *descry*] make known, observe.

35–6. *Lo . . . palace*] The stage probably had two 'houses', wooden frames covered with canvas, one depicting the city and one the palace; see p. 33.

35. *Syracuse*] the most important Greek town in Sicily, sacked by Rome in 212 BC. For pronunciation see p. 98.

37. *just*] accurate, appropriate.

38. *tragical comedy*] This play may be the first tragi-comedy written in English.

40. *mean . . . that*] This disclaimer, of course, actually does invite comparison with Elizabeth I's court.

41. *who*] i.e. he who, whoever. This usage is common throughout the play.

42. *authors*] (*a*) all those who have written on the story, (*b*) those who instigated the performance at court or the subsequent publication.

43. *shent*] blamed.

4. *frame*] In this play Aristippus is repeatedly said to 'shape himself' to circumstances (4.8. 13.148, 14.59); see p. 48.

5. *skill*] discrimination, understanding.

I say that I am a philosopher still.
Lovers of wisdom are termed '*philosophi*',
Then who is a philosopher so rightly as I?
For in loving of wisdom, proof does this try,
That '*Frustra sapit, qui non sapit sibi*'.   10
I am wise for myself, then tell me of troth,
Is not that great wisdom as the world go'th?
Some philosophers in the street go ragged and torn
And feed on vile roots—whom boys laugh to scorn—
But I in fine silks haunt Dionysius' palace,   15
Wherein with dainty fare myself I do solace.
I can talk of philosophy as well as the best,
But the strait kind of life I leave to the rest,
And I profess now the courtly philosophy,
To crouch, to speak fair—myself I apply—   20
To feed the King's humour with pleasant devices,
For which I am called '*regius canis*'.

---

7. Lovers . . . '*philosophi*'] *This ed.*; Lovers . . . Philosophie *Q*; Loving of wisdom is termed philosophy *Hazlitt (sugg. Collier)*.   14. feed] *Q2*; feedes *Q*.

---

7. *philosophi*] philosophers, from Gk *philos*, loving; *sophia*, wisdom. Pythagoras was reputedly the first person to call himself a philosopher. He believed in *loving* wisdom since *being* wise is a human impossibility. This and other philosophical commonplaces used in the play can be found in William Baldwin's *A Treatise of Morall Phylosophie, Contaynyng the Sayinges of the Wyse* (eighteen editions between c.1547 and 1640).

9. *proof*] evidence.

try] test.

10. Frustra . . . sibi] 'He knows nothing that knows not himself', referring to the famous proverb written over the entrance to Apollo's oracle at Delphi, 'know thyself' (often rendered in English as the more worldly saying 'He is not wise that is not wise for himself', Tilley W532).

11. *troth*] truth.

14. *roots*] roots or root vegetables. Diogenes Laertius (2.8.68) tells how Diogenes the cynic (cf. note ll. 24–5 below), 'washing the dirt from his vegetables saw [Aristippus] passing and jeered at him in these terms, "If you had learnt to make these your diet, you would not have paid court to kings," to which his rejoinder was, "And if you knew how to associate with men, you would not be washing vegetables".' Diogenes Laertius tells the same story of Plato (2.6.58) and of Theodorus (2.8.103).

15. *haunt*] frequent, hang about.

18. *strait*] austere.

20. *crouch*] bow, cringe, fawn.

fair] (*a*) flatteringly, (*b*) in an educated, polished manner.

apply] (*a*) work hard, (*b*) submit, bend both mind and body. Cf. William Baldwin, *Mirror for Magistrates*, ed. L. B. Campbell (Cambridge: Cambridge University Press, 1938): 'Thus clymyng and contendyng alway to the top / . . . That of kinge Richards counsayle we came to be full nye: / To crepe into whose favour we were full fyne and slye' ('The Tragedy of Robert Tresilian', 78–82).

21. *pleasant*] pleasing, merry.

devices] (*a*) conversation, counsel, (*b*) fanciful conceits, mottoes, plays, entertainments etc. Edwards performed exactly the same role at both Mary's and Elizabeth's courts.

22. regius canis] (Lat.) royal dog, implying 'fawning lapdog'.

But wot you who named me first the King's dog?
It was the rogue Diogenes, that vile grunting hog.
Let him roll in his tub to win a vain praise,   25
In the court pleasantly I will spend all my days,
Wherein what to do, I am not to learn—
What will serve mine own turn I can quickly discern.
All my time at school I have not spent vainly—
I can help one. Is not that a good point of philosophy?   30

Enter CARISOPHUS.

Carisophus. Ay, beshrew your fine ears, since you came from school,
In the court you have made many a wise man a fool,
And though you paint out your feigned philosophy,
So God help me, it is but a plain kind of flattery
Which you use so finely in so pleasant a sort,   35
That none but Aristippus now makes the King sport.
Ere you came hither, poor I was somebody—
The King delighted in me—now I am but a noddy.
Aristippus. In faith, Carisophus, you know yourself best,
But I will not call you 'noddy' but only in jest,   40
And thus I assure you, though I came from school
To serve in this court, I came not yet to be the King's fool,
Or to fill his ears with servile scurrility—
That office is yours, you know it right perfectly.
Of parasites and sycophants you are a grave bencher,   45
The King feeds you often from his own trencher.
I envy not your state, nor yet your great favour,
Then grudge not at all if in my behaviour
I make the King merry with pleasant urbanity,

---

23. *wot*] know.
24–5.] The philosopher Diogenes (c.400–c.325 BC) reputedly inured himself to the weather by living in a tub. He ate only the barest necessities and believed that no natural function was indecent. This, and his snarling attitude, earned him the nickname 'dog-like' (Gk *cynicus*—hence cynic school of philosophy). The occasion on which he turned the 'dog' epithet on Aristippus is told by Diogenes Laertius, 2.8.66.
27. *I . . . learn*] i.e. I do not need to learn, I already know.
29. *at school*] (a) (in the classical sense) studying philosophy with a master, (b) at a school for boys.
30. *one*] i.e. himself; proverbial (Tilley O50), 'it is good to save one'.
32–42. *fool . . . fool*] The role of 'parasite' was marked by a parti-coloured costume, similar to that of a court jester.
33. *paint out*] display in full colour.
feigned] alleged, imagined.
35. *finely*] (a) delicately, consummately, (b) cunningly, artfully.
38. *noddy*] fool.
39. *know . . . best*] a joking reference to the proverb 'know thyself' (cf. l. 10n).
40. *but only*] = only (*OED*, 6c).
45. *bencher*] someone who sits on a bench as a mark of office (magistrate, member of the Inns of Court) or of life style (in a tavern or at a dining table).
46. *trencher*] plate.
49. *urbanity*] polished, witty talk.

Whom I never abused to any man's injury.   50
Carisophus. By cock sir, yet in the court you do best thrive,
    For you get more in one day than I do in five.
Aristippus. Why man, in the court do you not see
    Rewards given for virtue to every degree?
    To reward the unworthy, that world is done—   55
    The court is changed. A good thread has been spun
    Of dogs' wool heretofore, and why? Because it was liked,
    And not for that it was best trimmed and picked.
    But now men's ears are finer, such gross toys are not set by,
    Therefore to a trimmer kind of mirth myself I apply—   60
    Wherein though I please, it comes not of my desert
    But of the King's favour.
Carisophus. It may so be, yet in your prosperity,
    Despise not an old courtier (Carisophus is he),
    Which has long time fed Dionysius' humour,   65
    Diligently to please, still at hand—there was never rumour
    Spread in this town of any small thing, but I
    Brought it to the King in post by and by.
    Yet now I crave your friendship, which, if I may attain,
    Most sure and unfeigned friendship I promise you again.   70
    So we two linked in friendship, brother and brother,
    Full well in the court may help one another.
Aristippus. By'r lady, Carisophus, though you know not
    philosophy,
    Yet surely you are a better courtier than I,
    And yet I not so evil a courtier that will seem to despise   75
    Such an old courtier as you, so expert and so wise.
    But whereas you crave mine and offer your friendship so
    willingly,

---

50. *abused*] deceived.
51. *By cock*] a corruption of 'by God'.
54. *degree*] rank.
57. *dogs' wool*] Thread can indeed be spun from dog fur, but the primary sense here is that Diogenes's snarling cynic philosophy (cf. l. 24n) is out of fashion. There may be an urbanely veiled jibe at Carisophus's brand of abusive, 'mongrel' behaviour. Cf. proverbs 'not worth the wool of a dog', 'His thread is spun' (i.e. he has had his time, is dead) and 'You have spun a fine thread' (Tilley W752, T249, T252).
58. *trimmed . . . picked*] cleaned, refined, exquisitely fashioned.
59. *set by*] valued.
60. *trimmer*] more refined.
64. *is he*] 'is the one I mean'.
66. *still*] always.
67. *but*] except that, unless.
68. *in post*] speedily.
70. *again*] in return.
71–2.] *friendship . . . court*] Cf. proverb, 'Better is a friend in court than a penny in purse' (Tilley F687).
73. *By'r lady*] 'by our Lady', the Virgin Mary.
75. *evil*] bad (i.e. at being a courtier).

With heart I give you thanks for this your great courtesy,
Assuring of friendship both with tooth and nail,
Whilst life lasts, never to fail.   80
Carisophus. A thousand thanks I give you, O friend Aristippus.
Aristippus. O friend Carisophus.
Carisophus. How joyful am I since I have to friend Aristippus now!
Aristippus. None so glad of Carisophus' friendship as I, I make
     God a vow—
     I speak as I think, believe me.   85
Carisophus. Since we are now so friendly joined, it seems to me
     That one of us help each other in every degree.
     Prefer you my cause when you are in presence.
     To further your matters to the King, let me alone in your
         absence.
Aristippus. Friend Carisophus, this shall be done as you would wish,   90
     But I pray you tell me thus much by the way,
     Whither now from this place will you take your journey?
Carisophus. I will not dissemble—that were against friendship.
     I go into the city some knaves to nip,
     For talk with their goods to increase the King's treasure—   95
     In such kind of service, I set my chief pleasure.
     Farewell, friend Aristippus, now for a time.   *Exit.*
Aristippus. Adieu, friend Carisophus. In good faith now,
     Of force I must laugh at this solemn vow.
     Is Aristippus linked in friendship with Carisophus?   100
     Quid cum tanto asino, talis philosophus?
     They say, '*Morum similitudo conciliat amicitias*'.

---

102. *conciliat*] *sugg. Steevens*; *consuit Hazlitt*; *consultat Q.*

---

79. *with ... nail*] proverbial (Tilley T422), 'with might and main', 'completely', but here also suggesting aggression.

83. *to friend*] as a friend.

87. *one ... other*] i.e. each should help the other.

every degree] in all details.

88. *in presence*] in the presence of the King.

89. *let ... alone*] trust me to do it.

94. *knaves*] Carisophus means lowborn, ordinary people, those without influence, rather than scoundrels.

nip] (*a*) censure, rebuke, (*b*) arrest, (*c*) thieves' slang for 'pick a pocket'.

95. *talk*] commerce, intercourse. Carisophus earns Dionysius's favour by arresting people upon a pretext and confiscating their goods for the state. He also takes his own cut in the process, as did any Tudor court official.

99. *Of force*] on compulsion, inevitably.

101. Quid ... philosophus] 'What is a philosopher like me doing with such an ass?'

102. Morum ... amicitias] 'similarity of habit makes friendship'. This speech rehearses the arguments of Cicero's *De amicitia* (14.48–50) and loosely quotes his *De officiis* (1.17.56): '*Nihil autem est amabilius nec copulatius quam morum similitudo bonorum*', see pp. 47–8. With regard to the choice of Latin reading: *Conciliat* = joins together, makes friendly; *consuit* = knits together, but the word is extremely rare and has too few strokes to account for Q *consultat* ('considers'), which makes no sense in this context.

Then how can this friendship between us two come to pass?
We are as like in conditions as Jack Fletcher and his bolt—
I brought up in learning, but he is a very dolt   105
As touching good letters. But otherwise such a crafty knave,
If you seek a whole region, his like you cannot have.
A villain for his life, a varlet dyed in grain—
You lose money by him if you sell him for one knave, for he
    serves for twain—
A flattering parasite, a sycophant also,   110
A common accuser of men, to the good an open foe.
Of half a word he can make a legend of lies
Which he will avouch with such tragical cries
As though all were true that comes out of his mouth—
Where indeed to be hanged by and by,   115
He cannot tell one tale but twice he must lie.
He spares no man's life to get the King's favour,
In which kind of service he has got such a savour
That he will never leave. Methink then that I
Have done very wisely to join in friendship with him, lest
    perhaps I   120
Coming in his way might be nipped, for such knaves in presence
We see oft times put honest men to silence.
Yet I have played with his beard in knitting this knot,
I promised friendship, but you love few words: I spoke it but I
    meant it not.
Who marks this friendship between us two,   125
Shall judge of the worldly friendship without any more ado—

---

104. *like ... bolt*] proverbial expression of dissimilarity (Tilley J14); *conditions* = natures, circumstances; *Jack* = generic name for 'fellow'; *fletcher* = (*a*) arrow maker, (*b*) archer; *bolt* = arrow.
    106. *touching*] with regard to.
    letters] learning.
    107. *like*] match, equal.
    108. *varlet*] (*a*) menial servant, (*b*) knave.
    dyed in grain] proverbial, 'A knave in grain' (Tilley K128), i.e. 'a knave through and through'. Wool dyed in the raw state before being spun has more lasting colour.
    109. *serves ... twain*] i.e. he is villainous enough for two knaves.
    110. *parasite*] hanger-on, toady, someone who lives at another's expense.
    sycophant] (*a*) informer, (*b*) impostor, deceiver, (*c*) parasite.
    112. *legend*] i.e. entire story.
    114. *all ... true*] proverbial.
    115. *indeed ... and by*] even if he was about to be hanged.
    118. *savour*] taste for it.
    119. *leave*] stop.
    121. *nipped*] caught out, checked, disadvantaged.
    in presence] in attendance on the King.
    122. *put ... silence*] (*a*) out-talked, out-faced, (*b*) put to death.
    123. *played ... beard*] pretended to his face (*OED*, *sb.* 1 e).
    124. *love ... words*] with reference to the proverb 'A word to a wise man is enough' (Tilley W781).

It may be a right pattern thereof, but true friendship indeed,
Of nought but of virtue does truly proceed.
But why do I now enter into philosophy,
Which do profess the fine kind of courtesy?   130
I will hence to the court with all haste I may,
I think the King be stirring, it is now bright day.
To wait at a pinch still in sight I mean,
For wot you what?—a new broom sweeps clean.
As to high honour I mind not to climb,   135
So I mean in the court to lose no time,
Wherein, happy man be his dole, I trust that I
Shall not speed worst, and that very quickly.   *Exit.*

[Scene 2]

> *Enter* DAMON *and* PYTHIAS *like mariners.*

Damon. O Neptune, immortal be thy praise,
For that so safe from Greece we have passed the seas
To this noble city Syracuse, where we
The ancient reign of the Romans may see,
Whose force Greece also heretofore has known,   5
Whose virtue the shrill trump of fame so far has blown.

---

127. pattern] *Q2*; Patron *Q*.

---

127. *right . . . thereof*] convincing image of worldly friendship. ('Patron', *Q*, is an old form of 'pattern').
127–8. *friendship . . . proceed*] Cf. Cicero, *De amicitia* (6.20), 'virtue is the parent and preserver of friendship and without virtue friendship cannot exist at all'.
130. *fine*] elegant, refined.
133. *at a pinch*] when needed in a crisis.
still] always.
mean] intend.
134. *wot*] know.
new . . . clean] proverbial (Tilley B682), i.e. as a new courtier he does the job assiduously. But Aristippus perhaps varies the sense for his own ends, suggesting that he is sweeping away all other contenders for Dionysius's favour.
135. *As to*] since.
mind not] i.e. would not mind, would like.
137. *happy . . . dole*] proverbial (Tilley M158), 'every man to his fate', or 'happy man, happy fate'.
138. *speed*] thrive, succeed.

0.1. *like mariners*] see pp. 34–5.
1. *Neptune*] Roman god of the sea.
4. *Romans*] The Romans sacked Syracuse in 212 BC. The line anachronistically conceives of Syracuse as a modern town with a Roman and earlier Greek ancient history, whereas the story is set in the Greek period. For the metre and pronunciation of Syracuse here see p. 98.
5–6. *Whose*] i.e. Syracuse. Originally a Corinthian Greek colony, Syracuse had been helped by Spartan forces to overcome Athenian invasion in 413 BC, shortly before the reign of Dionysius I.
6. *trump*] trumpet, regularly used to denote personifications of Fame.

Pythias. My Damon, of right high praise we ought to give
    To Neptune and all the gods that we safely did arrive.
    The seas, I think, with contrary winds never raged so,
    I am even yet so seasick that I faint as I go.   10
    Therefore let us get some lodging quickly—
    But where is Stephano?

        Enter STEPHANO [*weighed down with baggage*].

Stephano. Not far hence. A pox take these mariner knaves.
    Not one would help me to carry this stuff. Such drunken slaves
    I think be accursed of the gods' own mouths—   15
Damon. Stephano, leave thy raging and let us enter Syracuse.
    We will provide lodging, and thou shalt be eased of thy burden
      by and by.
Stephano. Good master, make haste, for I tell you plain,
    This heavy burden puts poor Stephano to much pain.
Pythias. Come on thy ways, thou shalt be eased, and that anon.

                               Exeunt.   20

[Scene 3]

        Enter CARISOPHUS.

Carisophus. It is a true saying that oft has been spoken,
    'The pitcher goes so long to the water, that it comes home
      broken'.
    My own proof this has taught me, for truly since I
    In the city have used to walk very slyly
    And to creep into men's bosoms some talk for to snatch,   5
    By which into one trip or other I might trimly them catch
    And so accuse them, now not with one can I meet
    That will join in talk with me—I am shunned like a devil in the
      street.
    My credit is cracked where I am known, but yet I hear say
    Certain strangers are arrived—they were a good prey   10

2.12.1. *weighed . . . baggage*] *This ed.*
2. it] *Q2;* he *Q.*   4.] *Q then adds* 'Not with one can I meete, that will in talke ioyne with mee,'.

  16. *raging*] mad, foolish talk.
  Syracuse] *Q* original spelling 'Syracusae' rhymes with 'by'.

  2. *pitcher . . . broken*] proverbial (Tilley P501) i.e. 'things get worn out with use'. Carisophus's scams are too well known and he has had no luck. He is therefore tired and fed up.
  4.] *Q* additional line anticipates ll. 7–8. See p. 96.
  6. *trip . . . catch*] a common metaphor from wrestling, i.e. trip and throw them into a fall.
  trimly] neatly, cleverly.
  9. *cracked*] broken, ruined; 'cracked credit' is a common phrase.

If haply I might meet with them. I fear not I
But in talk I should trip them, and that very finely,
Which thing, I assure you, I do for mine own gain,
Or else I would not plod thus up and down, I tell you plain.
Well, I will for a while to the court to see   15
What Aristippus does. I would be loath in favour he should
   overrun me—
He is a subtle child, he flatters so finely, that I fear me
He will lick all the fat from my lips and so outweary me.
Therefore I will not be long absent, but at hand,
That all his fine drifts I may understand.   *Exit.*   20

[Scene 4]

Enter WILL *and* JACK.

Will. I wonder what my master Aristippus means nowadays
That he leaves philosophy and seeks to please
King Dionysius with such merry toys.
In Dionysius' court now he only joys,
As trim a courtier as the best,   5
Ready to answer, quick in taunts, pleasant to jest,
A lusty companion to devise with fine dames
Whose humour to feed, his wily wit he frames.
Jack. By cock, as you say, your master is a minion—
A foul coil he keeps in this court. Aristippus alone   10
Now rules the roost with his pleasant devices,
That I fear he will put out of conceit my master Carisophus.

11–12. *I fear . . . But*] i.e. I do not doubt that.

16. *I . . . me*] i.e. I do not want him to surpass me in the King's favour.

17. *child*] used contemptuously to mean 'man', and often suggesting craftiness (*OED*, 7), but playing here on the fact of the child actor.

18. *lick . . . lips*] i.e. cheat me of my gains.

outweary] wear out, exhaust.

19. *at hand*] nearby.

20. *drifts*] (*a*) insinuations, (*b*) schemes, plots, aims.

5–20.] Plutarch describes Cicero in much the same way: 'Truely pleasaunt tawntes doe grace an orator, and sheweth a fine witte: but yet Cicero used them so commonly, that they were offensive unto many, and brought him to be counted a malicious scoffer and spightfull man' (Plutarch, vol. 5, 318).

5. *trim*] proper, fine.

7. *lusty*] (*a*) cheerful, vigorous, (*b*) lustful.

devise] (*a*) chat, (*b*) scheme.

7–8. *dames . . . frames*] This portrayal of Aristippus is satirically autobiographical. Cf. Edwards's flattering poem to Mary I's ladies-in-waiting, CT 1, pp. 187–8.

8. *humour*] desires, whims.

9. *By cock*] By God.

minion] (*a*) lover, (*b*) favourite, (*c*) servile creature.

10. *coil*] fuss, bustle, disturbance.

12. *out of conceit*] (*a*) out of favour (with Dionysius), *OED*, *sb.* 5, (*b*) out of confidence (in himself).

Will. Fear not that, Jack, for like brother and brother
    They are knit in true friendship, the one with the other.
    They are fellows you know, and honest men both,   15
    Therefore the one to hinder the other they will be loath.
Jack. Yea, but I have heard say there is falsehood in fellowship.
    In the court sometimes, one gives another finely the slip,
    Which when it is spied, it is laughed out with a scoff,
    And with sporting and playing, quietly shaken off.   20
    In which kind of toying thy master has such a grace,
    That he will never blush—he has a wooden face!
    But Will, my master has bees in his head,
    If he find me here prating, I am but dead.
    He is still trotting in the city, there is somewhat in the wind—   25
    His looks bewrays his inward troubled mind.
    Therefore I will be packing to the court by and by—
    If he be once angry, Jack shall cry, 'woe the pie'.
Will. By'r lady, if I tarry long here, of the same sauce shall I taste,
    For my master sent me on an errand, and bade me make haste,   30
    Therefore we will depart together.   *Exeunt.*

[Scene 5]

Enter STEPHANO.

Stephano. Oft-times I have heard, before I came hither,
    That no man can serve two masters together—
    A sentence so true as most men do take it,
    At any time false that no man can make it.
    And yet by their leave that first have it spoken,   5

---

    15. *fellows*] well-matched companions.

    17. *falsehood in fellowship*] proverbial (Tilley F41).

    18. *gives ... slip*] cleverly outwits another.

    20. *quietly*] calmly, without fuss, as befits an urbane courtier. The word is used repeatedly throughout the play to indicate wise and/or courtly behaviour (cf. 8.88; 11.42).

    22. *blush ... face*] The more usual form of the proverb is 'brazen face' (Tilley F8); *wooden*] dull, blockish, collocates jokingly with 'head' l. 23.

    23. *bees ... head*] proverbial (Tilley H255), 'he's mad, obsessive'.

    24. *but dead*] as good as dead.

    26. *bewrays*] shows, exposes; the third person singular, used as a plural.

    28. *woe ... pie*] probably 'woe for a thrashing' in reference to the proverb, 'give some lamb pie', i.e. give a thrashing (Tilley L38), and playing on the proverb 'merry as a pie' i.e. magpie (Tilley P281).

    29. *same ... taste*] proverbial (Tilley S99), i.e. 'the same will happen to me' (playing on 'sauce' and 'pie').

    1–48.] See p. 53 for the poetic form of Stephano's language here.

    2. *no ... together*] 'No man can serve two masters. For ether he shal hate the one, and love the other, or els leane to the one, and despyse the other' (Bible, Matt. 6.24, which goes on to warn against caring about what one eats or wears, cf. 8.13–38).

    3. *sentence*] maxim, saying.

    4. *make*] think (OED, *vb*.19).

How that may prove false, even here I will open.
For I, Stephano, lo, so named by my father,
At this time serve two masters together,
And love them alike. The one and the other
I duly obey—I can do no other,   10
A bondman I am, so nature has wrought me.
One Damon of Greece, a gentleman, bought me.
To him I stand bound, yet serve I another,
Whom Damon my master loves as his own brother—
A gentleman too, and Pythias he is named,   15
Fraught with virtue, whom vice never defamed.
These two, since at school they fell acquainted,
In mutual friendship at no time have fainted,
But loved so kindly and friendly each other,
As though they were brothers by father and mother.   20
Pythagoras' learning, these two have embraced,
Which both are in virtue so narrowly laced,
That all their whole doings do fall to this issue:
To have no respect but only to virtue.
All one in effect. All one in their going,   25
All one in their study, all one in their doing,
These gentlemen both, being of one condition,
Both alike of my service have all the fruition.
Pythias is joyful if Damon be pleased,
If Pythias be served, then Damon is eased.   30
Serve one, serve both. So near, who would win them?
I think they have but one heart between them.
In travelling countries, we three have contrived

---

6. *open*] disclose, explain.

12. *gentleman*] (*a*) well born (though not a nobleman), (*b*) generous, courteous man.

13. *bound*] i.e. as a slave.

16. *Fraught*] freighted, filled with.

18. *fainted*] lost heart, flagged.

21. *Pythagoras' learning*] For examples, see 5.25n; 7.71–4n; 8.28n; 15.228n; 15.238n.

22. *narrowly*] tightly (cf. 'straitlaced').

23. *fall . . . issue*] have this outcome.

24. *respect . . . to*] regard for anything except.

25. *one*] In Pythagorean doctrine true friends become one person: 'for when two people have the same ideals and the same tastes, it is a natural consequence that each loves the other as himself; and the result is, as Pythagoras requires of ideal friendship, that several are united in one.' Cicero, *De officiis* (1.17.56).

effect] actuality, reality.

28. *Both . . . fruition*] share the fruits of my service alike.

30. *eased*] comforted, benefited.

31. *Serve . . . both*] Stephano's aphorism here seems a response to the proverb, 'He that serves everybody is paid by nobody' (Tilley S244).

near] close.

win] winnow, separate.

33. *contrived*] passed time (*OED*, *vb*.2).

Full many a year, and this day arrived
At Syracuse in Sicily, that ancient town 35
Where my masters are lodged, and I up and down
Go seeking to learn what news here are walking,
To hark of what things the people are talking.
I like not this soil. For as I go plodding,
I mark there two, there three, their heads always nodding 40
In close, secret wise, still whispering together.
If I ask any question, no man does answer,
But shaking their heads, they go their ways speaking,
I mark how with tears their wet eyes are leaking.
Some strangeness there is that breeds this musing. 45
Well, I will to my masters, and tell of their using,
That they may learn, and walk wisely together.
I fear we shall curse the time we came hither.   *Exit.*

[Scene 6]

Enter ARISTIPPUS *and* WILL.

Aristippus. Will, didst thou hear the ladies so talk of me?
    What ails them? From their nips shall I never be free?
Will. Good faith sir, all the ladies in the court do plainly report
    That without mention of them, you can make no sport.
    They are your plainsong to sing descant upon— 5
    If they were not, your mirth were gone.
    Therefore master, jest no more with women in any wise.
    If you do, by cock, you are like to know the price.
Aristippus. By'r lady Will, this is good counsel. Plainly to jest
    Of women, proof has taught me it is not best. 10

---

35. *Syracuse in*] The final syllable 'ae' of Q standard spelling *Siracusae* would here
be elided with 'in'.
36–7.] Cf. John Skelton's satirical poem *Colin Clout* (1522): 'Thus I, Colin Clout, /
As I go about, / And wandering as I walk / I hear the people talk' (ed. Philip
Henderson (London: Dent, 1959), p. 258); *walking* = circulating (*OED*, *vb*.3.b).
39. *soil*] country.
41. *close*] (*a*) secret, (*b*) close together.
46. *their using*] the behaviour of the Syracusans.
47. *wisely*] carefully.

2. *nips*] rebukes, complaints, sarcasm; cf. 4.7n.
5. *plainsong*] simple melody.
descant] (*a*) a tune for a higher voice harmonising on a given melody, (*b*) verbal comments on a given theme.
7. *wise*] manner.
8. *by cock*] by God, but in this context with a sexual pun.
9. *Plainly*] openly, frankly.
10. *proof*] experience.

I will change my copy—howbeit, I care not a quince,
I know the galled horse will soonest wince.
But learn thou secretly what privily they talk
Of me in the court. Among them slyly walk,
And bring me true news thereof.   15
Will. I will sir. Master thereof have no doubt, for I,
    Where they talk of you, will inform you perfectly.
Aristippus. Do so, my boy. If thou bring it finely to pass,
    For thy good service, thou shalt go in thine old coat at
    Christmas.   *Exeunt.*

[Scene 7]

                 Enter DAMON, PYTHIAS [*and*] STEPHANO.

Damon. Stephano, is all this true that thou hast told me?
Stephano. Sir, for lies hitherto you never controlled me.
    O that we had never set foot on this land
    Where Dionysius reigns with so bloody a hand.
    Every day he shows some token of cruelty,   5
    With blood he has filled all the streets in the city.
    I tremble to hear the people's murmuring,
    I lament to see his most cruel dealing.
    I think there is no such tyrant under the sun—
    O my dear masters, this morning what has he done!   10
Damon. What is that? Tell us quickly.
Stephano. As I this morning passed in the street,
    With a woeful man going to his death did I meet.
    Many people followed, and I of one secretly
    Asked the cause why he was condemned to die,   15

---

11. *change . . . copy*] proverbial (Tilley C648); *copy* = (*a*) behaviour, image, (*b*) copiousness or variety of language (Lat. *copia*), (*c*) possible pun on 'printer's copy' and 'proof'.

howbeit] however

I . . . quince] (*a*) cf. 'I don't care a fig'; quince = the hard, acid fruit of the quince tree; (*b*) punning on the verb quince or quinch, 'to start, flinch'. This is an example of the courtier quietly accommodating himself without fuss to the situation no matter what he really thinks (cf. 4.20).

12. *galled . . . wince*] proverbial (Tilley H700), i.e. 'the women are only objecting because I've touched their sore points by making the correct observation'; *galled* = rubbed sore; *wince* = kick.

14. *slyly*] (*a*) secretly, (*b*) with pun on deceitfully.

19. *go . . . Christmas*] perhaps 'go in your own skin (i.e. unbeaten) as far as Christmas'; cf. proverb 'to pay one's jacket' i.e. give a thrashing (Tilley J13). Servants were customarily given new suits at Christmas and there may be a meta-theatrical joke here perhaps concerning the non-arrival of liveries in Elizabeth's cash-strapped court. Either way, the joke is that Aristippus is not offering anything extra in return for Will's good service.

2. *controlled*] disciplined.
12. *passed*] moved about, walked.

Which whispered in mine ear, 'Nought has he done but thus:
In his sleep he dreamed he had killed Dionysius,
Which dream told abroad was brought to the King in post,
By whom condemned for suspicion, his life he has lost.'
Marsyas was his name as the people said.   20
Pythias. My dear friend Damon, I blame not Stephano
For wishing we had not come hither, seeing it is so
That for so small cause, such cruel death does ensue.
Damon. My Pythias, where tyrants reign, such cases are not new,
Which fearing their own state for great cruelty,   25
To sit fast as they think, do execute speedily
All such as any light suspicion have tainted.
Stephano. With such quick carvers I list not be acquainted.
Damon. So are they never in quiet, but in suspicion still,
When one is made away, they take occasion another to kill,   30
Ever in fear, having no trusty friend, void of all people's love,
And in their own conscience a continual hell they prove.
Pythias. As things by their contraries are always best proved,
How happy are then merciful princes, of their people beloved.
Having sure friends everywhere, no fear does touch them,   35
They may safely spend the day pleasantly—at night '*secure
dormiunt in utramque aurem*'.
O my Damon, if choice were offered me, I would choose to be
Pythias

---

16. Which] *This ed.*; He *Dods.*; Who *Hazlitt; Q omits.*   20. Marsyas] Marcia *Q.*
36. *utramque*] *Hazlitt; vtranque Q.*

---

16. *Which*] The text consistently uses 'which' where modern English would use 'who'.

18. *in post*] speedily.

20. *Marsyas*] Cf. Plutarch, 'Life of Dion' (vol. 6, 135) '[Dionysius] sayed he was affrayed of his frendes . . . bicause he knewe that they desired rather to rule, th[a]n to be ruled . . . He slewe one of his Captaines called Marsyas . . . bicause he dreamed that he killed him: saying that he dreamed of this in the night, bicause that waking in the day he had determined to kill him.'

25. *fearing . . . cruelty*] fearful for their own safety (*state*) because of their cruelty [to others]. The fearfulness and sleeplessness of Kings is a commonplace: Cicero quotes the poet Ennius, 'Whom they [the people] fear they hate. And whom one hates, one hopes to see him dead' (*De officiis*, 2.7.23–5).

26. *sit fast*] make themselves secure.

28. *quick*] speedy.

carvers] (*a*) cutters, i.e. here, 'executioners', (*b*) those who please themselves.

list not be] do not want to be.

30. *one . . . away*] one person is killed.

32. *prove*] experience, suffer (*OED*, *vb*.B2).

33. *contraries . . . proved*] proverbial. Cf. Elyot, *Of Knowledge*, 'For every thinge sheweth moste perfectely, and after the common proverbe of marchantis, best to the sale, whan it is joyned or compared with his contrary' (cited Tilley C630).

36. *secure . . . aurem*] 'free from care they sleep soundly' (lit. 'sleep on both ears'); cf. Erasmus, *Adagia*, 307B; Tilley E24; also Terence, *The Self-tormentor*, l. 342, where the Latin reads, '*in aurem utramvis otiose ut dormias*'.

As I am, Damon's friend, rather than to be King Dionysius.
Stephano. And good cause why—for you are entirely beloved of one,
  And as far as I hear, Dionysius is beloved of none.   40
Damon. That state is most miserable. Thrice happy are we
  Whom true love has joined in perfect amity.
  Which amity first sprung—without vaunting be it spoken that is
    true—
  Of likeliness of manners, took root by company, and now is
    conserved by virtue.
  Which virtue always through worldly things does not frame,   45
  Yet does she achieve to her followers immortal fame,
  Whereof, if men were careful, for virtue's sake only
  They would honour friendship, and not for commodity.
  But such as for profit in friendship do link,
  When storms come, they slide away sooner than a man will
    think.   50
  My Pythias, the sum of my talk falls to this issue:
  To prove no friendship is sure but that which is grounded on
    virtue.
Pythias. My Damon, of this thing, there needs no proof to me—
  The gods forbid but that Pythias with Damon in all things
    should agree.
  For why is it said, '*Amicus alter ipse*'?   55
  But that true friends should be two in body but one in mind,
  As it were one transformed into another—which against kind
  Though it seem, yet in good faith, when I am alone
  I forget I am Pythias, methink I am Damon.
Stephano. That could I never do, to forget myself. Full well I know,   60
  Wheresoever I go, that I am *pauper Stephano*.
  But I pray you sir, for all your philosophy,

---

45. does] *This ed.;* do *Q.*   55. is it] *Dods.;* it is *Q.*

38. *be . . . Dionysius*] Cf. the story of Damocles (poem *PDD*, 10).
44. *likeliness*] similarity.
  took . . . company] i.e. rooted in long exposure to each other's company.
  45. *virtue . . . frame*] 'virtue does not always prosper in a worldly context' (*frame* =
'prosper', *OED*, *vb.*2.obs.). Q 'do' (singular, now only dialectical) was not an uncommon construction (cf. 13.307), although it may be a slip occasioned by the plural
'worldly things'. It is here regularised to 'does'. Cf. 15.184. The syntax here led Dodsley
to amend 'through' to 'though' which reverses the sense to 'worldly things do not
always shape themselves (*frame*, *OED*, *vb.*5.e) to virtue'.
  46. *immortal fame*] i.e. not transient, worldly fame.
  48. *commodity*] profit, advantage (in the world).
  49. *such as*] i.e. those who.
  50. *they*] fair-weather friends.
  51. *issue*] outcome, conclusion.
  52. *no . . . virtue*] Cf. 1.127–8n.
  55. Amicus . . . ipse] 'a friend is a second self', proverbial (Tilley F696; Erasmus,
Adagia, 14F); see 5.25n.
  57. *kind*] nature.
  61. pauper Stephano] Stephano the poor man.

See that in this court you walk very wisely.
You are but newly come hither—being strangers you know,
Many eyes are bent on you in the streets as you go.   65
Many spies are abroad, you cannot be too circumspect—
Damon. Stephano, because thou art careful of me thy master, I do
    thee praise.
Yet think this for a surety: no state to displease
By talk or otherwise, my friend and I intend. We will here
As men that come to see the soil and manners of all men of
    every degree.   70
Pythagoras said that this world was like a stage
Whereon many play their parts. The lookers-on the sage
Philosophers are, says he, whose part is to learn
The manners of all nations, and the good from the bad to
    discern.
Stephano. Good faith sir, concerning the people, they are not gay   75
And as far as I see they be mummers, for nought they say
For the most part whatsoever you ask them.
The soil is such, that to live here I cannot like.
Damon. Thou speakest according to thy learning, but I say,
    '*Omne solum forti patria*'—a wise man may live everywhere.   80
Therefore my dear friend Pythias,
Let us view this town in every place
And then consider the people's manners also.
Pythias. As you will my Damon—but how say you Stephano,
Is it not best ere we go further to take some repast?   85

---

70. come] *Dods.;* coms *Q.*   80. *Omne . . . patria*] *Hazlitt; Omnis solum fortis patria Q.*

---

63. *wisely*] carefully.

66.] The hanging half-couplet here, and Damon's refusal to consider what Stephano is saying, suggests that he interrupts; see pp. 52–3.

67. *careful of*] full of care for.

69. *will*] i.e. will be, will behave.

70. *see . . . degree*] Cf. quotation, 8.73–4; *soil* = country.

71–4. *Pythagoras . . . discern*] Pythagoras is supposed to have said that the wisest men went to the games to watch the behaviour of other people: cf. p. 40; Cicero, *Tusc.*, 5.3.9; Shakespeare, *AYLI*, 2.7.137–40.

76. *mummers*] actors in a dumb-show.

77–80.] The lack of rhyme here again perhaps indicates a breakdown in communication between Damon and Stephano, smoothed over by Pythias at l. 84.

78. *soil*] country.

79. *Thou . . . learning*] i.e. you are too uneducated to know better.

80. Omne . . . patria] 'every soil (place) is home to a steadfast man'; see Ovid, *Fasti*, 1.493 (*omne solum forti patria est*), where it refers to bravery in the face of banishment from one's country. Damon's translation, though not an uncommon form of the proverb (cf. Tilley M426), is perhaps an indication of folly and pride on his part. Cf. 'The wise man knows himself to be a fool, the fool thinks he is wise' (Tilley M425, W522).

85. *ere*] before.

Stephano. In faith, I like well this question, sir. For all your haste,
    To eat somewhat I pray you, think it no folly,
    It is high dinnertime, I know by my belly.
Damon. Then let us to our lodging depart. When dinner is done
    We will view this city as we have begun.   *Exeunt.*   90

[Scene 8]

Enter CARISOPHUS.

Carisophus. Once again in hope of good wind, I hoist up my sail—
    I go into the city to find some prey for mine avail.
    I hunger while I may see these strangers that lately
    Arrived. I were safe if once I might meet them haply.
    Let them bark that list at this kind of gain,   5
    He is a fool that for his profit will not take pain.
    Though it be joined with other men's hurt, I care not at all.
    For profit I will accuse any man—hap what shall.
    [*To audience*] But soft sirs, I pray you hush, what are they that
      comes here?
    By their apparel and countenance some strangers they appear.   10
    I will shroud myself secretly even here for a while,
    To hear all their talk that I may them beguile.
[*Carisophus hides.*]

Enter DAMON and STEPHANO.

Stephano. 'A short horse soon curried'—my belly waxes thinner,
    I am as hungry now as when I went to dinner.
    Your philosophical diet is so fine and small   15
    That you may eat your dinner and supper at once, and not
      surfeit at all.
Damon. Stephano, much meat breeds heaviness, thin diet makes thee
    light.
Stephano. I may be lighter thereby, but I shall never run the faster.

---

5. list] *This ed.;* lust *Q.*   9.SD] *This ed.*   12.SD] *This ed.*

---

1. *wind . . . sail*] Cf. p. 109n.3
2. *avail*] advantage.
3. *while*] until.
4. *safe*] 'safely arrived at my destination' i.e. successful.
haply] by chance.
5. *bark*] object, cry out.
list] wish.
13. *short . . . curried*] proverbial (Tilley H691), i.e. 'that was quick'; *curried* = (*a*)
groomed, rubbed down, (*b*) beaten.
16. *not surfeit*] not have too much to eat.
17. *light*] Damon means (*a*) nimble, quick-witted, (*b*) cheerful. Cf. proverb, 'A fat
belly does not engender a subtle wit' (Erasmus, *Adagia*, 833C, Tilley B293, also P123).
Stephano, however, needs food for energy so that he can run his errands. The humour
for the audience is that the word also has connotations with 'light weight', 'trivial'.

Damon. I have had sufficiently discourse of amity
    Which I had at dinner with Pythias, and his pleasant company   . 20
    Has fully satisfied me. It does me good to feed mine eyes on him.
Stephano. Course or discourse, your course is very coarse, for all
      your talk,
    You had but one bare course, and that was pike, rise and walk,
    And surely for all your talk of philosophy,
    I never heard that a man with words could fill his belly.   25
    'Feed your eyes', quoth you, the reason from my wisdom
      swerves—
    I stared on you both, and yet my belly starves.
Damon. Ah Stephano, small diet makes a fine memory.
Stephano. I care not for your crafty sophistry.
    You two are fine, let me be fed like a gross knave still.   30
    I pray you license me for a while to have my will
    At home to tarry while you take view of this city—
    To find some odd victuals in a corner, I am very witty.
Damon. At your pleasure sir, I will wait on myself this day,
    Yet attend upon Pythias, which for a purpose tarries at home.   35
    So doing, you wait upon me also.
Stephano. With wings on my feet I go.   [*Exit* STEPHANO].

---

22. coarse] *Hazlitt;* course *Q.*   37.SD] *Dods.*

19–30. *discourse . . . knave*] Cf. the argument that true friendship is sustained by
discourse, whereas what Erasmus called the 'friendship of the pot' ('*Ollae amicitia*',
Adagia, 190C), or 'trencher friendship' (cf. 'cupboard love'), is the mark of a dependent, hanger-on or sycophant.

22–3.] Extensive puns on *course*: (*a*) the action of running, picking up *run the faster*
(l. 17); (*b*) habit, course of action; (*c*) course of a meal; and *coarse* (ordinary, not fine).
At ll. 38–40 Damon regrets that Stephano is a coarse (i.e. lowborn and greedy) feeder.

23. *pike*] (*a*) make off with oneself, depart, (*b*) with possible puns on 'pick' (behave
pickily, fastidiously) and perhaps pike as a coarse (i.e. freshwater) fish, since fish were
eaten on fast days. Cf. *Jack Juggler*, 421, 'Pike and walke a knave'.

25. *words . . . belly*] Cf. proverb, 'Fair words butter no parsnips' (Tilley W791).

26. *Feed . . . eyes*] a common phrase. Cf. proverb, 'Better fill a glutton's belly than
his eyes' (Tilley G146); Plato, *Phaedrus*, 249–51, where virtuously directed enjoyment
of the sight of a beloved person leads to spiritual insight.

reason . . . swerves] (*a*) the reason is beyond his capacity to understand it, (*b*) it is
driving him mad (his reason departing from his mental capacity).

28. *memory*] Pythagoras demanded that his followers should remember rather than
write down his teachings. He had strict instructions for a frugal diet without meat or
beans, and only rarely allowed fish.

30. *fine*] refined.

31. *license me*] (*a*) give me leave, permission, (*b*) let me leave you.

33. *in a corner*] (*a*) hidden away, (*b*) in a tight spot, difficult situation; with possible reference to the proverbs: 'A friend in a corner' (Tilley F692); 'a friend in need is
a friend in deed' (F693); and 'better fed than taught' (F174). Stephano's real refuge and
support is food, not friendship or learning.

witty] clever, efficient.

37. *wings . . . go*] This recalls Plautus's comedy *Amphitruo* (source for *Jack Juggler*)
in which a slave is impersonated by the god Mercury, often depicted with winged
sandals.

Damon. Not in vain the poet says, '*Naturam furca expelles, tamen*
    usque recurret',
    For train up a bondman never to so good a behaviour,
    Yet in some point of servility he will savour.   40
    As this Stephano, trusty to me his master, loving and kind,
    Yet touching his belly, a very bondman I him find.
    He is to be borne withal, being so just and true,
    I assure you I would not change him for no new.
    But methinks this is a pleasant city,   45
    The seat is good, and yet not strong, and that is great pity—
Carisophus. [*Aside*] I am safe, he is mine own.
Damon. The air subtle and fine. The people should be witty
    That dwell under this climate in so pure a region—
    A trimmer plot I have not seen in my peregrination.   50
    Nothing mislikes me in this country
    But that I hear such muttering of cruelty.
    Fame reports strange things of Dionysius,
    But kings' matters, passing our reach, pertain not to us.
Carisophus. [*Coming forward*] 'Dionysius', quoth you? Since the
    world began,   55
    In Sicily never reigned so cruel a man.
    A despiteful tyrant to all men, I marvel I
    That none makes him away, and that suddenly.
Damon. My friend, the gods forbid so cruel a thing,
    That any man should lift up his sword against the King,   60
    Or seek other means by death him to prevent,
    Whom to rule on earth the mighty gods have sent.
    But my friend, leave off this talk of King Dionysius.
Carisophus. Why sir? He cannot hear us.
Damon. What then? '*An nescis longas regibus esse manus?*'   65

---

38. *Naturam . . . recurret*] Hazlitt; *Natura furca expellas, tamen vsque recurrit* Q.
47. *Aside*] Hazlitt.   55.SD] *This ed.*

---

    38. Naturam . . . recurret] Lit., 'you can thrust out nature with a fork, nevertheless
it runs back all the way', Horace, *Epistles*, 1.10.24, i.e. it is not possible to dig out
(eradicate) a man's basic instincts. The word order in Horace is '*Naturam expelles
furca*', etc.
    39. *train . . . behaviour*] i.e. even if you train a servant in the very best manners.
    40. *savour*] show traces (*OED*, *vb*.4).
    43. *borne withal*] put up with.
    46–51] Strabo, *Geography*, 6.2.7, describes Syracuse as a favoured, wealthy town,
'an acropolis by the sea'.
    46. *seat*] (*a*) situation, (*b*) seat of government.
    48. *subtle*] fine, rarefied, i.e. pure.
    49. *climate*] (*a*) region, (*b*) weather conditions.
    54. *pertain . . . to*] do not concern.
    57.] The repetition of 'I' is a colloquial form of emphasis.
    61. *prevent*] forestall, stop.
    65. An . . . manus] 'do you not know that kings have long hands?', Ovid, *Heroides*,
17.166; proverbial, Tilley K87.

It is no safe talking of them that strikes afar off.
But leaving kings' matters, I pray you show me this courtesy
To describe in few words the state of this city.
A traveller I am, desirous to know
The state of each country wherever I go, 70
Not to the hurt of any state, but to get experience thereby.
It is not for nought that the poet does cry,
'*Dic mihi musa, virum captae post tempora Troiae*
Multorum hominum mores qui vidit et urbes',
In which verses, as some writers do scan, 75
The poet describes a perfect wise man.
Even so, I being a stranger, addicted to philosophy,
To see the state of countries, myself I apply.
Carisophus. Sir, I like this intent, but may I ask your name without
    scorn?
Damon. My name is Damon, well known in my country, a
    gentleman born. 80
Carisophus. You do wisely to search the state of each country
    To bear intelligence thereof whither you list. [*Aside*] He is a
    spy.—
    Sir, I pray you, have patience awhile, for I have to do hereby.
    View this weak part of this city as you stand, and I very quickly
    Will return to you again, and then will I show 85
    The state of all this country, and of the court also.   *Exit.*
Damon. I thank you for your courtesy. This chances well that I
    Met with this gentleman so happily,
    Which as it seems, mislikes some thing,
    Else he would not talk so boldly of the King, 90
    And that to a stranger—but lo where he comes in haste.

---

73. *tempora*] Dods.; *tempore* Q.   74. *urbes*] Dods.; *vrbis* Q.   82. whither]
Dods.; whether Q.   list] lust Q.   Aside] Hazlitt.   91. where] Q2; were Q.

73–4. Dic . . . urbes] 'Tell me, Muse, about the man who after the capture of Troy
saw the customs and towns of many peoples'. Damon is quoting (albeit with a slightly
different word order) Horace, *On the Art of Poetry*, ll. 141–2, which is in turn a sim-
plified Latin translation from Greek of the opening lines of Homer's *Odyssey*.

75. *some writers*] These lines from the *Odyssey* have always excited much commentary. Roger Ascham quotes the Homeric passage in order to warn at length about
the dangers of allowing young men to travel to Italy unless they also have both the
wisdom and wariness of Ulysses, plus a guardian to protect them (as Ulysses had the
goddess Pallas). He adds that Plato found in Dionysius's Sicily 'every Citie full of vanitie,
full of factions, even as Italie is now' (*Schoolmaster*, 222–6). Damon is blissfully and
hubristically unaware of his problematic situation.

scan] interpret.

77–8. *philosophy . . . countries*] Cf. *Tusc.*, 4.19.44, 'Pythagoras, Democritus, Plato
journeyed to the ends of the earth for they judged it their duty to go where there was
something to be learnt'.

79. *without scorn*] i.e. without being scorned (for my ignorance).

82. *whither . . . list*] to whatever place you wish.

83. *have . . . hereby*] have business to attend to near here.

88. *happily*] felicitously, by good fortune.

Enter CARISOPHUS *and* SNAP.

Carisophus. This is he, fellow Snap, snap him up. Away with him.
Snap. Good fellow, thou must go with me to the court.
Damon. To the court sir, and why?
Carisophus. Well, we will dispute that before the King. Away with
    him quickly.   95
Damon. Is this the courtesy you promised me, and that very lately?
Carisophus. Away with him I say.
Damon. Use no violence, I will go with you quietly.   *Exeunt omnes.*

[Scene 9]

Enter ARISTIPPUS [*and* WILL].

Aristippus. Ah sirrah, by'r lady, Aristippus likes Dionysius' court
    very well,
    Which in passing joys and pleasures does excel,
    Where he has *Dapsiles cenas, geniales lectos, et auro*
    Fulgentem tyranni zonam.
    I have plied the harvest, and struck when the iron was hot.   5
    When I spied my time, I was not squeamish to crave, God wot,
    But with some pleasant toy I crept into the King's bosom,
    For which Dionysius gave me *Auri talentum magnum*—
    A large reward for so simple services.
    What then? The King's praise stands chiefly in bountifulness,   10
    Which thing, though I told the King very pleasantly,
    Yet can I prove it by good writers of great antiquity,

---

92. he, fellow] *Farmer;* he fellow *Q;* the fellow *Q2.*
0.1. *and* WILL] *This ed.*   3–4. Dapsiles . . . zonam] *Hazlitt (dapsiles); Dapsilae
coenas, gemalis lectes, & auro. / Fulgentii turgmani zonam Q.*   5. struck] *This ed.;*
strock *Q2;* stroke *Q.*   8. Auri] *Dods.;* Aure *Q.*

---

98. *Use no violence*] This is probably a joke relying on a difference in size between
the two actors. Snap, the shortest role, is likely to have been played by the youngest
and smallest boy.

2. *passing*] (*a*) everyday, regular, (*b*) ephemeral, (*c*) surpassing.

3–4. Dapsiles . . . zonam] 'sumptuous suppers, bridal beds and a king's money belt
with glittering gold'; i.e. he has everything conducive to sensual pleasure: food, sex and
money. See p. 48. Cicero condemns Aristippus's pursuit of pleasure as weakness (*Tusc.,*
2.6.15).

5. *plied the harvest*] Cf. proverb 'Make hay while the sun shines' (Tilley H235);
plied = worked away at.

struck . . . hot] proverbial (Tilley I94).

8. Auri . . . magnum] 'a full talent of gold' (talent = a measurement by weight). The
Syracusan talent had a reputation for being under-weight.

10. *praise*] praiseworthiness, reputation.

stands] consists.

bountifulness] Cf. 10.190–213.

11. *pleasantly*] lightly, i.e. without citing serious, philosophical authorities.

But that shall not need at this time since that I have
   abundantly—
When I lack hereafter, I will use this point of philosophy.
But now, whereas I have felt the King's liberality,   15
As princely as it came, I will spend it as regally.
Money is current, men say, and 'current' comes of *currendo*.
Then will I make money 'run', as his nature requires I trow.
For what becomes a philosopher best,
But to despise money above the rest?   20
And yet not so despise it, but to have in store
Enough to serve his own turn, and somewhat more.
With sundry sports and taunts, yesternight I delighted the King,
That with his loud laughter, the whole court did ring,
And I thought he laughed not merrier than I when I got this
   money—   25
But mumbudget, for Carisophus I espy
In haste to come hither. I must handle the knave finely.

Enter CARISOPHUS [and JACK].

O Carisophus, my dearest friend, my trusty companion,
What news with you? Where have you been so long?
Carisophus. My best beloved friend Aristippus, I am come at last.   30
   I have not spent all my time in waste,
   I have got a prey, and that a good one I trow.
Aristippus. What prey is that?—fain would I know.
Carisophus. Such a crafty spy I have caught, I dare say,
   As never was in Sicily before this day,   35
   Such a one as viewed every weak place in the city,
   Surviewed the haven and each bulwark—in talk very witty,
   And yet by some words himself he did bewray.

27.1.SD] *Occurs after l. 29 in Q;* [*and* JACK] *this ed.*

---

13. *have abundantly*] i.e. have money in abundance.
14. *lack*] need money.
15. *felt*] sensed, perceived (with the sense of weighing the gold in the hand).
16. *princely*] (*a*) graciously, (*b*) magnificently, munificently.
17. *is current*] circulates, runs (from hand to hand).
currendo] (Lat.) running.
18. *his*] its.
trow] believe.
20-2. *despise . . . more*] As usual, Aristippus turns a well-known maxim to his own use: since money has no moral value, he will get rid of it (i.e. use it to buy things), while reserving an ample nest-egg. Cf. Horace, *Satires*, 2.3.99–110, where a famous story about Aristippus throwing all his money away (from Diogenes Laertius, 2.77) is juxtaposed with an injunction to spend freely.
26. *mumbudget*] a cry for silence, perhaps from a children's game.
27. *finely*] (*a*) with skill, cunningly, (*b*) handsomely, flatteringly.
31. *in waste*] (*a*) idly, (*b*) in conspicuous consumption (with the suggestion that that is what Aristippus has been doing). Originally spelt 'wast' and rhyming with 'last'.
37. *surviewed*] surveyed, inspected, perhaps with the sense of looking down from a high vantage place.

Aristippus. I think so in good faith, as you did handle him.
Carisophus. I handled him clerkly, I joined in talk with him
    courteously,   40
    But when we were entered, I let him speak his will and I
    Sucked out thus much of his words that I made him say plainly
    He was come hither to know the state of the city,
    And not only this, but that he would understand
    The state of Dionysius' court and of the whole land.   45
    Which words when I heard, I desired him to stay
    Till I had done a little business of the way,
    Promising him to return again quickly, and so did convey
    Myself to the court for Snap the tipstaff which came and
    upsnatched him,
    Brought him to the court and in the porter's lodge dispatched
    him.   50
    After, I ran to Dionysius as fast as I could,
    And bewrayed this matter to him which I have you told,
    Which thing when he heard, being very merry before,
    He suddenly fell in a dump and foaming like a boar.
    At last he swore in a great rage that he should die   55
    By the sword or the wheel, and that very shortly.
    I am too shamefast for my travail and toil,
    I crave nothing of Dionysius but only his spoil.
    Little has he about him but a few moth-eaten crowns of gold—
    I've pouched them up already, they are sure in hold—   60
    And now I go into the city, to say sooth,
    To see what he has at his lodging to make up my mouth.
Aristippus. My Carisophus, you have done good service, but what is
    the spy's name?
Carisophus. He is called Damon, born in Greece, from whence lately
    he came.
Aristippus. By my troth, I will go see him and speak with him too if
    I may.   65

---

38. *bewray*] expose.
39. *handle him*] manipulate him, set him up.
40. *clerkly*] skilfully.
41. *entered*] engaged in conversation.
47. *of the way*] Cf. 'by the way'.
49. *upsnatched*] snatched up, arrested.
50. *dispatched him*] disposed of him, settled his business, *OED*, *vb.*3.
52. *bewrayed*] revealed, discovered.
54. *dump*] depression.
foaming] i.e. at the mouth, with rage.
56. *wheel*] instrument of torture and execution.
57. *shamefast*] modest.
58. *his spoil*] i.e. the goods and possessions confiscated from Damon.
59. *Little . . . gold*] i.e. Damon had very little money on him.
62. *make . . . mouth*] compensate me, make up the shortfall; proverbial (Tilley M1263).

Carisophus. Do so I pray you, but yet by the way,
    As occasion serves, commend my service to the King.
Aristippus. 'Dictum sapienti sat est'—friend Carisophus, shall I
    forget that thing?
    No I warrant you, though I say little to your face,
    I will lay on with my mouth for you to Dionysius when I am in
    place.   70
    [*To audience*] If I speak one word for such a knave, hang me.
                               Exit [*with* WILL].
Carisophus. Our fine philosopher, our trim learned elf,
    Is gone to see as false a spy as himself.
    Damon smatters as well as he of crafty philosophy
    And can turn cat in the pan very prettily,   75
    But Carisophus has given him such a mighty check,
    As I think in the end will break his neck.
    What care I for that? Why would he then pry
    And learn the secret estate of our country and city?
    He is but a stranger, by his fall let others be wise,   80
    I care not who fall, so that I may rise.
    As for fine Aristippus, I will keep in with him,
    He is a shrewd fool to deal withal—he can swim!
    And yet by my troth, to speak my conscience plainly,
    I will use his friendship to mine own commodity.   85
    While Dionysius favours him, Aristippus shall be mine,
    But if the King once frown on him, then goodnight Tomaline—
    He shall be as strange as though I never saw him before.
    But I tarry too long, I will prate no more.
    Jack, come away.
Jack.   At hand sir.
Carisophus.   At Damon's lodging if that you see   90

---

70. on . . . mouth] *Q2;* one month *Q.*   71. *To audience*] *This ed.*   with WILL]
This ed.   72. trim] trimme *Q2;* timme *Q1.*

---

68. Dictum . . . est] proverbial, 'a word to the wise is sufficient' (Tilley W781).
70. *on with my mouth*] i.e. I'll speak on your behalf (cf. 'lay it on thick').
72. *elf*] tricksy, malicious person, with possible reference to the small size of the boy actor.
74. *smatters*] chatters, babbles.
75. *turn . . . pan*] proverbial (Tilley C172), i.e. turn things inside out or make them seem the opposite of what they are. This describes the practice of sophistry rather than philosophy.
76. *check*] interruption to his accustomed course, restraint.
79. *estate*] condition, situation.
83. *swim*] float above all difficulties; cf. proverb 'sink or swim' (Tilley S485).
85. *commodity*] convenience, profit.
87. *goodnight Tomaline*] i.e. 'that's it, no more'. 'Goodnight, Nicholas' is proverbial (Tilley N170), but Tomaline, a poetic form of Thomas, is used here for its rhyme and scansion.
88. *strange*] i.e. unknown to me.

Any stir to arise, be still at hand by me.
Rather than I will lose the spoil, I will blade it out.

[Exeunt.]

[Scene 10]

Enter PYTHIAS *and* STEPHANO.

Pythias. What strange news are these, ah my Stephano?
Is my Damon in prison, as the voice does go?
Stephano. It is true, O cruel hap, he is taken for a spy,
And as they say, by Dionysius' own mouth condemned to die.
Pythias. To die?—alas for what cause?   5
Stephano. A sycophant falsely accused him. Other cause there is
      none,
   That—O Jupiter, of all wrongs the revenger,
   Seest thou this injustice, and wilt thou stay any longer
   From heaven to send down thy hot consuming fire
   To destroy the workers of wrong which provoke thy just ire?   10
   Alas master Pythias, what shall we do,
   Being in a strange country, void of friends and acquaintance too?
   Ah poor Stephano, hast thou lived to see this day,
   To see thy true master unjustly made away?
Pythias. Stephano, seeing the matter is come to this extremity, 15
   Let us make virtue our friend of mere necessity.
   Run thou to the court and understand secretly
   As much as thou canst of Damon's cause, and I
   Will make some means to entreat Aristippus.
   He can do much, as I hear, with King Dionysius.   20
Stephano. I am gone, sir. Ah, I would to God my travail and pain
   Might restore my master to his liberty again.   *[Exit.]*
Pythias. Ah woeful Pythias, since now I am alone,
   What way shall I first begin to make my moan?

92.SD] *Reed.*
7. That—O] *This ed.;* That oh *Q;* That oh, *Q2;* But, oh *Dods.;* Thou *conj. Brown,*
Wilson.   22.SD] *This ed.*

---

91. *stir*] commotion, brawl.
92. *blade it out*] fight (with a sword); cf. 'tough it out'.

2. *as . . . go*] as it is rumoured.
6–8.] Whatever the punctuation here, the syntactical awkwardness serves to express
Stephano's desperation (indicated also by the lack of rhyme, l. 6). Substantive emendation is unnecessary.
8. *stay*] delay, hesitate.
10. *just ire*] A pause after this would promote a laugh when, of course, no thun-
derbolt ensues.
16. *virtue . . . necessity*] proverbial, 'Make a virtue of necessity' (Tilley V73), but
also with the sense here of being forced by the situation to make a virtue out of dubious
actions like spying and making new friends only to enlist their aid (l. 64); *of* = out of;
mere = utmost.
24. *moan*] complaint, lamentation.

What words shall I find apt for my complaint?   25
Damon—my friend, my joy, my life—is in peril, of force I must
    now faint.
But O music, as in joyful tunes, thy merry notes I did borrow,
So now lend me thy yearnful tunes, to utter my sorrow.

    Here PYTHIAS *sings, and the regals play.*

Awake you woeful wights,
    that long have wept in woe,   30
Resign to me your plaints and tears,
    my hapless hap to show.
My woe no tongue can tell,
    nor pen can well descry,
O, what a death is this to hear,   35
Damon my friend must die!

The loss of worldly wealth,
    man's wisdom may restore,
And physic has provided too
    a salve for every sore.   40
But my true friend once lost,
    no art can well supply,
Then what a death is this to hear,
Damon my friend must die!

My mouth refuse the food   45
    that should my limbs sustain,
Let sorrow sink into my breast
    and ransack every vein.
You Furies all at once,
    on me your torments try,   50
Why should I live since that I hear,

---

44. must die] *Q*; is judged to die *Add. 15117; Cott. Vesp. A25 and subsequently.*

---

25. *complaint*] This word was often used for the titles of poems expressing grief.
26. *faint*] lose heart or courage.
28.1. *regals*] portable organs with reed pipes. The sound was often reckoned to be equivalent to that of the human voice. The words for the song are also preserved in Cott. Vesp. A.xxv fol. 135, and Add. 15117, fol. 3. For the music see pp. 245–7.
29. *wights*] creatures.
31. *Resign*] give, surrender.
plaints] lamentations, audible expressions of grief.
32. *hapless hap*] unlucky fate.
34. *descry*] proclaim.
39. *physic*] medicine.
40. *salve . . . sore*] proverbial (Tilley S84).
42. *art*] scientific, medical or magical skill.
45. *My mouth*] i.e. May my mouth.
48. *ransack*] search, penetrate.
49. *Furies*] the three Fates, responsible for spinning, weaving and cutting off the thread of a person's life.

Damon my friend must die?
Gripe me, you greedy griefs
   and present pangs of death,
You sisters three, with cruel hands,   55
   with speed now stop my breath.
Shrine me in clay alive,
   some good man stop mine eye,
O death, come now, seeing I hear,
Damon my friend must die.   60

He speaks this after the song.

In vain I call for death which hears not my complaint,
But what wisdom is this, in such extremity to faint?
'*Multum juvat in re mala animus bonus*'.
I will to the court myself to make friends, and that presently—
I will never forsake my friend in time of misery.   65
But do I see Stephano amazed hither to run?

Enter STEPHANO.

Stephano. O Pythias, Pythias, we are all undone,
   Mine own ears have sucked in mine own sorrow—
   I heard Dionysius swear that Damon should die tomorrow.
Pythias. How camest thou so near the presence of the King   70
   That thou mightest hear Dionysius speak this thing?
Stephano. By friendship I got into the court, where in great audience,
   I heard Dionysius with his own mouth give this cruel sentence
   By these express words: that Damon the Greek, that crafty spy,
   Without further judgement, tomorrow should die.   75
   Believe me Pythias, with these ears I heard it myself.
Pythias. Then how near is my death also, ah woe is me.
   Ah my Damon, another myself, shall I forgo thee?

---

52. must] *Q2*; should *Q*.   63. *Multum . . . bonus*] *Dods.*; *Multum iuua in re mala annimas bonus Q*.

---

52. *must*] The *Q* reading is a mistake caused by the use of 'should' in the previous line.
53. *Gripe*] (a) clutch, grip, (b) afflict.
55. *sisters three*] the three Fates.
57. *Shrine*] entomb. The soul, traditionally said to be enshrined or imprisoned in the 'clay' of the body, would be set free at death. This grief, as Pythias himself says (ll. 62–3), is excessive.
   clay] earth.
63. Multum . . . bonus] 'A good mind is a great help in a bad situation', a paraphrase of Plautus, *The Captives*, l. 202, '*in re mala animo si bono utare, adiuvat*'.
64. *presently*] immediately.
66. *amazed*] bewildered, out of his mind (with grief).
68. *sucked in*] 'heard the information and extracted [sorrow] from it' (*OED, vb.*5).
70–1.] The 'est' endings should probably be elided to 'cam'st', 'might'st'.
72. *got*] *Q* reads 'gate' which is the old form of the past tense.
78. *another myself*] See 7.55n.
   forgo thee] lose you, let you go.

Stephano. Sir, there is no time of lamenting now. It behoves us
    To make means to them which can do much with Dionysius,   80
    That he be not made away ere his cause be fully heard, for we
      see
    By evil report, things be made to princes far worse than they be.
    But lo, yonder comes Aristippus, in great favour with King
      Dionysius.
    Entreat him to speak a good word to the King for us,
    And in the mean season I will to your lodging, to see all things
      safe there.   85
Pythias. To that I agree,   *Exit* [STEPHANO].
              but let us slip aside, his talk to hear.
                        [Stands aside.]

        Enter ARISTIPPUS.

Aristippus. Here is a sudden change indeed, a strange
    metamorphosis.
    This court is clean altered—who would have thought this?
    Dionysius, of late so pleasant and merry,
    Is quite changed now into such melancholy   90
    That nothing can please him—he walked up and down
    Fretting and chafing—on every man he does frown.
    In so much that when I in pleasant words began to play,
    So sternly he frowned on me and knit me up so short—
    I perceive it is no safe-playing with lions, but when it please
      them,   95
    If you claw where it itch not, you shall dis-ease them

---

86. *Exit*] *Q after l. 85.*   *Stands aside.*] *This ed.; Pithias retires. Farmer.*   93. play]
Q; sport *conj. Brown, Wilson.*

85. *mean season*] meantime.

86. *us*] i.e. 'me' (colloquial and dialect usage), although it could conspiratorially
include the audience.

87. metamorphosis] The word was already normal English usage but, like the other
Latin quotations in this play, *Q* prints it in roman, rather than black-letter. This might
be compositorial, or it may indicate that Aristippus is showing off his erudition. The
Metamorphoses, a collection of tales of transformation by the Latin poet Ovid, was
taught in schools.

93. *play*] i.e. entertain deftly and wittily. Brown and Wilson suggested emending for
the sake of the rhyme. However a lack of rhyme (ll. 93–4), combined with the confusion of tenses (ll. 90–2), may constitute characterisation of Aristippus's confusion and
anxiety. Hazlitt amended 'walked' to 'walketh' to preserve the tense.

94. *knit me up*] snubbed (*OED*, *vb.*10.b), shut me up.

short] (*a*) crossly, curtly, (*b*) quickly, immediately.

95–6. *no safe-playing . . . dis-ease them*] a combination of proverbs: 'claw (scratch)
where it does not itch' i.e. flatter where it is not wanted (Tilley M49, B17); 'Itch and
ease can no man please' and 'An itch is worse than a smart' (I106, 107); 'No playing
with short daggers/an old cat' (P405, P406), i.e. it is dangerous to play with those older,
wiser or more powerful.

dis-ease] discomfort.

And so perhaps get a clap. Mine own proof taught me this:
That it is very good to be merry and wise.
The only cause of this hurly-burly is Carisophus, that wicked
    man
Which lately took Damon for a spy—a poor gentleman—   100
And has incensed the King against him so despitefully
That Dionysius has judged him tomorrow to die.
I have talked with Damon, whom though in words I found very
    witty,
Yet was he more curious than wise in viewing this city.
But truly for aught I can learn, there is no cause why   105
So suddenly and cruelly he should be condemned to die.
Howsoever it be, this is the short and long:
I dare not gainsay the King, be it right or wrong.
I am sorry, and that is all I may or can do in this case—
Nought avails persuasion, where froward opinion takes place.   110
Pythias. [*Coming forward*] Sir, if humble suits you would not
    despise,
Then bow on me your pitiful eyes.
My name is Pythias, in Greece well known,
A perfect friend to that woeful Damon—
Which now a poor captive in this court does lie,   115
By the King's own mouth, as I hear, condemned to die—
For whom I crave your mastership's goodness,
To stand his friend in this his great distress.
Nought has he done worthy of death, but very fondly,
Being a stranger, he viewed this city,   120
For no evil practices but to feed his eyes.
But seeing Dionysius is informed otherwise,
My suit is to you, when you see time and place,
To assuage the King's anger and to purchase his grace—
In which doing, you shall not do good to one only,   125
But you shall further two, and that fully.
Aristippus. My friend, in this case I can do you no pleasure.
Pythias. Sir, you serve in the court as fame does tell.
Aristippus. I am of the court indeed, but none of the counsel.

111.SD] *Farmer.*   126. two] *Q2;* too *Q.*

---

97. *clap*] (*a*) sudden blow (of lion's paw), (*b*) misfortune, (*c*) punning on 'venereal disease' (cf. 'a tailor might scratch her where'er she did itch', Shakespeare, *Temp.*, 2.2.51).
98. *good . . . wise*] proverbial (Tilley G324).
101. *despitefully*] (*a*) scornfully, (*b*) maliciously.
107. *short and long*] proverbial (Tilley L419).
110. *froward*] perverse.
takes place] takes precedence, has influence or official position.
119. *fondly*] foolishly.
126. *further*] advance, support.
129. *court . . . counsel*] proverbial (Tilley C727), i.e. I am a courtier but not privy to any secrets; *counsel* = (*a*) confidential adviser, counsellor, (*b*) council.

Pythias. As I hear, none is in greater favour with the King than you
at this day. 130
Aristippus. The more in favour, the less I dare say.
Pythias. It is a courtier's praise to help strangers in misery.
Aristippus. To help another and hurt myself, it is an evil point of
courtesy.
Pythias. You shall not hurt yourself to speak for the innocent.
Aristippus. He is not innocent whom the King judges nocent. 135
Pythias. Why sir, do you think this matter past all remedy?
Aristippus. So far past that Dionysius has sworn Damon tomorrow
shall die.
Pythias. This word my trembling heart cuts in two.
Ah sir, in this woeful case, what wist I best to do?
Aristippus. Best to content yourself when there is no remedy— 140
He is well relieved that foreknows his misery.
Yet if any comfort be, it rests in Eubulus,
The chiefest counsellor about King Dionysius,
Which pities Damon's case in this great extremity,
Persuading the King from all kind of cruelty. 145
Pythias. The mighty gods preserve you for this word of comfort.
Taking my leave of your goodness, I will now resort
To Eubulus that good counsellor— [*A trumpet sounds.*]
But hark, methink I hear a trumpet blow.
Aristippus. The King is at hand, stand close in the press. Beware. If
he know 150
You are a friend to Damon he will take you for a spy also.
[*Pythias hides.*]
Farewell, I dare not be seen with you. [*Exit.*]

Enter King DIONYSIUS, EUBULUS *the counsellor, and*
GROANO *the hangman.*

Dionysius. Groano, do my commandment, strike off Damon's irons
by and by,
Then bring him forth. I myself will see him executed presently.
Groano. O mighty King, your commandment will I do speedily. 155
[*Exit.*]
Dionysius. Eubulus, thou hast talked in vain, for sure he shall die.

---

137. far] Q2; fare Q.   148.SD] *This ed.*   151.SD] *This ed.*   152.SD] *This ed.*

131. *more . . . say*] i.e. the closer I am to the King, the less I dare say about him.
132. *praise*] virtue, act of praiseworthiness.
135. *nocent*] guilty, harmful.
139. *wist*] know (pseudo-archaic).
141. *relieved*] comforted.
142. *comfort*] aid, support.
145. *kind*] variety, types.
150. *close*] hidden.
press] crowd. Pythias probably hides among the audience.
153. *irons*] fetters.

Shall I suffer my life to stand in peril of every spy?
Eubulus. That he conspired against your person, his accuser cannot
    say.
He only viewed your city, and will you for that make him away?
Dionysius. What he would have done, the guess is great. He minded
    me to hurt   160
That came so slyly to search out the secret estate of my court.
Shall I still live in fear? No, no, I will cut off such imps betime,
Lest that to my further danger, too high they climb.
Eubulus. Yet have the mighty gods immortal fame assigned
To all worldly princes which in mercy be inclined.   165
Dionysius. Let Fame talk what she list, so I may live in safety.
Eubulus. The only mean to that is to use mercy.
Dionysius. A mild prince the people despiseth.
Eubulus. A cruel king the people hateth.
Dionysius. Let them hate me, so they fear me.   170
Eubulus. That is not the way to live in safety.
Dionysius. My sword and power shall purchase my quietness.
Eubulus. That is sooner procured by mercy and gentleness.
Dionysius. Dionysius ought to be feared.
Eubulus. Better for him to be well beloved.   175
Dionysius. Fortune makes all things subject to my power.
Eubulus. Believe her not, she is a light goddess, she can laugh and
    lower.
Dionysius. A king's praise stands in the revenging of his enemy.
Eubulus. A greater praise to win him by clemency.
Dionysius. To suffer the wicked live, it is no mercy.   180
Eubulus. To kill the innocent, it is great cruelty.
Dionysius. Is Damon innocent, which so craftily undermined
    Carisophus

155.SD] *This ed.*

157–87.] Cf. Seneca, *Octavia*, 437–81, in which the philosopher Seneca counsels the
emperor Nero against tyranny, in particular: (*a*) 'Nero. Am I to tolerate conspiracy /
Against my life, and make no retribution?' (*b*) 'Nero. Steel is the emperor's guard. *Sen.*
Trust is a better. *Nero.* A Caesar should be feared. *Sen.* Rather be loved. *Nero.* Fear is a
subject's duty'; (*c*) 'Nero. I, thanks to Fortune, may do anything' (trans. Watling, 1966).
    160. *the guess is great*] is great cause for speculation.
    minded] intended.
    162. *imps*] (*a*) young shoots of a plant (which could therefore be 'cut off'), hence
(*b*) 'offspring'—both 'young men' (referring to the character), and 'children', particularly mischievous children (referring to the actor).
    betime] (*a*) early, (*b*) promptly, in season.
    164. *fame*] reputation, renown.
    167. *mean to*] way of achieving.
    169–71. *cruel . . . safety*] cf. 7.25n.
    177. *light*] wanton, faithless.
    lower] lour, scowl.
    178. *praise*] reputation, renown.
    revenging] punishment.
    179. *win*] (*a*) conquer, (*b*) persuade, i.e. win over.
    182. *undermined*] questioned in a secret, underhand manner (*OED*, *vb.* 6.) but, in

To understand what he could of King Dionysius?
Which surviewed the haven and each bulwark in the city
Where battery might be laid, what way best to approach? Shall I   185
Suffer such a one to live that works me such despite?
No, he shall die, then I am safe. A dead dog cannot bite.
Eubulus. But yet, O mighty, my duty binds me
To give such counsel as with your honour may best agree.
The strongest pillars of princely dignity,   190
I find this: justice with mercy; and prudent liberality.
The one judges all things by upright equity,
The other rewards the worthy, flying each extremity.
As to spare those which offend maliciously,
It may be called no justice but extreme injury,   195
So upon suspicion of such things not well proved,
To put to death presently whom envious flattery accused,
It seems of tyranny. And upon what fickle ground all tyrants do
    stand
Athens and Lacedemon can teach you if it be rightly scanned,
And not only these citizens, but who curiously seeks   200
The whole histories of all the world, not only of Romans and
    Greeks,
Shall well perceive of all tyrants the ruinous fall,
Their state uncertain, beloved of none but hated of all.

---

188. mighty] *Q*; mighty King *Q2*.   191. this: justice] *This ed.*; this justice *Q*; is
justice *Dods.*   196. such] *conj. Brown, Wilson*; each *Q*.

---

the light of the following lines, punning on the word's primary military meaning: to
dig a mine underneath the opposing army's position. The historical Dionysius reputedly had a secret cavern in which he could overhear what was being said about him.

184–5. *bulwark . . . laid*] 'part of the city defensive walls and earthworks which
might best be attacked by artillery bombardment', but also possibly suggesting 'section
of the wall which might contain batteries (cannon emplacements)', and which should
therefore be avoided by attackers.

186. *despite*] outrage, defiance.

187. *dead . . . bite*] proverbial (Tilley D448). Cf. Erasmus, *Adagia*, 857D, 'Dead
men bite not'.

188. *mighty*] Q2's reading is the usual form in the play and, combined with full
pronunciation of the original 'eth' ending on 'binds', would render 188–9 as regular
poulter's measure. The remainder of the speech, however, is irregular, which better suits
the urgency of Eubulus's appeal. The use of 'mighty' as a quasi-noun is not uncommon
in this period.

189. *honour . . . agree*] 'best matches your high status, reputation and good name'
playing on 'which will be most agreeable to your Honour'.

191. *prudent*] wise, discreet, politic.

liberality] bountifulness, largesse.

192. *equity*] natural justice, which tempers justice with mercy by paying attention
to the circumstances of each case, rather than imposing the letter of the law.

193. *flying*] shunning. The examples which follow suggest that prudence must be
applied to the 'pillars' of both justice and liberality.

199. *Athens*] reputedly the birthplace of civic freedom.

Lacedemon] i.e. Sparta in Greece, whose inhabitants were renowned for living
simple, highly disciplined lives.

if . . . scanned] i.e. if the history of Athens and Lacedemon is properly examined.

Of merciful princes to set out the passing felicity
I need not—enough of that, even these days do testify.   205
They live devoid of fear, their sleeps are sound, they dread no
    enemy,
They are feared and loved, and why? They rule with justice and
    mercy,
Extending justice to such as wickedly from justice have swerved,
Mercy unto those where, in opinion, simpleness have mercy
    deserved.
Of liberty nought I say but only this thing: 210
Liberty upholds the state of a king.
Whose large bountifulness ought to fall to this issue:
To reward none but such as deserve it for virtue.
Which merciful justice, if you would follow, and provident
    liberality,
Neither the caterpillars of all courts—'*et fruges consumere nati*', 215
Parasites with wealth puffed up—should not look so high,
Nor yet for this simple fact, poor Damon should die.
Dionysius. With pain mine ears have heard this vain talk of mercy.
I tell thee, fear and terror defends kings only.
Till he be gone whom I suspect, how shall I live quietly   220
Whose memory with chilling horror fills my breast day and night
    violently?
My dreadful dreams of him bereaves my rest. On bed I lie
Shaking and trembling, as one ready to yield his throat to
    Damon's sword.
This quaking dread, nothing but Damon's blood can stay—
Better he die, than I to be tormented with fear alway.   225
He shall die, though Eubulus consent not thereto—
It is lawful for kings as they list all things to do.

---

209. where, in opinion,] *This ed.;* where opinion, *Q;* who in opinion of *Hazlitt.*
227.1. *with* SNAP] *and* Snap Hazlitt.

---

   204. *passing*] surpassing, extreme.
   209. *where . . . deserved*] i.e. where it is widely felt that the accused are acting from simple ignorance without malicious intent, and therefore deserve mercy.
   211. *state . . . king*] (*a*) state of being a king, (*b*) stateliness and magnificence of kingship, (*c*) suggesting also 'the state, country'.
   214–17.] i.e. If Dionysius were to exercise merciful justice and be provident in his liberality, the parasites of the court would not get above themselves and Damon would not die.
   214. *if . . . follow*] if you would follow justice (perhaps also with the sense of 'if you would follow my argument').
   215. et fruges . . . nati] 'born indeed to consume the fruits of the earth', Horace, *Epistles,* 1.2.27. This epistle praises Homer because he tells of the suffering caused by the tyrannous passions of kings.
   217. *fact*] action (i.e. in following justice).
   221. *Whose memory*] i.e. 'my memory of whom'.

Here GROANO [*with* SNAP] *brings in* DAMON, *and*
PYTHIAS *meets him by the way.*

Pythias. O my Damon.
Damon. O my Pythias, seeing death must part us, farewell for ever.
Pythias. O Damon, O my sweet friend.   230
Snap. Away from the prisoner, what a press have we here!
Groano. As you commanded, O mighty King, we have brought
    Damon.
Dionysius. Then go to, make ready, I will not stir out of this place
    Till I see his head strucken off before my face.
Groano. It shall be done sir. [*To Damon*] Because your eyes have
    made such ado,   235
    I will knock down this your lantern, and shut up your shop
    window too.
Damon. O mighty King, whereas no truth my innocent life can save,
    But that so greedily you thirst, my guiltless blood to have—
    Albeit even for thought for aught against your person—
    Yet now I plead not for life, nor will I crave your pardon.   240
    But seeing in Greece, my country where well I am known,
    I have worldly things fit for mine alliance when I am gone,
    To dispose them ere I die, if I might obtain leisure,
    I would account it, O King, for a passing great pleasure,
    Not to prolong my life thereby, for which I reckon not this,   245
    But to set my things in a stay. And surely I will not miss—
    Upon the faith which all gentlemen ought to embrace—
    To return again, at your time to appoint, to yield my body here
    in this place.
    Grant me O King, such time to dispatch this invent'ry,

---

235. *To Damon*] Hazlitt.   238. thirst] *Q2*; thrust *Q*.   249. invent'ry] *This ed.*;
iniurie *Q*; inquiry *Hazlitt*.

228–32.] The lack of rhyme indicates separate, parallel snatches of dialogue; see
p. 52.

235. *eyes ... do*] 'your spying has made such a commotion'.

236. *knock ... lantern*] 'chop off your head', punning on 'sconce', (*a*) lantern, can-
dlestick, (*b*) head.

shut ... window] Proverbial: 'shut the shop windows for lack of merchandise' (Tilley
S394), and used as a metaphor for going to sleep in William Baldwin's *Beware the Cat*
(entered 1568–9, ed. J. O. Halliwell (London: Chiswick Press, 1864), p. 95). Here it
puns on the practice of blindfolding the condemned person; cf. Edwards's source, 'the
officer of justice had closed his eyes with a kerchief, and had drawn his sword to have
stricken off his head, his fellow came running and crying that the day of his appointment was not yet past' (*Governor*, 2.11) and compare 15. 128–31.

239. *even ... aught*] i.e. just for thinking something. Of course Damon is not guilty
even of this supposed crime.

242. *alliance*] kinsmen and friends.

246. *set ... stay*] finalise my affairs, put them in order.

248. *at ... appoint*] at whatever time you stipulate.

249. *dispatch*] dispose of, distribute.

invent'ry] the collection of goods which are the subject of an inventory or list (*OED,
sb.* 3).

And I will not fail, when you appoint it, even here my life to
    pay.   250
Dionysius. A pleasant request—as though I could trust him absent,
    Whom in no wise I cannot trust being present!
    And yet, though I swore the contrary, do that I require:
    Give me a pledge for thy return and have thine own desire.
    [*Aside*] He is as near now as he was before.   255
Damon. There is no surer nor greater pledge than the faith of a
    gentleman.
Dionysius. It was wont to be, but otherwise now the world does
    stand,
    Therefore do as I say, else presently yield thy neck to the sword.
    If I might with mine honour, I would recall my word.
Pythias. Stand to your word, O King, for kings ought nothing say   260
    But that they would perform, in perfect deeds alway.
    A pledge you did require when Damon his suit did move,
    For which, with heart and stretched hands, most humble thanks
    I give,
    And that you may not say but Damon has a friend
    That loves him better than his own life and will do to his end,   265
    Take me, O mighty King, my life I pawn for his,
    Strike off my head if Damon hap at his day to miss.
Dionysius. What art thou that chargest me with my word so boldly
    here?
Pythias. I am Pythias, a Greek born, which hold Damon my friend
    full dear.
Dionysius. Too dear perhaps to hazard thy life for him—what
    fondness moves thee?   270
Pythias. No fondness at all, but perfect amity.
Dionysius. A mad kind of amity. Advise thyself well: if Damon fail
    at his day
    Which shall be justly appointed, wilt thou die for him, to me his
    life to pay?

---

250. appoint it] *conj. Brown, Wilson;* appointed *Q;* appoint *Q2.*   pay] *Q;* yeelde
speedely *Q2.*   253. swore] *This ed.;* sware *Q.*   255. Aside] *Hazlitt.*

    252. *wise*] way.
    253. *though*] even if.
    255. *near*] (*a*) 'close to succeeding in his request', (*b*) with the sense of 'closely bound
to me'. Dionysius wants Damon dead yet offers to free him if he can find someone to
stand in his place. He gives his word to this, believing that it will not happen.
    258. *presently*] immediately.
    259. *word*] i.e. the promise to free Damon.
    261. *perfect*] (*a*) beyond reproach, (*b*) completed, fully carried out.
    262. *move*] Q uses the old spelling 'meeue' here for the sake of a closer rhyme with
'give' (old spelling 'geue') l. 263.
    264. *but*] i.e. 'anything except that'.
    270. *to hazard*] i.e. if you are prepared to hazard.
    272. *Advise thyself well*] consider carefully.

Pythias. Most willingly, O mighty King. If Damon fail, let Pythias
    die.
Dionysius. Thou seemest to trust his words that pawnest thy life so
    frankly.   275
Pythias. What Damon says, Pythias believes assuredly.
Dionysius. Take heed for life—worldly men break promise in many
    things.
Pythias. Though worldly men do so, it never haps amongst friends.
Dionysius. What callest thou friends? Are they not men—is not this
    true?
Pythias. Men they be, but such men as love one another only for
    virtue.   280
Dionysius. For what 'virtue' dost thou love this spy, this Damon?
Pythias. For that virtue which yet to you is unknown.
Dionysius. Eubulus, what shall I do? I would dispatch this Damon
    fain,
    But this foolish fellow so charges me, that I may not call back
    my word again.
Eubulus. The reverent majesty of a King stands chiefly in keeping his
    promise.   285
    What you have said, this whole court bears witness.
    Save your honour, whatsoever you do.
Dionysius. For saving mine honour, I must forbear my will. Go to.
    Pythias, seeing thou tookest me at my word, take Damon to
    thee.
    For two months he is thine—unbind him, I set him free—   290
    Which time once expired, if he appear not the next day by noon,
    Without further delay, thou shalt lose thy life, and that full soon.
    Whether he die by the way or lie sick in his bed,
    If he return not then, thou shalt either hang or lose thy head.
Pythias. For this, O mighty King, I yield immortal thanks.—O joyful
    day!   295
Dionysius. Groano, take him to thee, bind him, see him kept in
    safety.
    If he escape, assure thyself, for him thou shalt die.
    Eubulus, let us depart to talk of this strange thing within.
Eubulus. I follow.   *Exit* [DIONYSIUS *and* EUBULUS].
Groano. Damon, thou servest the gods well today, be thou of
    comfort.   300

---

277. heed for life—] *This ed.*; heed for life, *Q*; heed, for life, *Q2*; heed, for [your] life
Hazlitt.

<hr>

  275. *frankly*] freely, unconditionally.
  282. *unknown*] i.e. because Dionysius is a tyrant.
  283. *dispatch*] kill, but with a pun on 'send away'.
  284. *charges me*] presses me.
  call . . . word] 'go back on what I have vowed to do', proverbial (Tilley W777);
cf. 255n.
  288. *Go to*] This expression of protest here signifies reluctant acquiescence.
  300. *servest . . . well*] i.e. you must have done something amazing to deserve this.

[*To Pythias*] As for you sir, I think you will be hanged in sport.
You heard what the King said? I must keep you safely.
By cock so I will—you shall rather hang than I.
Come on your way.

Pythias. My Damon, farewell, the gods have thee in keeping.   305
Damon. O my Pythias, my pledge, farewell, I part from thee
        weeping,
But joyful at my day appointed I will return again,
When I will deliver thee from all trouble and pain.
Stephano will I leave behind me to wait upon thee in prison
        alone,
And I, whom fortune has reserved to this misery, will walk
        home.   310
Ah my Pythias, my pledge, my life, my friend, farewell.
Pythias. Farewell, my Damon.
Damon. Loath I am to depart. Since sobs my trembling tongue does
        stay,
O music sound my doleful plaints when I am gone my way.
                                                            [*Exit.*]
Groano. I am glad he is gone, I had almost wept too. Come Pythias,   315
        So God help me, I am sorry for thy foolish case.
        Wilt thou venture thy life for a man so fondly?
Pythias. It is no venture. My friend is just for whom I desire to die.
Groano. Here is a mad man, I tell thee. I have a wife, whom I love
        well,
        And if I would die for her—would I were in hell!   320
        Wilt thou do more for a man, than I would for a woman?
Pythias. Yea, that I will.
Groano. Then come on your ways, you must to prison in haste.
        I fear you will repent this folly at last.
Pythias. That shalt thou never see, but O music, as my Damon
        requested thee,   325
        Sound out thy doleful tunes, in this time of calamity.   *Exeunt.*

301.SD] *This ed.*   314. *Exit*] *Dods.*   326. *Exeunt*] EXIT Q.

301. *you will*] i.e. you would be willing to be.
in sport] as a game.
309. *wait ... prison*] Wealthy prisoners would normally have access to their servants and other creature comforts.
310. *walk*] travel (not necessarily on foot).
313. *Loath ... depart*] 'Loath to depart' is the title of a popular ballad tune dating
from the medieval period. The words are lost, but this phrase is commonly quoted in
plays and poems. Several late sixteenth-century musical arrangements survive, including one by John Dowland. The tune was presumably played as the 'mourning song' at
the ensuing scene break.
314. *plaints*] lamentations.
323–4.] This is a possible verbal echo of the proverb 'No haste to hang true men'
(Tilley H201); cf. *Jack Juggler*, l. 327, 'I feare hanging wher unto no man is hastie'.

[Scene 11]

> *Here the regals play a mourning song, and* DAMON *comes in,*
> *in mariner's apparel, and* STEPHANO *with him.*

Damon. Weep no more Stephano, this is but destiny.
    Had not this happed yet I know I am born to die,
    Where or in what place, the gods know alone,
    To whose judgement myself I commit, therefore leave of thy
      moan,
    And wait upon Pythias in prison till I return again,   5
    In whom my joy, my care and life does only remain.
Stephano. O my dear master, let me go with you, for my poor
      company
    Shall be some small comfort in this time of misery.
Damon. O Stephano, hast thou been so long with me
    And yet dost not know the force of true amity?   10
    I tell thee once again, my friend and I are but one—
    Wait upon Pythias, and think thou art with Damon.
    Whereof I may not now discourse, the time passes away,
    The sooner I am gone, the shorter shall be my journey.
    Therefore farewell Stephano, commend me to my friend Pythias,   15
    Whom I trust to deliver in time out of this woeful case.   [*Exit.*]
Stephano. Farewell my dear master, since your pleasure is so.
    O cruel hap, O poor Stephano,
    O cursed Carisophus that first moved this tragedy.
    But what a noise is this? [*To audience*] Is all well within, trow
      ye?   20
    I fear all be not well within. I will go see.
    [*Calling*] Come out you weasel, are you seeking eggs in Damon's
      chest?
    Come out I say, wilt thou be packing?—by cock, you were best.
Carisophus. [*Within*] How durst thou, villain, to lay hands on me?
Stephano. Out sir knave, or I will send ye.   25

16–49. SDs] *This ed.*

0.2. *mariner's apparel*] See pp. 34–5.
2–3. *know . . . know alone*] proverbial (Tilley N311), 'Nothing more certain than death and nothing more uncertain than the time of its coming'.
4. *leave . . . moan*] put lamentation aside. The standard modernisation would be 'leave off', but this would encourage a stress on 'off' rather than on 'leave' and 'moan'.
11. *friend . . . one*] Cf. 7.55n.
16. *case*] circumstance, predicament, plight.
22.SD] Stephano can remain visible while grappling with Carisophus off-stage.
weasel . . . eggs] This refers to the proverbial cheapness of eggs (i.e. there is nothing worth stealing in Damon's chest), and to the supposed sneaking and actual egg-thieving habits of weasels. Cf. also, 'he that will steal an egg will steal an ox' (Tilley E73).
chest] travel trunk.
23. *be packing*] clear off, leave.
25. *send*] eject with force.

[*Enter* CARISOPHUS *with some of Damon's possessions.*
JACK *follows.*]

Art thou not content to accuse Damon wrongfully,
But wilt thou rob him also, and that openly?
Carisophus. The King gave me the spoil to take mine own. Wilt thou
    let me?
Stephano. Thine own, villain? Where is thine authority?
Carisophus. I am authority of myself, dost thou not know?   30
Stephano. By'r lady, that is somewhat, but have you no more to
    show?
Carisophus. What if I have not?
Stephano. Then for an earnest penny, take this blow—[*Hits
    Carisophus.*]
    I shall bumbaste you, you mocking knave, I'll put '*pro*' in my
    purse for this time.
Carisophus. Jack, give me my sword and target.   35
Jack. I cannot come to you, master, this knave does me let. Hold,
    master.
Stephano. [*To Jack*] Away Jack-napes, else I will colpheg you by and
    by,
    [*To Carisophus*] You slave, I will have my pennyworths of thee
    therefore if I die.
    [*To Jack*] About villain.

---

28. *gave . . . own*] allowed me to confiscate Damon's property for my own use.
let] stop.
29. *authority*] right, authorisation.
30. *I . . . myself*] 'I am my own authority'.
31. *somewhat*] (*a*) a start, a minimum requirement, (*b*) mockingly interprets Carisophus's statement as 'author' (creator) of himself.
have . . . show] i.e. 'have you not got some kind of official warrant?'
33. *earnest penny*] instalment, down payment.
34. *bumbaste you*] thrash you soundly, possibly 'beat you on the bottom'.
pro] This is obscure, but it is possibly the Latin prefix meaning 'instead of' ('substitute', therefore here an 'I.O.U.') with a pun on *earnest* 'real', 'serious'. Since money-bags are often used as emblems of memory by classical authors (cf. 'male', 13.94n), there is also a sense of 'image' or 'memento' (cf. l. 51 below). Hence the whole speech signifies, 'I'll put in my purse the "pro" (image, reminder, I.O.U.) for the pennyworth (revenge, l. 38) that I mean to extract from you, and give you an "earnest penny" (a real blow as a first instalment)'. With likely reference to the proverbial sayings, 'Put money in your purse', and 'A friend in court is better than a penny in purse'. Images of payment, part payment and debt are repeated extensively in the play (cf. Pythias as Damon's 'pledge' or 'pawn', 10.254, 266, 273, 311).
35. *target*] light, round shield.
36. *me let*] stop me.
37. *Jack-napes*] Someone who is full of tricks like a monkey.
colpheg] a corruption of 'colaphise', buffet.
38. *have my pennyworths*] have my revenge.
therefore] The word is used to make an emphatic conclusion to a statement (*OED* B).
if I die] Cf. 'if I swing for it'.

Carisophus. [To *audience*] O citizens, help to defend me.   40
Stephano. Nay, they will rather help to hang thee.
Carisophus. Good fellow, let us reason this matter quietly, beat me
    no more.
Stephano. Of this condition: I will stay if thou swear as thou art an
    honest man
    Thou wilt say nothing to the King of this when I am gone.
Carisophus. I will say nothing—here is my hand, as I am an honest
    man.   45
Stephano. Then say on thy mind. [To *audience*] I have taken a wise
    oath on him have I not, trow ye?
    To trust such a false knave upon his honesty?
    As he is an honest man, quoth you, he may bewray all to the
      King,
    And break his oath for this never a whit. [To *Carisophus*] But
    my franion, I tell you this one thing,
    If you disclose this, I will devise such a way   50
    That whilst thou livest thou shalt remember this day.
Carisophus. You need not devise for that, for this day is printed in
    my memory,
    I warrant you I shall remember this beating till I die.
    But seeing of courtesy you have granted that we should talk
    quietly,
    Methinks, in calling me knave, you do me much injury.   55
Stephano. Why so, I pray thee heartily?
Carisophus. Because I am the King's man. Keeps the King any
    knaves?
Stephano. He should not, but what he does it is evident by thee.
    And as far as I can learn or understand,
    There is none better able to keep knaves in all the land.   60
Carisophus. O sir, I am a courtier. When courtiers shall hear tell
    How you have used me, they will not take it well.
Stephano. Nay, all right courtiers will ken me thank, and wot you
    why?
    Because I handled a counterfeit courtier in his kind so finely.
    What sir, all are not courtiers that have a counterfeit show—   65
    In a troop of honest men, some knaves may stand you know,
    Such as by stealth creep in under the colour of honesty,
    Which sort, under that cloak, do all kind of villainy.

---

43. *stay*] stop.
46. *say . . . mind*] speak freely.
48. *bewray*] expose.
49. *franion*] reckless fellow.
52. *devise*] (*a*) plan, design, (*b*) draw (thus punning on *printed*).
63. *ken me thank*] express thanks to me.
wot] know.
64. *in his kind*] in his own manner, appropriately.
66. *stand*] (*a*) be set, exist, (*b*) possibly 'stand for', appear to be, (*c*) with pun on
'creep in' (l. 67).

A right courtier is virtuous, gentle and full of urbanity,
Hurting no man, good to all, devoid of all villainy,   70
But such as thou, art fountains of scurrility and vain delights,
Though you hang by the courts, you are but flatt'ring parasites
As well deserving the right name of courtesy,
As the coward knight, the true praise of chivalry.
I could say more, but I will not for that I am your well willer—   75
In faith Carisophus, you are no courtier but a caterpillar,
A sycophant, a parasite, a flatterer and a knave.
Whether I will or no, these names you must have.
How well you deserve this, by your deeds it is known,
For that so unjustly thou hast accused poor Damon,   80
Whose woeful case the gods help alone.

Carisophus. Sir, are you his servant that you pity his case so?
Stephano. No, bum troth, goodman Grumb, his name is Stephano.
    I am called Onaphets, if needs you will know.
    [*To audience*] The knave begins to sift me, but I turn my name
       in and out,   85
    Cretiso cum Cretense, to make him a lout.
Carisophus. What mumble you with yourself, Master Onaphets?
Stephano. I am reckoning with myself how I may pay my debts.
Carisophus. You have paid me more than you did owe me—
Stephano. Nay, upon a further reckoning, I will pay you more if I
      know   90
    Either you talk of that is done, or by your sycophantical envy
    You prick forth Dionysius the sooner that Damon may die.
    I will so pay thee that thy bones shall rattle in thy skin.
    Remember what I have said, Onaphets is my name.   *Exit.*
Carisophus. The sturdy knave is gone, the devil him take,   95

---

79. deserve] Q2; deserne Q.   85.SD] *This ed.; Aside. Dods.*   89. owe me—] *This ed.;* owe me. Q; owe *conj. Brown, Wilson.*

---

69. *gentle*] well born and well behaved.

72. *hang . . . courts*] 'are hangers-on at court', punning on the proverbial phrase, 'hang by the wall'. Clothes hung up out of use are subject to attack by moth (cf. *caterpillar* l. 76), suggesting that Carisophus is not even the image of a courtier but the moth that attacks a courtier's cast-off clothes; cf. 10.215, and 14.52.

83. *bum troth*] by my troth.

Grumb] groom, fellow (here used contemptuously).

84. *Onaphets*] In this backward spelling 'ph' is considered as the single Greek letter phi. Cf. 12.8–13n.

86. Cretiso] (non-classical Lat. from Gk *Kretize*), 'I play the Cretan'.

cum Cretense] (Lat.) 'with a Cretan'. Idomeneus, leader of the Cretan troops at the siege of Troy was once asked by Thetis and Medea to adjudicate a beauty contest between them. He chose Thetis. Medea cursed his entire race, condemning them never to tell the truth, saying 'All Cretans are liars'.

89. *owe me*—] Brown and Wilson's suggested emendation was for the sake of the rhyme. The lack of rhyme, however, combined with Stephano's 'Nay', suggests that he interrupts before Carisophus finishes speaking.

91. *that is done*] what has happened.

92. *prick . . . die*] provoke Dionysius to advance the date of Damon's execution.

95. *sturdy*] violent, rough, surly.

He has made my head, shoulders, arms, sides and all to ache.
Thou whoreson villain boy, why didst thou wait no better?
As he paid me, so will I not die thy debtor.   [*Starts to beat Jack.*]
Jack. Master, why do you fight with me? I am not your match you
  see—
 You durst not fight with him that is gone, and will you wreak
  your anger on me?   100
Carisophus. Thou villain, by thee I have lost mine honour,
 Beaten with a cudgel like a slave, a vagabond or a lazy lubber,
 And not given one blow again. Hast thou handled me well?
Jack. Master, I handled you not, but who did handle you very
  handsomely, you can tell.
Carisophus. Handsomely, thou crack-rope?   105
Jack. Yea sir, very handsomely, I hold you a groat
 He handled you so handsomely that he left not one mote in your
  coat.
Carisophus. O I had firked him trimly, thou villain, if thou hadst
 given me my sword.
Jack. It is better as it is, master, believe me at a word.
 If he had seen your weapon, he would have been fiercer   110
 And so perhaps beat you worse, I speak it with my heart—
 You were never yet at the dealing of fence blows but you had
  four away for your part.
 It is but your luck—you are man good enough,
 But the Welsh Onaphets was a vengeance knave and rough.
 Master, you were best go home and rest in your bed,   115
 Methinks your cap waxes too little for your head.
Carisophus. What, does my head swell?
Jack. Yea, as big as a cod's-head, and bleeds too.
Carisophus. I am ashamed to show my face with this hue.
Jack. No shame at all—men have been beaten far better than you.   120

98.SD] *This ed.; Strikes him. Hazlitt.*

---

 97. *wait*] attend me, serve.
 103. *again*] in return.
 105. *crack-rope*] rogue fit for the gallows.
 106. *hold*] bet, wager.
 107. *handled . . . coat*] Cf. 'to dust one's coat', a proverbial expression for a beating
(cf. 6.19); also 'to reduce to dust'; 'mote' = speck of dust.
 108. *firked*] beaten, thrashed.
 109. *at a word*] in short.
 110. *weapon*] with *double entendre* on 'penis', playing on the sexual immaturity of
the boy actor.
 112. *fence*] i.e. fencing, swordplay.
 four . . . part] overcome by a factor of four to one.
 114. *Welsh*] Jack adopts a common stereotype of the period and assumes that
'Onaphets's' outlandish name and wild behaviour must mean that he is Welsh.
 vengeance] extreme, violent.
 118. *cod's-head*] (*a*) lit. the large head of a codfish, (*b*) fig. a fool, (*c*) sexual *double
entendre* (*cod* = scrotum) collocating with *handled, weapon, bed.*
 120. *men . . . you*] much better men than you have been beaten.

Carisophus. I must go to the surgeon's. What shall I say when I am
    a-dressing?
Jack. You may say truly, you met with a knave's blessing.   *Exeunt.*

[Scene 12]

                Enter ARISTIPPUS.

Aristippus. By mine own experience, I prove true that many men tell:
    To live in court not beloved—better be in hell.
    What crying out, what cursing is there within of Carisophus
    Because he accused Damon to King Dionysius!
    Even now, he came whining and crying into the court for the
        nonce   5
    Showing that one Onaphets had broke his knave's sconce,
    Which strange name when they heard, every man laughed
        heartily,
    And I by myself scanned his name secretly,
    For well I knew it was some madheaded child
    That invented this name, that the logheaded knave might be
        beguiled.   10
    In tossing it often with myself to and fro,
    I found out that Onaphets backward, spelled Stephano.
    I smiled in my sleeve how to see by turning his name he dressed
        him,
    And how for Damon his master's sake, with a wooden cudgel he
        blessed him.
    None pitied the knave, no man nor woman, but all laughed him
        to scorn.   15
    To be thus hated of all—better unborn.
    Far better Aristippus has provided I trow,
    For in all the court I am beloved both of high and low.
    I offend none, in so much that women sing this to my great
        praise:

---

   122. *knave's blessing*] i.e. beating.

   2. *live . . . hell*] Cf. 7.32; 10.320.
   5. *for the nonce*] specifically, for the purpose of.
   6. *sconce*] head.
   8–13.] The fact that Aristippus is so proud of decoding something that the audience
already knows about indicates the presence of a further joke. Onaphets seems to be a
Greek pun from *onos* ('ass') and *aphettos* (freely, set loose, rambling, also used of a
freed slave)—hence 'free-wheeling ass'. It suggests that Stephano kicks Carisophus as
well as beating him in the previous scene, and that Aristippus is an ass for not recog-
nising the pun.
   9. *child*] Cf. 3.17n.
   13. *smiled . . . sleeve*] smiled secretly; proverbial (Tilley S535).
   dressed] prepared, manipulated.
   16. *better unborn*] Cf. proverb, 'better unborn than untaught', sometimes rendered
as 'better unborn than unbred' (Tilley U1).
   17. *provided*] served, filled the role (of court philosopher).

[*Sings.*] '*Omnis Aristippum decuit color, et locus et res*'.   20
But in all this jollity, one thing 'mazes me,
The strangest thing that ever was heard or known
Is now happened in this court by that Damon
Whom Carisophus accused: Damon is now at liberty,
For whose return Pythias his friend lies in prison, alas in great
    jeopardy.   25
Tomorrow is the day, which day by noon if Damon return not,
    earnestly
The King has sworn that Pythias should die,
Whereof Pythias has intelligence very secretly,
Wishing that Damon may not return till he have paid
His life for his friend. Has it been heretofore ever said   30
That any man for his friend would die so willingly?
O noble friendship, O perfect amity,
Thy force is here seen, and that very perfectly.
The King himself muses hereat, yet is he far out of square
That he trusts none to come near him—not his own daughters
    will he have   35
Unsearched to enter his chamber, which he has made barbers, his
    beard to shave.
Not with knife or razor—for all edge tools he fears—
But with hot burning nutshells, they singe off his hairs.
Was there ever man that lived in such misery?
Well, I will go in with a heavy and pensive heart too,   40
To think how Pythias this poor gentleman tomorrow shall die.
                                    Exit.

---

20. *Sings.*] *This ed.*

---

20. Omnis . . . res] 'Every colour, place and thing suited Aristippus' (Horace, *Epistles*, 1.17.23, which reads '*et status* [manners, dress] *et res*'), i.e. he did not allow anything to prevent his pursuit of sensual pleasure; cf. John Northbrooke, *A Treatise wherein Dicing Daunsing, Vaine Plays or Enterluds . . . Are Reproved* (1577), 'Aristippus daunced in purple [a woman's robe] and being reproved, he made an excuse, that he was made never a whit the worse by that dauncing : but might in that softnesse kepe still his philosophicall minde chast' (R2v); the story is originally in Diogenes Laertius, 2.77.

21. '*mazes*] amazes.

26. *earnestly*] (*a*) in all seriousness, (*b*) recalling Pythias's function as an earnest or pledge for Damon (cf. 11.34n.).

27–30.] i.e. Pythias has somehow learnt that Dionysius has swom to have him executed. He hopes that he will be able to give up his life for his friend before Damon returns.

34. *out of square*] out of balance, disordered, suspicious.

36. *which*] i.e. the daughters. This slightly confusing usage is standard in this play. Hazlitt, perhaps also for decorum's sake, amended to 'while'.

38. *hot . . . hairs*] This story is commonplace, occurring in Cicero, *Tusc.*, 5.20.58, *De officiis*, 2.7.25 and (minus the daughters) in Plutarch's 'Life of Dion' (vol. 6, 135).

[Scene 13]

Enter JACK and WILL.

Jack. Will, by my honesty, I will mar your monk's face if you so
    fondly prate.

Will. Jack, by my troth, seeing you are without the court gate,
    If you play Jack-napes in mocking my master and despising my
      face,
    Even here with a pantacle I will you disgrace.
    And though you have a far better face than I,   5
    Yet who is better man of us two, these fists shall try,
    Unless you leave your taunting.

Jack. Thou began'st first. Didst thou not say even now
    That Carisophus my master was no man but a cow
    In taking so many blows and gave never a blow again?   10

Will. I said so indeed. He is but a tame ruffian
    That can swear by his flask and touch-box and God's precious
      potstick,
    And yet he will be beaten with a faggot stick.
    These barking whelps were never good biters,
    Nor yet great crackers were ever great fighters.   15
    But seeing you egg me so much, I will somewhat more recite:
    I say Carisophus thy master is a flatt'ring parasite,

---

1. monk's] *This ed.;* monckes *Q;* monkey's *Hazlitt.*   4. pantacle] *Q;* faire pantacle
Q2.   12. potstick] *This ed.;* lady *Q.*

---

  1. *monk's*] i.e. 'holier than thou', sanctimonious; perhaps 'dishonest'. Hazlitt
amended to read 'monkey's', but the collocation with the word 'prate' (speak dishon-
estly) supports an anti-Catholic joke.

  2. *without*] outside.

  court gate] This was the name of the gate at Whitehall palace which opened on to
the court around which the Great Hall, kitchens and other domestic offices were situated.

  3. *play Jack-napes*] play the knave.

  4. *pantacle*] pantofle, variously a slipper, overshoe or exotic footwear; cf. Gosson,
School of Abuse, 1579 (OED), 'The litle crackhalter that carrieth his maisters pan-
touffles'. Will threatens Jack by wielding a shoe as a weapon (probably taking off one
of his own).

  9. *cow*] i.e. coward, but also 'dumb beast'.

  12. *flask*] gunpowder flask.

  touch-box] box for touch-powder (fine gunpowder for priming a musket).

  potstick] stick for stirring a pot. This oath is also used in *Jack Juggler*, 148, where
Axton suggests a possible pun on 'Lat. *posticus*: posterior'. The *Q* reading 'precious
lady' (the Virgin Mary), is much less coarse, disrupts the rhyme, makes less connection
with 'faggot stick' and thus suggests censorship.

  13. *faggot stick*] small stick from a bundle of brushwood.

  14-15. *barking . . . fighters*] proverbial (Tilley B85, B86, B591): 'Great braggers
commonly be least fyghters, and most cowardes even as the mooste barkying dogges
be for the most parte lest biters', Richard Taverner, *Proverbs* (1552), 66v.

  15. *crackers*] boasters.

Gleaning away the sweet from the worthy in all the court.
What tragedy has he moved of late! The devil take him, he does
  much hurt.
Jack. I pray you, what is Aristippus thy master? Is not he a parasite
  too,   20
That with scoffing and jesting in the court makes so much ado?
Will. He is no parasite, but a pleasant gentleman, full of courtesy.
Thy master is a churlish lout, the heir of a dung fork, as void of
  honesty
As thou art of honour.
Jack. Nay, if you will needs be prating of my master still,   25
In faith, I must cool you, my friend dapper Will.
Take this at the beginning.   [*Strikes him.*]
Will. Praise well your winning—my pantacle is as ready as yours.
Jack. By the mass, I will box you.
Will. By cock, I will fox you.   30
Jack. Will, was I with you?
Will. Jack, did I fly?
Jack. Alas pretty cock'rel, you are too weak.
Will. In faith doting dottrel, you will cry creak.

                      Enter SNAP.

Snap. Away you crack-ropes, are you fighting at the court gate?   35
An I take you here again, I will swinge you both—what?   *Exit.*
Jack. I beshrew Snap the tipstaff, that great knave's heart that hither
  did come.

27.SD] *Hazlitt.*   33. cock'rel] *This ed.;* cockerell *Q.*   34. doting dottrel] *Hazlitt;*
Dutting Duttell *Q;* Dutting Duttrell *Q2.*   36. An] *This ed.;* And *Q.*

---

   18. *Gleaning away*] carrying away, i.e. screwing favours ('sweets') out of more
worthy courtiers, or depriving more worthy courtiers of preferment.
   23. *heir . . . fork*] (*a*) someone born to use a dung fork, (*b*) the dung itself, (*c*) recalling the Latin quotation at 8.38 to suggest that both those qualities are completely
engrained in him.
   26. *dapper*] pretty, little and lively.
   28. *Praise . . . winning*] i.e. 'don't boast until you've won'. Cf. proverbs, 'He laughs
that wins' and 'He plays best that wins' (Tilley L93, P404). Jack either takes off his
own shoe or snatches Will's.
   29. *box*] thrash.
   33. *cock'rel*] young cock, sexually immature and therefore 'weak'. The pronunciation needs to be disyllabic to rhyme with dottrel, l. 34.
   34. *doting dottrel*] stupid fool. A dottrel or dotterel is a 'species of plover so called
from the apparent simplicity with which it allows itself to be approached and taken'
(*OED*); with play on 'cock'rel', both aurally and in the contrast between 'youth' and
'dotage', senility, second childhood.
   cry creak] 'give in', possibly playing on 'creaking' old age.
   36. *An*] If.
   swinge] thrash.
   37. *beshrew*] curse.
   great . . . heart] i.e. with the sense that Snap is the very essence of a knave or that
he is a boon companion with knaves.

Had he not been, you had cried ere this *victus, victa, victum*.
But seeing we have breathed ourselves, if you list
Let us agree like friends, and shake each other by the fist.   40
Will. Content am I, for I am not malicious, but on this condition:
    That you talk no more so broad of my master as here you have
    done.
    But who have we here? Is *Colax epi* coming yonder?
Jack. Will, let us slip aside and view him well.

Enter GRIM *the collier whistling [carrying a sack of charcoal on his*
    shoulder. He speaks with a regional accent].

Grim. What devil! I ween the porters are drunk. Will they not dup
    the gate today?   45
    [*Calling aloud*] Take in coals for the King's own mouth. Will
    nobody stir, I say?—
    I might have lain two hours longer in my bed.
    I've tarried so long here, that my teeth chatter in my head.
Jack. [*To Will*] Will, after our falling out, wilt thou laugh merrily?
Will. Ay marry Jack, I pray thee heartily.   50
Jack. Then follow me, and hem in a word now and then.
    [*Aloud*] What brawling knave is there at the court gate so early?
Will. It is some brainsick villain, I durst lay a penny.
Jack. It was you sir, that cried so loud, I trow,
    And bid us take in coals for the King's mouth, even now?   55
Grim. 'Twas I indeed.
Jack. Why sir, how dare you speak such petty treason?
    Does the King eat coles at any season?

---

43. Colax epi] *This ed.; Cobex epi Q;* coals I spy *Hazlitt.*   44.1–2. *carrying…
accent] This ed.*   46–100. SDs] *This ed.*

---

38. victus … victum] conquered (the Lat. past participle in its masculine, feminine
and neuter forms) i.e. 'I've been conquered completely', parodying Caesar's statement,
Veni, vidi, vici, 'I came, I saw, I conquered'.

39. *breathed ourselves*] had some exercise: both (*a*) got out of breath, and (*b*) got
our breaths back.

42. *broad*] rudely.

43. Colax epi] This is a combination of Gk (*epi* = on top of) and classicised English,
i.e. 'coals on top', referring to the sack on Grim's shoulder. It also puns on *Colax* (Gk
and Lat. flatterer or sycophant), i.e. 'arch flatterer'. Cf. p. 49.

44.1. *collier*] charcoal dealer. The devil was commonly referred to as a collier
because of his blackened appearance (cf. *Twelfth Night,* 3.3.112). For Grim's use of
language see p. 98.

45. *ween*] think.
dup] open.

46. *King's … mouth*] pertaining to the provision of food for the King.

48. *chatter*] i.e. presumably with cold and tiredness from being up so early.

49. *falling out*] Cf. the proverbial refrain to the poem 'In going to my naked bed':
'the falling out of faithful friends, is the renewing of love' (*PDD,* 9, p. 208).

51. *hem in*] throw in (lit. cough in).

58. *coles*] cabbages, cheap proletarian food. Pythagoras extolled the virtue of eating
cabbage.

Grim. Here is a gay world!—boys now sets old men to school.
    I said well enough. What Jack-sauce, think'st I'm a fool?   60
    At bake-house, buttery-hatch, kitchen and cellar,
    Do they not say 'for the King's mouth'?
Will. What then, goodman collier?
Grim. What then? Seeing without coals they cannot finely dress the
    King's meat,
    May I not say, 'take in coals for the King's mouth', though coals
    he do not eat?   65
Jack. In the name of Christ, came ever from a collier an answer so
    trim?
    You are learnèd, are you not, Father Grim?
Grim. Grim is my name indeed. I'm not learnèd, and yet the King's
    collier.
    This forty winter I've been to the King a servitor,
    Though I be not learnèd, yet I've mother-wit enough whole and
    some.   70
Will. So it seems—you have so much mother wit, that you lack your
    father's wisdom.
Grim. 'Mass, I'm well be-set. Here's a trim cast of merlins.
    What be you, my pretty cockerels, that ask me these questions?
Jack. Good faith, master Grim, if such merlins on your pouch may
    light,
    They are so quick of wing that quickly they can carry it out of
    your sight.   75
    [*Aside*] And though we are cockerels now, we shall have spurs
    one day
    And shall be able perhaps to make you a capon.

---

66. In . . . Christ] *This ed.;* James Christe *Q.*   72. beset. Here's] be set: heres is *Q;*
be set, heeres *Q2.*

---

61. *buttery-hatch*] the half-door which acted as a serving counter for provisions
from the buttery (storeroom for liquor).
    64. *dress*] prepare.
    68. *King's collier*] with aural pun on 'King's scholar'. Chapel children often became
King's (or Queen's) scholars at Oxford or Cambridge. It is possible that Grim was
played by one of the Gentlemen of the Chapel, perhaps Edwards himself; see pp. 87–8.
    69. *forty*] This is a conventional round number, although Edwards would also have
been about forty at the time.
    70. *whole and some*] altogether, in every particular.
    72. *'Mass*] by the mass.
    be-set] surrounded.
    cast] hawking term for the number of hawks cast up to fly at once.
    merlins] smallest but boldest of European birds of prey. The 'Jack' (male) bird has
striking plumage. Corrected *Q* 'murleons' perhaps rhymes with 'questions', l. 73.
    73. *cockerels*] young cocks, i.e. sexually immature.
    76. *spurs*] sharp projections on the backs of the legs, used by the mature cock for
fighting.
    77. *capon*] castrated cock. The lack of rhyme is probably to mark the lines as an
aside, but it caused Hazlitt to suppose that something was missing and he added 'to
your pay' after 'capon'.

[*To Grim*] But to tell you truth, we are the porters' men, which
    early and late,
Wait on such gentlemen as you, to open the court gate.
Grim. Are you servants then?   80
Will. Yea sir, are we not pretty men?
Grim. 'Pretty men', quoth you? Nay, you are strong men else you
    could not bear these breeches.
Will. Are these great hose? In faith goodman collier, you see with
    your nose.
By mine honesty, I have but for one lining in one hose, but seven
    ells of rug.
Grim. That is but a little! yet it makes thee seem a great bug.   85
Jack. How say you goodman collier, can you find any fault here?
Grim. Nay, you should find fault—marry here's trim gear!
    Alas little knave, dost not sweat?—thou goest with great pain,
    These are no hose, but water-budgets, I tell thee plain,
    Good for none but such as have no buttocks.   90
    Did you ever see two such little robin ruddocks
    So laden with breeches? I'll say no more, lest I offend.
    Who invented these monsters first, did it to a ghostly end
    To have a male ready to put in other folks' stuff.

---

83. great] *Q*; such great *Q2*.   93. monsters] *Q*; hose at *Q2*.

80. *servants*] with possible pun, unintended by Grim, on 'service', (*a*) sexual performance, (*b*) impregnation.
    81. *pretty*] (*a*) proper, (*b*) skilful, artful, (*c*) implying 'well made up (as men)'.
    83. *great hose*] very long baggy breeches fashionable in the 1560s, reaching well
below the knee, often lined and slashed and using yards of material. The suggestive-
ness of the collocation here—i.e. 'nose' (l. 83), 'buttocks' (l. 90) and 'male' (l. 94, see
note)—allows an aural (and sodomitic) pun on 'holes' (anuses) since a hose is also the
socket on any tool into which a wooden handle can be inserted.
    see . . . nose] (*a*) look into things that don't concern you, (*b*) nose out faults, (*c*) a
joke about body smells.
    84. *seven ells*] more than eight metres, an excessive amount even for adult-sized
breeches, see pp. 23–4, 32–3.
    rug] coarse woollen cloth.
    85. *but a little*] Grim is being sarcastic.
    bug] (*a*) evil spirit, object of terror to frighten children, (*b*) possibly 'person of
assumed importance' (*OED*, *sb*.1b, although the references are much later).
    86. *find . . . fault*] referring to anti-theatrical propaganda on the sins of dressing up.
    88. *pain*] difficulty.
    89. *hose*] here playing on 'hose-pipe'.
    water-budgets] pair of leather pouches, slung on a yoke or across a horse's back for
carrying water.
    90. *buttocks*] with pun on 'prostitutes' (*OED*, *sb*.5, although the earliest instance
of this usage given is 1673), and loose, aural pun on 'budgets'.
    91. *robin ruddocks*] robin redbreasts, (*a*) i.e. 'little innocents', (*b*) with the sense of
a boy's reddened buttocks after he has been 'breeched' (beaten); cf. John Pikeryng,
Horestes (1567), C4v, 'Wyth ruddockes red. Be at a becke. / Beware the arse, breake
not thy necke.'
    93. *ghostly*] spiritual.
    94. *male . . . stuff*] This comments ironically on the anti-theatrical attacks frequently
made by Protestant divines on boy actors as objects of homosexual desire; *male* = com-

We see this evident by daily proof—   95
One preached of late not far hence, in no pulpit but in a wain
    cart,
That spoke enough of this, but for my part
I'll say no more. Your own necessity
In the end will force you to find some remedy.
Jack. [*To Will*] Will, hold this railing knave with a talk when I am
    gone—   100
  I will fetch him his filling ale for his good sermon.   [*Exit.*]
Will. Go thy way.—Father Grim, gaily well you do say.
  It is but young men's folly that list to play
  And mask awhile in the net of their own device.
  When they come to your age, they will be wise.   105
Grim. Bum troth, but few such roisters come to my years at this day,
  They be cut off betimes, ere they have gone half their journey.
  I will not tell why, let them guess that can—I mean somewhat
    thereby.

       Enter JACK *with a pot of wine and a cup to drink on.*

Jack. Father Grim, because you are stirring so early,
  I have brought you a bowl of wine to make you merry.   110
Grim. Wine? Marry, that is welcome to colliers, I'll swap't off by
    and by,

---

96. a wain] *Q2;* Waayne *Q.*   100. Will] *Dods.;* well *Q.*   101.SD] *Hazlitt.*

partmentalised travelling bag or strong-box, used figuratively to denote a compendium
of stories or ideas, probably punning on (*a*) 'mail', eyelet hole for lacing clothes, hence
'hole' (anus), (*b*) Lat. *male*, evil; *stuff* = (*a*) belongings, (*b*) material, (*c*) rubbish, nonsense, (*d*) pun on the action of fornication. Hence the boys are the sink and repository
of other people's filthy thoughts—even if not their deeds. 'Stuff' pronounced with a
long vowel sound, common in English regional accents, virtually rhymes with 'proof'.
  96. *One . . . cart*] i.e. a 'hedge priest' or itinerant nonconformist preacher, likely to
disapprove of the wickedness of playacting. It may, however, be a more specific reference. Bishop Ally preached a famous sermon at court (April 1560) against all forms of
licentiousness, playing and drunkenness (Nichols, 83). At Whitehall palace, a yard near
the court gate (cf. 13.2n) was known as the 'preaching place'. Cf. l.101, n.
  98–9. *Your . . . remedy*] Grim jests that although the appearance of the children will
furnish others with material for moral sermons, their own discomfort is likely to force
them to change their breeches for less excessive garments.
  101. *his . . . sermon*] (*a*) Jack jokes that Grim must be habitually filled with drink
to sound off in this way; (*b*) possibly a satirical reference to 'church ales' (saints' day
celebrations in which ale was sold in aid of church funds), regarded as the cause of
licentiousness by church reformers; (*c*) possible aural pun on ale/Ally.
  104. *mask*] disguise themselves.
  net . . . device] i.e. see-through invention of their own; proverbial, 'dance in a net
and think nobody sees' (Tilley N130).
  106. *come . . . years*] live to be as old as I.
  107. *be . . . betimes*] die early.
  108. *guess . . . thereby*] Grim is pruriently alluding to sexually transmitted and
alcohol-induced diseases.
  108.1. *on*] i.e. from.
  111. *swap't off*] drink it up quickly.

I was stirring so early that my very soul is dry.   [*Drinks.*]
Jack. This is stoutly done. Will you have it warmed, father Grim?
Grim. No, it is warm enough. It is very luscious and trim—
    'Tis muscadine I ween—of fellowship, let me have another spurt,   115
    I can drink as easily now as if I sat in my shirt.
Jack. By cock and you shall have it, but I will begin and that anon,
    Je bois à vous mon compagnon.
Grim. Jhar vow pledge, petty zawne.
Jack. Can you speak French? Here is a trim collier by this day!   120
Grim. What man? I learned this when I was a soldier,
    When I was a lusty fellow, and could yerk a whip trimly,
    Better than these boy colliers that come to the court daily—
    When there were not so many captious fellows as now
    That would toruppe men for every trifle, I wot not how,   125
    As there was one Damon not long since taken for a spy,
    How justly I know not, but he was condemned to die.
Will. [*To Jack*] This wine has warmed him, this comes well to pass,
    We shall know all now, for *in vino veritas.*
    [*To Grim*] Father Grim, who accused this Damon to King
      Dionysius?   130
Grim. A vengeance take him, 'twas a gentleman, one master
    Crowsphus.
Will. Crowsphus? You clip the King's language, you would have said
    'Carisophus',

112.SD] *This ed.*   115. muscadine] Musselden *Q.*   118. *Je ... compagnon*] *Stevens;* Jebit avow mon companion *Q;* Iebit avou mon companyon *Q2.*   128. *To Jack*] *This ed; Aside Hazlitt.*

---

113. *stoutly*] bravely, manfully. The word is commonly applied to drinking capacity.
    warmed] Wine and ale were often drunk warmed.
    115. *muscadine*] red or white wine made from muscatel grapes. *Q* may indicate mispronunciation by Grim.
    ween] suppose, believe.
    spurt] i.e. quick drink.
    116. *in my shirt*] perfectly relaxed, at ease.
    117. *I ... anon*] 'I'll have one now too'.
    118–19.] It is difficult to distinguish here between printing errors in *Q* and intentional attempts to render different levels of inaccurate French, but *Q* suggests, realistically, that Jack is at least attempting French whereas Grim is speaking bastard English.
    Je ... compagnon] = 'I drink to you my companion'.
    Jhar ... zawne] i.e. 'I pledge you, little zany' (zany = *commedia dell'arte* character, a servant or assistant who plays the fool and imitates his superiors).
    121–7.] This rambling sentence progresses by association and shows Will that Grim is indeed getting drunk.
    121. *soldier*] Grim is presented as the figure of *Miles Gloriosus*, the braggart soldier, a stock character in Greek and Roman comedy and the title of a play by Plautus.
    122. *lusty*] vigorous, strong, courageous.
    yerk] strike (with a whip), crack.
    124. *captious*] quarrelsome.
    125. *toruppe*] probably a drunken rendition of 'trip', catch out, blame.
    129. in ... veritas] 'wine brings out the truth'.
    132. *clip*] (*a*) mispronounce, (*b*) mutilate, cut short.

But I perceive now, either the wind is at the south,
Or else your tongue cleaves to the roof of your mouth.
Grim. A murrain take thik wine, it so intoxicate my brain,   135
   That to be hanged by and by, I cannot speak plain.
Jack. [*Aside*] You speak knavishly plain, seeing my master you do
      mock.
   In faith, ere you go I will make you a lobcock.
   [*To Grim*] Father Grim, what say they of this Damon abroad?
Grim. All men are sorry for him, so help me God,   140
   They say a false knave 'cused him to the King wrongfully,
   And he is gone, and should be here tomorrow to die,
   Or else his fellow which is in prison, his room shall supply—
   I'll not be his half for forty shillings, I tell you plain,
   I think Damon be too wise to return again.   145
Will. Will no man speak for them in this woeful case?
Grim. No, I'll warrant you. One master Stippus is in place
   Where he may do good, but he frames himself so
   Whatsoever Dionysius wills to, that he will not say no.
   'Tis a subtle fox, he will not tread on thorns for none,   150
   A merry hare-cop 'tis and a pleasant companion,
   A right courtier, and can provide for one.
Jack. [*To Will*] Will, how like you this gear? Your master Aristippus
      also
   At this collier's hand has had a blow.
   [*To Grim*] But in faith Father Grim, cannot you colliers   155
   Provide for yourselves far better than courtiers?
Grim. Yes I trow, black colliers go in threadbare coats,
   Yet so provide they that they have the fair white groats.

137.SD] *Hazlitt.*

---

133. *wind . . . south*] A south wind was regarded as beneficent (cf. proverb, 'When the wind is in the south it blows the bait into the fish's mouth', Tilley W443), i.e. Will can see the plot is working.

135. *murrain*] plague.

thik] This is a dialect form of 'this' but here also suggests a hiccup.

136.] i.e. he is so drunk that to save his life he could not speak without slurring his words.

138. *lobcock*] country bumpkin.

143. *his . . . supply*] shall take his place.

144. *half*] agent, representative (here, 'substitute').

150. *not . . . none*] This is a combination of the proverbs 'to tread upon thorns' (implying both haste and anxiety) and 'I will not pull the thorn out of your foot and put it into my own' (Tilley T239, T231).

151. *hare-cop*] probably 'giddy head, hare-brained', but it is a nonce word and also suggests a drunken hiccup.

152. *provide . . . one*] look after himself (cf. 1.30n).

153. *gear*] matter, stuff, goings on.

158. *provide*] (a) provide supplies for others for profit, (b) make provision for themselves with care and foresight.

white] silver.

groats] very small silver coins with face value of four pennies, thus archetypally signifying a very small sum of money.

I may say in counsel, though all day I moil in dirt,
I'll not change lives with any in Dionysius' court,   160
For though their apparel be never so fine,
Yet sure their credit is far worse than mine,
And by cock I may say, for all their high looks,
I know some sticks full deep in merchants' books,
And deeper will fall in, as fame me tells,   165
As long as instead of money they take up hawks' hoods and
    bells,
Whereby they fall into a swelling disease which colliers do not
    know,
'T'has a mad name, it is called I ween, *centum pro cento*.
Some other in courts make others laugh merrily,
When they wail and lament their own estate secretly.   170
Friendship is dead in court, hypocrisy does reign,
Who is in favour now, tomorrow is out again.
The state is so uncertain that I by my will,
Will never be courtier, but a collier still.
Will. It seems that colliers have a very trim life.   175
Grim. Colliers get money still. Tell me of truth,
    Is not that a trim life now as the world goeth?
    All day, though I toil with main and might,
    With money in my pouch, I come home merry at night,
    And sit down in my chair by my wife, fair Alison,   180
    And turn a crab in the fire, as merry as Pope Joan.
Jack. That Pope was a merry fellow of whom folk talk so much.
Grim. Had to be merry withal—had gold enough in his hutch.
Jack. Can gold make men merry? They say, 'who can sing so merry a
    note
    As he that is not able to change a groat?'   185
Grim. Who sings in that case, sings never in tune, I know for my
    part
    That a heavy pouch with gold makes a light heart,

---

175. very] *Q*; merie *Q2*.   181. Pope Joan] *This ed.*; Pope John *Q*.

---

159. *in counsel*] in confidence.
moil] (*a*) defile myself, make myself dirty, (*b*) toil.
164. *sticks . . . books*] i.e. are overwhelmingly in debt to tradesmen.
165. *fame*] (*a*) rumour, (*b*) their reputation.
166. *hawks' . . . bells*] i.e. expensive and frivolous pastimes.
168. *'T'has*] It has.
centum . . . cento] cent per cent, i.e. 100 per cent interest.
178. *main and might*] proverbial, i.e. 'all my strength'.
181. *turn . . . fire*] roast a crab-apple. This would then be added to hot, spiced drink.
Pope Joan] the legendary Pope whose female identity was discovered when she gave
birth. She is proverbially 'merry'.
183. *gold . . . hutch*] lewdly suggesting a child in the womb; *hutch* = chest, coffer.
184-5. *who . . . groat*] proverbial (Tilley N249), i.e. the happiest people are those
without any money.
187. *heavy . . . heart*] proverbial (Tilley P655).

Of which I have provided for a dear year good store,
And these 'benters I trow shall anon get me more.
Will. By serving the court with coals, you gained all this money?   190
Grim. By the court only, I assure you.
Jack. After what sort, I pray thee tell me?
Grim. Nay, 'there bate me an ace', quod Bolton, I can wear a horn
  and blow it not.
Jack. By'r lady, the wiser man!
Grim. Shall I tell you by what sleight I got all this money?   195
  Then I were a noddy indeed. No, no, I warrant ye,
  Yet in few words I tell you this one thing,
  He is a very fool that cannot gain by the King.
Will. Well said, Father Grim, you are a wily collier and a brave—
  I see now there is no knave to the old knave.   200
Grim. Such knaves have money when courtiers have none.
  But tell me, is it true that abroad is blown?
Jack. What is that?
Grim. Has the King made those fair damsels his daughters,
  To become now fine and trim barbers?   205
Jack. Yea truly, to his own person.
Grim. Good fellows, believe me as the case now stands,
  I would give one sack of coals to be washed at their hands—
  If I came so near them, for my wit could not give three chips
  If I could not steal one swap at their lips.   210
Jack. [*To Will*] Will, this knave is drunk, let us dress him,
  Let us rifle him so that he have not one penny to bless him,
  And steal away his debenters too.
Will. [*To Jack*] Content. Invent the way and I am ready.
Jack. Faith, and I will make him a noddy.   215
  [*To Grim*] Father Grim, if you pray me well, I will wash you
  and shave you too,

211–16. SDs] *This ed.*

---

188. *dear year*] bad time when prices are high.

189. *'benters*] debenters or debentures, i.e. certificates given by government departments and the royal household for goods and services supplied, used by the supplier to
claim payment. Grim is showing the contents of his purse, which enacts the proverb
'He that shows his purse longs to be rid of it' (Tilley P654).

193. *bate . . . Bolton*] proverbial (Tilley A20), lit. abate, leave off a bit (cf. 'leave it
out').

wear . . . not] proverbial (Tilley H618), i.e. keep my own counsel.

196. *noddy*] fool. Jack seems to take this as a personal insult (see l. 215). There is
also a visual joke if he has been nodding in reply to the previous question.

200. *no . . . knave*] proverbial, also suggesting the proverb, 'there's no fool like an
old fool' (Tilley K131, F506).

202. *that . . . blown*] that which is being said publicly.

209. *could . . . chips*] would not mind. Cf. proverbs, 'Not to care a chip', and 'As
merry as three chips' (Tilley C355, C356).

210. *swap*] kiss.

211. *dress him*] Cf. 'fit him up'

212. *rifle*] ransack and rob.

216. *pray . . . well*] ask me nicely.

Even after the same fashion as the King's daughters do.
In all points as they handle Dionysius, I will dress you trim and
    fine.
Grim. I'd fain learn that. Come on then, I'll give thee a whole pint of
    wine
At tavern for thy labour, when I've money for my benters here.   220

Here WILL *fetches a barber's basin, a pot with water, a razor, and*
    cloths and a pair of spectacles [*and a chair*].

Jack. Come mine own Father Grim, sit down.
Grim. 'Mass to begin withal, here is a trim chair.
Jack. What man? I will use you like a prince. Sir boy, fetch me my
    gear.
Will. Here sir.
Jack. Hold up, Father Grim.   225
Grim. Meseem my head does swim.
Jack. My costly perfumes make that.
                [*Takes Grim's pouch and gives it to Will.*]
                   Away with this, sir boy, be quick,
Aloyse, aloyse, how, how pretty it is, is not here a good face?
A fine owl's eyes, a mouth like an oven,
Father, you have good butter teeth full seen—   230
You were weaned, else you would have been a great calf.
Ah trim lips—to sweep a manger. Here is a chin—
As soft as the hoof of a horse.
Grim. Does the King's daughters rub so hard?
Jack. Hold your head straight, man, else all will be marred.   235
    By'r lady, you are of a good complexion—

220.2 *and a chair*] This ed.   227.SD] This ed.

---

222. *trim chair*] By calling attention to an ordinary item of furniture, Grim perhaps
unwittingly suggests the proverb, 'As common as a barber's chair, fit for every buttock'
(Tilley B73, B74).

227–33.] This succession of semi-asides is indicated by the complete lack of
rhyme.

228–37.] This seems to be a parodic reference to Cicero's discussion of the nature
of the 'good': 'but take such insignificant things—we have to *call* them good—as white
teeth, fine eyes, fresh colour . . . if we are to reckon such things as good, what shall we
find to describe as more serious and elevated in the seriousness of the philosopher?'
(*Tusc.*, 5.16.46).

228. *Aloyse, aloyse*] This might represent 'aloynez' = carry it away (addressed to
Will), which turns on its repetition into 'alose' = praise be (in order to distract Grim).

    how, how] Although this could be a printing error, the repetition allows some
humour and suggests Jack thinking on his feet for something to say.

229. *owl's eyes*] Owls were considered blind since they blink in the sunlight
(cf. Tilley O92).

    mouth . . . oven] proverbial, 'to gape against (just like) an oven' (Tilley G33), i.e. he
has a big mouth, always open, talking too much.

230. *butter teeth*] buck teeth, but here probably referring to their colour and with
play on 'milk teeth'.

A right Croydon sanguine, beshrew me.
Hold up, Father Grim.—Will, can you bestir ye?
Grim. Methinks after a marvellous fashion you do besmear me.
Jack. It is with *unguentum* of *Daucus maucus* that is very costly,   240
    I give not this washing ball to everybody.
    After you have been dressed so finely at my hand,
    You may kiss any ladies' lips within this land.
    Ah, you are trimly washed, how say you, is not this trim water?
Grim. It may be wholesome, but it is vengeance sour.   245
Jack. It scours the better. Sir boy, give me my razor.
Will. Here at hand, sir.   [*Gives Jack a large kitchen knife.*]
Grim. God's ayness, 'tis a chopping knife, 'tis no razor.
Jack. It is a razor and that a very good one,
    It came lately from Palermo, it cost me twenty crowns alone.   250
    Your eyes dazzle after your washing—these spectacles put on.
    Now view this razor: tell me, is it not a good one?
Grim. They be gay barnacles, yet I see never the better.
Jack. Indeed, they be a young sight, and that is the matter,
    But I warrant you, this razor is very easy.   255
Grim. Go to then, since you begun, do as please ye.
Jack. Hold up, Father Grim.
Grim. O your razor does hurt my lip.
Jack. No, it scrapes of a pimple, to ease you of the pip.
    I have done now. How say you, are you not well?   260
Grim. I'm lighter than I was, the truth to tell.
Jack. Will you sing after your shaving?
Grim. 'Mass content, but I'll be polled first ere I sing.
Jack. Nay that shall not need—you are polled near enough for this
    time.

247.SD] *This ed.*   248. ayness] *This ed.;* aymes *Q.*   250. Palermo] *Steevens;*
Palarrime *Q.*

237. *Croydon*] The town south of London, famous for charcoal made in the surrounding forest, hence 'black', 'dirty'.
   sanguine] ruddy complexion (and cheerful manner).
240. *unguentum*] Lat. ointment.
   Daucus] Lat., carrot—used medicinally as a poultice for ulcerous sores.
   maucus] a nonsense word to rhyme with *Daucus*.
241. *washing ball*] ball of soap.
244. *water*] cosmetic preparation, perhaps urine, which was sometimes used as an
astringent.
245. *vengeance*] extremely.
   sour] bitter, unpleasant, and perhaps astringent.
248. *ayness*] everlastingness.
250. *Palermo*] famous for its razors.
253. *barnacles*] spectacles, colloquially derived from 'barnacle', a hinged instrument
to pinch the nose of a horse to stop it biting.
254. *young sight*] i.e. only suitable for young eyes. There is scope for much comic
business here: Will perhaps peers through the spectacles, as if to check their power.
259. *pip*] spot, probably here a 'whitehead'.
263. *'Mass . . . content*] i.e. by the mass I am happy to do so.
   be polled] 'have my hair cut'. In the next line Jack puns on the meaning 'plundered,

Grim. Go to then lustily, I will sing in my man's voice,   265
    I've a troubling base buss.
Jack. You are like to bear the bob, for we will give it.
    Set out your bussing base, and we will quiddle upon it.

Grim sings bass.

Jack sings. To-nidden, and to-nidden.
Will sings. To-nidden, and toodle, toodle do-nidden,   270
    Is not Grim the collier most finely shaven?

Grim. Why my fellows, think I am a cow, that you make such to-
    ing?
Jack. Nay by'r lady, you are no cow by your singing,
    Yet your wife told me you were an ox.
Grim. Did she so? 'Tis a pestilent quean, she is full of such mocks.   275
    But go to, let us sing out our song merely.

---

272. to-ing] *This ed.;* tooying *Q;* toying *Hazlitt.*   275. pestilent] *This ed.;* pestens *Q.*

robbed'. The episode is an expansion of a passage in Plautus in which a haircut is used as a metaphor for deception: 'the old fellow is in the barber's chair . . . we have the clippers on him. And master not even willing to throw a towel over him to keep his clothes clean! . . . he'll dock him handsomely' (*The Captives*, l. 266–9).

265. *lustily . . . man's voice*] Grim perhaps puns unwittingly on 'polled' (castrated) and 'lusty'.

266. *troubling*] uneven, unpleasant.

base] unrefined, punning on 'bass voice'.

buss] bass voice, picking up references to 'buss' (kiss) throughout the scene.

267. *bear the bob*] (*a*) join in the chorus, (*b*) be made a fool of, be cheated, (*c*) with an undercurrent of sexual puns on 'bob': dock a tail/penis; bob up and down (perhaps suggesting 'masturbate').

give it] i.e. 'give the bob', make a sharp rebuke or bitter jest.

268. *base*] (*a*) bottom (bass) part, (*b*) starting point, (*c*) place, home base (for kissing).

quiddle . . . it] i.e. descant on it foolishly.

269. *To-nidden*] perhaps a corruption of Lat. *tondeo* (I prune, shear, shave), see p. 107n.129.

271. *shaven*] punning on 'stripped of money, robbed'.

272. *to-ing*] i.e. lowing, animal sound.

273. *cow*] someone who has been cowed, (*a*) beaten, (*b*) polled, clipped.

273–4. *singing . . . ox*] Grim's bass voice indicates that the part was played by an adult (cf. l. 68), but Jack's joke questions his masculinity and his intelligence: ox = (*a*) a castrated (polled) bovine used as a draught animal, (*b*) a fool; cf. Shakespeare, *Merry Wives*, 5.5.116–17, '*Falstaff*: I do begin to perceive that I am made an ass. *Ford*: Ay, and an ox too.'

275. *quean*] hussy.

276. *merely*] (*a*) 'for its own sake' (i.e. with the sense 'let's forget what my wife says'), (*b*) an obsolete form of 'merrily', (i) pleasantly, (ii) in jest, (iii) with alacrity, briskly).

The song at the shaving of the collier

Jack. Such barbers God send you at all times of need,
Will. That can dress you finely and make such quick speed,
Jack. Your face like an inkhorn now shineth so gay,
Will. That I with your nostrils of force must needs play.   280
            With to-nidden and to-nidden,
Jack.   With to-nidden and toodle, toodle do-nidden,
[*All.*]   Is not Grim the collier most finely shaven?

Will. With shaving, you shine like a pestle of pork,
Jack. Here is the trimmest hog's flesh from London to York,   285
Will. It would be trim bacon to hang up awhile,
Jack. To play with this hogling, of force I must smile.
            With to-nidden, and to-nidden,
Will.   With to-nidden and toodle, toodle do-nidden,
[*All.*]   Is not Grim the collier most finely shaven?   290

Grim. Your shaving does please me, I am now your debtor,
Will. Your wife now will buss you, because you are sweeter,
Grim. Near would I be polled, as near as I'm shaven,
Will. Then out of your jerkin needs must you be shaken!
Grim.   With to-nidden and to-nidden,   295
            With to-nidden and toodle, toodle do-nidden,
[*All.*]   Is not Grim the collier most finely shaven?

Grim. It is a trim thing to be washed in the court,
Will. Their hands are so fine that they never do hurt,
Grim. Methink I am lighter than ever I was,   300
Will. Our shaving in the court has brought this to pass.
            With to-nidden, and to-nidden,
Jack.   With to-nidden and toodle, toodle do-nidden,
[*All.*]   Is not Grim the collier most finely shaven?   *Finis.*

Grim. This is trimly done. Now I'll pitch my coals not far hence,   305
    And then at the tavern I'll bestow whole two pence.   [*Exit.*]
Jack. Farewell cock. Before the collier again do us seek,
    Let us into the court to part the spoil—share and share like.
Will. Away then.   *Exeunt.*

                    Enter GRIM.

Grim. Out alas, where shall I make my moan?   310

279. inkhorn] *Hazlitt;* Inco rne Q.   283. *All*] *This ed., and subsequently.*
306.SD] *Hazlitt.*   309. *Exeunt*] *Dods.;* EXIT *Q.*

---

   278. *dress*] prepare, treat, minister.
   279.] Inkhorns were so called because originally made from animal horns, which would be polished and therefore shiny but also yellowish.
   280. *nostrils . . . play*] This implies 'lead by the nose', 'dupe'.
   284. *pestle*] haunch.
   287. *hogling*] little pig.
   294. *jerkin . . . shaken*] Implies 'you'll have the very clothes stolen from your back'.
   306. *bestow . . . pence*] 'buy two pennyworth of drinks'.
   308. *share . . . like*] share out equally (proverbial, Tilley S286).

My pouch, my benters and all is gone.
Where is that villain that did me shave?
Has robbed me, alas, of all that I have.

Enter SNAP.

Snap. Who cries so at the court gate?
Grim. I, the poor collier, that was robbed of late.   315
Snap. Who robbed thee?
Grim. Two of the porters' men that did shave me.
Snap. Why, the porters' men are no barbers.
Grim. A vengeance take them, they are quick carvers.
Snap. What stature were they of?   320
Grim. As little dapper knaves as they trimly could scoff.
Snap. They were lackeys, as near as I can guess them.
Grim. Such lackeys make me lack—an halter beswinge them—
      I'm undone, they have my benters too.
Snap. Dost thou know them if thou seest them?   325
Grim. Yea, that I do.
Snap. Then come with me. We will find them out and that quickly.
Grim. I follow, mast' tipstaff. They be in the court, it is likely.
Snap. Then cry no more, come away.   *Exeunt.*

[Scene 14]

Enter CARISOPHUS *and* ARISTIPPUS.

Carisophus. If ever you will show your friendship, now is the time,
      Seeing the King is displeased with me, of my part without any
          crime.
Aristippus. It should appear it comes of some evil behaviour,
      That you so suddenly are cast out of favour.
Carisophus. Nothing have I done but this: in talk I over-thwarted
          Eubulus   5
      When he lamented Pythias' case to King Dionysius,
      Which tomorrow shall die but for that false knave Damon—
      He has left his friend in the briars and now is gone.
      We grew so hot in talk, that Eubulus protested plainly
      Which held his ear open to parasitical flattery.   10

---

319. *carvers*] cutters, (*a*) 'cutpurses', (*b*) those who castrate animals.
321. *scoff*] mock, deride unjustifiably.
322. *lackeys*] attendants, but with pun 'lacking sexual maturity', since 'lack' in the
next line picks up on the established wordplay on 'polling' (thieving and castration).
323. *beswinge*] beat soundly.
328. *mast'*] master.

5. *over-thwarted*] went up against, opposed.
7. *Which*] i.e. Pythias.
8. *left . . . briars*] proverbial (Tilley B673), 'left him in the lurch'.
9. *plainly*] simply, directly, without rhetorical flourish.
10. *Which*] i.e. Dionysius.

And now in the King's ear like a bell he rings,
Crying that flatterers have been the destroyers of kings,
Which talk in Dionysius' heart has made so deep impression,
That he trusts me not as heretofore in no condition,
And some words broke from him as though that he   15
Began to suspect my truth and honesty,
Which you of friendship I know will defend, howsoever the
     world goeth.
My friend, for my honesty will you not take an oath?
Aristippus. To swear for your honesty, I should lose mine own.
Carisophus. Should you so indeed? I would that were known.   20
     Is your void friendship come thus to pass?
Aristippus. I follow the proverb, '*Amicus usque ad aras*'.
Carisophus. Where can you say I ever lost mine honesty?
Aristippus. You never lost it for you never had it, as far as I know.
Carisophus. Say you so, friend Aristippus, whom I trust so well? 25
Aristippus. Because you trust me, to you the truth I tell.
Carisophus. Will you not stretch one point to bring me in favour
     again?
Aristippus. I love no stretching—so may I breed mine own pain.
Carisophus. A friend ought to shun no pain to stand his friend in
     stead.
Aristippus. Where true friendship is, it is so in very deed.   30
Carisophus. Why sir, has not the chain of true friendship linked us
     two together?
Aristippus. The chiefest link lacked thereof, it must needs de-sever.
Carisophus. What link is that? Fain would I know.
Aristippus. Honesty.
Carisophus. Does honesty knit the perfect knot in true friendship? 35
Aristippus. Yea truly, and that knot so knit will never slip.
Carisophus. Belike then, there is no friendship but between honest
     men.

---

22. *aras*] Hazlitt; *auras* Q.

---

11. *like ... rings*] he (i.e. Eubulus) keeps speaking like a tolling bell calling people
to church.

21. *void*] worthless, empty.

22. Amicus ... aras] 'a friend as far as the altar', proverbial (Erasmus, *Adagia*,
1055A; Tilley F690), i.e. be a friend only as far as conscience permits.

28. *stretching ... pain*] This is a satirical reduction of the idea that happiness can
be defined as the absence of pain (see p. 57); cf. *Tusc.*, 2.6.15, 'Aristippus ... had no
hesitation in pronouncing pain to be the chief evil; next Epicurus lent himself quite
obediently to the support of this backboneless view'; *stretching* = (a) extreme exertion,
(b) torture on the rack.

29. *stand*] (a) remain steadfast to, (b) support, (c) punning on the opposite of
'stretching'.

stead] support (*OED* 13).

35. *honesty ... friendship*] Cf. 1.127–8. Carisophus is shocked by this axiom both
because he does not expect Aristippus to put virtue above pleasure and because he has
been relying on the contrasting concept of 'honour among thieves'.

Aristippus. Between the honest only, for '*Amicitia inter bonos*', says
    a learnèd man.
Carisophus. Yet evil men use friendship in things unhonest, where
    fancy does serve.
Aristippus. That is no friendship but a lewd liking, it lasts but a
    while.   40
Carisophus. What is the perfect'st friendship among men that ever
    grew?
Aristippus. Where men loved one another, not for profit but for
    virtue.
Carisophus. Are such friends both alike in joy and also in smart?
Aristippus. They must needs, for in two bodies they have but one
    heart.
Carisophus. Friend Aristippus, deceive me not with sophistry,   45
    Is there no perfect friendship, but where is virtue and honesty?
Aristippus. What a-devil then meant Carisophus,
    To join in friendship with fine Aristippus,
    In whom is as much virtue, truth and honesty
    As there are true feathers in the Three Cranes of the Vintry?   50
    Yet these feathers have the shadow of lively feathers the truth to
      scan,
    But Carisophus has not the shadow of an honest man.
    To be plain, because I know thy villainy
    In abusing Dionysius to many men's injury,
    Under the cloak of friendship, I played with his head   55
    And sought means how thou with thine own fancy might be led.
    My friendship thou soughtest for thine own commodity
    As worldly men do, by profit measuring amity,

---

38. *bonos*] Dods.; *bonus* Q.

---

38. *Amicitia . . . bonos*] Cf. *amicitiam nisi inter bonos esse non posse*, 'friendship
cannot exist except among good men' (Cicero, *De amicitia*, 18.65).
  39. *where . . . serve*] wherever the whim prompts.
  40. *lewd*] vulgar, worthless.
  43. *smart*] pain.
  49. *whom*] i.e. Carisophus.
  50. *Three Cranes*] well-known London tavern (referring here to its inn sign).
  Vintry] This area of wine-merchants' houses in the City of London is still to be found
north of modern Southwark Bridge.
  51. *shadow*] exact image, but in the next line with the sense 'merest imitation' i.e.
the inn sign depicts an accurate image of reality, but Carisophus has not the slightest
imitation of honesty. Ironically, Aristippus's costume may have included feathers to
denote the vanity of his character; cf. *Liberality and Prodigality* (1574–5), where a
costume with multi-coloured feathers, 'plainely pictures perfect Vanitie' (cited T. W.
Craik, *The Tudor Interlude* (Leicester: Leicester University Press, 1967), 66).
  lively] living.
  54. *abusing*] misleading.
  55. *friendship*] to Carisophus.
  played . . . head] i.e. let something slip about Carisophus that seemed innocent but
which Dionysius would interpret sinisterly.
  56. *sought . . . led*] cf. 'gave himself enough rope to hang himself'.

Which I perceiving, to the like myself I framed—
Wherein I know, of the wise I shall not be blamed.   60
If you ask me, 'Quare?'
I answer, 'Quia prudentis est multum dissimulare'.
To speak more plainer, as the proverb does go,
In faith Carisophus, 'cum Cretense cretiso'.
Yet a perfect friend I show myself to thee in one thing: 65
I do not dissemble now I say I will not speak for thee to the
   King,
Therefore sink in thy sorrow, I do not deceive thee,
A false knave I found thee, a false knave I leave thee.   *Exit.*
Carisophus. He is gone. Is this friendship, to leave his friend in the
   plain field?
Well I see now, I myself have beguiled   70
In matching with that false fox in amity,
Which has me used to his own commodity,
Which, seeing me in distress, unfeignedly goes his ways.
Lo, this is the perfect friendship among men nowadays,
Which kind of friendship toward him I used secretly,   75
And he with me the like has requited me craftily.
It is the gods' judgement, I see it plainly,
For all the world may know, 'Incidi in foveam quam feci'.
Well I must content myself, none other help I know,
Until a merrier gale of wind may hap to blow.   *Exit.*   80

[Scene 15]

[*Enter* EUBULUS.]

Eubulus. Who deals with kings in matters of great weight
   When froward will does bear the chiefest sway,

61–2.] This ed.; *printed as one line in Q.*   78. incidi] Dods.; *incide* Q.
0.1 SD] Hazlitt.

---

   59. *like . . . framed*] behaved in the same way.
   61. Quare?] why, wherefore?
   62. Quia . . . dissimulare] Because it is wise to dissimulate much.
   64. cum . . . cretiso] I play the Cretan (i.e. I am dishonest) with a Cretan (cf. 11.86n).
   69. *plain field*] open battle field.
   72. Which] i.e. who.
   73. *unfeignedly*] i.e. only now behaving as he really thinks.
   78. Incidi . . . feci] 'I fell into the pit which I made'. This is a version in the first person of Psalm 7.15, 'He hath graven and dygged up a pytte, & is falen hym selfe into the destruccyon that he made (for other)'. The psalm also contains the verse 'Yf I have rewarded evyll unto him that dealt frendly with me, ye[a], I have delyvered hym, that without any cause is myne enemye. Then lett myne enemye persecute my soule, and take me.' This is the only Latin spoken by Carisophus.

   1–26.] See p. 54.
   2. *froward will*] evilly disposed or perverse desire.

Must yield of force. There need no subtle sleight
Nor painted speech the matter to convey—
No prayer can move when kindled is the ire,   5
The more you quench, the more increased is the fire.

This thing I prove in Pythias' woeful case,
Whose heavy hap with tears I do lament.
The day is come when he in Damon's place
Must lose his life—the time is fully spent.   10
Nought can my words now with the King prevail,
Against the wind and striving stream I sail.

For die thou must, alas, thou seely Greek,
Ah Pythias, now come is thy doleful hour,
A perfect friend—none such a world to seek—   15
Though bitter death shall give thee sauce full sour.
Yet for thy faith, enrolled shall be thy name
Among the gods within the book of fame.

Who knows his case and will not melt in tears?
His guiltless blood shall trickle down anon.   20

Then the Muses sing [and are revealed].

Muses. Alas what hap hast thou, poor Pythias, now to die,
          Woe worth the man which for his death has given us cause
             to cry.
Eubulus. Methink I hear, with yellow, rented hairs,
          The Muses frame their notes thy state to moan,
          Among which sort as one that mourns with heart,   25
          In doleful tunes, myself will bear a part.

1–26.] *Division into stanzas, this ed.*   8. heavy] *Q2;* hauuy *Q.*   20.1. *and are revealed*] *This ed.*   22. man which] *Q2;* which man *Q.*   24. thy] *Dods.;* my *Q.*

3–5. *There . . . move*] i.e. there is no need for courtly devices or language because not even prayers can succeed.

6. *more . . . fire*] referring to the proverbs 'do not blow the fire you would quench', and 'to quench fire with oil' (Tilley F251, F287).

12. *wind . . . sail*] This is a standard image of the storm of fortune (cf. poems CT 4, PDD, 5).

13. *seely*] (a) blessed, (b) innocent, pitiable.

15. *none . . . seek*] 'no other such person to be found in all the world'.

20.1.SD] It is possible that the Muses were revealed seated on a rock (see pp. 33–4).

22. *Woe worth*] cursed be, woe to.

his] i.e. Pythias's.

23–6.] Eubulus continues with his established rhyme scheme although interrupted by the Muses.

23. *yellow . . . hairs*] The Muses were probably wearing wigs made from yellow silk threads.

rented] torn, dishevelled. Tearing the hair is a standard representation of grief.

25. *sort*] group (of people), i.e. the Muses.

with heart] with true emotion.

Muses. [*Sing.*] Woe worth the man which for his death has given
us cause to cry.

Eubulus. [*Sings.*] With yellow, rented hairs come on you Muses
nine,
  Fill now my breast with heavy tunes, to me your plaints
  resign,
  For Pythias I bewail which presently must die,   30
  Woe worth the man which for his death has given us cause
  to cry.
Muses. Woe worth the man which for his death has given us
  cause to cry.

Eubulus. Was ever such a man that would die for his friend?
  I think even from the heavens above, the gods did him
  down send
  To show true friendship's power, which forced thee now to
  die.   35
  Woe worth the man which for his death has given us cause
  to cry.
Muses. Woe worth the man which for his death has given us
  cause to cry.

Eubulus. What tiger's whelp was he, that Damon did accuse?
  What faith hast thou, which for thy friend thy death does
  not refuse?
  O heavy hap hadst thou to play this tragedy,   40
  Woe worth the man which for his death has given us cause
  to cry.
Muses. Woe worth the man which for his death has given us
  cause to cry.

Eubulus. Thou young and worthy Greek that shows such perfect
  love,
  The Gods receive thy simple ghost into the heavens above.
  Thy death we shall lament with many a weeping eye,   45
  Woe worth the man which for his death has given us cause
  to cry.
Muses. Woe worth the man which for his death has given us
  cause to cry.

                                             Finis.

Eubulus. Eternal be your fame, you Muses, for that in misery
  You did vouchsafe to strain your notes to walk.
  My heart is rent in two with this miserable case,   50
  Yet am I charged by Dionysius' mouth, to see this place

---

36. his] thy *Q and at 41, 47.*   47. given] genen *Q.*

49. *strain*] (*a*) sing, (*b*) with the sense of 'exert, suffer'.
walk] i.e. in the sense that ghosts or spirits 'walk' or appear.

At all points ready for the execution of Pythias.
Need has no law. Will I or nil I, it must be done—

[*Enter* GROANO.]

But lo, the bloody minister is even here at hand.
Groano, I came hither now to understand   55
If all things are well appointed for the execution of Pythias.
The King himself will see it done here in this place.
Groano. Sir, all things are ready. Here is the place, here is the hand,
    here is the sword,
    Here lacks none but Pythias, whose head at a word,
    If he were present, I could finely strike off—   60
    You may report that all things are ready.
Eubulus. I go with an heavy heart to report it.—Ah woeful Pythias,
    Full near now is thy misery.   [*Exit.*]
Groano. I marvel very much under what constellation
    All hangmen are born, for they are hated of all, beloved of none,   65
    Which hatred is showed by this point evidently:
    The hangman always dwells in the vilest place of the city.
    That such spite should be, I know no cause why,
    Unless it be for their office's sake which is cruel and bloody.
    Yet some men must do it to execute laws—   70
    Methink they hate me without any just cause.
    But I must look to my toil—Pythias must lose his head at one
    blow
    Else the boys will stone me to death in the street as I go.
    But hark, the prisoner comes, and the King also.

Enter SNAP [*with* PYTHIAS *and* STEPHANO. *They stand aside*].

Enter DIONYSIUS *and* EUBULUS.

I see there is no help, Pythias his life must forgo.   75
Dionysius. Bring forth Pythias that pleasant companion,
    Which took me at my word and became pledge for Damon.
    It pricks fast upon noon—I do him no injury
    If now he lose his head, for so he requested me
    If Damon return not, which now in Greece is full merry—   80
    Therefore shall Pythias pay his death, and that by and by.
    He thought belike if Damon were out of the city,

53.1.SD] *This ed.; Hazlitt after l. 54.*   63.SD] *Hazlitt.*   74.1.SD] *This ed.; Here
entreth Snap. Q after l. 85.*   74.2.SD] *This ed.; Here entreth Dionysius and Eubulus.
Q after l. 75.*

---

   52. *At all points*] in every detail.
   53. *Need . . . law*] proverbial (Tilley N76); i.e. law is law, irrespective of need or
desire.
   Will . . . I] whether I will or no.
   72. *look . . . toil*] 'see I do the job properly'. He might sharpen his sword at this point.
   78. *pricks . . . upon*] fast approaches.
   82. *belike*] probably.

I would not put him to death, for some foolish pity.
But seeing it was his request, I will not be mocked, he shall die.
Bring him forth.   85
Snap. Give place, let the prisoner come by, give place.
Dionysius. How say you, sir? Where is Damon your trusty friend?
    You have played a wise part, I make God a vow.
    You know what time of day it is. Make you ready.
Pythias. Most ready I am, mighty King, and most ready also   90
    For my true friend Damon this life to forgo
    Even at your pleasure.
Dionysius. A true friend?—a false traitor that so breaks his oath!
    Thou shalt lose thy life though thou be never so loath.
Pythias. I am not loath to do whatsoever I said,   95
    Nor at this present pinch of death am I dismayed.
    The gods now I know have heard my fervent prayer,
    That they have reserved me to this passing great honour,
    To die for my friend, whose faith even now I do not mistrust.
    My friend Damon is no false traitor, he is true and just.   100
    But since he is no god but a man, he must do as he may,
    The wind may be contrary, sickness may let him, or some
        misadventure by the way,
    Which the eternal gods turn all to my glory,
    That fame may resound how Pythias for Damon did die.
    He breaks no oath which does as much as he can—   105
    His mind is here, he has some let, he is but a man.
    That he might not return, of all the gods I did require,
    Which now to my joy, do grant my desire.
    But why do I stay any longer, seeing that one man's death
    May suffice, O King, to pacify thy wrath?   110
    [*To Groano*] O thou minister of justice, do thine office by and
        by,
    Let not thy hand tremble, for I tremble not to die.
    Stephano, the right pattern of true fidelity,
    Commend me to thy master, my sweet Damon, and of him crave
        liberty
    When I am dead, in my name—for thy trusty services   115
    Has well deserved a gift far better than this.
    O my Damon, farewell now forever, a true friend to me most
        dear.

111.SD] *This ed.*   113. pattern] patrone *Q.*

82–3. *city . . . pity*] Cf. proverb, 'Foolish pity mars a city' (Tilley P366).
    101. *must . . . may*] 'he can only do what he is able to do', proverbial: 'Men must do as they may, not as they would', and 'Men are but men' (Tilley M554, M541); cf. Aristotle, *Nic. Eth.*, 'Friendship asks a man to do what he can, not what is proportional to the merits of the case' (8.14.1163b).
    102. *let*] hinder, prevent.
    106. *let*] hindrance.
    107. *That . . . require*] i.e. 'I begged all the gods that he might not return'.
    108. *Which*] who (i.e. the gods).
    113. *pattern*] Q1 gives the obsolete spelling 'patrone' here (cf. 1.127).

Whilst life does last, my mouth shall still talk of thee,
And when I am dead, my simple ghost, true witness of amity,
Shall hover about the place wheresoever thou be.   120
Dionysius. Eubulus, this gear is strange, and yet because
Damon has falsed his faith, Pythias shall have the law.
Groano, despoil him, and eke dispatch him quickly.
Groano. It shall be done. Since you came into this place,
I might have strucken off seven heads in this space.   125
By'r lady, here are good garments, these are mine by the rood—
It is an evil wind that blows no man good.
Now Pythias kneel down, ask me blessing like a pretty boy,
And with a trice thy head from thy shoulders I will convey.

Here enters DAMON *running and stays the sword.*

Damon. Stay, stay, stay, for the King's advantage stay.   130
O mighty King, mine appointed time is not yet fully past,
Within the compass of mine hour, lo here I come at last,
A life I owe, a life I will you pay.
O my Pythias, my noble pledge, my constant friend,
Ah woe is me, for Damon's sake how near were thou to thy end!   135
Give place to me, this room is mine, on this stage must I play,
Damon is the man—none ought but he to Dionysius his blood to
    pay.
Groano. Are you come sir? You might have tarried if you had been
    wise,
For your hasty coming you are like to know the price.
Pythias. [*To Groano*] O thou cruel minister, why didst not thou thine
    office?   140
Did not I bid thee make haste in any wise?
Hast thou spared to kill me once that I may die twice?
Not to die for my friend, is present death to me, and alas
Shall I see my sweet Damon slain before my face?
What double death is this! But O mighty Dionysius,   145
Do true justice now—weigh this aright thou noble Eubulus.
Let me have no wrong—as now stands the case,
Damon ought not to die, but Pythias.
By misadventure, not by his will, his hour is past, therefore I,
Because he came not at his just time, ought justly to die.   150
So was my promise—so was thy promise, O King,
All this court can bear witness of this thing.
Damon. Not so, O mighty King. To justice it is contrary

---

121. *gear*] matter, affair, business.
123. *despoil him*] remove his clothes.
126. *garments . . . mine*] The condemned man's clothes traditionally became the
property of the hangman.
127. *evil . . . good*] proverbial (Tilley W421).
128. *pretty*] proper.
129.1–130.] Cf. 10.236n.
136. *stage . . . play*] Cf. 7.71–4n.
143. *present*] immediate.

That for another man's fault, the innocent should die.
Nor yet is my time plainly expired—it is not fully noon 155
Of this my day appointed, by all the clocks in the town.
Pythias. Believe no clock, the hour is past by the sun.
Damon. Ah my Pythias, shall we now break the bonds of amity?
    Will you now over-thwart me, which heretofore so well did
        agree?
Pythias. My Damon, the gods forbid but we should agree, 160
    Therefore agree to this: let me perform the promise I made for
        thee,
    Let me die for thee. Do me not that injury
    Both to break my promise and to suffer me to see thee die
    Whom so dearly I love. This small request grant me,
    I shall never ask thee more—my desire is but friendly. 165
    Do me this honour, that fame may report triumphantly
    That Pythias for his friend Damon was contented to die.
Damon. That you were contented for me to die, fame cannot deny.
    Yet fame shall never touch me with such a villainy
    To report that Damon did suffer his friend Pythias for him
        guiltless to die. 170
    Therefore content thyself—the gods requite thy constant faith—
    None but Damon's blood can appease Dionysius' wrath.
    And now, O mighty King, to you my talk I convey
    Because you gave me leave my worldly things to stay.
    To requite that good turn ere I die, for your behalf this I say: 175

    Although your regal state Dame Fortune decketh so,
    That like a king in worldly wealth abundantly you flow,
    Yet fickle is the ground whereon all tyrants tread,
    A thousand sundry cares and fears do haunt their restless
        head.
    No trusty band, no faithful friends do guard thy hateful state, 180
    And why?—
    Whom men obey for deadly fear, sure them they deadly hate.

    That you may safely reign, by love get friends whose constant
        faith
    Will never fail, this counsel gives poor Damon at his death.
    Friends are the surest guard for Kings—gold in time does wear
        away 185

176–94] *Division into stanzas, this ed.*   181.] *This ed.; lineated with l. 182 in Q.*
185. Kings—gold in time does] kings, gold . . . does *Hazlitt, modernising Dods.;*
kinges golden time doo *Q.*

---

   159. *over-thwart*] cross, oppose.
   168. *contented . . . die*] i.e. willing to die for me.
   174. *stay*] finalise, put in order.
   182. *men . . . hate*] Cf. Seneca, *Thyestes*, 200, 'Men compelled by fear To praise,
may be by fear compelled to hate'. Cf. 7.25n.
   185. *Friends . . . guard*] Cf. Aristotle, *Nic. Eth.*, 8.1, 'how can prosperity be guarded
and preserved without friends?'. Cf. 7.45n.
   gold . . . away] Cf. Surrey's poem 'The winter with his ugly storms': 'For slipper
wealth will not abide / Pleasure will wear away' (see p. 22).

And other precious things do fade, friendship will never decay.
Have friends in store therefore—so shall you safely sleep.
Have friends at home—of foreign foes so need you take no
  keep.

Abandon flatt'ring tongues, whose clacks truth never tells,
Abase the ill, advance the good in whom Dame Virtue dwells,   190
Let them your play-fellows be, but O you earthly kings,
Your sure defence and strongest guard stands chiefly in faithful
  friends.
Then get you friends by liberal deeds, and here I make an end,
Accept this counsel, mighty King, of Damon, Pythias' friend.

O my Pythias, now farewell for ever. Let me kiss thee ere I die.   195
My soul shall honour thee—thy constant faith above the heavens
  shall fly.
Come Groano do thine office now—why is thy colour so dead?
My neck is so short that thou wilt never have honesty in striking
  off this head!
Dionysius. Eubulus, my spirits are suddenly appalled, my limbs wax
  weak,
This strange friendship amazes me so, that I can scarce speak.   200
Pythias. O mighty King, let some pity your noble heart move.
You require but one man's death, take Pythias, let Damon live.
Eubulus. —O unspeakable friendship.
Damon. Not so, he has not offended, there is no cause why
My constant friend, my Pythias, for Damon's sake should die.   205
Alas, he is but young, he may do good to many.
[*To Groano*] Thou coward minister, why dost thou not let me
  die?
Groano. —My hand with sudden fear quivers.
Pythias. O noble King, show mercy on Damon, let Pythias die.
Dionysius. Stay, Groano—my flesh trembles—Eubulus, what shall I
  do?   210
Were there ever such friends on earth as were these two?
What heart is so cruel that would divide them asunder?
O noble friendship, I must yield—at thy force I wonder.
My heart, this rare friendship has pierced to the root
And quenched all my fury. This sight has brought this about,   215

---

198. is so] *Q2;* is so is *Q.*   207.SD] This ed.

187. *in store*] in abundance.
188. *keep*] heed, care.
189. *clacks*] chattering din.
198. *short*] (*a*) inadequate, powerless (*OED*, I.g.), (*b*) breakable (*OED*, IV), with
possible reference to the phrase, 'made shorter by the head', i.e. beheaded. Sir Thomas
More reputedly made the same joke at his execution in 1535.
  honesty] respect, credit (thus bearing out Groano's fears at 15.64–73).
199. *appalled*] dismayed, weakened.
214. *pierced*] penetrated.

Which thy grave counsel, Eubulus, and learned persuasion could
   never do.

O noble gentlemen, the immortal gods above
Has made you play this tragedy, I think, for my behove.
Before this day, I never knew what perfect friendship meant,
My cruel mind, to bloody deeds was full and wholly bent.   220

My fearful life, I thought with terror to defend,
But now I see there is no guard unto a faithful friend,
Which will not spare his life at time of present need—
O happy kings, within your courts, have two such friends
   indeed.

I honour friendship now, which that you may plainly see,   225
Damon, have thou thy life, from death I pardon thee.
For which good turn, I crave this honour do me lend,
O friendly heart, let me link with you to you—make me the
   third friend.

My court is yours, dwell here with me, by my commission
   large,
Myself, my realm, my wealth, my health, I commit to your
   charge.   230
Make me a third friend, more shall I joy in that thing,
Than to be called as I am, 'Dionysius the mighty King'.

Damon. O mighty King, first for my life most humble thanks I give,
   And next I praise the immortal gods that did your heart so
     move,
That you would have respect to friendship's heavenly lore,   235
Foreseeing well, he need not fear which has true friends in
   store.

For my part, most noble King, as a third friend, welcome to our
   friendly society,

217–36.] *Division into stanzas, this ed.*   228. you to you—make] *This ed.;* you, to
you make *Q;* you two, to, make *Q2.*

217–36.] Dionysius's transformation is marked by breaking into a regular metre.
Damon comments in imitation, before lapsing into more irregular, conversational
style.

218. *behove*] benefit. As befits this theatrical defence of the theatre, Dionysius's
moral transformation has been accomplished by watching a 'play' not by listening to
moral injunctions (cf. 7.71–4, and p. 40).

221. *fearful*] (*a*) frightened, wary, (*b*) causing fear.

222. *unto*] to compare with.

224. *have*] i.e. that have.

228. *you to you*] Dionysius presumably gestures to Damon and Pythias in turn.

third friend] Cf. Cicero, *Tusc.*, 5.22.63, where Dionysius likewise asks to be made
the third friend. Three is a significant number in Pythagorean numerology as it is the
sum of the monad (perfect unity) and the dyad (two; considered unstable or 'feminine').

229. *commission large*] wide-ranging authority and freedom.

But you must forget you are a king, for friendship stands in true
    equality.
Dionysius. Unequal though I be in great possessions,
    Yet full equal shall you find me in my changed conditions.   240
    Tyranny, flattery, oppression, lo here I cast away,
    Justice, truth, love, friendship shall be my joy.
    True friendship will I honour unto my life's end,
    My greatest glory shall be to be counted a perfect friend.
Pythias. For this your deed, most noble King, the gods advance your
    name,   245
    And since to friendship's lore you list your princely heart to
    frame,
    With joyful heart, O King, most welcome now to me,
    With you will I knit the perfect knot of amity,
    Wherein I shall instruct you so, and Damon here your friend,
    That you may know of amity the mighty force and eke the joyful
    end,   250
    And how that kings do stand upon a fickle ground,
    Within whose realm at time of need, no faithful friends are
    found.
Dionysius. Your instruction will I follow, to you myself I do commit.
    Eubulus, make haste to fetch new apparel fit
    For my new friends.   255
Eubulus. I go with a joyful heart—O happy day.   *Exit.*
Groano. [*To audience*] I am glad to hear this word—though their
    lives they do not lose
    It is no reason the hangman should lose his fees,
    [*Taking up the clothes*] These are mine, I am gone with a trice.
                      Exit [GROANO *and* SNAP].

          Enter EUBULUS *with new garments.*

Dionysius. Put on these garments now, go in with me, the jewels of
    my court.   260
Damon and Pythias. [*Going*] We go with joyful hearts.
Stephano. O Damon, my dear master, in all this joy remember me.
Dionysius. My friend Damon, he asks reason.
Damon. Stephano, for thy good service, be thou free.
Stephano. O most happy, pleasant, joyful, and triumphant day!   265
    Poor Stephano now shall live in continual joy—
    Vive le roi—with Damon and Pythias in perfect amity.
               [*Exeunt all but* STEPHANO.]

257–9. SDs] *This ed.*   257. lose] leese *Q.*   261.SD] *This ed.*   267.SD] *sugg.*
Collier; Dam. Pithias. *in margin at l. 263, and* EXEUNT. DION *at l. 264, Q.*

238. *friendship . . . equality*] This is one of Pythagoras's precepts and is proverbial
(Tilley F761); *stands* = consists.
    246. *list*] desire.
    257. *lose*] *Q* uses the old verb 'leese' (= lose) for the sake of the rhyme.
    259. *with*] in.
    261.SD] *Q* marginal 'Dam. Pithias.' at l. 263 may indicate a re-entry or coming
forward after a partial exit here.
    267. *Vive le roi*] long live the king.

Vive tu Stephano, in thy pleasant liberality,
Wherein I joy as much as he that has a conquest won—
I am a free man, none so merry as I now under the sun.   270
[*To audience*] Farewell my lords, now the gods grant you all that
    sum of perfect amity
And me long to enjoy my long desired liberty.   *Exit.*

[Scene 16]

Enter EUBULUS *beating* CARISOPHUS.

Eubulus. Away villain, away you flatt'ring parasite,
    Away the plague of this court. Thy filed tongue that forged lies,
    No more here shall do hurt. Away false sycophant, wilt thou
        not?
Carisophus. I am gone sir, seeing it is the King's pleasure.
    Why whip you me alone? A plague take Damon and Pythias!
        Since they came hither   5
    I am driven to seek relief abroad, alas I know not whither,
    Yet, Eubulus, though I be gone, hereafter time shall try,
    There shall be found, even in this court, as great flatterers as I.
    Well, for a while I will forgo the court, though to my great pain,
    I doubt not but to spy a time when I may creep in again. *Exit.* 10
Eubulus. The serpent that eats men alive, flattery with all her brood,
    Is whipped away in princes' courts which yet did never good.
    What force, what mighty power, true friendship may possess,
    To all the world Dionysius' court now plainly does express,
    Who since to faithful friends he gave his willing ear,   15
    Most safely sits in his seat and sleeps devoid of fear.
    Purged is the court of vice, since friendship entered in,
    Tyranny quails, he studies now with love each heart to win.
    Virtue is had in price and has his just reward,
    And painted speech that gloses for gain, from gifts is quite
        debarred.   20
    One loves another now for virtue, not for gain,
    Where virtue does not knit the knot, there friendship cannot
        reign,
    Without the which, no house, no land, nor kingdom can endure,
    As necessary for man's life, as water, air and fire,
    Which frames the mind of man, all honest things to do—   25

271.SD] *This ed.*

268. Vive tu Stephano] long live you, Stephano.

2. *filed*] (*a*) smooth, lying, (*b*) defiled, polluting.
7. *try*] put to the test.
12. *which*] i.e. flattery.
19. *Virtue . . . reward*] proverbial, 'virtue is its own reward' (Tilley V81).
had in price] held in high value.
20. *gloses*] flatters, talks speciously.

Unhonest things friendship nor craves, nor yet consents thereto.
In wealth a double joy, in woe a present stay,
A sweet companion in each state, true friendship is alway.
A sure defence for kings, a perfect trusty band,
A force to assail, a shield to defend the enemy's cruel hand,   30
A rare and yet the greatest gift that god can give to man,
So rare that scarce four couple of faithful friends have been since
    the world began,
A gift so strange and of such price, I wish all kings to have,
But chiefly yet, as duty binds, I humbly crave,
True friendship and true friends full fraught with constant faith,   35
The giver of friends, the Lord grant her, most noble Queen
    Elizabeth.

                                Finis.

The last song

    The strongest guard that kings can have
    Are constant friends their state to save.

True friends are constant, both in word and deed,
True friends are present and help at each need,
True friends talk truly, they glose for no gain,   5
When treasure consumes, true friends will remain,
True friends for their true prince, refuse not their death,
The Lord grant her such friends, most noble Queen Elizabeth.

Long may she govern in honour and wealth,
Void of all sickness, in most perfect health,   10
Which health to prolong, as true friends require,
God grant she may have her own heart's desire,
Which friends will defend with most steadfast faith,
The Lord grant her such friends, most noble Queen Elizabeth.

                                Finis.

1–2.] *Italic, this ed.*

  26. *nor . . . nor*] neither . . . nor.
  27. *present*] ever present, immediate.
stay] support.
  30. *defend*] ward off, repel, hinder.
  32. *scarce . . . couple*] Elyot (*Governor*, 2.11–12) lists three pairs of famous friends: Damon and Pythias; Orestes and Pylades (who are likewise prepared to die for each other) and Titus and Gisyppus (source for Shakespeare's *Two Gentlemen of Verona*). Cicero's *De amicitia*, written as a discourse between Laelius and others, cites only Laelius and Scipio Aemilianus (Cicero's ideal of the true prince).

  1–2.] These two lines are in the nature of a thematic title for the song, cf. *PDD*, 7.
  6. *When . . . consumes*] 'when wealth is all used up'; cf. proverb 'a friend in need is a friend in deed' (Tilley F693).

POEMS

The poems are grouped according to their principal source. Other occurrences, if any, are listed in the commentary. Variants are recorded in the
collation only where the copy text has been emended or where the variant
indicates a particularly interesting aspect of the transmission of the text.
Spelling and punctuation have been modernised according to the principles set out on pp. 97–100.

The commentary for each poem from *The Paradise of Dainty Devices*
starts with the page signature and date of its earliest appearance in the
various editions. Unless otherwise stated, all the poems occur in all subsequent editions. Not all the following poems are by Edwards, and
some appear under different names in different editions. Ascriptions in
this edition follow the earliest printing in each case, with commentary as
necessary.

In the collation, variant readings from individual editions of *PDD* are
given by date. When editions agree, this is indicated by '*PDD*'.

PRINCIPAL PRINTED AND MANUSCRIPT SOURCES

British Library, Cotton MS Titus A.xxiv

For a full discussion see pp. 16ff. The poems by Edwards in this manuscript were transcribed by Leicester Bradner (1927). He made several substantive errors, in both CT 2 and CT 5, which have not been collated
here.

The Paradise of Dainty Devices

See pp. 40ff. The first edition is collated A4, A–L4. The first gathering
(A) contains the title page, the address to the patron, Sir Henry Compton,
with his coat-of-arms, and four unnumbered poems. Numbering of the
poems starts on the second gathering (A) and continues through to no.
55 on the last page of G. An old-spelling, critical edition by Hyder Rollins
was published in 1927. There is a facsimile edition by Scolar Press (1972).

British Library Add. 26737

This is a mid-seventeenth-century compilation of genealogies and copies of documents relating to land-holdings mostly connected with the county of Yorkshire, written in a clear hand. It also contains (fols 106bff.), copies of the following poems by Edwards: 'May'; 'The Sailing Ships'; 'In going to my naked bed'; 'The subtle slyly sleights' (*PDD*, 1, 5, 9, 16) and 'When women first' (CT 3). Most valuably it preserves one and perhaps two songs from Edwards's lost play *Palamon and Arcyte*: 'The songe of Emelye per Edwardes'; and the fullest known version of the text of 'O death (see pp. 80–1). Most of the poems in this MS, like those in CT and unlike those in *PDD*, are copied with line breaks at the caesurae.

Bodleian Library Tanner 306.1

This is a compilation MSS containing two leaves which preserve two poems in the same sixteenth-century hand, both printed here. The second is attributed to Edwards and the attribution might be understood to be doing duty for the first poem as well, since the two poems share a similar style and format.

J. Stow, The Summary of English Chronicles (1566)

This is a pocket-size version of the *Chronicles*, perhaps for the lighter end of the market as it contains the challenge in verse for the Bedford Wedding tournament which does not occur in other, larger-format editions.

OTHER SOURCES

Arundel Harington MS

This is one of the largest surviving sixteenth-century collections of poetry, consisting of some ten thousand lines (probably three hundred and twenty four poems, either in whole or in part) on 145 leaves. It originally contained a further eighty-three leaves. The collection was started by John Harington, who served Henry VIII and Elizabeth both before and after her coronation. It then passed to his son, Sir John Harington of Kelston, translator of the verse epic the *Orlando Furioso*. Extracts from it were printed by a Harington descendant in 1769 as *Nugae Antiquae* but, instead of transcripts, the original leaves were used as printer's copy and a number of them are known to have been destroyed in the process (Ruth Hughey, ed., *The Arundel Harington MS of Tudor Poetry*, 2 vols (Columbus: Ohio State University, Press, 1960), I, 11–18). The poems are written in a number of different hands over many years and are generally not ascribed to authors. There are three known to be by Edwards (CT 4, 'O Lord that rulest'; *PDD*, 4, 'In youthful years'; *PDD*, 16, 'The subtle slyly sleights'). The manuscript also contains a poem in praise of six ladies of the Princess Elizabeth's court, perhaps written by John Harington between 1554 and 1558 (Hughey, II, 409) very different in style from Edwards's poem in praise of the eight ladies attending Queen Mary. John Harington's own verse style is characterised by its metrical smoothness. This explains the majority of the variants in the transcripts of the three Edwards poems, which accordingly have not been collated here.

British Library, Add. 15233

This MS, shaped like a music part-book, contains organ music and the interlude *Wit and Weather* by John Redford (Master of the Children at St Paul's), with poems by a number of other authors, including Edwards's 'In youthful years' (fols 38v–39r).

Dow MS, Christ Church

See p. 250.

FIVE POEMS FROM BRITISH LIBRARY COTTON MS TITUS A.XXIV

I

My fancy fawned on me, somewhat of you to say,
Good ladies all, accept my will, this thing I only pray.
1 Howard is not haughty, but of such smiling cheer
That would allure each gentle heart, her love to hold full dear.
2 Dacres is not dangerous, her talk is nothing coy, 5

---

1. My . . . say,] My fance fanned onne me somewhat of y[ow] / to see *CT.*
2. pray] *Bradner;* pr *CT.* 3. Howard] Hawarde *CT.* haughty] hawghte *CT.*
4. dear] der *CT.* 5. Dacres] Dacars *CT.*

The right-hand edge of the manuscript has been cropped, removing some letters in this poem. See Appendix, p. 231, for the identities of these women.

1. *fancy*] (*a*) imagination, (*b*) desire.
fawned on] cajoled.
say] The scribe also uses the spelling 'see' for 'say' (CT 2.15) and for 'sea' (CT 4.3).
2. *will*] desire, determination, punning on sexual desire.
3. *cheer*] (*a*) face, (*b*) expression, (*c*) disposition, manner.
5. *dangerous*] difficult to please, fastidious, dainty (*OED*, 1b).
coy] (*a*) disdainful, (*b*) quiet, reserved, (*c*) falsely appearing to be quiet and reserved, (*d*) coaxing, enticing, alluring, with the sense of a 'decoy' (hence 'dangerous').

Her noble stature may compare with Hector's wife of Troy.

3   Baynam is as beautiful as Nature can devise,
    Steadfastness possess her heart and chastity her eyes.

4   Arundel is ancient in these her tender years,
    In heart, in voice, in talk, in deed, a matron's wit appears.   10

5   Dormer is a darling, and of such lively hue
    That whoso feeds his eyes on her may soon her beauty rue.

6   Mansell is a merry one and is right worthy love,
    Whom Nature wrought so featously her cunning for to
        prove.

7   Cooke is comely, and thereto in books sets all her care,   15
    In learning with the Roman dames, of right she may
        compare.

8   Bridges is a blessed wight, and prays with heart and voice,
    Which from her cradle has been taught in virtue to rejoice.

These eight now serves one noble Queen, but if power were in
    me,
For beauty's praise and virtue's sake, each one a queen should
    be.   20

                                                    Finis R. E.

                                    2

                Truth with the touchstone tries
                    each thing we daily see,
                If truth with you be had in price,
                    then hear the truth of me.

---

10. deed] deade *CT.*   appears] appere *CT.*

---

6. *Hector's wife*] Andromache was noted for her love for her husband, Hector, the noblest of the Trojan heroes, and for her endurance following the slaughter of her father, brothers, husband and son (*Iliad*, 6.395ff.).

7.] Mrs Baynam was middle-aged when the poem was written.

8. *Steadfastness ... eyes*] Either 'may steadfastness and chastity possess (be situated in) her heart and eyes' or 'may steadfastness possess her heart and chastity possess her eyes'.

9. *is ancient*] has the experience of age.

tender] young.

11. *hue*] appearance, complexion.

12. *feeds his eyes*] a common phrase (cf. *D&P*, 8.26).

rue] i.e. regret that she is beautiful because he cannot possess her.

14. *featously*] beautifully.

her cunning] i.e. Nature's skill.

15. *comely*] (*a*) morally decent, (*b*) pretty, pleasing.

16. *Roman*] This praises Cooke's skill in Latin while commenting obliquely on her Protestantism.

17. *wight*] creature.

1. *touchstone*] The purity of gold and silver alloys was tested by rubbing on a dark quartz stone.

tries] tests.

3. *had in price*] valued highly.

Where spite has spun the twine   5
  and wrath has woven the web,
There wrong has won the flowing stream
  and driven the truth to ebb.

What wonder is it then,
  though ladies suffer blame,   10
Since men of spite has framed their wits
  and will to do the same?

When fancy's hammer beats
  their fond and idle brains,
The women are the cause, say they,   15
  of all their cruel pains.

The fish may swim at large
  and not himself annoy;
Who bade him snatch that pleasant bait
  that does him thus destroy?   20

The fly plays with the candle light
  even of his own desire,
Who by his vain delight at last
  un'wares falls in the fire.

Even so you fondlings all,   25
  none can it well deny,
Truth with the touchstone tries this true:
  you are the fish, you are the fly.

Nor yet are women such
  that daily sigh for new;   30
Who makes account of both your faiths
  shall find men most untrue.

And if that one may say
  she found her lover true,
A thousand, for their changing minds,   35
  has just cause men to rue.

---

19. bait] beate *CT*.   24. falls] false *CT*.

5–8. *spite . . . ebb*] The image, which recalls the three Fates spinning, weaving and cutting off the thread of each person's life, suggests that truth is the water of life; *won* = reclaimed as dry land (*OED*, *vb*. 1, 5c).

12. *will*] desire.

do the same] i.e. drive the truth away, pervert it.

13. *fancy's*] (*a*) desire's, (*b*) imagination's, later (l. 42) with the sense 'delusion'.

14. *fond*] foolish.

idle] empty, void (*OED*, *a*.1).

17. *at large*] at liberty.

18. *annoy*] harm.

21. *fly*] i.e. moth.

25. *fondlings*] (*a*) foolish people, (*b*) those who have been fondled (i.e. by a lover).

30. *new*] i.e. new lovers.

36. *rue*] regret, deplore.

Their filed, flattering tongues
   such trains do put in ure,
That simple hearts they do reclaim
   as hawks unto the lure.   40

With feigned sighs they groan
   till fancy frames his toy,
As crocodiles with tears do train
   such as they would destroy.

When women's wisdom shouts out will   45
   that is men's only page,
Like tigers spoiled of their whelps
   then do they chiefly rage.

And in that mood their tongues
   do chat so many lies,   50
That reason says the ground is nought
   whereof such folly rise.

Therefore content yourselves
   and let them work their spite;
Against women, who jangles most,   55
   at length must yield of right.

In whom, of all good gifts
   and virtues lies such store,

---

40. hawks] *This ed.;* hakes *CT.*

37. *filed*] (a) smooth, (b) defiled, dishonourable.
38. *trains*] (a) consequences, series of events, (b) training (e.g. of a hawk, l. 40), also the tethered, live birds used to train a hawk, (c) tricks.
in ure] in use.
39. *reclaim*] (a) recall a hawk, (b) control, tame.
40. *hawks*] CT 'hakes' (whiting, a common fish) is probably a mis-reading occasioned by ll. 17–20, 28.
lure] A small leather pouch swung on a string which, when training a hawk, contains food.
41–4.] Since the woman imagines the man's false sighs to be the expression of genuine love, she is set up (framed and trained) as a plaything of both his fancifulness and her imagination; *frames* = constructs; *his* = (a) imagination's, (b) the man's; *toy* = trifling, amorous action or speech, plaything.
43–4. *crocodiles . . . destroy*] Crocodiles were proverbially described as luring their victims by pretending to weep for them (Tilley C831); *train* = allure, entice.
45. *shouts out*] deplores, cries out against (i.e. denies men's will).
will] sexual desire, punning on the name Will (i.e. for a page, l. 46).
46. *page*] attendant.
47. *spoiled*] despoiled, deprived. It is ironic that men's frustrated libido should be likened to tigers losing their cubs.
49. *mood*] (a) fierce anger, (b) frame of mind.
50. *chat*] babble, gossip.
51–2. *reason . . . rise*] i.e. 'There is no justification for their raging foolishness'.
54. *work*] wear out (*OED, vb.* 38.d).
55. *Against . . . most*] those who most wrangle and complain against women.
56. *of right*] rightfully, of necessity.
57. *whom*] i.e. women.

That sooner may we tell the sands
   upon the salt flood shore.   60

And thus I make an end:
   if women do amiss,
The wicked man, as truth does try,
   is only cause of this.

                       Finis R. E.

3

When women first Dame Nature wrought,
'All good,' quoth she, 'none shall be nought,
All wise shall be, none shall be fools,
For wit shall spring from women's schools,
In all good gifts they shall excel,   5
Their virtues all no tongue can tell.'
   Thus Nature said—I heard it, I,
   I pray you ask them if I do lie.

By Nature's grant this must ensue:
No woman false, but all are true,   10
None sow debate, but love maintain,
None joys to see her lover's pain,
As turtles true, their chosen one
They love and pine when he is gone.
   This is most true, none can deny,   15
   I pray you ask them if I do lie.

No lamb so meek as women be,
Their humble hearts from pride are free,
Rich things they wear—and wot you why?
Only to please their husband's eye!   20

---

6. virtues] *Add. 26737;* goodness *Ash. 48;* nature *CT.*   8. I do] *CT;* I *Add. 26737 and subsequently; Ash. 48.*   12. joys . . . her lover's] ioies . . . hir lovers *CT;* ioye . . . their husbandes *Add. 26737.*   14. when] *Add. 26737;* where *CT.*

59–60. *sooner . . . shore*] proverbial, 'As difficult as to number the sands in the sea' (Tilley S91); *tell* = count. This hyperbole is, of course, ironic.
  63. *try*] determine, prove.
  64. *only*] i.e. the only.

The poem also occurs in Add. 26737, 107v. There is a later imitation in Bodleian MS. Ashmole 48, fol. 127.
  2. *nought*] (*a*) bad quality, (*b*) immoral, wicked.
  4. *schools*] punning on 'flocks', 'bevies' (of animals or birds).
  6. *virtues*] CT would mean 'the nature of all of them' but is probably the result of the scribe's eye skipping to the next line.
  no . . . tell] is beyond description, a common phrase (cf. *D&P*, 10.33).
  10. *all are true*] 'All is true' is a common saying.
  11. *sow debate*] spread strife and argument.
  13. *turtles*] turtle doves, whose fidelity is both actual and proverbial.
  19. *wot*] know.

They never strive their wills to have,
Their husband's love, nought else they crave,
 Vain talk in them none can espy,
 I pray you ask them if I do lie.

If vice the earth should overcome   25
And no wight left under the sun,
If wealth would wring the poor, and might
With open force would suppress right,
If no rule were left on the ground
In women yet it might be found,   30
 The star of goodness in them does lie,
 I pray you ask them if I do lie.
The eagle with his piercing eye

Shall burn and waste the mountains high,
Huge rocks shall fleet as ship with sail,   35
The crab shall run, swim shall the snail,
Springs shall return from whence they came,
Sheep shall be wild and tigers tame,
 Or these my words false you shall try—
 Ha, ha, methinks I make a lie.   40

          Finis R. E.

4

O Lord that rulest both land and sea
 even by thy heavenly power,

36.] *CT;* Swimme shall the stone, runne shall the snaile *Add.* 26737. 37. came] c *CT.*
1. Lord] *CT;* god *AH.* land and sea] *Bradner;* lande seae *CT;* sea and land *AH.*

---

25. *vice . . . overcome*] i.e. depravity should cause the complete destruction of the world.

26. *wight*] creature.

27. *wring*] oppress.

might] powerful people.

29. *rule*] rule of law.

33. *eagle . . . eye*] It was thought that sight was achieved by means of beams of light emanating from the eye, but the ability to burn mountain tops is both humorously excessive even for the proverbially strong-sighted eagle, and a reversal of its supposed ability to gaze unharmed upon the sun (Tilley E3, E6); *piercing* = penetrating.

34. *waste*] lay waste, destroy.

35. *fleet*] float, sail.

36.] CT is not entirely satisfactory unless running is regarded as an entirely forward movement, but *Add.* 26737 is inferior both in its rhetorical structure and its use of 'stone' to follow 'rocks'.

39. *Or*] ere, before.

false . . . try] pick out as false.

40. *make*] write poetry (*OED, vb.* 5).

lie] This puns on the idea that all poetry is lies. Cf. Shakespeare, *AYLI*, 3.3.16, 'the truest poetry is the most feigning'.

Occurs also in AH. See pp. 16–17.

1–3.] Cf. Psalm 89.9, 'Thou rulest the ragynge of the see, thou stillest the waves therof, when they aryse'.

Grant I may pass these raging seas
   now in this happy hour.

For as the deer that sees the dart   5
   his bane does dread full sore,
So do I fear the winds, the sea,
   and eke the drenching shore.

But if thou wilt my corpse to pine
   amidst the drenching waves,   10
I yield my sprite to thee, O Lord,
   that all the world saves.

And to the fish I give my flesh,
   a worthy food to be,
Woe worth the time that chances thus   15
   my country for to fly.

For lo, even now my ears do hear
   how these same waves do roar,
That shall forth drive my drenched corpse
   unto the sounding shore.   20

And there some man shall see me lie
   upon the shining sands,
And thus shall pray unto the Lord
   with lifting up his hands:

'O Lord, my friends and children all   25
   guide with thy holy hand,
And grant they fly the raging seas
   and die upon the land.

---

8. shore] *AH;* showre *CT.*   18. these] theise *AH;* this *CT.*

---

5. *dart*] arrow.
6. *bane*] (*a*) death, (*b*) cause of death.
sore] (*a*) grievously, extremely, (*b*) with the sense of painfulness.
8. *eke*] also.
drenching] (*a*) drowning, overwhelming, (*b*) soaking.
shore] The spelling 'showre' (in CT) can signify both 'shore' and 'shower'.
9. *corpse*] body (whether alive or dead). The spellings 'corps' and 'corse' were interchangeable at this period. CT gives 'corse' throughout this poem and 'corps' at 5.1.
pine] afflict with pain and suffering.
11. *sprite*] spirit.
12. *world*] This word, spelt with a final 'e' in CT, needs almost to be pronounced disyllabically to fill up the metre; AH accordingly gives 'whole world'.
14. *worthy*] suitable, excellent.
15. *Woe worth*] 'may evil befall on', a common curse (cf. *D&P,* 15.22ff.).
19. *drenched*] drowned.
20. *sounding shore*] (*a*) shallow coastal waters where ships are wrecked and mariners must use a sounding lead (line with lead weight) to ascertain the depth and nature of the sea floor, (*b*) shore reverberating with the sound of waves.
22. *shining*] glistening with water.
27. *fly*] (*a*) sail freely with loosed sails, (*b*) flee, shun.

'For so even here I see one lie
    while he this race did run,   30
Amidst the cruel seas he caught
    his bane alas too soon.

'It is alas a ruthful thing
    to see this woeful wight,
Make thou, O Lord, his seely soul   35
    partaker of thy light.

'And I to show the fervent love
    I bear to Christian blood,
Here will I take the corpse unknown
    and wind it in a shroud,   40

'And bring it to the holy church
    the Christian rites to have,
And so within the hallowed ground
    will put him in a grave.

'Upon his grave shall stand a stone   45
    as witness of his case,
And shall forbid all such as sail
    to attempt that dreadful place.'

Thus shall I die, thus shall I lie,
    this is my destiny,   50
But woe worth me, that shall give cause
    each wight the seas to fly.

Woe worth the man that framed the ship
    whereby we cut the seas
And see the countries far apart   55
    our fancies for to please.

But woe worth me yet once again
    that thus shall lie unknown,
And shall not place my wretched corpse
    under some English stone.   60

---

29. *so*] Ironically, the poet dead on the land, died trying to fly (escape) the sea.
30. *while*] The pronoun 'who' is also implied.
    race] (*a*) period of his life, (*b*) name given to certain dangerous currents in the sea, (*c*) the action of sailing swiftly.
32. *bane*] death, ruin, fate.
35. *seely*] (*a*) miserable, helpless, often used with respect to a soul about to receive divine judgement (*OED*, 6.b), (*b*) spiritually blessed (*OED*, 3).
40. *wind*] wrap.
46. *case*] plight.
48. *to attempt*] The 'o' should be elided (as in AH).
53. *framed*] constructed.
54. *cut*] cleave, pass quickly through.

O Lord, why dost thou take me now
    amidst the drowning seas,
And shorten thus my springing youth
    and eke my pleasant days?

But now O Lord, but now I say   65
    begins my youthly prime,
Take me in age and let me live
    as yet a longer time,

That I may wail my wicked ways
    and eke my wanton will,   70
And learn to hate all earthly joys
    of which I had my fill.

But woe is me, I pray in vain
    even clean against thy will,
For in my sins and wickedness   75
    O Lord, thou wilt me kill.

Thy will be done in land and sea,
    to die myself I bend,
O death come now, for God my Lord
    appointed me this end.   80

O death how sharp art thou to such
    as be in tender age,
Which by repentance thinks at length
    their sins for to assuage.

But die I must, undoubtedly—   85
    what needs me further talk?—
And in the salt sea flood, my corpse
    unto the shore shall walk.

I yield my sprite into thy hands
    that died upon the rood,   90
For thou hast bought me, God of truth,
    even with thy precious blood.

I am beset with sin alas,
    I am the child of ire,

---

64. days] dayes *AH;* deas *CT.*

61–8. *O Lord . . . longer time*] Cf. Psalm 102.24, 'He brought downe my strength
in my journey, and shortened my dayes. But I sayed: O my God, take me not away in
the myddest of myne age.'
63. *springing*] burgeoning.
78. *bend*] submit.
83. *at length*] later, after a long time.
84. *assuage*] mitigate, lessen.
88. *walk*] travel.
90. *rood*] cross.

Keep thou, O Lord, my seely soul   95
    from everlasting fire.

In thee, in thee I trust O Lord,
    thy blood, thy blood I crave,
Forget my sins and grant my sprite
    the heavenly joys to have.   100

Lo now I sink, lo now I drown,
    and drink the mortal flood,
O Christ, O Christ, take thou my sprite
    that trusteth in thy blood.

                              Finis R. E.

5   *Mr Wilson*

O caitiff corpse that long hast felt
    the present pangs of death,
Shall that not be thy chance at last
    to yield thy natal breath?
But still to stay and not revolve   5
    nor yet from flame return,
But ay, alas, with troubling heart
    in Etna still to burn.
Alas what heavy hap have I
    that still must love obey   10
Till that my daunted heart shall moan,
    and still in it can stay.

97. In . . . Lord] *CT*; In thee o Lorde I putt my trust *AH*.   98. thy blood, thy blood]
CT; thie bloode onlye *AH*.   99. my sprite] me sprite *CT*.   100. the] *CT*; thie *AH*.
103. O . . . Christ] *CT*; O Christe make speede *AH*.   sprite] *CT*; sowle *AH*.

97–8.] AH adopts a more measured tone; cf. Psalms 31.1 and 71.1, 'In the[e],
O Lord, have I put my trust'.
    102. *mortal*] fatal.

0.1 Mr Wilson] The meaning of this evidently ambiguous poem depends on the
context supplied by the identity of this person; see p. 17.
    1. *caitiff*] (*a*) miserable, wretched, (*b*) captive.
corpse] living body (cf. 4.9n).
    4. *natal*] dating from the day of birth.
    5. *revolve*] return.
    7. *ay*] always.
    8. *Etna*] Europe's highest active volcano, in Sicily. Cf. the lament of the Cyclops,
Polyphemus, for Galatea, 'O Nereid; your anger is more deadly than the lightening
flash . . . For oh, I burn, and my hot passion, stirred to frenzy, rages more fiercely within
me; I seem to carry Etna let down into my breast with all his violence. And you, Galatea,
do not care at all' (Ovid, *Metamorphoses*, 13.858–69).
    11. *moan*] lament.
    12. *in it*] i.e. in love.

O greedy gripes, come late my guest,
   no longer let me stay,
O Furies all with cruel hand   15
   do all my limbs array.
Let me not be in thraldom thus
   by love as one aghast,
O death ere she that death shall cause
   come change my case at last.   20
Come change my case that I sustain,
   or speedy hand shall give
Unnatural death—which long I wished
   so loath I am to live.
Alas Leander, why do I   25
   impute to thee a blame
For yielding life to earnest love
   where I do mean the same?
Nothing can quench my parching flames,
   in vain for help I call,   30
In fine therefore, O sacred dame,
   thou shalt have life and all.
To one I come not yet—that sure
   that better does deserve—
Therefore my last and gasping hest   35
   to honour thee shall serve.

                  Finis per meum. R. E.

---

13. gripes] griphes *CT;* guest] geste *CT.*   25–6. I / impute] I impute / *CT.*

---

13. *greedy gripes*] voracious, grasping spasms. As the CT spelling indicates, there is some slippage between 'gripe' and 'grief', i.e. physical as well as mental pain, (*OED*, 'gripe' *vb*.7). 'Griping griefs' is a common poetic phrase at this period for intense (lit. stomach-churning) emotional pain; cf. *D&P*, 10.53; *PDD*, 14.1.
   come . . . guest] i.e. be belatedly welcome.
  16. *array*] prepare, dress, arrange, in the ironical sense of 'disfigure', 'discomfort'; perhaps 'tear limb from limb'.
  18. *aghast*] struck with terror.
  19. *she*] i.e. the cruel lover.
  20. *case*] (*a*) situation, condition, (*b*) body.
  25. *Leander*] This young man nightly swam the Hellespont (Dardanelles) to visit his lover Hero until he was drowned in a storm (Ovid, *Heroides*, 18, 19).
  31–6.] These lines are perhaps necessarily obscure and evidently sum up the poet's dilemma. Both the 'sacred dame' and the subject of the poem, Mr Wilson, can be encompassed in the pronouns 'one' (l. 33) and 'thee' (l. 36).
  31. *In fine*] (*a*) in the end, (*b*) in short.
  35. *hest*] vow, promise.
  36.1. Finis per meum] (*a*) 'The end as far as it concerns me', an ironic comment in the light of this poem calling on the speaker's death, (*b*) 'Finished by me', a phrase which sometimes indicates an autograph MS.

POEMS FROM *THE PARADISE OF DAINTY DEVICES*

1 *M. Edwards'* MAY

When MAY is in his prime, then may each heart rejoice,
When MAY bedecks each branch with green, each bird strains
   forth his voice.
The lively sap creeps up into the blooming thorn,
The flowers, which cold in prison kept, now laugh the frost to
   scorn.
All nature's imps triumph while joyful MAY does last,   5
When MAY is gone, of all the year the pleasant time is past.

MAY makes the cheerful hue, MAY breeds and brings new blood,
MAY marches throughout every limb, MAY makes the merry
   mood.
MAY pricketh tender hearts, their warbling notes to tune,
Full strange it is yet some we see do make their MAY in June.   10
Thus things are strangely wrought while joyful MAY does last,
When MAY is gone, of all the year the pleasant time is past.

All you that live on earth, and have your MAY at will,
Rejoice in MAY, as I do now, and use your MAY with skill.
Use MAY while that you may, for MAY has but his time,   15
When all the fruit is gone it is too late the tree to climb.

---

3. creeps] *PDD;* shoutes *Add. 26737.*   4. flowers . . . cold] *PDD;* flowers with colde
Dow; flower long *Add. 26737.*   laugh] *Dow;* laughes *PDD.*   5. triumph while]
Dow; Add. 26737; triumphes, whyles *PDD.*   6. pleasant] *PDD;* pleasantst *Dow and
subsequently.*   8. limb] limme *PDD;* tyme *Dow.*   12. When . . . year] *Dow; PDD
prints l. 18 here.*   14. I] *PDD; Dow;* we *Add. 26737.*   with skill] *PDD; Dow;* at
will *Add. 26737.*

A1r–v, *1576.* This song may belong to *Palamon and Arcyte;* see p. 80. The words
and music occur in the Dow MS; see pp. 250–4. Lines 1–6 and 13–16 occur in Add.
26737, fol. 108.

0.1 *M. Edwards' MAY*] This title suggests that by the time of its printing in 1576
the poem was already well known, and perhaps that the MS copy for this particular
poem did not belong to Edwards himself. The signature 'M[aster] Edwardes' was added
to the end of the poem in 1578 and subsequently. Here, and in poems 2 and 3 below,
the authors play on the word 'may' both as a noun, (*a*) the name of the month, (*b*)
bloom, prime, (*c*) flowers of the hawthorn tree, (*d*) maiden, virgin; and as a verb: (*a*)
engage in May games and rituals, (*b*) be able, (*c*) have permission, (*d*) the auxiliary
verb of conditionality and uncertainty.

3. *lively*] life-bearing. The scribe for Add. 26737 probably understood 'quick-
moving', hence his reading 'shouts' (presumably an error for 'shoots').

thorn] hawthorn (*crataegus monogyna*), a common small tree or shrub, usually in
flower by 1 May in the old Julian calendar, hence 'may-tree'.

5. *imps*] (*a*) young men (*OED, sb.* 6), (*b*) young shoots (*OED, sb.* 1).

9. *pricketh*] (*a*) spurs, (*b*) writes music [in].

12.] The Dow MS order for ll. 12 and 18 is more climactic than the *PDD* version
and fits the use of imperatives in the third stanza.

16. *When . . . climb*] A similar phrase occurs at *PDD,* 5.6, but it does not seem to
be a conventional proverb, indeed it rather contradicts the proverb, 'The higher he
climbs the greater his fall' (Tilley C414).

Your liking and your lust is fresh while MAY does last,
Take MAY in time, when MAY is gone the pleasant time is past.

Finis.

2   *A reply to M. Edwards' 'May'*

I read a maying rhyme of late delighted much my ear,
It may delight as many more as it shall read or hear.
To see how there is showed how May is much of price,
And eke to may when that you may, even so is his advice.
It seems he meant to may himself, and so to use his skill,   5
For that the time did serve so well, in May to have his will.
His only May was ease of mind, so far as I can guess,
And that his May his mind did please, a man can judge no less.

And as himself did reap the fruits of that his pleasant May,
He wills his friend the same to use in time when as he may.   10
He is not for himself it seems, but wishes well to all,
For that he would they should take May in time when it does fall.
So use your May, you may, it cannot hurtful be,
And May well used in time and place may make you merry glee.
Modest maying meetest is, of this you may be sure,   15
A modest maying, quietness to mayers does procure.

Who may and will not take, may wish he had so done,
Who may and it does take, may think he took too soon,
So join your May with wisdom's lore and then you may be sure
Who makes his May in other sort his unrest may procure.   20
Some may before May come, some may when May is past,
Some make their May too late, and some do May post-haste.
Let wisdom rule I say your May, and thus I make an end,
And may that when you list to may, a good May God you send.

Finis. M. S.

3   *Master Edwards his 'I may not'*

In May, by kind, Dame Nature wills all earthly wights to sing,
In May the new and coupled fowls may joy the lively spring,

18. Take . . . gone] *Dow. PDD prints l. 12 here.*

---

17. *lust*] desire.

D3, *1578*. Whoever M.S. was, he lacks Edwards's sangfroid; see pp. 42 and 80.
2. *more . . . hear*] i.e. 'more people as shall read or hear it'.
6. *will*] desire.
14. *glee*] (*a*) sport, enjoyment, (*b*) music.
17. *Who . . . take*] i.e. 'He who has the opportunity and does not grasp it'.
18. *may . . . soon*] Cf. proverbs, 'Men must do as they may, not as they would',
'Who that may not as they would, will as they may' (Tilley M554, M769).
20. *in . . . sort*] i.e. unwisely.

M3r–v, *1585*. The title led Rollins and Bradner to ascribe the poem to Edwards, but
it is clumsier than *PDD*, 1, above. The list of animals is conventional, and similar to
that in Surrey's 'The soote season'; the poem has no redeeming irony.
1. *by kind*] (*a*) naturally, (*b*) by species (each in its own way).
wights] creatures.

In May the nightingale her notes does warble on the spray,
In May the birds their mossy nests do timber as they may.
In May the swift and turning hare her bagged belly slacks,   5
In May the little sucking wats do play with tender flax,
All creatures may in May be glad, no May can me remove,
I sorrow in May since I may not in May obtain my love.

The stately hart in May does mew his old and palmed beams,
His state renews, in May he leaps to view Apollo's streams,   10
In May the buck his horned tops does hang upon the pale,
In May he seeks the pastures green in ranging every dale.
In May the ugly, speckled snake does cast his loathsome skin,
In May the better that he may increase his scaly skin.
All things in May I see they may rejoice like turtle dove,   15
I sorrow in May since I may not in May obtain my love.

Now may I mourn in fruitful May, who may or can redress,
My May is sorrow since she that may, withholds my 'may'
    afresh.
Thus I must may in pleasant May till I may may at will
With her in May, whose 'may', my life, now may both save and
    spill.   20

---

12. every] *1585*; over the *1600; Bradner.*   13. his] *This ed.;* her *1585.*   14. skin]
1585; kin *conj. Rollins; Bradner.*   18. My] *Rollins;* May *1585.*

4. *timber*] build.
5. *bagged*] pregnant, distended.
slacks] allows to diminish, subside i.e. gives birth. *PDD* prints the related older word
'slakes'.
6. *wats*] hares.
7. *remove*] change, move (to joy).
9. *hart*] male deer, particularly a red deer that is more than five years old and therefore with impressive horns.
mew] shed.
palmed beams] antlers; *beams* = the main trunk of the horn (*OED*, 12); *palmed* =
breaking into finger-like divisions.
10. *Apollo's streams*] i.e. sunbeams.
11. *buck*] male fallow deer.
pale] fence, boundary of an enclosure, i.e. the edge of the forest.
14. *skin*] Emendation to 'kin' here saves the author from the repetition of 'skin' but
perhaps goes against the subject of the stanza which, apart from the confusion caused
by *PDD* 'her' (cf. collation l. 13), is the growth and rejuvenation of the male body;
female fecundity is the subject of the first stanza; cf. *PDD*, 16.10–11 (collation), for a
similar switch of gender.
18. *she ... afresh*] she that might [do so] still withholds permission for me [to enjoy
her].
19. *must may*] must do as I please.
may may at will] am able to (*a*) go maying, (*b*) do what I really want to do.
20. '*may*'] i.e. permission.
spill] kill, with pun on spilling the poet's 'life', i.e. vivifying essence (semen).

Contented hearts that have your hope, in May you may at large
Unfold your joys, expel your cares, and bask in pleasure-barge,
Save I alone in May that may lament for my behove,
I mourn in May till that I may in May obtain my love.

Finis.

4   *Fair words make fools fain*

In youthful years when first my young desires began
To prick me forth to serve in court, a slender, tall, young man,
My father's blessing then I asked upon my knee,
Who blessing me with trembling hand, these words gan say to me:
'My son, God guide thy way, and shield thee from mischance,   5
And make thy just deserts in court, thy poor estate to advance.
Yet when thou art become one of the courtly train,
Think on this proverb old,' quoth he, 'that fair words makes
    fools fain'.

This counsel gravely given, most strange appeared to me,
Till tract of time, with open eyes had made me plainly see   10
What subtle sleights are wrought by painted tales' device,
When hollow hearts with friendly shows the simple do entice
To think all gold that shines, to feed their fond desire
Whose shivering cold is warmed with smoke, instead of flaming
    fire.
Since talk of tickle trust does breed a hope most vain,   15

---

22. Unfold] *Rollins;* Untolde *1585.*   pleasure-barge] pleasure barge *1585;* pleasure's
barge *Rollins.*
1. youthful] *PDD; Dallis;* youthlye *Add. 15117.*   9. appeared] *AH;* appeares *PDD.*
12. shows] *1578;* shoes *1576.*

---

22. *pleasure-barge*] broad, flat-bottomed river boat, used for ceremonial trips and
recreation.
23. *behove*] benefit, advantage.

A1v–A2, *1576.* Occurs in Add. 15233, fols 38v–39r; AH, fol. 166 (where those
variants which offer credible readings tend to smooth the style); and with music in Add.
15117. See pp. 4–5 and 247–9.
0.1. *Fair . . . fain*] proverbial (Tilley W794); *Fair words* = promises; *fain* = glad,
pleased.
2. *prick*] urge, drive.
slender] (*a*) slim, graceful, (*b*) immature, ill prepared.
tall] (*a*) proper, handsome, bold, (*b*) tall in height.
4. *gan*] did, began to.
6. *to advance*] The metre seems to demand elision, i.e. *t'advance* (as in AH and
PDD, 1590 onwards); however the full syllable is set to music in Add. 15117.
10. *tract*] passage, duration.
13. *all . . . shines*] proverbial, 'all that glisters is not gold' (Tilley A146).
13–14. *feed . . . fire*] proverbial, 'The smoke of fair words will serve to feed fools'
(Tilley S575). Cf. 'It is no fire that gives no heat' (Tilley F261).
15. *tickle*] uncertain, unreliable.

This proverb true by proof I find, that fair words makes fools
fain.

Fair speech alway does well, where deeds ensue fair words,
Fair speech again alway does evil, that bushes gives for birds.
Who hopes to have fair words, to try his lucky lot,
If I may counsel let him strike it while the iron is hot.   20
But them that feed on clods instead of pleasant grapes,
And after warning often given, for better luck still gapes,
Full loath I am, yet must I tell them in words plain,
This proverb old proves true in them, that fair words makes
fools fain.

Woe worth the time that words so slowly turn to deeds,   25
Woe worth the time that fair sweet flowers are grown to rotten
weeds,
But thrice woe worth the time that truth away is fled,
Wherein I see how simple hearts with words are vainly fed.
Trust no fair words therefore where no deeds do ensue,
Trust words as skilful falconers do trust hawks that never flew.   30
Trust deeds, let words be words which never wrought me gain,
Let my experience make you wise, and let words make fools fain.
                                                M. Edwards.

   5   Wanting his desire he complains

The sailing ships with joy at last do touch the long desired port,
The hewing axe the oak does waste, the batt'ring cannon breaks
the fort,

---

1. last . . . touch] *conj.* Rollins; length . . . touche *1578* (lenght *1576*); last . . . reach
Add. *26737*.

   18. *evil*] This should be elided to one syllable (ev'l) for the sake of the metre.
   bushes . . . birds] Cf. proverb, 'one [person] beats the bush and another catches the
bird' (Tilley B740); *for* = instead of.
   20. *strike . . . hot*] proverbial (Tilley I94).
   21–2. *feed . . . gapes*] Cf. proverbs: 'He that gapes until he be fed, well may he gape
until he be dead'; 'One cannot gather grapes of thorns or figs of thistles' (Tilley G31,
G411).
   23. *loath . . . tell*] Cf. proverbs 'Few words are best', 'Few words show men wise'
(Tilley W798, W799), i.e. wise men do not speak too much; also 'A word to a wise
man is enough' (Tilley W781), i.e. those who need to be told repeatedly must be foolish.
   25, 26, 27. *Woe worth*] cursed be.
   25. *words . . . deeds*] Cf. proverb, 'From words to deeds is a great space' (Tilley
W802).
   26. *flowers . . . weeds*] Cf. proverb, 'The weeds overgrow the corn (Tilley W242).
   30. *Trust . . . flew*] Cf. proverb, 'Try [i.e. test] before you trust' (Tilley T595).
   31. *deeds . . . words*] Cf. proverb, 'Not words but deeds' (Tilley W820), i.e. 'let
words which have done me no good, be just words'.

   C2r–v, *1576*. Occurs in BL Add. 26737, entitled 'The vain hopes of a lover'.
   1. *last*] This emendation initiates a sequence of mid-line caesural rhymes and is

Hard, haggard hawks stoop to the lure, wild colts in time the
    bridle tames,
There is nothing so out of ure, but to his kind long time it
    frames.
    Yet this I find in time: no time can win my suit,   5
    Though oft the tree I climb, I cannot catch the fruit.

And yet the pleasant branches oft, in yielding wise to me do bow,
When I would touch, they spring aloft—soon are they gone, I
    wot not how.
Thus I pursue the fleeting flood like Tantalus in hell below,
Would God my case she understood, which can full soon relieve
    my woe—   10
    Which if to her were known, the fruit were surely mine,
    She would not let me groan, and browse upon the rime.

But if my ship with tackle torn, with rented sails must needs
    retire,
And stream and wind had plainly sworn by force to hinder my
    desire,
Like one that strikes upon the rocks, my weary wrack I should
    bewail   15

---

12. rime] *This ed.;* rine *PDD* (riue *1576*).   13. torn] *1578; Add. 26737;* turne *1576*.

probably correct. However 'length' would pun on (*a*) the length of a ship, (*b*) the sense
of riding at anchor at length from the shore, which would likewise enhance the sense
of just 'touching' the port.
    touch] make a brief stop during a journey.
    2–3. *oak ... tames*] Cf. proverbs, 'In time / the sturdy oak will bow / the haggard
hawks will be trained to the lure / the ox will bear the yoke' (Tilley T304, T298, T303);
waste = destroy.
    3. *Hard*] (*a*) difficult to deal with, (*b*) slow (to learn).
    haggard] untrained hawk.
    stoop] swoop, fly down.
    lure] See CT 2.40n.
    4. *ure*] use, habit, custom.
    kind ... frames] eventually shapes itself to its own nature. Cf. proverb, 'Custom
(use) is a second nature' (Tilley C932).
    6. *tree ... fruit*] perhaps proverbial (cf. 'May', *PDD*, l. 16).
    7. *yet*] as yet, still.
    wise] manner.
    9. *fleeting*] flowing, vanishing.
    Tantalus] For disclosing the secrets of the Feast of the Gods, Tantalus was tormented
in hell by being chained up to his chin in water beneath an overhanging fruit tree: 'Thy
lips can catch no water, Tantalus, and the tree that overhangs ever eludes thee' (Ovid,
Metamorphoses, 4.457–9).
    10. *which*] who.
    12. *rime*] frozen mist, hoarfrost with likely pun on 'rime' (*a*) poetic metre (*OED,
sb.* 1), (*b*) rhymed verse (*OED, sb.* 2).
    13–16. *ship ... mocks*] A storm-tossed ship is a common emblem of the vicissitudes
of fortune; *rented* = torn; *wrack* = obsolete form of 'wreck' but is retained here because
of the aural pun on 'wracked' (racked, tortured, l. 18).

And learn to know false Fortune's mocks, who smiles on me to
    small avail.
Yet since she only can my rented ship restore,
To help her wracked man but once, I seek no more.

Finis. M. Edwards.

6   *Of Fortune's power*

Polycrates whose passing hap caused him to lose his fate,
A golden ring cast in the seas to change his constant state,
And in a fish yet at his board, the same he after found,
Thus Fortune lo, to whom she takes, for bounty does abound.

The misers unto might she mounts—a common case we see—   5
And mighty in great misery, she sets in low degree.
Whom she today does rear on high upon her whirling wheel,
Tomorrow next she dingeth down, and casteth at her heel.

No measure has she in her gifts, she does reward each sort—
The wise that counsel have, no more than fools that maketh sport.   10
She uses never partial hands for to offend or please,
'Give me good Fortune,' all men says, 'and throw me in the seas'.

---

18. man but once,] man, but once *PDD;* but once *Add.* 26737.

---

17. *she only*] only she, i.e. Fortune, who is cast in this poem in the role of disdain-ful mistress.

18. *man but once,*] This edition alters the punctuation to promote the sense, but readers should register the internal caesural rhyme on can/man as a moment of inter-rupted momentum.

C4v–D1, *1576.* See pp. 44–5.

1. *Polycrates*] This tyrant of the island of Samos (fl. 540–522 BC) was noted for his piratical mastery of the sea and for his good fortune. He was advised to break his luck lest he anger the gods and be brought to complete ruin, so he decided to throw his most precious possession, a ring, into the sea. It was found in the belly of a fish, and he continued fortunate until he was trapped and crucified by Oroetes (Herodotus, 3). The story of a ring cast into the sea and found inside a fish is a staple of world folk tale.

passing] surpassing.

hap] fortune.

2. *constant state*] i.e. of good fortune.

3. *board*] table.

5. *misers*] (*a*) miserable wretches, (*b*) people who hoard their wealth. Great princes were expected to demonstrate their power by a conspicuous display of wealth.

unto . . . mounts] she raises to positions of power.

6. *mighty*] i.e. powerful people.

7. *whirling wheel*] Fortune is commonly depicted with a wheel, raising some people up and casting others down.

8. *dingeth*] strikes, dashes.

9. *measure*] moderation.

sort] class of person.

11. *partial*] favouring a particular person as a matter of policy.

12. *Give . . . seas*] proverbial (Tilley M146), i.e. a fortunate person will survive any eventuality.

It is no fault or worthiness that makes men fall or rise,
I rather be born fortunate than to be very wise.
The blindest man right shoots that by good Fortune guided is,   15
To whom that pleasant Fortune pipes, can never dance amiss.

Finis. M. Edwards.

7   *Though triumph after bloody wars, the greatest brags do bear,*
Yet triumph of a conquered mind, the crown of Fame shall wear.

Whoso does mark the careless life of these unhappy days,
And sees what small and slender hold the state of virtue stays,
He finds that this accursed trade proceedeth of this ill:
That men be given too much to yield to their untamed will.

In lack of taming witless will, the poor we often see   5
Envies the rich, because that he his equal cannot be.
The rich advanced to might by wealth, from wrong does not
   refrain,
But will oppress the weaker sort, to heap excessive gain.

If Fortune were so blind to give to one man what he will,
A world would not suffice the same, if he might have his fill.   10
We wish, we search, we strive for all, and have no more therein
Than has the slave, when death does come, though Croesus'
   wealth we win.

In getting much, we get but care, such brittle wealth to keep—
The rich within his walls of stone does never soundly sleep,
When poor in weak and slender house do fear no loss of wealth   15

---

15. shoots] *This ed.;* soone *PDD.*
8. opress the] *conj. Rollins;* opresseth *PDD.*

---

14. *rather . . . wise*] proverbial, 'It is better to be happy (fortunate) than wise' (Tilley
H140), cf. Cicero, quoting, with some reservation, Theophrastus, 'Fortune not wisdom
rules the life of man', *Tusc.*, 5.9.25.
    15. *blindest . . . shoots*] proverbial, 'A blind man can sometimes hit the mark', i.e.
by chance (Tilley M81). Ironically, Fortune herself is usually represented as blind (cf.
PDD, 7.9). A similar proverb refers to fools (Tilley F516); cf. l. 14.
    16. *To . . . amiss*] proverbial, 'He dances well to whom Fortune pipes' (Tilley F611).

D11-v, *1576*. See pp. 44–5.
    3. *trade*] way of life, habit.
    4. *be given*] tend, are prone.
    9. *blind*] Fortune is regularly depicted as blind because her gifts and tribulations are
distributed indiscriminately.
    he will] i.e. he would have.
    10. *suffice the same*] satisfy him.
    12. *Croesus*] King of Lydia (c.560–546 BC) was proverbially famous for his wealth
(Herodotus, 1).
    13–14. *care . . . sleep*] proverbial: 'A rich man and a miserable'; 'Much coin, much
care' 'Riches bring care and fears' (Tilley M363, C506, R109, R108); *brittle* = fragile.
    15–16. *wealth . . . health*] proverbial, 'He that has his health is rich enough' (Tilley
H288); cf. Herodotus, 1, 'Great wealth can make a man no happier than moderate

And have no further care but this: to keep themselves in health.

Affection may not hide the sword of sway, in judgement seat,
Lest partial favour execute the law in causes great;
But if the mind in constant state, affection quite do leave,
The higher state shall have their rights, the poor no wrong
    receive.   20

It is accounted greater praise to Caesar's lofty state,
Against his vanquished foes, in wars, to bridle wreakful hate,
Than when to Rome he had subdued the people long
    unknown—
Whereby as far as land was found, the fame abroad was blown.

If honour can self-will refuse, and justice be upright,   25
And private state desires but that which good appears in sight,
Then virtue shall with sovereign show, to every eye reveal
A heavenly life, a wealful state, a happy commonweal.

Let virtue then the triumph win, and govern all your deeds,
Your yielding to her sober hests immortal glory breeds.   30
She shall uprear your worthy name, shining unto the skies,
Her beams shall blaze in grave obscure where shrined carcass
    lies.

Finis. M. Edwards.

8   *Of perfect wisdom*

Whoso will be accounted wise, and truly claim the same,
By joining virtue to his deeds, he must achieve the fame,

---

18. favour] *1578;* law doe *1576.*   24. fame] *conj. Rollins;* same *PDD.*   31.
shining unto] *1600;* shining into *1578;* shew then vnto *1576.*   32. blaze] *1578;*
shine, *1576.*
2. fame] *conj. Rollins;* same *PDD.*

---

means, unless he has the luck to continue in prosperity to the end . . . for though the
rich have the means to satisfy their appetites and to bear calamities . . . the poor . . .
will have besides the blessings of a sound body'; *slender* = poor, straitened.
    17. *Affection . . . seat*] i.e. those who sit in judgement should not be irrational or
influenced by their emotions when wielding the sword of power.
    18. *execute*] bring into effect or operation.
    20. *higher state*] i.e. rich and powerful people.
    22. *vanquished . . . hate*] Cf. Cicero, *De officiis,* 2.8.26, 'as long as the empire of
the Roman People maintained itself by acts of service, not of oppression, wars were
waged in the interest of our allies or to safeguard our supremacy; the end of our wars
was marked by acts of clemency or by only a necessary degree of severity'; *wreakful* =
vengeful.
    24. *Whereby . . . blown*] i.e. the fame of which spread to the ends of the earth.
    28. *wealful*] happy, prosperous, fortunate.
commonweal] commonwealth.
    30. *hests*] commands.
    32. *shrined carcass*] i.e. the body enclosed in its coffin.

DIV–D2, *1576.* See pp. 44–5.
2. *fame*] The compositor probably mistook 'f' for long 's'.

But few there be that seek thereby true wisdom to attain—
O God, so rule our hearts therefore, such fondness to refrain.

The wisdom which we most esteem, in this thing does consist: 5
With glorious talk to show in words our wisdom when we list.
Yet not in talk, but seemly deeds our wisdom we should place,
To speak so fair and do but ill does wisdom quite disgrace.

To bargain well and shun the loss a wisdom counted is,
And thereby through the greedy coin no hope of grace to miss;   10
To seek by honour to advance his name to brittle praise,
Is wisdom which we daily see increases in our days.

But heavenly wisdom soe'er seems too hard for them to win—
But weary of the suit they seem when they do once begin.
It teaches us to frame our life while vital breath we have,   15
When it dissolveth earthly mass, the soul from death to save.

By fear of God to rule our steps from sliding into vice,
A wisdom is which we neglect, although of greater price.
A point of wisdom also this, we commonly esteem,
That every man should be indeed that he desires to seem.   20

To bridle that desire of gain which forces us to ill,
Our haughty stomachs Lord repress, to tame presuming will;
This is the wisdom that we should above each thing desire—
O heavenly God from sacred throne, that grace in us inspire,

And print in our repugnant hearts the rules of wisdom true,   25
That all our deeds in worldly life may like thereof ensue.
Thou only art the living spring from whom this wisdom flows,
O wash therewith our sinful hearts, from vice that therein grows.
                                                  Finis M. Edwards

---

13. soe'er] sower *PDD*.

___

6–7. *words . . . deeds*] proverbial, cf. *PDD*, 4.25n, 31n.

10. *grace*] i.e. worldly honour (not the eternal grace that true spiritual wisdom should attain).

11. *by honour*] by courtesy or flattery (in order to gain honours and titles as a reward).

brittle] fragile, mortal.

13. *soe'er*] soever i.e. whenever, always.

14. *suit*] pursuit.

when . . . begin] as soon as they begin.

15. *frame*] shape, order.

vital breath] the breath of life.

16. *When . . . save*] i.e. [so that] the soul is saved from death when the solid earthly body dissolves; cf. 2 Cor. 5.1.

17. *fear of God*] Cf. Psalm 111.10, 'The feare of the lord is the beginning of wisdome'.

20. *that*] that which, what.

25. *repugnant*] resisting, hostile.

26. *like . . . ensue*] may flow from such [rules of wisdom].

9   *Amantium irae amoris redintegratio est*

In going to my naked bed as one that would have slept,
I heard a wife sing to her child that long before had wept.
She sighed sore and sang full sweet to bring the babe to rest,
That would not cease but cried still in sucking at her breast.
She was full weary of her watch, and grieved with her child,   5
She rocked it and rated it, until on her it smiled.
   Then did she say, 'Now have I found this proverb true to prove:
   The falling out of faithful friends is the renewing of love'.

Then took I paper, pen and ink, this proverb for to write,
In register for to remain of such a worthy wight.   10
As she proceeded thus in song unto her little brat,
Much matter uttered she of weight, in place whereas she sat,
And proved plain there was no beast, nor creature bearing life,
Could well be known to live in love without discord and strife.
   Then kissed she her little babe and swore by God above,   15
   'The falling out of faithful friends is the renewing of love'.

She said that neither king nor prince nor lord could live aright,
Until their puissance they did prove, their manhood and their
    might.
When manhood shall be matched so, that fear can take no place,
Then weary works makes warriors each other to embrace   20
And leave their force that failed them, which did consume the rout,
That might by force with love have lived the term of nature out.
   Then did she sing as one that thought no man could her reprove,
   'The falling out of faithful friends is the renewing of love'.

0.1. *redintegratio*] redintigratia *PDD*.   3. and] *PDD;* yet *Add. 26737.*   sweet]
1578; Add. 26737; sore *1576.*   4. cease] *1578; Add. 26737;* rest *1576.*   7. this]
1578; the *1576.*   8. is the renewing] *1576; Add. 26737;* reneuing is *1578, and subsequently.*   22. by force ... term of] *Add. 26737; Bradner;* before haue liued their
tyme, and *1576.*

F1–v, *1576.* The words are also in Add. 26737. See pp. 56, 98, and music, p. 238.
  0.1 Amantium ... est] 'the anger of friends is the renewing of love'; proverbial
(Erasmus, *Adagia,* 740b; Tilley F40, Terence, *Andria,* l. 555).
  1. *naked*] (*a*) He is going naked to bed—the usual poetic meaning, cf. *Venus and
Adonis,* 397f.: 'Who sees his true-love in her naked bed, / Teaching the sheets a whiter
hue than white'; (*b*) possibly implying that the bed is otherwise empty and unoccupied
(*OED,* III.8).
  8. *is ... renewing*] This is metrically irregular (resulting in a fifteen-syllable line) but
it elegantly underlies the musical setting. The regularised 1578 reading is syntactically
and musically awkward.
  10. *register*] record.
  18. *puissance*] power.
  prove] test.
  20. *weary works*] exhausting troubles, afflictions (*OED, sb.* 6a).
  21. *consume*] destroy.
  rout] troop, rabble.
  22. *by ... love*] by the force or virtue of love.
  lived ... out] lived out the natural length of their lives.

She said she saw no fish nor fowl nor beast within her haunt,   25
That met a stranger in their kind, but could give it a taunt.
Since flesh might not endure, but rest must wrath succeed
And force the fight to fall to play in pasture where they feed,
So noble nature can well end the works she has begun,
And bridle well that will not cease her tragedy in some.   30
   Thus in her song she oft rehearsed, as did her well behove,
   'The falling out of faithful friends is the renewing of love'.

'I marvel much, perdie,' quoth she, 'for to behold the rout,
To see man, woman, boy and beast, to toss the world about.
Some kneel, some crouch, some beck, some check, and some can
   smoothly smile,   35
And some embrace others in arms, and there think many a wile.
Some stand aloof at cap and knee, some humble and some stout,
Yet are they never friends indeed until they once fall out.'
   Thus ended she her song and said before she did remove,
   'The falling out of faithful friends is the renewing of love'.   40
                                   M. Edwards.

10   *Prudence: the history of Damocles and Dionysius*

Whoso is set in princely throne and craveth rule to bear,
Is still beset on every side with peril and with fear.

1. throne] *1578;* trone *1576.*

---

25. *her*] i.e. their, but perhaps here signifying female animals, or animals thought of as showing female characteristics, such as the hare or mouse.
haunt] habitual living or feeding place of an animal or bird.
26. *in . . . kind*] of the same species.
but could] i.e. and could not.
taunt] gibe, challenge.
27. *flesh . . . endure*] living things may not continue to live.
rest] tranquillity, mental peace (*OED, sb.* 4.d).
29–30. *noble . . . some*] i.e. those of noble nature will control anger, which in others will end in tragedy.
31. *her . . . behove*] well befitted her, well became her.
33. *perdie*] certainly, by God.
rout] crowd, disorderly gathering.
35. *crouch*] cringe, fawn.
beck] a bow or other sign of respect.
check] evil trick, reprimand
36. *wile*] plot, stratagem.
37. *stand . . . knee*] refrain from doffing their caps or kneeling and bowing.
stout] (*a*) proud, arrogant, (*b*) firm, courageous.
39. *did remove*] went away.

F4–G1, *1576;* first ascribed to Edwards in *1578.* See p. 45.
0.1. Prudence] Scholastic philosophy recognised four cardinal or principal virtues: Prudence; Fortitude; Justice; Temperance.
history . . . Dionysius] The story occurs in *Tusc.,* 5.20. Dionysius was the infamous tyrant of Syracuse in Sicily: see *D&P* and p. 110n.10.

High trees by stormy winds are shaked and rent up from the
   ground,
And flashy flakes of lightning's flames on turrets do rebound
When little shrubs in safety lurk in covert all a-low   5
And freshly flourish in their kind, whatever wind do blow.
The cruel King of Sicily, who fearing barbers' hands,
Was wont to singe his beard himself with coal and firebrands,
Has taught us this—the proof whereof full plainly we may see,
Was never thing more lively touched, to show it so to be.   10
This King did seem to Damocles, to be the happiest wight,
Because he thought none like to him, in power or in might,
Who did alone so far excel the rest in his degree,
As does the sun in brightness clear the darkest star we see.
'Wilt thou,' then said this cruel King, 'prove this my present state? 15
Possess thou shalt this state of mine and so be fortunate.'
Full gladly then this Damocles this proffered honour took,
And shooting at a princely life, his quiet rest forsook.
In honour's seat then was he placed according to his will,
Forthwith a banquet was prepared that he might feast his fill.   20
Nothing did want wherein 'twas thought that he would take
   delight
To feed his eye, to fill his mouth or please the appetite.
Such store of plate, I think in Greece, there scarcely was so much,
His servitors did angels seem, their passing shape was such.
No dainty dish, but there it was and thereof was such store,   25
That throughout Greece so princely cheer was never seen before.

3–6. *High . . . blow*] proverbial: 'The highest trees abide (suffer) the sharpest storms'; 'High cedars are shaken when low shrubs remain' (Tilley T509, C208); *flakes* = flashes of lightning (*OED* 2).

5. *a-low*] (*a*) low-growing, (*b*) below.

7–8. *King . . . brands*] Dionysius feared assassination and did not allow himself to be shaved with a razor; cf. *D&P*, 12.34–9; Cicero, *De officiis*, 2.7.25, *Tusc.*, 5.20.58, Plutarch, 'Life of Dion' (vol. 6, 135).

10. *lively touched*] depicted so true to life.

12. *he*] Damocles.

him] Dionysius.

13. *degree*] rank (of king).

15. *prove*] try out, test.

16. *state*] (*a*) status, position, (*b*) chair of state, throne, (*c*) punning on 'state of mind'.

18. *shooting*] aiming.

21. *did want*] was lacking.

24. *passing*] surpassing.

25. *No . . . was*] i.e. There was no delicacy that was not included.

store] plentiful supply.

26. *cheer*] entertainment, provision.

Thus while in pomp and pleasure's seat this Damocles was placed,
And did begin with gladsome heart each dainty dish to taste,
At length by chance cast up his eyes and gan the house to view,
And saw a sight that him enforced his princely state to rue.   30
A sword forsooth with downward point, that had no stronger
    thread
Than one horse hair that peised it, direct upon his head.
Wherewith he was so sore amazed and shook in every part,
As though the sword that hung above had struck him to the
    heart.
Then all his pleasures took their leave and sorrow came in place,   35
His heavy heart the tears declared that trickled down his face.
And then forthwith with sobbing voice, besought the King of
    grace
That he would license him with speed to depart out of that
    place.
And said that he full long enough had tried now with fear
What 'tis to be a happy man and princely rule to bear.   40
This deed of thine, O Dionys, deserves immortal fame—
This deed shall always live with praise though thou didst live
    with shame.
Whereby, both kings be put in mind their dangers to be great,
And subjects be forbid to climb high steps of honour's seat.

11   *Fortitude: a young man of Egypt, and Valerian*

Each one deserves great praise to have—but yet not like I
    think—
Both he that can sustain the yoke of pains and does not shrink,
And he whom Cupid's covert craft can nothing move at all
Into the hard and tangled knots of Venus' snares to fall.
Bestir you then, who so delights in virtue's race to run,   5

---

35. his] *conj. Rollins; their PDD.*

32. *peised*] (*a*) suspended (*OED*, *vb*.3), (*b*) punning on 'drive down by impact of a
heavy body' (*OED*, *vb*.5), cf. l. 34.
36. *heavy . . . declared*] i.e. his tears showed the heaviness of his heart.
38. *license*] permit, allow.
39–40. *tried . . . bear*] i.e. tried out fearfully what it is to be a fortunate man with
princely power.

G1–G1v, *1576*; first ascribed to Edwards, *1578*. See pp. 45–6.
0.1. Fortitude] One of the four cardinal virtues and defined by Sir Thomas Elyot
(quoting Cicero) as 'the contempt of death and of grief' (*Governor*, 3.9); cf. *PDD*,
10.0.1.n, and p. 17.
Valerian] Roman emperor AD 253–60. This story of Valerian and the young
Christian closely follows the version in *Governor*, 3.18, where it is used as an illustration of virtuous continence.
1. *like*] identical.

The flying boy with bow ybent, by strength to overcome,
As one did once when he was young and in his tender days,
Whose stout and noble deed of his has got immortal praise.
The wicked Romans did pursue the seely Christians then,
What time Valerian Emperor was, a wicked cruel man,   10
Who spared not with bloody draughts to quench his own desire,
Dispatching all that stuck to Christ, with hot, consuming fire.
At length a man of tender years was brought before his sight,
Such one as Nature seemed to make a witness of her might,
For every part so well was set that nothing was depraved,   15
So that the cruel King himself would gladly have him saved,
So loath he was to see a work so rare of nature's power,
So finely built, so suddenly destroyed within an hour.
Then means he sought to overcome, or win him at the least,
To slip from Christ, whom he before had earnestly professed—   20
A bed prepared, so finely decked, such divers pleasant smells,
That well it might appear a place where pleasure only dwells.
By him he laid a naked wench, a Venus darling sure,
With sugared speech and lovely toys that might his mind allure.
Such wanton lures as these, he thought, might easily him entice,   25
Which things he knew with lusty youth had always been in price.
Such ways I think the Gods themselves could have invented none,
For flattering Venus overcomes the senses every one,
And he himself was even at point to Venus to consent,
Had not his stout and manly mind resisted his intent.   30
When he perceived his flesh to yield to pleasure's wanton toys,
And was by sleight almost provoked to taste of Venus' joys,
More cruel to himself than those that glad would him undo,
With bloody tooth his tender tongue, bit quite and clean in two.
Thus was the pain so passing great, of this his bloody bit,   35

---

6. *flying boy*] Cupid.
ybent] archaic form of 'bent'.
9. *seely*] hapless.
10. *What time*] when.
14. *Nature . . . might*] i.e. so beautiful that he seemed to be proof of the power of Nature.
19. *he*] Valerian.
him] the young Christian.
20. *he*] the young Christian.
21. *divers*] various, but with the sense of 'opposed to what is good' (*OED*, *sb*.2).
24. *toys*] amorous tricks, flirtations.
25. *easily*] The *1576* spelling suggests disyllabic pronunciation.
26. *in price*] held in high esteem, desired.
29. *he himself*] the young Christian.
even at point] almost, on the point of. The metre demands elision of 'even' to a single syllable, *e'en*, or *ev'n*.
30. *stout*] brave, firm.
35. *bit*] mouthful.

That all the fire and carnal lust was quenched every whit.
Do ill, and all thy pleasures then full soon will pass away,
But yet the shame of those thy deeds will never more decay.
Do well, and though thy pains be great, yet soon each one will
    cease,
But yet the praise of those thy deeds will evermore increase.   40
Finis.

12   *Justice: Zaleuch and his son*

Let rulers make most perfect laws to rule both great and small,
If they themselves obey them not, it booteth not at all.
As laws be nought but rulers' doom containing equal might,
So rulers should be speaking laws to rule by line of right.
Zaleuch, the prince of Locrine once, appointed by decree   5
Each lecher should be punished with loss of either eye.
His son by chance offended first, which when his father saw,
Lord God, how earnest then was he to execute the law.
Then ran the people all by flocks, to him with weeping eyes,
Not one among the rout there was but, 'Pardon, pardon,' cries.   10
By whose outcries and earnest suit, his son in hope did stand
That he thereby should then obtain some pardon at his hand.
But all in vain, for he is found to be the man he was,
And maketh haste so much the more to have the law to pass.
The people yet renewed their suit, in hope of some relief,   15
Whose faces all besprent with tears did testify their grief,
And cried all, 'For pity's sake, yield now to our request,
If all you will not clean remit, yet ease the pain at least'.

GIV–G2, *1576*; first ascribed to Edwards, *1578*; see pp. 45–7. A ballad by the title of 'The Just Judgement of Zaleucus against Whoredom' was registered in 1568–9 (cf. H. E. Rollins, *An Analytical Index to the Ballad-Entries, 1557–1709, in the Register of the Company of Stationers* (Chapel Hill: University of North Carolina Press, 1924), no. 1343), but has not survived.

0.1. *Justice*] One of the four cardinal virtues, cf. *PDD* 10.0.1n.

Zaleuch] Zaleucus (c.660 BC), King of Locris (a Greek state in South Italy), was anachronistically believed to be a pupil of Pythagoras (cf. Diodorus Siculus, 12.20). His code of law, which was reputedly the first ever to be written down, stipulated a severe fixed penalty for each offence.

2. *booteth*] profits, helps.

3. *doom*] opinion.

containing . . . might] i.e. matched by equivalent power, with play on 'equal', equitable, just, impartial.

4. *by line*] in lineal descent, i.e. (*a*) the ruler should have inherited the right to rule, (*b*) the laws should be derived from a concept of right justice.

6. *either*] each (of the two).

8. *execute*] bring into operation.

10. *rout*] crowd.

13. *the man . . . was*] i.e. as honourable and just as he had ever been.

16. *besprent*] sprinkled.

18. *least*] *PDD* spelling, 'lest', rhymes with request.

Then somewhat was the father moved with all the people's voice,
And every man did give a shout, to show they did rejoice.   20
'Well then,' quoth he, 'it shall be thus, the law shall be fulfilled,
And yet my son shall favour have, according as you willed.
One eye of his shall be pulled out, thus has his lewdness got,
And likewise so shall one of mine, though I deserve it not.'
This word no sooner was pronounced but straight the deed was
      done,   25
Two eyes, no more, were left between the father and the son.
Say now who can, and on my faith Apollo he shall be,
Was he more gentle father now, or juster judge, trow ye?
This man would not his laws be like the webs that spiders
      weave
Wherein they lurk when they intend the simple to deceive,   30
Wherewith small flies full soon be caught and tangled ere they
      wist,
When great ones fly and 'scape away, and break them as they list.
                                                                      Finis.

13   *Temperance: Spurinna and the Roman ladies*

If nature bear thee so great love that she in thee have beauty
      placed,
Full hard it is, as we do prove, to keep the body clean and
      chaste—
            Twixt comeliness and chastity,
            A deadly strife is thought to be.
For beauty, which some men suppose to be as 'twere a golden ill,   5
Provoketh strife and many foes that seek on her to work their
      will—

---

6. their] *1600;* her *1576.*

---

27. *Say ... be*] i.e. 'he who can tell this is a very god in judgement', cf. Virgil,
Eclogues, 3.104, 'Tell me, whoever you are, and you shall seem to me to be great
Apollo'. *Apollo* = Greek sun god, associated with law-giving and high moral principle,
cf. Herodotus, 1.65.6 and 6.86.15
28. *more ... judge*] i.e. a kinder father than he was a just judge or a juster judge
than he was a kind father.
trow ye?] do you think?
29. *would not*] did not want.
31. *wist*] know, are aware.
32. *them*] i.e. laws, webs.
list] wish, desire.

   G2r-v, *1576*; signed F.M. in *1576*, M.E. in *1578* and *1580*, and M. Edwards subsequently. The poem may well not be by Edwards; cf. p. 47. The story can be found
in Valerius Maximus, 4.5.ext 1; Gower tells this story about one Phyryas, *Confessio
Amantis,* 5.6372-84; Petrarch tells it without mentioning the young man, Spurinna, by
name, 'The Triumph of Chastity', 271-4; cf. also Hoccleve, *The Regiment of Princes,*
1412.

Assaults to towns if many make,
　　No town so strong but may be take.
And this Spurinna witness can, who did for beauty bear the bell,
So clean a wight, so comely made, no dame in Rome but loved
　　well—   10
　　　　Not one could cool her hot desire,
　　　　So burning was the flame of fire.
Like as when bait cast in the flood forthwith does cause the fishes
　　come,
That pleasantly before did play, now presently to death to run,
　　　　For when they see the bait to fall,   15
　　　　Straightway they swallow hook and all.
So when Spurinna they did see, to him they flocked out of
　　hand—
She, happest dame was thought to be that in his favour most
　　did stand—
　　　　Not knowing under sweet deceits,
　　　　How Venus hides her poisoned baits.   20
But when he saw them thus to rage, whom Love had linked in his
　　chain,
This means he sought for to assuage these ladies of their grievous
　　pain:
　　　　His shape intending to disgrace,
　　　　With many wounds he scotched his face,
By which his deed it came to pass that he that seemed an angel
　　bright,   25
Even now so clean disfigured was that he became a loathsome
　　wight,
　　　　And rather had be foul and chaste
　　　　Than fair and filthy joys to taste.
What pen can write, or tongue express, the worthy praises of
　　this deed?
Methink that God can do no less than grant him heaven for his
　　meed,   30
　　　　Who for to save himself upright,
　　　　Himself has first destroyed quite.
　　　　　　　　　　　　　　　　　　Finis. q. F. M.

---

11. cool] cole *PDD*.   20. hides] hids *PDD*.   24. scotched] *1578*; skotch *1576*.
30. Methink] *1578*; My think *1576*.

---

10. *clean*] pure, unsullied.
18. *happest*] most fortunate.
21. *his*] i.e. Love's.
22. *assuage . . . pain*] calm the women's raging emotion.
24. *scotched*] gashed.
29. *pen . . . express*] Cf. *D&P*, 10.33–4.
30. *meed*] reward.
31. *upright*] morally pure.
32.1. q.] Either (*a*) Lat. *qua*, in the capacity of, i.e. by, or (*b*) 'quoth', said.

14   *In commendation of music*

Where griping grief the heart would wound, and doleful dumps
   the mind oppress,
There music with her silver sound is wont with speed to give
   redress,
Of troubled mind, for every sore, sweet music has a salve
   therefore.

In joy it makes our mirth abound, in grief it cheers our heavy
   sprites,
The careful head release has found by music's pleasant, sweet
   delights.   5
Our senses—what should I say more?—are subject unto music's
   lore.

The gods by music have their pray—the soul therein does joy—
For as the Roman poets say, in seas, whom pirates would
   destroy,
A dolphin saved from death most sharp, Arion playing on his
   harp.

A heavenly gift that turns the mind, like as the stern does rule
   the ship,   10
Music whom the gods assigned to comfort man whom cares
   would nip,
Since thou both man and beast dost move, what wise man then
   will thee reprove?

Finis M. Edwards

---

1. Where . . . grief] *PDD;* When . . . griefs *Mulliner.*   the mind] *1578;* thē *1576.*
10. A] *1576;* O *1578.*

G4, *1576.* Attributed to Edwards in *1576* but printed anonymously thereafter. It
occurs in BL Cotton MS Vespasian A. xxv. Shakespeare quotes and satirises it in *R&J,*
4.5.120ff. See p. 40 and music, p. 241–2.

   1. *dumps*] melancholy, depression.
   2. *silver*] purely resonating, cf. 'The Muses nine' l. 5, p. 228.
   redress] remedy, relief
   3. *Of . . . therefore*] i.e. music has a remedy (salve) for every grief (sore) of the troubled mind. The musical setting matches the ambiguous structure of the poetic writing
which can be understood either endstopped between lines 2 and 3, as here, or enjambed,
i.e. music gives speedy relief or correction (redress, *OED, sb.*4) to a troubled mind, and
provides a salve for every sore.
   5. *careful*] full of care.
   7.] The music is able to stretch this short line to a standard length.
   pray] praise.
   9. *Arion*] A poet and musician (c.626 BC) who was reputedly saved by a dolphin
after being thrown overboard, cf. Ovid, *Fasti,* 2.79–118; Herodotus, 1.23.
   12. *wise . . . reprove*] Some religious extremists of the period were as opposed to
music as they were to theatre.

15   *He requests some friendly comfort affirming his constancy*

The mountains high whose lofty tops do meet the haughty sky,
The craggy rock that to the sea free passage does deny,
The aged oak that does resist the force of blust'ring blast,
The pleasant herb that everywhere a fragrant smell does cast,
The lion's force whose courage stout declares a prince-like
   might,   5
The eagle that for worthiness is borne of kings in fight,
The serpent eke whose poisoned jaws do belch out venom vile,
The loathsome toad that shunneth light and liveth in exile,
These, these I say and thousands more by tract of time decay,
And like to time do quite consume and vade from form to clay,   10
But my true heart and service vowed shall last time out of mind,
And still remain as thine by doom, as Cupid has assigned.
My faith, lo here, I vow to thee, my troth thou knowest right
   well,
My goods, my friends, my life is thine, what need I more to tell?
I am not mine but thine I vow, thy hests I will obey,   15
And serve thee as a servant ought, in pleasing, if I may.
And since I have no flying wings to see thee as I wish,
Nor fins to cut the silver streams as does the gliding fish,
Wherefore leave now forgetfulness and send again to me,
And strain thy azured veins to write, that I may greeting see.   20
And thus farewell, more dear to me than chiefest friend I have,
Whose love in heart I mind to shrine till Death his fee do crave.

                                      M. Edwards

---

7. jaws] *1578*; waies *1576*.

H1v, *1576*.
   1. *haughty*] high, *OED*, 3.
   3. *oak . . . blast*] Cf. the proverbs, 'The highest trees abide (suffer) the sharpest storms' and 'In time the sturdy oak will bend and bow' (Tilley T509, T304).
   5. *stout*] firm, brave.
   6. *borne . . . fight*] i.e. depicted on kings' shields.
   8. *exile*] barren impoverishment (*OED*, *sb.*1, 2), i.e. a cold, dark place.
   9. *tract*] duration.
   10. *consume*] waste away. Cf. proverbs: 'Time consumes all things'—including, of course, itself; 'Time flees away' (Tilley T326, T327).
   vade . . . clay] i.e. disintegrate into dust; *vade* = fade, depart, flee; *form* = bodily shape.
   11. *true . . . mind*] Cf. proverbs: 'Time tries the truth'; 'Time tries friends' (Tilley T338, T337); and the common saying, 'time out of mind', i.e. beyond memory.
   13. *troth*] truth, faith.
   15. *hests*] commands.
   17. *flying wings*] Cf. proverb, 'Time has wings' (Tilley T327).
   22. *mind*] intend.
   fee] due right, i.e. my life.
   crave] demand.

16   *Evil to him that evil thinks*

The subtle, slyly sleights that worldly men do work,
The friendly shows under whose shade most craft does often lurk,
Enforces me alas, with yearnful voice to say:
Woe worth the wily heads that seeks the simple man's decay.

The bird that dreads no guile is soonest caught in snare,   5
Each gentle heart devoid of craft is soonest brought to care—
Good nature soonest trapped—which gives me cause to say:
Woe worth the wily heads that seeks the simple man's decay.

I see the serpent vile that lurks under the green,
How subtly he shrouds himself that he may not be seen,   10
And yet his foster's bane his leering looks bewray,
Woe worth the wily heads that seeks the simple man's decay.

Woe worth the feigning looks, on favour that do wait,
Woe worth the feigned, friendly heart that harbours deep deceit,
Woe worth the viper's brood—oh thrice woe worth I say   15
All worldly, wily heads that seeks the simple man's decay.
                                                    Finis. M. Edwards

17   *Complaining to his friend, he replies wittily*

A. The fire shall freeze, the frost shall fry the frozen mountains
   high.
B. What strange things shall Dame Nature force, to turn her
   course awry!
A. My Lady has me left, and taken a new man.
B. This is not strange, it haps oft times, the truth to scan.

0.1.] *1576 omits.*   1. men] *PDD;* wittes *AH; Add. 26737.*   10. he ... himself ...
he] *PDD; AH;* she ... herself ... she *Add. 26737.*   13. feigning] *PDD;* fawneinge
Add. 26737.

H2v–H3, *1576,* without a title. Occurs in AH, fol. 166v, and Add. 26737, fol. 107r.
1. *slyly*] i.e. skilful, sly.
sleights] cunning dealings, deceits.
2. *shade*] protection, cover.
3. *yearnful*] earnest (cf. *D&P,* 10.28).
4. *Woe worth*] 'May evil afflict' (cf. *D&P,* 15.22).
6. *care*] grief, suffering.
10. *subtly*] This needs to be pronounced with three syllables to fit the metre.
11. *foster's bane*] nurse's or protector's murderer (evoking the proverb 'nourish a
viper in one's bosom' (Tilley V68); *bane* = murderer; cf. *PDD,* 3.14n.
leering looks] sly, sidelong glances.
bewray] reveal, expose.

H3v–H4, *1576.* See p. 43.
1–2.] B ridicules A's paradoxical reversal of ice and fire which, following Petrarch,
is a common conceit in Elizabethan love poetry; *force* = bring about, constrain.
4. *scan*] scrutinise, examine.

A. The more is my pain.
B.   Her love then refrain.   5
A. Who thought she would flit?
B.   Each one that has wit.
A. Is not this strange?
B.   Light love will change.

A. By skilful means I her reclaim to stoop unto my lure.
B. Such haggard hawks will soar away, of them who can be sure?
A. With silver bells and hood, my joy was her to deck.   10
B. She was full gorged, she would the sooner give the check.
A. The more is my pain.
B.   Her love then refrain.
A. Who thought she would flit?
B.   Each one that has wit.
A. Is not this strange?
B.   Light love will change.

A. Her chirping lips would chirp to me sweet words of her desire.   15
B. Such chirping birds, who ever saw to perch still on one briar?
A. She said she loved me best, and would do till she die.
B. She said in words, she thought it not—as time does try.
A. The more is my pain.
B.   Her love then refrain.
A. Who thought she would flit?
B.   Each one that has wit.   20
A. Is not this strange?
B.   Light love will change.

A. Can no man win a woman so, to make her love endure?
B. To make the fox his wiles to leave, what man will put in ure?
A. Why then there is no choice, but all women will change.

---

8. reclaim] *PDD;* reclaimed *conj. Rollins.*   16. perch] preach *PDD.*

5. *Her ... refrain*] i.e. 'Stop loving her'.
7. *Light*] wanton, fickle.
8. *reclaim*] call back a flying, trained hawk.
stoop] swoop (said of a hawk flying to its quarry or to the lure).
lure] See CT 2.40n.
9. *haggard*] wild, untamed hawk. The term was also applied to uncontrolled women.
10. *bells and hood*] hawking equipment.
11. *full gorged*] hawking term for 'well fed' (hawks were trained by being starved). Applied to a woman, it implies that she had complete licence.
check] (*a*) a false stoop, when the hawk flies at something other than the intended quarry, (*b*) taunt, rebuke.
18. *time ... try*] proverbial, 'Time tries all things' (Tilley T336); *try* = test, ascertain the truth.
23. *put in ure*] achieve, put into practice.
24. *but*] unless.

B. As men do use, so some women do love to range. 25
A. The more is my pain.
B.   Her love then refrain.
A. Who thought she would flit?
B.   Each one that has wit.
A. Is not this strange?
B.   Light love will change.

A. Since slipper gain falls to my lot, farewell that gliding prey.
B. Since that the dice do run awry, betimes leave off thy play. 30
A. I will no more lament the thing I may not have.
B. Then by exchange, the loss to come, all shalt thou save.
A. Love will I refrain.
B.   Thereby thou shalt gain.
A. With loss I will leave.
B.   She will thee deceive.
A. That is not strange.
B.   Then let her range. 35

                                        M. Edwards

18   *The fruits of feigned friends*

In choice of friends what hap had I to choose one of Sirenes' kind!
Whose harp, whose pipe, whose melody could feed my ears
        and make me blind,
Whose pleasant noise made me forget that in sure trust was great
        deceit.

In trust I see is treason found, and man to man deceitful is,
And whereas treasure does abound, of flatterers there do not miss, 5

---

1. hap] happ *1578;* happy *1576.*

25. *do use*] behave.
29. *slipper*] slippery, unreliable.
gliding] (*a*) flying like a bird of prey, (*b*) slippery, elusive (*OED, vb.*5b).
prey] the action of preying (*OED, sb.*4), i.e. 'preying thing', here representing the woman herself.
30. *leave off*] abandon, cf. *D&P,* 11.4n.
32. *by . . . save*] i.e. 'by giving up the woman, you save the loss that would otherwise come [when she abandons you], and therefore save everything [because you lose nothing]'. This rhetorical flourish constitutes the witty reply referred to in the title; *exchange* = change of one thing for another (*OED, sb.*6a), i.e. (*a*) change of behaviour, (*b*) the rhetorical term 'metonymy'. This is the substitution of an attribute of a thing (here 'gain') for the name of a thing (here 'loss'). In this instance it also results in an 'antithesis' or opposite.

I1, *1576,* assigned to W.H. (William Hunnis). The couplet ascribed to Edwards first appears in 1578 (I3); see p. 42.
1. *Sirenes' kind*] 'like one of the Sirens', mythical birds with women's faces which supposedly lived on the South coast of Italy, luring sailors ashore by their songs and then killing them. 'Sirenes' is trisyllabic, and is the correct Latin plural.
5. *whereas . . . miss*] i.e. where there is wealth, there is no lack of flatterers.

Whose painted speech and outward show do seem as friends and
    be not so.

Would I have thought in thee to be the nature of the crocodil?
Which if a man asleep may see, with bloody thirst desires to kill,
And then with tears awhile gan weep the death of him thus slain
    asleep.

O flatterer false, thou traitor born, what mischief more might thou
    devise   10
Than thy dear friend to have in scorn, and him to wound in
    sundry wise?
Which still a friend pretends to be, and art not so by proof I see.
    Fie, fie, upon such treachery.

                             Finis W. H.

If such false ships do haunt the shore,
Strike down the sail and trust no more.

                             M. Edwards

    19   *Being importunate, at the length he obtains*

A. Shall I no way win you to grant my desire?
B. What woman will grant you the thing you require?
A. You only to love me is all that I crave.
B. You only to leave me is all I would have.
A. My dear alas, now say not so.   5
B. To love you best, I must say no.
A. Yet will I not flit.
B.   Then play on the bit.
A. I will.
B.   Do still.
A.   Yet kill not.
B.   I will not.
A. Make me your man.
B.   Beshrew me then.

A. The swifter I follow, then you fly away.   10
B. Swift hawks in their flying oft times miss their pray.

---

3. I] *omitted 1576, 1596.*

  7. *crocodil*] crocodile, which was popularly believed to pretend to weep for those it
killed.
  9. *gan*] began to.

  I1r–v, *1576*; assigned to M.B. (Master Bewe); attributed to Edwards from *1578*; see
p. 43.
  7. *play . . . bit*] 'control (bridle) your desire' but with the sense of maintaining
amorous play.
  8. *kill not*] (*a*) 'do not be unkind', (*b*) 'do not cause me to die' (with the usual
Elizabethan pun on 'die'—achieve orgasm).
  9. *then*] *PDD*'s standard spelling for this period ('than') of course rhymes with
'man'.

A. Yet some killeth deadly that fly to the mark.
B. You shall touch no feather, thereof take no cark.
A. Yet hope shall further my desire.
B. You blow the coals and raise no fire.   15
A. Yet will I not flit.
B.   Then play on the bit.
A. I will.
B.   Do still.
A.   Yet kill not.
B.   I will not.
A. Make me your man.
B.   Beshrew me then.

A. To love is no danger where true love is meant.
B. I will love no ranger, lest that I repent.   20
A. My love is no ranger, I make God a vow.
B. To trust your smooth sayings, I sure know not how.
A. Most truth I mean, as time shall well try.
B. No truth in men, I oft espy.
A. Yet will I not flit.
B.   Then play on the bit.   25
A. I will.
B.   Do still.
A.   Yet kill not.
B.   I will not.
A. Make me your man.
B.   Beshrew me then.

A. Some women may say nay and mean love most true.
B. Some women can make fools of as wise men as you.
A. In time I shall catch you, I know when and where.   30
B. I will soon dispatch you, you shall not come there.
A. Some speed at length, that oft have missed.
B. I am well armed, come when you list.
A. Yet will I not flit.
B.   Then play on the bit.
A. I will.
B.   Do still.
A.   Yet kill not.
B.   I will not.   35

---

32. speed] *This ed.*; speeds, *1580*; speds, *1576*.

---

13. *cark*] burden; hence trouble, pains, anxiety.
20. *ranger*] rover, someone who 'ranges', hunts for pray, hence inconstant lover, libertine.
28. *woman . . . true*] Cf. proverb, 'a woman says no and means aye' (Tilley W660).
29–33.] B's put-downs involve sexual puns on 'come'.
32. *speed at length*] succeed at last. *PDD* 'speeds' regards the noun 'some' as singular.
missed] failed.
33. *armed*] prepared, with the sense that she will not 'miss' (l. 31) her aim.

A. Make me your man.
B.   Beshrew me then.

A. Yet work your kind kindly, grant me love for love.
B. I will use you friendly as I shall you prove.
A. Most close you shall find me, I this do protest.
B. Then sure you shall bind me to grant your request.   40
A. O happy thread now have I spun,
B. You sing before the conquest won.
A. Why then, will you swerve?
B.   Even as you deserve.
A. Love still.
B.   I will.
A.   Yet kill not.
B.   I will not.

A. Make me your man.
B.   Come to me then.   45

Finis. M. B.

20   *Of a friend and a flatterer*

A faithful friend is rare to find, a fawning foe may soon be got,
A faithful friend bear still in mind, but fawning foe regard thou
      not.
A faithful friend no cloak does crave to colour knavery withal,
But sycophant a gown must have to bear a port whate'er befall.
A nose to smell out every feast, a brazen face to set it out,   5
A shameless child or homely guest whose life does like to range
      about,
A fawning foe while wealth does last, a thief to rob and spoil his
      friend,
As strong as oak till wealth does waste, but rotten stick does prove
      in the end.

1. faithful] *1596;* trusty *1578.*   8. waste] *This ed.;* last *1578.*

---

37. *work . . . kindly*] perform your natural inclinations in a kind manner.
38. *use . . . prove*] i.e. 'I will treat you as I find you'.

E4v, *1578.* It is likely that only lines 9–12 are by Edwards; see p. 42.
   1. *faithful . . . foe*] Cf. proverb, 'better to have an open foe than a dissembling friend'
(Tilley F410).
   4. *gown*] rich garment, sometimes a mark of office.
   port] grand, expensive style.
   5. *nose . . . feast*] Cf. proverb, 'Fiddlers, dogs and flatterers come to feasts uncalled'
(Tilley F206).
   6. *child*] youth of gentle birth.
   homely] household.
   life . . . about] i.e. someone who gains his livelihood by staying as a house guest with
one person after another.

Look first, then leap, beware the mire,
Burnt child is warned to dread the fire.   10
Take heed my friend, remember this,
Short horse, they say, soon curried is.

Finis. M. Edwards

21   *Being in love he complains*

My haught desire to hie that seeketh rest,
My fear to find where hope my help should give,
My sighs and plaints sent from unquiet breast,
The hardened heart that will not truth believe,
Bids me despair, and reason says to me,   5
'Forsake for shame the suit that shameth thee'.

But when mine eyes behold the alluring cays,
Which only me to Cupid's spoil have trained,
Desire anew does work his wonted ways,
Thus shall I freeze, and yet I fry in pain—   10
O quenchless fire to quail and quick again.

Such is the flame where burning love does last,
As high nor low can bear with reason's bit,
And such is love, wherein is settled fast,
That nought but death can ease his fervent fit,   15
Then cannot I, nor love will me forsake,
Sweet is the death, that faithful love does make.

Finis. M. Edwards

---

9. *Look . . . leap*] proverbial (Tilley L429).

10. *Burnt . . . fire*] proverbial (Tilley C297), i.e. it is not until one has had the experience that one is aware of the danger.

12. *Short . . . curried*] proverbial (Tilley H691), *curried* = groomed; i.e. either 'an inadequate friend will soon be found wanting', or here, perhaps, 'an inconsequential poem is soon read'. Cf. *D&P*, 8.13.

M2, *1580* only. This lacks both the twist in the tail and the humorous vigour which normally characterises Edwards's work and is probably not by him. The fourth line of stanza 2 appears to be missing.

0.1. *Being . . . complains*] Five other poems in *PDD* share this title, three by Lord Vaux, one by the Earl of Oxford and one by R.L.

1. *haught*] high, extreme.

hie] hasten onwards, go.

2. *fear . . . find*] fear that I shall not find [any place].

hope . . . give] i.e. hope should give help to me.

7. *cays*] shoals, coral reefs, a Spanish word, related to key (quay).

11. *quail*] destroy.

quick] revive, rekindle.

13. *bit*] mouthpiece of a bridle, i.e. those so burnt by love cannot be controlled by reason.

16. *cannot . . . forsake*] i.e. I cannot forsake love nor will love forsake me.

FROM *THE SUMMARY OF ENGLISH CHRONICLES*

Verses for the Bedford wedding tournament

You that in warlike ways and deeds of arms delight,
You that for country's cause or else for ladies' love dare fight,
Know you four knights there be that come from foreign land,
Whose haughty hearts and courage great has moved to take in hand
With sword, with spear and shield, on foot, on horseback too,   5
To try what you by force of fight or otherwise can do.
Prepare yourselves therefore, this challenge to defend,
That trump of fame, your prowess great abroad may sound and send.
And he that best can do, the same shall have the prize,
The day, the place and form and sight, lo here before your eyes.   10

TWO POEMS FROM BL ADD. 26737

1   An elegy on the death of a sweetheart

Come follow me you nymphs
    whose eyes are never dry,
Augment your wailing numbers now
    with me poor Emily.
Give place you to my plaints   5
    whose joys are pinched with pain,
My love, alas, through foul mishap,
    most cruel death has slain.

What wit can will, alas,
    my sorrows to indite?   10
I wail to want my new desire,
    I lack my new delight.
Gush out my trickling tears
    like mighty floods of rain,
My knight, alas, through foul mishap   15
    most cruel death has slain.

O hap, alas, most hard—
    O death, why didst thou so?

---

10. sight] *This ed.; fight Stow.*

From *The Summarie of English Chronicles* (1566), P. 196; see pp. 62–3.

Fol. 106v. Emily's song from *P&A*, presumably sung after the death of Arcyte. It is similar in form and content to Pythias's lament (*D&P*, 10.29–60) and can be sung to the same tune, pp. 245–7. See p. 83.

1–2. *nymphs . . . dry*] The wives of the dead Theban knights who greet Theseus in tears at the beginning of Chaucer's 'The Knightes Tale'.

10. *my . . . indite*] 'give words and poetic form (indite *OED*, *vb*.3) to my sorrows'.

11, 12. *new*] recently found, still fresh.

17–20. *hap . . . woe*] i.e. 'O most hard fate . . . that gave me such misery'.

Why could not I embrace my joy?—
    for me that bid such woe.   20
False fortune, out, alas,
    woe worth thy subtle train
Whereby my love, through foul mishap
    most cruel death has slain.

Rock me asleep in woe,   25
    you woeful sisters three,
O cut you off my fatal thread,
    dispatch poor Emily.
Why should I live, alas,
    and linger thus in pain?   30
Farewell my life, since that my love
    most cruel death has slain.

                  The song of Emily per Edwards

2

O death, O death, rock me asleep,
Bring me to quiet rest,
Let pass my weary, guiltless ghost
Out of my careful breast.
    Toll on thou passing bell,   5
    Ring out my doleful knell,
    Let thy sound my death tell,
        For I must die,
        There is no remedy.

My pains, my pains, who can express?   10
Alas they jar so strong,
My dolours will not suffer strength
My life for to prolong.
    Toll on etc.

Alone, alone in prison strong   15
I wail my destiny,

---

4. careful] *Add. 26737;* teareful *Add. 15117.*   5. thou] *Add. 15117;* the *Add. 30481;* your *Add. 26737.*   6. my] *Add. 26737;* the *Add. 30481.*   7. Let ... tell] *Add. 15117;* Thy sound my deathe abroad will tell *Add. 26737.*   14. Toll on etc.] *Add. 26737 omits, and subsequently.*

---

22. *subtle*] deceitful, treacherous.
train] retinue, agents.
26. *sisters three*] The three Fates who spin, weave and cut off the thread of human life (cf. *D&P,* 10.55).
27. *fatal*] pertaining to Fate.
32.1. *per*] Lat. by.

This is perhaps another song from *P&A;* see pp. 80–1, and music, pp. 255–7.
4. *careful*] full of cares.
12. *dolours*] sufferings.

Woe worth this cruel hap that I
Must taste this misery.
   Toll on etc.

Farewell, farewell my pleasures past,   20
Welcome my present pain,
I feel my torment so increased,
That life cannot remain.
   Cease now, thou waking bell,
   Ring out my doleful knell,   25
   For thou my death dost tell,
     Lord pity thou my soul,
     Death does draw nigh,
     Sound dolefully,
     For now I die,   30
     I die, I die.

TWO POEMS FROM BODLEIAN MS TANNER 306.1

I

If all the gods would now agree
   to grant the thing I would require,
Madam, I pray you, what judge ye
   above all thing I would desire?
In faith no kingdom would I crave,   5
   such idle thoughts I never have.

Nor Croesus would I wish to be
   to have in store great hoards of gold,
Apelles' gift liketh not me—
   of riddles dark the truth to unfold.   10
Nor yet to honour would I climb—
   amidst the streams I love to swim.

Nought I regard that most men crave,
   and yet a thing I have in mind

Fol. 175. The poem is not signed but it seems to be a companion piece to the next poem, 'The Muses nine'. Its wordplay, topic (see pp. 11–12) and similarities of phrasing with his other works supports ascription to Edwards.

   7. *Croesus*] Cf. *PDD*, 7.12n.

   9. *Apelles*] celebrated court painter to Philip of Macedon and his son Alexander the Great (fourth century BC).

   gift] (*a*) Apelles fell in love with Alexander's mistress Campaspe while drawing her portrait. Alexander gave her to him. (*b*) Perhaps also Apelles' legendary ability to draw so well that his subjects seemed alive.

   10. *riddles*] (*a*) the legends about Apelles and his work, (*b*) the riddle that Croesus was told by the oracle at Delphi, which he mistakenly interpreted as good news when in fact it foretold the destruction of his empire.

   12. *streams*] i.e. rank and file, general run of people.

Which if by wishing I might have   15
    like luck to me could not be assigned.
But will you know what liketh me?
    Madam, I wish your fool to be.

Whom you might bob whenas you list
    and out and taunt in your sweet talk,   20
About whose head your little fist
    for your disport might often walk,
Which finely might your chamber keep
    and, when you list, whist you asleep.

And warm your slipper when you rise,   25
    and make the bed wherein you slept,
But you to see in any wise,
    each thing you do be closely kept.
For all my service, this grant me:
    Madam, your chamber fool to be.   30

2

The Muses nine that cradle rocked
    wherein my noble mistress lay,
And all the Graces then they flocked
    so joyful of that happy day,
That then with silver sounding voice   5
    gan altogether to rejoice.

Their chirping charm did Nature praise
    whose fame aloud they all did ring,

---

16. *like luck*] i.e. 'similar good fortune', with possible reference to the proverb, 'If wishes might prevail, beggars would be kings' (Tilley W535, although all references there are much later).

18. *fool*] (*a*) abject servant, (*b*) licensed man, entertainer.

19. *bob*] (*a*) strike with the fist, buffet, (*b*) make a fool of.

whenas] whenever.

20. *out*] put out, abuse.

23. *Which*] i.e. who.

24. *whist . . . asleep*] whisper, murmur you to sleep.

27. *wise*] manner, fashion, habit, action (*OED*, *sb*.1).

28. *closely kept*] kept secret.

30. *chamber fool*] gentleman of the chamber, personal servant.

Fol. 176. The poem may be connected with *P&A*; see p. 65.

1. *Muses*] These nine, beautiful demi-goddesses, governing all intellectual pursuits, were regarded as intercessors between humankind and the gods, and are regularly depicted singing and dancing.

3. *Graces*] Three nymphs usually named Chastity, Passion and Beauty, representing the different aspects of Venus, goddess of love.

5. *silver sounding*] (*a*) sounding clear and pure as silver, bell-like, cf. *PDD*, 14.2; (*b*) silvery and resounding.

6. *altogether*] (*a*) in consort together, (*b*) completely.

7. *charm*] the singing of many birds (*OED*, *sb*.2).

Of royal line, that she did raise,
    a princess by that noble King   10
Whose memory does yet revive
    all courtly wights that be alive.

And when this solemn song was done,
    in council grave they sat straight way,
With smiling cheer then one began—   15
    fair orator—these words to say:
'Behold,' quod she, 'my sisters dear,
    how Nature's gifts do here appear.

'Let us therefore not seem unkind;
    as Nature has the body decked,
So let our gifts adorn the mind—   20
    of the gods lest we be checked—
And you three Graces in like sort,
    await upon her princely port.'

To this with hands cast up on high,   25
    these ladies all gave their consent,
And kissing her most lovingly,
    from whence they came, to heaven they went.
Their gifts remain yet here behind
    to beautify my mistress' mind.   30

Which given to her in tender years,
    by tract of time have so increased,
A peerless prince that she appears,
    and of her kind passing the rest
As far in skill, as does in sight   35
    the sun excel the candle light.

No wonder then, though noble hearts
    of sundry sorts her love does seek,

---

17. sisters] *This ed.;* sister *Tanner.*   32. have] *This ed.;* of *Tanner.*   33. A peer-less] *This ed.;* apreles *Tanner.*

9–10. *Of . . . King*] i.e. that Nature did raise a princess from the royal line of Henry VIII.

11–12. *Whose . . . alive*] i.e. who remains in the living memory of those at court.

15. *cheer*] face.

one] i.e. one of the Muses.

22. *checked*] reprimanded.

23. *like sort*] the same way.

24. *await . . . port*] (*a*) take care of (await, *OED*, *vb*. 4b) her behaviour, carriage, stately bearing, (*b*) attend upon her as part of her retinue (port, *OED*, *sb*.4. 2b).

32. *tract*] passage.

34. *of . . . rest*] surpassing all other princes and monarchs.

37–8. *noble . . . sorts*] many different noble suitors.

Her will to win they play their parts,
  happy is he whom she shall like.
To God yet is this my request: 40
  him to have her that loves her best.

Finis, qd Edwards

---

39. *will*] (*a*) willingness (to marry), (*b*) desire, love.

42.1. qd] either (*a*) quod (quoth) said; or (*b*) quasi dixit (Lat.) 'as if he [Edwards] said'.

This courtly compliment (recalling Aristippus's behaviour in *Damon and Pythias*, 6.3–6) is based on the rhetorical exercise of finding a flattering but sometimes teasing adjective to alliterate with each lady's name. The poem addresses a select list of ladies connected with Mary's court. These include former attendants who had become old friends, current gentlewomen of the chamber and young maids of honour. It may therefore mark a particular occasion or gathering. It is a more tightly constructed literary game than a poem in AH addressed to six gentlewomen attending the Princess Elizabeth at Hatfield written between 1554 and 1558.

Women are usually of interest to genealogists only when they marry and are then referenced under their husbands' names (see G. E. Cockayne, *Complete Peerage*, 1887–98). This makes identification extremely difficult. The poem must have been written before December 1555 when Katherine Bridges became Katherine Sutton. A more precise date depends on the identification of Howard and Arundel. The preferred identifications below put the date of the poem prior to March 1555 when Mary Fitzalan, daughter of the Earl of Arundel, became Mary Howard.

Howard. This is probably either the wife or the daughter, both named Mary, of William Howard, who was created Baron of Effingham in 1554 for his part in suppressing Wyatt's rebellion, but who also befriended Princess Elizabeth. Howard's daughter became the third wife of Katharine Bridges's husband, Edward Sutton.

Other possibilities are Mary Fitzalan who married Thomas Howard in March 1555 (see Arundel below), or Jane Howard, daughter to the poet Henry Howard, Earl of Surrey, some of whose poems occur in CT. Jane was commanded to attend Elizabeth at her coronation (Add. 25460) and married Charles Neville, Earl of Westmorland, in 1563–4. Neville was attaindered under Elizabeth I for attempting to free Mary, Queen of Scots.

Dacres. Magdalene Dacre (1538–1608), maid of honour, was daughter of William, 3rd Lord Dacre of the North (one of the twelve mourners at the funeral of Henry VIII and one of four peers who protested against the Book of Common Prayer). Immediately after the death of Queen Mary she became the second wife of Antony Browne, Viscount Montagu, Master of Horse to Mary's husband, King Philip, and one of Mary's executors. He later opposed the Act of Supremacy separating England from the Roman Catholic church. He was implicated in the plot to marry the Duke of Norfolk to Mary, Queen of Scots, but was one of the commissioners at her trial in 1586.

Baynam. Mrs Frances Baynam had served Mary since at least 1538.

Arundel. This is probably Mary Fitzalen (c.1540–57), daughter of Henry Fitzalen, Earl of Arundel, Lord Steward of the household, and Katherine Grey (daughter of Thomas, 2nd Marquis of Dorset). Mary, her brother Henry, and elder sister Joanna (Lady Lumley), were famously well educated. Mary's New Year's gifts to her father of certain Latin translations are preserved in BL MS Royal, Ai–iv, while her brother was described by Roger Ascham (*Scholemas-*

ter, 219) as such an example 'to the Court for learnyng, as our tyme may rather wishe than looke for agayne'. Mary's youth and education thus fit the description. She married Thomas Howard, Duke of Norfolk, in March 1555 and died in childbirth.

Her stepmother, also Mary, was the second wife of the Earl of Arundel, the widow of Robert Radclyffe, and daughter of Sir John Arundel of Lanherne. She was thus an Arundel twice over but, although the surname fits her better, the description does not match unless Edwards was being ironic about her age. See J. P. Yeatman, *The Early Geneological History of the House of Arundel* (1882), 268–74.

Dormer. Jane Dormer attended Mary throughout her reign and is listed as Gentlewoman of the Privy Chamber in the funeral expense accounts. Immediately after Mary's death in 1558 she married the Duke of Feria (courtier to King Philip) and returned with him to Spain. Henry Clifford's *Life of Jane Dormer* (transcribed E. E. Estcourt, 1887), celebrates her Catholic piety.

Mansell. Cicely, daughter of John Dabridgecourt, served the young Princess Mary for at least two years, accompanying her on her vice-regal progress to the Welsh marches in 1525. She became the third wife of Sir Rhys Mansell and wrote from Wales to Cromwell, 3 August 1535, that the King had commanded her husband 'my bedfellow' to go to fight the Irish, notwithstanding the needs of his wife, children, lands and goods. She complains that 'most of his living is encumbered with jointures and other charges'; that she is a 'stranger in these parts', and if he should die, 'I and my children are undone'. Princess Mary's Privy Purse accounts (ed. Madden (London, 1831)), record gifts from both of them. She rode in state in Mary's coronation procession and appears in the lists for her funeral (Cott. Vesp. cxiv), but had died two months earlier on 20 September. Sir Rhys leaves to his daughter, Mary, two of Cicely's special dresses, one black and one red (the latter presumably for the coronation) together with a jewel given to his wife by Queen Mary (E. P. Statham, *History of the Family of Maunsell*, 1917–20, vol. 1, 329ff.).

Cooke. The five daughters of Sir Anthony Cooke, a tutor of Edward VI and one of the Marian Protestant exiles, were all extremely well educated, and had a reputation for their forthright intelligence. The eldest, Mildred, had already married William Cecil (future Secretary of State under Elizabeth). This woman is either Anne (d. 1610, a gifted translator of several major Protestant texts, and the mother of Francis Bacon) or Margaret (who married Ralph Powlet in 1558, on which occasion Mary made her a grant of a life interest in land). Jane Dormer's husband in a letter to the King of Spain (29 December 1558) describes Anne as 'a tiresome bluestocking who belonged to the bedchamber of the late Queen who is in heaven' (*CSP, Spanish*, 1.18).

Bridges. Katherine, gentlewoman in ordinary, was the daughter of John Brydges (elevated Lord Chandos of Sudeley, 1554, brother to Sir Rhys Mansell's first wife, Ann). When Katherine married Edward Sutton, Lord Dudley, Mary made extensive grants of land and manors, 'To hold to Lord Dudley and Katherine and the heirs of their bodies', 31 December 1555 (*Patent Rolls*).

MUSIC

In 1573 Claudius Desainliens published a French phrase book with parallel English translation, *The French School-master*, containing model conversations for all social situations. One passage, supposedly suitable for after-dinner music-making, praises Edwards and perhaps recalls the shaving song in *Damon and Pythias* in its reference to bacon and to hose:

> if I should not drink, I should become as dry as a gammon of bacon hung on a chimney . . . I perceive, you cannot tell the song which begins 'I had rather go without hose than forbear drinking'.
> . . . There is a good song. I do marvel who hath made it.
> It is the Master of the Children of the Queen's Chapel.
> What is his name?
> Master Edwards.
> Is he alive? I heard say that he was dead.
> It is already a good while ago—there are at the least five years and a half.
> Truly it is pity. He was a man of a good wit, and a good poet: and a great player of plays. (130–4, modernised spelling)

On the evidence of the surviving manuscript music commonplace books, which so often juxtapose sacred and profane music, families and friends who enjoyed singing together would happily move between religious and secular songs. Tunes themselves were often re-used and likewise frequently crossed between different categories of music. The most ubiquitous example of this is probably the use of the plainsong Vespers antiphon *Gloria tibi trinitas* from the Salisbury rite. John Taverner made it the basis for all the movements in a mass of the same name, but the Benedictus, which starts with the words '*In nomine*', inspired countless purely instrumental versions by other composers. All give the plainsong melody in long notes, usually in the tenor part, but nevertheless create very different variations on the theme. This same plainsong melody seems also to form the basis for one of Edwards's own compositions, 'O the silly man' (pp. 242–5).

In much the same way, Pythias's song from *Damon and Pythias* set a fashion for declamatory songs in choirboy plays. The tune, although uncomfortably shortened to fit, appears on a broadsheet ballad published in 1568 entitled, 'A new Ballade of a Lover / Extollinge his Ladye' (BL Huth collection).[1] Other ballads are likewise headed with the instruction that they should be sung 'to the tune of Damon and Pithias'.[2] One of these is in *A Handefull of Pleasant Delights* (1584), a book of love songs collected by Clement Robinson and published by Richard Jones, the broadside publisher and printer also responsible for the printing of *Damon and Pythias*. This book is unashamedly aimed at the women's market. Jones advertises his wares like a pedlar selling haberdashery: 'Here may you have such pretie thinges, as women much desire, / Here may you have of sundrie sorts, such Songs as you require. / . . . Doubt not to buy this pretie Booke, the price is not so deare' (A1v). Again, unfortunately, the music, like second-hand clothes, fits the words where it touches.

Edwards's poem 'In youthful years' (*PDD*, 4) may have been sold as a ballad in its own right. Broadside ballads with the same title ('Fair words make Fools Fain') were certainly registered for publication by William Griffith (1563–4) and Thomas Colwell (1565–6). The phrase is proverbial, however, and the ballads have not survived so we cannot tell if in fact it was this poem that was printed.[3]

Music was thus recycled for different occasions. It would also be sung or played according to whatever instruments were to hand. The original stage direction for Pythias's song in the play calls for an accompaniment on the regals (a small portable organ). The surviving version gives the tune with an accompaniment in tablature for the lute. Conversely, three settings of poems by Edwards, probably originally for broken consort in five parts, survive only in later transcriptions for keyboard in the Mulliner Book, and are identifiable as songs only by their titles.

Most of the settings included here are not ascribed in the original MSS and it is not possible to state categorically that they are by Edwards since so little music firmly attributed to him survives. Nevertheless, the exuberance that we have noted both in *Damon* and in the account of the performance of *Palamon* is mirrored in the bold harmonies of his arrangement of the famous '*Vater unser*' chorale (pp. 237–8). A sense of the dramatic can also be discerned in most of the other settings included here, most remarkably in the tolling bell effect in 'O death' and the wonderfully rhythmic setting for 'May' (see pp. 255–7 and 250–4). Both of these are found in manuscripts copied in Oxford between 1560 and 1588, which certainly does not detract from the idea that they were written by him, nor from the suggestion that they both belong to *Palamon and Arcyte*. Besides the arrangement of the Lord's Prayer, only one piece of religious music ascribed to Edwards survives. This is a proportional motet in five parts '*In terrenum*' for which only four partbooks survive (Cambridge University Library, Peterhouse MSS 471–4).

There has long been considerable antiquarian interest in Elizabethan song. There are four collections of Tudor partsongs in the Royal College of Music, for example, all copied in the late eighteenth or early nineteenth centuries, and all containing songs by Edwards which are otherwise only known from *Mulliner*.[4] It is possible that in fact they are separations into four separate parts of Mulliner's keyboard transcriptions rather than copies of an independent source. These manuscripts concur that 'O the silly man' is a setting for Francis Kindelmarsh's *PDD* poem, 'By painted words, the silly simple man', and extract the first six lines from this three-stanza poem to provide a verbal underlay in each part. The music is not a good fit, however, and I doubt that it was originally intended to go with these words. More recently there have been various attempts at reconstruction into four parts of 'In going to my naked bed'.[5] The composer Peter Warlock included 'O death', arranged for voice and string quartet, in his *Third Book of Elizabethan Songs*, with a transcription of the Dow MS setting of 'May' in the *Second Book*, while John Ireland set 'May' to a new tune for voice and piano under the title 'The Sweet Season'.[6]

All known examples of English sixteenth-century keyboard music and consort song have now been edited in the series *Musica Britannica*. The volumes containing music by Edwards are: *Mulliner Book* (vol. 1, ed. Stevens), *Consort Songs* (vol. 22, ed. Brett) and *Tudor Keyboard Music* (vol. 66, ed. Caldwell).

TEXT AND INTERPRETATION

The aim, in the transcriptions that follow, is to enable individual readers to sing and play the music for themselves with a keyboard. The tablature of the Swarland Book is therefore transcribed. The keyboard transcriptions of 'O death' and those in *Mulliner* are presented with the tune duplicated in a separate voice part with words underlaid. The partsongs 'May' and the 'Lord's Prayer' are presented in close score, the direction of the tails indicating the throughline of each part. Notational values are halved, both for the sake of modernisation and in order to make this clearer (since the many semibreves in the original notation do not have tails).

Early music was written without bar-lines. The modern bar conveys both metre (the number and type of beats in the bar) and accent (the stress that naturally falls on the first beat).[7] In early music metre is indicated by mensuration marks (usually at the beginning, and sometimes in the course of the piece to indicate changes in the proportional length of the notated notes). The accent given to a piece by performers, however, will be affected by the combinations of note lengths to be found in individual groups of notes and, in the case of song, by the sense of the words (see pp. 49–52). Transcription into modern regular bars according to the mensuration of the piece thus sometimes fails to capture the sprung rhythms that are the hallmark of this music. I have therefore used changes of time signature in order to indicate the playful relationship between rhythm and metre that unbarred music achieves. For example, the MS source for

'May' has the mensuration sign ₵ which indicates imperfect or duple time (i.e. two beats to the bar) with each beat subdivided in three. This translates into the modern time signature $\frac{6}{4}$. But the natural accent of the words sometimes creates a different rhythm. Bars 29–34 demonstrate that the composer made these changes deliberately, entirely alive to the formal rhetorical qualities of the verse as well as its sense. While the piece normally dances along in dotted minim beats (dotted semibreves in the original notation), here it marches in minims, albeit punctuated every four beats with a crotchet rest. This glancingly illustrates the meaning (marching), reinforces the rhetorical form of the words (giving a strong beat to each alliterative syllable) and reflects the natural accent of the sentence. It effectively turns the duple $\frac{6}{4}$ metre (1̲ 2 3 4 5 6) into the triple $\frac{3}{2}$ (1̲2 3̲4 5̲6). Elsewhere in this piece duple and triple rhythms are present in different parts simultaneously.

The rhythms in the piece as a whole are also reminiscent of some forms of the sixteenth-century basse dance. Thomas Elyot (*Governor*, 1.22–5) gives an extensive treatment of this dance as an exemplum of the virtue of 'Prudence', using its various steps as metaphors for the different qualities that contribute to that virtue. The particular succession of steps that he describes fits the music for the first stanza quite closely, while the music for the second stanza suits the five-step tordion or cinquepace (a kind of galliard) which was often paired with the basse dance.

The treatment of keys and accidentals is even more problematic. Music at this period was written in modes corresponding to the successive white notes of the piano keyboard, each with a different feel depending on the different ordering of tones and semitones caused by the starting note. It was, however, simultaneously understood according to the sol fa system invented by Guido d'Arezzo for teaching sight-singing (see plate 2). This was a system of overlapping hexachords (runs of six notes labelled ut, re, mi, fa, sol, la) with the initial ut on bottom G. The subsequent hexachord started on C and the third on F (with a flattened B in order to keep the same relative intervals); the fourth started on the G an octave higher than the first—and so on. This is a therefore a relative system of pitch, and most notes thus occur with different sol fa names in two or even three hexachords. Whether a B is considered flat or natural will depend on the hexchord in which it is understood to occur at that point in the piece. The demands of harmony, however, resulted in the addition of other accidentals according to the uncertain principles of *musica ficta*. For example, any minor third in the final chord of a cadence may be sharpened; in places where a line rises or falls by a single step and then returns, the interval may be flattened or sharpened to make a semitone; the tritone (an augmented interval of three whole tones) should be avoided by flattening or sharpening as appropriate. The result, by the end of the sixteenth century, was the break-up of the modal system into our present system of keys, each in one of two modes, minor or major.

Accidentals are mostly supplied in the Lord's Prayer from Day's Psalter (p. 238), a publication that was aimed at the musically inexperienced. More often they were left to the performer—which is where the problem lies. It is often very difficult to know how to treat instances in which two or more conflicting principles apply simultaneously—an indication that the rules were not applied consistently, but rather according to taste. It is easy to overdo the addition of accidentals, regularising the effect in accordance with our modern understanding of harmony, which is probably not appropriate. Musicologists disagree as to whether an accidental in one part should be considered as affecting all the other parts in the same beat. In the songs that follow, for example, there are several instances in which B flat sounds against B natural and F natural against F sharp. This sounds strange to modern ears but was probably intentional. In 'O death' the lute tablature makes it clear that the second *musica ficta* principle listed above has sharpened the Cs in the accompaniment in bars 22, 25, etc., but this principle does not apply to the Cs in the melody. The result wonderfully mimics the clang of a bell. In the transcriptions below suggested additional accidentals not in the original MS are supplied in brackets.

Music also changes in more personal ways between text and performance. Sixteenth-century performers would have ornamented the bare outline of the notated music, adding turns and filling in interval jumps with extra notes. In strophic songs such as these they would have used different ornamentation in each succeeding stanza for the sake of variation and to display their own musical skill. This music, therefore, is for participation.

THE 'LORD'S PRAYER' FROM *THE WHOLE BOOK OF PSALMS*, 1563

The book contains three settings (by Cawston, W P[arsons] and Edwards) of Richard Cox's metrical translation of Martin Luther's version of the Lord's Prayer. All use the famous German chorale tune 'Vater unser', which is probably also by Luther. Edwards's arrangement, perhaps more than the other two, exploits the harmonic instability of the mode. At this period, following the custom of religious polyphonic music, the tune was usually written in the tenor part, with the counter-tenor weaving in and out around it. In this transcription the relationship between tenor and counter-tenor has been retained but the chorale tune has been duplicated an octave higher to make it easier to hear. There is a case for flattening the B in the counter-tenor part of bar 6 since that phrase belongs to the hexachord starting on F, whereas the next phrase is within the compass of the G hexachord.

Our Fa – ther which in hea – ven art, and mak'st us all one bro – ther – hood

To call up – on Thee with one heart, our heaven–ly Fa – ther and our God,

Grant we pray not with lips a – lone, but with the heart deep sigh and groan.

THREE SONGS FROM THE MULLINER BOOK: ADD. 30513

This is one of the most important sources for English sixteenth-century keyboard music and keyboard transcriptions of songs and other instrumental music, but little is known for certain about its compiler, Thomas Mulliner, except that he was *moderator organum* at Corpus Christi College, Oxford, in 1563. The eighteenth-century suggestion that he was master of St Paul's School when John Shepard and Thomas Tallis were scholars there is unsubstantiated.

PDD, 9: 'In going to my naked bed' (fol. 79v–80)

In this piece changes in the musical metre are used to reinforce both the sense of the words and the formal alliterative features of the verse. In bar

In go-ing to my na — ked bed as one that would have slept, I heard a wife sing to her child that long be – fore had wept. She sighed sore and sang full sweet to bring the babe to rest, That would not cease but cried still in suck – ing at her breast. She was full wear – y of her

watch,   and   grie – ved with her   child,   She   rock – ed   it   and

rat – ed,   it   un – til   on   her   it smiled.   Then   did   she   say, 'Now

have   I   found this   pro – verb true   to   prove :   The   fall – ing   out   of

faith – ful   friends   is   the re – new – ing of   love'.

28, beat 2 alto, Stevens amends to crotchet F (to avoid a tri tone) but introduces a tri tone in bar 30 by naturalising alto B (beat 3).

Add. 36526 (copied c.1600, fols 1, 6) preserves two parts of the same setting. The tenor part mostly corresponds to the Mulliner tenor line, but it contains phrases which in Mulliner appear in the alto and bass registers, and thus indicates that the parts from which Mulliner was transcribed were probably likewise originally interwoven, making reconstruction into parts quite problematic.

PDD, 14: 'Where griping grief' (fol. 108v)

The bold use of *musica ficta* here creates a piece which seems to shift ground continually through the modern keys of A, D and E (both major and minor). This and the diminished seventh leap (bars 6, 18)

paint an aural picture of the troubled mind comforted by the emotional power of music and, in stretching the rules to the utmost in the context of a *defence* of music, seem to be making a statement about intellectual freedom.

'O the silly man' (fol. 77v–78)

The music is reminiscent of the many '*In nomine*' consort pieces of the period. The plainsong melody on which these are based, *Gloria tibi trinitas*, is not immediately visible in Edwards's piece, but can be picked out, weaving through the parts. It has been added here, with minor alterations, as a separate part. Some confusion in Mulliner's transcription concerning the direction of the tails in bars 23–4 and the number of parts in bars 17–18 likewise indicates crossover between parts in the original consort setting, but this is now impossible to reproduce. Accordingly tail directions have been standardised here. The first two lines of Kindelmarsh's poem fit both the plainsong and Edwards's music, but thereafter the underlay is clumsy, even with considerable repetition of the words (see pp. 234–5).

Stanza 1 of Francis Kindelmarsh's three-stanza poem (*PDD*, 1576, B3):

> *Most happy is that state alone*
> *Where words and deeds agree in one.*

> By painted words, the silly simple man
> To trustless trap is trained now and then,
> And by conceit of sweet alluring tale,
> He bites the baits that breeds his bitter bale.
> To beauty's blast, cast not thy rolling eye,   5
> In pleasant green do stinging serpent lie.
> The golden pill hath but a bitter taste,
> In glittering glass, a poison rankest placed,
> So pleasant words, without performing deeds,
> May well be deemed to spring of darnel seeds.   10
> The friendly deed is it that quickly tries
> Where trusty faith and friendly meaning lies.
> That state therefore, most happy is to me,
> Where words and deeds most faithfully agree.

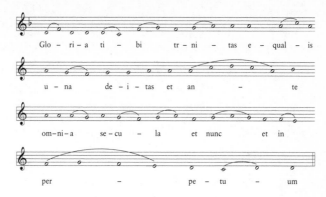

Glo – ri – a ti – bi tr – ni – tas e – qual – is

u – na de – i – tas et an – te

om – ni – a se – cu – la et nunc et in

per – pe – tu – um

TWO SONGS FROM THE SWARLAND BOOK: ADD. 15117

This MS is on paper dated between 1614 and 1616, but contains religious and secular music, some of which, like the song from *Damon and Pythias*, was written more than fifty years previously. It contains a considerable amount of theatre music, including Desdemona's 'Willow Song' from *Othello*, other songs by Ben Jonson and Thomas Campion, and the tolling bell version of 'O Death' (see below), all with accompaniments in tablature for lute. The manuscript is described by Mary Joiner (1969), and has been published in facsimile: Elsie Bickford Jorgens, ed., *English Song 1600–1675*, vol. 1 (London and New York: Garland, 1986).

'Awake you woeful wights' (fol. 3) from Damon and Pythias (10.29–60)

The MS gives the refrain as 'Damon my friend is judged to die'. The tune has nine notes for this line which probably indicates pronunciation of the 'ed' ending. The refrain as printed in the play, and used here, requires a repetition of the words 'my friend' in order to fit the music, with the extra note making a ligature on 'must'. This is both elegant and entirely in keeping with the declamatory style of the song.

A – wake you woe–ful wights,

that   long have wept in   woe,   Re – sign   to   me your

plaints and   tears,   my hap – less   hap to   show.   My

woe   no   tongue can   tell,   nor   pen   can   well de –

cry,   O,   what   a   death is   this to   hear,

PDD, 4: 'In youthful years' (fol. 14v)

The same tune also survives in the Dallis Book, dated Cambridge, 1583, and now in Trinity College, Dublin (MS D 3.30, 204–7). Both are transcriptions for lute tablature, but demand that the lute is tuned up a perfect fifth with d[1] as the highest note (rather than g as normal). The tuning, the contrapuntal nature of the setting and the fact that the harmonisation of each is broadly similar, although the arrangement is different, suggest that both are transcriptions of an original setting for a consort, perhaps for viols (Mary Joiner, 'B. M. Add. Ms. 15117, Commentary, Index and Bibliography' *RMA Research Chronicle* 7 (1969), pp. 51–109). The Dallis Book setting is ascribed to 'Mr Parsons'. This is probably Robert Parsons (1530–70). The *Cheque Book* of the Chapel Royal records that he was sworn in as a Gentleman in 1563 and that he drowned in the River Trent. He wrote a considerable amount of church music and is noted for his richly modulating harmonic style.

son, God guide thy way,   and shield thee from mis – chance,   And

make thy just des – erts   in court, thy poor es – tate to ad – vance.   Yet

when thou art be – come   one   of   the court – ly train,

Repeat from $

Think on this pro – verb old,' quoth he, 'that fair words makes fools   fain'.

DOW MS: OXFORD, CHRIST CHURCH, MS MUS 984–88

PDD, 1: 'May'

The Dow MS is a set of five music partbooks copied between 1581 and 1588 by Robert Dow, Fellow of All Souls' College, Oxford, and one of the most important and authoritative sources for the Elizabethan consort song. It contains this unascribed setting for 'May', together with settings for five other poems from *The Paradise of Dainty Devices*, all included in *Consort Songs* (ed. Brett, 1974).

Another setting can be found in Forbes, *Songs and Fancies* (1666 and 1682), and there is a lone bass part in PRO SP1/246 fol. 21v.

flowers, which cold in pri – son kept, now laugh the frost to scorn. All na-ture's imps tri-

umph while joy – ful May does last, When May is gone, of all the year the

plea – sant time is past, the plea – sant time is past is past

May makes the cheer-ful hue, May breeds and brings new blood, May march-es through-out

ev – er – y limb, May makes the me – rry mood. May pri-cketh ten – der

hearts, their war-bling notes to tune, Full strange it is yet some we see do

make their May in June. Thus things are strange-ly wrought while joy – ful May does

last, When May is gone, of all the year the plea – sant time is

past,   the plea – sant time is   past,   is past.

All you that live on earth, and have   your May at will,   Re –

joice   in May, as   I do   now,   and use   your May with   skill.   Use May

while that you may, for   May   has but his   time,   When all   the   fruit is

gone   it   is   too   late   the   tree   to   climb.   Your   li – king   and   your

lust   is   fresh while May   does   last,   Take May in   time   when

May   is   gone   the   plea – sant   time   is   past,   the   plea – sant   time   is

past,   is   past.

OXFORD CHRIST CHURCH, MS MUS 371

'O death'

Copied in the 1560s, this is a keyboard transcription of a consort song
with the melody, as usual, to be found weaving through the inner lines.
The same setting, together with the words to the first stanza and refrain,
but in a slightly different and less satisfactory arrangement for voice and
lute, is in Add. 15117.[8] With the aid of that version, however, it is possible to identify most of the melody notes in the Christ Church arrangement. I have transcribed the Christ Church version and reconstructed the
melody, doubling it as a separate voice part.[9]

Another arrangement occurs in a set of five part books for broken
consort, BL Add. MS 30480–4, copied between 1560 and 1590 and
belonging in 1615 to Thomas Hammond of Hawkedon, Suffolk. Here the
melody opens in much the same way and has a similar idea for the closing
'I die' bars, but the accompaniment is much more conventional. The
counter-tenor part contains the words relating to the first four stanzas in
Add. 26737, but in very garbled form. Other occurrences of this setting
include: Add. MSS 18936–9 (four out of five part books that probably
originated in the household of Edward Paston c.1600); and Bodleian
Library Tenbury MS 1464 (bass part only). This version is printed in
Musica Britannica, vol. 22.

Stanza 3

Lord pi-ty thou my soul, Death does draw nigh,

Sound dole-ful-ly, For now I die, I die, I die.

NOTES

1 John H, Long, 'Music for a song in Damon and Pithias', *Music and Letters* 48 (1967), 246–50.

2 'Can my poore harte be still' in the play *Patient Grissel* by John Phillip (C4, ll. 493–4, Malone Society Reprints); 'The lamentation of a woman being wrongfully defamed' in *A Handefull of Pleasant Delights* (1584, fols D4v–D5); Elviden, *Historie of Pesistratus and Catanea* (London, c.1570), C1. See Mary Joiner, 'B. M. Add. Ms. 15117, Commentary, Index and Bibliography', *RMA Research Chronicle* 7 (1969), p. 95, and John Ward, 'Music for A Handfull of Pleasant Delites', *Journal of the American Musicological Society* X (1957), 151–80.

3 Other pieces of music have in the past been attributed to Edwards but without foundation. Bodleian Library Tenbury MS 1464 contains music by Pewsey, Johnson, Byrde, Taverner and Tye and has been said to contain parts of a motet and mass by Edwards (fols 51v–54v). Unfortunately this is a misreading of the name Taverner. The name Edwards appears at the top of a piece called 'Madonna' for voice and accompaniment in lute tablature in Add. 4900 (fols 1, 62). This is an arrangement of an Italian madrigal, extremely popular in England and attributed in different MSS to a number of mid-sixteenth-century English composers (see Brett). It is not appreciably different from those.

4 'In going to my naked bed' is in RCM 722, 2111 and 36526; *O the silly man* is in RCM 722, 1196 and 2111; 'When griping griefs' (*sic*) is in RCM 1196.

5 J. Hawkins, *General History of Music* (London, 1776); E. H. Fellowes, *The English Madrigalists* (London: Stainer and Bell, 1920); H. Elliot Button, *Musical Times* LXIV (1923).

6 Peter Warlock, *Elizabethan Songs*, Books 2 and 3 (Oxford: Oxford University Press, 1926); John Ireland, *Five Sixteenth Century Poems for Voice and Piano* (London: Boosey and Hawkes, 1938).

7 See also Christopher F. Hasty, *Metre as Rhythm* (Oxford University Press, 1997).

8 Both versions are printed in Caldwell (ed.), *Musica Britannica*, vol. 66.

9 A great deal of confusion surrounds both the poetry and the music of this song. The poem has been romantically attributed variously to Anne Boleyn, or to her brother George, before their executions. However George Gascoigne referred to a poem called 'Soul-knell' which he says Edwards wrote 'in extremity of sickness'—a description which might equally fit CT4, but which J. W. Hebel and H. H. Hudson, *Poetry of the English Renaissance* (New York: Crafts, 1929), p. 920, identified with this poem. They also described the mid-seventeenth-century MS Add. 26737, the fullest source for the words, as dating from the reign of Henry VIII (a mistake repeated by Brett) which has effectively prevented anyone linking the poem with *Palamon and Arcyte*.

SELECT BIBLIOGRAPHY

Astington, John, *English Court Theatre, 1558–1642* (Cambridge: Cambridge University Press, 1999).

Attridge, Derek, *Well Weighed Syllables* (Cambridge: Cambridge University Press, 1974).

A–Z of Elizabethan London, The compiled A. Prockter and R. Taylor (London: London Topographical Society, no. 122, 1979).

Baldwin, T. W., *William Shakspere's Small Latine and Lesse Greeke*, 2 vols (Urbana: University of Illinois Press, 1944).

Baldwin, William, *The Mirror for Magistrates*, ed. L. B. Campbell (Cambridge: Cambridge University Press, 1938).

Baldwin, William, *A Treatise of Morall Philosophy*, 1579.

Barish, Jonas, *The Antitheatrical Prejudice* (Berkeley and Los Angeles: University of California Press, 1981).

Boas, F. S., *University Drama in the Tudor Age* (Oxford: Clarendon Press, 1914).

Breitenburg, Mark, ' "The hole matter opened": Iconic representation and interpretation in "The Quenes Majesties Passage" ', *Criticism* 28 (1986).

Brett, P., ed., *Consort Songs, Musica Britannica*, vol. 22, 2nd edn. (London: Stainer and Bell, 1974).

Caldwell, John, ed., *Tudor Keyboard Music, 1520–80, Musica Britannica*, vol. 66 (London: Stainer and Bell, 1995).

Chambers, E. K., *The Elizabethan Stage*, 4 vols (Oxford: Clarendon Press, 1923).

Cook, David and Wilson, F. P., eds., 'Dramatic Records in the Declared Accounts of the Treasurer of the Chamber, 1558–1642', *Collections* VI (Oxford University Press: Malone Society, 1961).

Craik, T. W., *The Tudor Interlude: Stage Costume and Acting* (Leicester: Leicester University Press, 1967).

Derrida, Jacques, *Politics of Friendship*, trans. George Collins (London and New York: Verso, 1997).

Elliott, John R. Jr, 'Queen Elizabeth at Oxford: New light on the royal plays of 1566', *English Literary Renaissance* 18:2 (1988), 218–29.

Gosson, Stephen, *The Schoole of Abuse* (London: 1579).

Gosson, Stephen, *Plays Confuted in Five Actions* (1582), introductory note by Peter Davison (New York: Johnson Reprint, 1972).

Guinle, Francis, 'Concerning a source of Richard Edwards' *Damon and Pithias*', *Cahiers Elisabethains* 30 (1986), 71–2.

Heinemann, Margot, *Puritanism and Theatre: Thomas Middleton and Opposition Drama under the Early Stuarts* (Cambridge: Cambridge University Press, 1980).

Holaday, Allan, 'Shakespeare, Richard Edwards, and the Virtues Reconciled', *Journal of English and Germanic Philology* 66 (1967), 200–6.

Hughey, Ruth, ed., *The Arundel Harington MS of Tudor Poetry*, 2 vols (Columbus: Ohio State University Press, 1960).

Iamblichus, 'The Life of Pythagoras', in *The Pythagorean Sourcebook and Library*, trans. Kenneth Sylvan Guthrie (Grand Rapids: Phanes Press, 1987).

Joiner, Mary, 'B.M. Add. Ms. 15117, commentary, index and bibliography', *RMA Research Chronicle* 7 (1969), 51–109.

Jorgens, Elise Bickford, ed., *English Song 1600–1675*, vol. 1 (London and New York: Garland, 1986).

King, Ros, 'Seeing the rhythm: An interpretation of sixteenth-century punctuation and metrical practice', J. Bray, M. Handley and A. Henry, eds., in *Ma[r]king the Text: The Presentation of Meaning on the Literary Page* (Aldershot: Ashgate, 2000).

Konstan, David, *Friendship in the Classical World* (Cambridge: Cambridge University Press, 1997).

Loades, David, *The Reign of Mary Tudor: Politics, Government and Religion in England 1553–58* (London: Longman, 2nd ed., 1991).

MacCulloch, Diarmaid, *Thomas Cranmer: A Life* (New Haven and London: Yale University Press, 1996).

Machyn, Henry, *Diary 1550–1563* (London: Camden Society, 1848).

Madden, F., *Privy Purse Expenses of Princess Mary* (London, 1831).

Marotti, Arthur F., *Manuscript, Print and the English Renaissance Lyric* (Ithaca and London: Cornell University Press, 1995).

Maynard, Winifred, 'The Paradyse of Daynty Deuises Revisited', *Review of English Studies* 24 (1973), 294–300.

Nelson, Alan H., *Early Cambridge Theatres: College, University and Town Stages 1464–1720* (Cambridge: Cambridge University Press, 1994).

Northbrooke, John, *A Treatise wherein Dicing Dauncing, Vaine Playes or Enterluds ... Are Reproved* (London, 1577).

Osborn, James M., ed., *The Quenes Maiesties Passage through the Citie of London to Westminster the Day before Her Coronacion* (New Haven: Yale University Press, 1960).

Puttenham, George, *The Arte of English Poesie* (London, 1589).

Rainoldes, John, *Th'Overthrow of Stage Plays* (Middleburg, 1599).

Rollins, Hyder Edward, ed., *The Paradise of Dainty Devices (1576–1606)* (Cambridge, Mass.: Harvard University Press, 1927).

Seneca, *Four Tragedies and Octavia*, trans. E. F. Watling (London: Penguin, 1966).

Stevens, Denis, ed., *The Mulliner Book, Musica Britannica*, vol. 1, 2nd edn. (London: Stainer and Bell, 1954).

Stevens, John, *Music and Poetry in the Early Tudor Court* (Cambridge: Cambridge University Press, 1979).

Streitberger, W. R., *Court Revels 1485–1559* (Toronto: Toronto University Press, 1994).

Stubbes, Philip, *The Anatomy of Abuses* (1583), introductory note by Peter Davison (New York: Johnson Reprint, 1972).

Vives, Jean Luis, *Tudor School-boy Life: Dialogues of Juan Luis Vives*, ed. Foster Watson (London: Dent, 1908).

Watson, Foster, ed., *Vives and the Renascence Education of Women* (London: Edward Arnold, 1912).

Webbe, William, *A Discourse of English Poetrie*, ed. Edward Arber (London, 1870).

Wickham, Glynne, *Early English Stages*, 2 vols (London: Routledge and Kegan Paul, 1959–72).

Wilson, Thomas, *The Arte of Rhetorique* (London, 1560).

INDEX

Edwards's poems are indexed by both title where applicable (in italic) and first line. Citations from editions in this book are given by page or page and note number.